kamera
BOOKS

www.kamerabooks.com

10,000
WAYS TO DIE

A DIRECTOR'S TAKE ON THE SPAGHETTI WESTERN

ALEX COX

kamera
BOOKS

First published in 2009 by Kamera Books
PO Box 394, Harpenden, Herts, AL5 1XJ.
www.kamerabooks.com

A CIP catalogue record for this book is available from the British Library.

ISBN: 978-1-84243-304-1

2 4 6 8 10 9 7 5 3 1

Typeset by Elsa Mathern
Printed and bound in the UK by J F Print Ltd, Sparkford, Somerset.

To Giulio Questi

Contents

Introduction

'I know death hath ten thousand several doors
For men to take their exits.'
John Webster, *The Duchess of Malfi* Act IV; Sc II

When I was trying to raise money for *Revengers Tragedy*, it sometimes helped to describe Frank Cottrell Boyce's adaptation of Thomas Middleton's Jacobean horror-comedy as a 'Spaghetti Western'.

The financiers' faces would brighten, slightly. But what did these words, 'Spaghetti Western', mean to them? Clint Eastwood, and a licence to print money? The desert, Europe, and the swinging sixties? Their twenties or their teenage years? Whatever they signified, it seemed to work in *Revengers'* favour. 'Oh!' the financier might exclaim. 'You can have flashbacks, then. And Morricone music!' And the frost on the chromium office fittings would thaw, albeit briefly. Spaghetti Westerns were familiar territory. They were established, acceptable.

It was not always thus. When Italian Westerns first appeared in England and the United States, they were derided; they were considered low brow even by low-brow standards. They were accused of being misogynistic and gratuitously violent, which they definitely were.

'Brutality is piled unskilfully on brutality in what appears to be a blatant plea for the X-certificate the censor has awarded it,' wrote Richard Davis in a review of *Fistful of Dollars*, for *films & filming*. For teenage boys, whether in southern Italy or northern England, this was good news indeed. American Westerns were on their last legs: either potboilers featuring old men like Elvis and John Wayne, or TV series like *Bonanza*, *The High Chaparral* and *The Virginian*, which celebrated the corporate hierarchy of Big Daddy's ranch. There was precious little action, and no violence worth the name. As teenagers, we hoped in vain for sex, and reasonably expected violence.

I grew up in an atmosphere of moderately mindless violence. Boys and girls were supervised and segregated. Teachers regularly beat their charges. Some had a sense of humour, like the form master who whacked my hand with a wooden ruler while yelling, 'School! Days! Are! The! Happiest! Days! Of! Your! Life!' And, in the absence of girls, school playgrounds were hotbeds of arbitrary cruelty. Punches were thrown, kicks to the groin occurred. Chanting mobs of boys gathered around any fight. On one occasion I was knocked down, hit my head on the asphalt, and was temporarily blinded. My classmates led me back into school when the bell rang. Gradually, as I sat at my desk, my sight returned. Another time, I and some mates heaved one of our enemies through a plate-glass window. Fortunately, he wasn't killed.

In the background, on television, played those bland corporate Westerns, endless documentaries about two world wars, and up-to-the-minute news of the latest one, in Vietnam. This was the least-sanitised war of my lifetime. Actual atrocities – perpetrated by 'our' side, the good side, the Americans – were reported while we ate our tea. Ongoing at this time were the violence, torture, shootings and bombings, which sustained the English colonial adventure in Ireland (though it was never described to us in quite those terms). And over-laying the fists and bombs and telly and suppressed sexuality was the consumerist violence of English car culture. When my grandfather was run over and killed outside our house, we were all sad, but there was no talk of getting rid of our two cars, or of the irresponsibility of the man who'd killed him: a bank manager who couldn't be bothered to walk a mile to work.

Violence – arbitrary, stupid violence, which could descend at any second from any side – seemed to be the norm. So, when a series of films appeared which depicted an atmosphere of mindless, inces-sant, childish, arbitrary violence, I was hooked – especially when these films, like the banned *Mars Attacks* bubblegum cards, annoyed the cultural establishment.

INTRODUCTION

As Richard Davis observed, these films were 'X' rated – which meant you had to be 16 or older to see them. But cinemas were never full, and ticket-sellers never asked boys how old they were. So, at the age of 13 or 14, I saw my first Italian Western double-bill: *Fistful of Dollars* and *For a Few Dollars More*. I was most impressed. Here was a world of arbitrary, stupid violence with a protagonist who dealt with it and survived it. It was also a world with an extraordinary visual aspect: ramshackle wooden towns surrounded by arid, dramatic deserts, the like of which I'd never seen. I watched most of these films, oddly enough, in Paris. As a teenage exchange student, I discovered a network of older, second-run movie houses in almost every *arrondissement*. They were playing Italian Westerns I'd heard about, but never seen: films reputedly banned by the censor, like *Django* and *The Big Silence*. I got a job in Paris as an office boy and runner for a distribution company: *les Films Marbeuf*. Riding the Metro back and forth across the city, copy of *Pariscope* in hand, I acquired pressbooks, scripts and stills. And I watched many, many Spaghetti Westerns.

I wrote a version of this book 30 years ago, when I was a graduate student at UCLA. It was almost published, but I made the mistake of getting an agent, who managed to wreck the deal. In retrospect, I'm grateful to that agent. The 1978 version of this book was very representative of a time when critics and theorists analysed films based on the symbols they saw in them. It was certainly a way of looking at things, but it seems arbitrary to me now. This volume aims to be a chronological history of important and worthwhile Italian Westerns, from a director's point of view.

It doesn't deal with every Italian Western – several hundred of which were made – but with the films I think are significant. The golden years of the Spaghetti Westerns were '67 and '68, and these are probably the most interesting chapters in this book. I don't think a single good Italian Western was made in the 1970s. But certain Spaghetti Westerns from that decade – *My Name is Nobody*, *Blindman*, the *Trinity* films – have a *phenomenal* quality which I address as well.

Is there a need for this? There are a number of good books about the Italian Western: Christopher Frayling's *Spaghetti Westerns* and his massive biography, *Sergio Leone*; Howard Hughes' *Once Upon a Time in the Italian West*; and Marco Giusti's massive *Dizionario del Western all'Italiana*, an epic work containing credits and analysis of over 800 Italian, and Italianate, Westerns. In '78 I was scouting territory into which Frayling, Hughes and Giusti have since led armies of settlers and prospectors. Now I'm walking in their footsteps, following the maps they've drawn.

I hope my standpoint as a film director will make this book a little different. By looking at the films in the order in which they were made – in the old *Monthly Film Bulletin* style of credits, story and analysis – I observe how the form developed. And I follow the parallel careers of Sergio Leone and Sergio Corbucci – co-creators of the Italian Western – and, for the first time, grant them equal importance.

And any attempt at 'chronology' is speculative. The hardest part of researching Italian Westerns is getting accurate information as to when they were made. There is contradictory information as to their release dates. Based on this, one has to guess when a film was shot: I've assumed that post-production was rapid – the same editors and composers were working on *a lot of films* – and that producers got the films into the cinemas quickly, if possible.

Likewise, what title to use can be problematic. Giulio Questi's film *Se Sei Vivo Spara* was titled *Django Kill* in Britain and the USA, to cash in on the success of Corbucci's banned Western. In some territories it was called *Oro Hondo*; in Mexico, *Si Eres Vivo... Dispara*. What to call Questi's picture, in an English-language book? The direct translation, *If You Live, Shoot*, is ridiculous. But its writer/director hates the familiar rip-off title, *Django Kill*.

And which version is the writer discussing, and the reader watching? *Se Sei Vivo Spara* was originally two hours long. The Italian censor and distributor reduced it to 115 minutes. When it played at the cinema in Britain, it ran only 101 minutes. Almost all Spaghetti Westerns were thus affected – including Leone's. In the *Dollars* movies, it's mostly short, censorship cuts, but his later, longer films were heavily edited by the distributors.

Dates, lengths and titles are all areas of confusion: in any book about Spaghetti Westerns the reader must sometimes 'triangulate' these three pieces of information, all of which may be wrong, to figure out which DVD they've rented. Generally, I'll use the most familiar title, and the short one if there's a choice (*¿Quien Sabe?* rather than *A Bullet for the General*). I call Corbucci's masterwork *The Big Silence* because I think it's a better title than *The Great Silence* (especially as a documentary about monks has stolen the original French title – *Le grand silence* – and is known as *Into Great Silence* in English). Spaghetti Westerns may have become 'respectable', but only Leone is accorded much respect; his DVDs alone are marketed as the 'director's cut'. Leone was the one bad boy allowed into the House of Culture; the door was then closed, and the rest of the *ragazzi* – Corbucci, Questi, Damiani, Petroni, Sollima – remain outside.

So, while this book deals with numerous films and filmmakers, it will return inevitably to Corbucci and Leone. They are the principal characters in its cast: first friends, then rivals, filmmakers of great influence and significance, whose careers ended in disappointment. Leone's West was one of uneasy alliances between god-like men: cat-like, innately violent westerners, cold, technological easterners, and Mexican bandits. Corbucci's West was a world without alliances, in which one man – usually crippled, maimed, or blind – was forced to confront two gangs of equal villainy. In Leone's world money was always the goal, and usually attainable. In Corbucci's world money was mentioned, then quickly forgotten in a downward spiral of torture, destruction and loss.

In conclusion, I'll deal with something which has long interested me: the mysterious yet striking parallel between the Italian Western and the Jacobean Revenge Tragedy. In both cases, several decades of original work in a new creative form led to works of exceptional brilliance, which were condemned by 'right-thinking' critics as immoral and degenerate. Renaissance drama was crudely but efficiently curtailed, by legislation and war. Italian Westerns consumed themselves, in a sprawl of self-parody and uninspired genre-breaking.

I would like to thank Chris Frayling, Howard Hughes and Marco Giusti, all of whom have been generous with information and insights over the years. I am most grateful to Katsumi Ishikuma – Stonebear – for assembling the 'Macaroni Western DVD Bible' and tracking down a copy of *Don't Touch the White Woman*; to Phil Hardcastle for turning me on to *Cemetery Without Crosses*; to Kim Newman for pointing me towards *Closed Circuit*; to Hannah Patterson and Anne Hudson, my editors; to Steven Davies, for the introduction to Kamera; and to Tod, Gray and Pearl for welcoming me back into the real world of beauty and compassion, when I emerged, squinty-eyed and twitching, from the insane mayhem of these films.

- Alex Cox

Background
Brando, Kurosawa & the Continental Op

'I hate writing. I suffer the tortures of the damned. I can't sleep and it feels like I'm going to die any minute. Eventually I lock myself away somewhere, out of reach of a gun, and get in on in one big push.' – **Sam Peckinpah**

L ike all drama, the Italian Westerns were influenced and formed by what had gone before: the American Western, a genre virtually invented by John Ford, who directed 56 of them during his long career. The events which happen in Italian Westerns, their dramatic conflicts, their plot structures, were usually recycled from American films made years before. Each film contains various examples: the crushing of the hero's hands in *Django* – so shocking that the film was banned – has one antecedent in an American Western, *The Man from Laramie* (1955, Anthony Mann), another in an early European Western *Savage Guns* (1961, Michael Carreras). In Mann's *Noir* Western, the villain, played by Alex Nichol, callously shoots James Stewart in his gun hand. In Carreras' British-Italian-Spanish coproduction, the hero's hands are crushed by wagon wheels. And the entire plot of *Once Upon a Time in the West* boils down to the thin premise of many an American two-reeler: the villains' plan to seize, by murder if necessary, land which the railroad must cross.

But some films influenced the Italian Western more than others did. And one of them wasn't a Western at all. So, before embarking on our chronological trip, I'd like to consider two features which had a major impact on the new form: Akira Kurosawa's *Yojimbo*, and Marlon Brando's *One-Eyed Jacks*.

Yojimbo was directed by Akira Kurosawa in l961, the year Marlon Brando's Western One-Eyed Jacks opened in the United States. As far as I can tell, Kurosawa didn't see Brando's film before making Yojimbo. But, as a keen observer of the Western cinema, he would quite likely have known of One-Eyed Jacks, and of its fate. Both films have one thing in common: an inexplicable and implausible tardiness on the part of the hero, who – confronted with a very dangerous situation of his own making – sits around doing nothing, and ends up suffering, as a result.

One-Eyed Jacks was based on a book by Charles Neider, The Authentic Death of Hendry Jones, which Brando had optioned. The actor/producer's first choice of a creative team was two strokes of genius. To direct, he hired Stanley Kubrick, who had made two striking, stylish independent thrillers; and for the screenplay, he chose a TV writer, one Sam Peckinpah. Brando quickly fell out with both men. His firing of Peckinpah seems to have been both acrimonious and memorable, as the film's theme of betrayal – by an old outlaw who has betrayed the outlaw code – became the central theme of all Peckinpah's work as a director. As a director, I can report that it is galling to work for a vainglorious, powerful 'star'. Actors are instinctive, essential creatures, but when they gain too much power they can be both stupid and amoral. Loyalty is a rare trait in most thespians, whereas it's something a managerial post – such as a film director – depends on. This is why 'stars' usually make such a bad job of directing: intrinsically shallow, isolated and self-pitying, they have a hard time managing any enterprise, or earning respect from their team.

Having fired Kubrick, Brando decided to direct One-Eyed Jacks himself. Paramount Pictures, smiling like a crocodile, agreed. Lacking discipline and a completed script, Brando couldn't keep a lid on things. The shoot began in December 1958. It was supposed to last two months. Instead, it stretched to six. Famously, when Brando and his co-star, Karl Malden, had to play drunk, the two Method actors became drunk: a short scene of inebriation then took days to film. The studio's two-million-dollar budget (not bad for a cowboy movie of the period) became six million. Why did Paramount permit it? Brando's biographer suggests a dark but familiar motive: 'chasten his arrogance, teach him

a lesson. How much can it cost? He whom Hollywood would humble, it first indulges. It is, perhaps, the most basic law of the business...'[1]

[1] Brando - A Life in Our Times
*by Richard Schickel, Atheneum,
1991, p 174*

Brando's first cut of *One-Eyed Jacks* was six hours long. The *auteur* had become confused and bored in the editing room. Unable to finish his picture, he wanted to be fired, so he could shift his burden of guilt onto the studio, and pretend his masterwork had been abused. Beaten up by the negative studio and critical response, he never directed again. Yet *One-Eyed Jacks* is a more-than-decent film. Brando's only real directorial failing is in the transitions (scenes are inevitably linked by dissolves, as in the very worst American Westerns). But the complexity of the plot and character, the visual aspect of the film, and the performances, are all excellent. His own performance is very good – but he gives plenty of screen time to Karl Malden, to Ben Johnson and his gang, and to additional odd characters such as Timothy Carey's. Brando is generous to the other actors, both as an actor and as a director.

Several elements from *One-Eyed Jacks* reappear in the Spaghetti Western. The film's stylish costumes are almost as specific and over-the-top as those of Nicholas Ray's *Johnny Guitar*. The Rio Kid dresses in the Mexican *vaquero* style, and sometimes wears a *serape*: points not lost on Carlo Simi when he prepared his costume designs for Corbucci and Leone. The plot device of the revenge-seeking hero who escapes/is released from jail would be re-used many times. The teeth-grinding intensity with which Rio pursues his revenge became the stock-in-trade of many actors, American and Italian, who starred in these films. But the most 'Italianate' aspect of the film, for me, is Rio's mysterious tardiness.

When Rio tracks Dad down, he ought to kill him right away. Dad anticipates a gunfight. Rio's gang expects one, too. Instead, Rio sets about seducing Dad's adopted daughter, and then – even after that ignoble goal has been achieved – delays killing Dad. After killing Howard (Timothy Carey) in a barroom brawl, Rio knows his time is short, his options are limited. Yet he continues to hang around the bar, drinking.

Squandering his advantage, the hero is ambushed, whipped, and (as in *The Man from Laramie*) his gun-hand is smashed by Longworth, who now has a revenge motive of his own. Rio escapes, and slowly, painfully recuperates, once again plotting his long-delayed revenge.

Exactly the same thing occurs in Yojimbo.

Kurosawa's cynical samurai drama began production at Toho Studios in January 1961. As a director, the 51-year-old Kurosawa was the opposite of the 37-year-old Brando: disciplined, hard-working, and – at this stage of his career – famously fast. It seems impossible to believe, but *Yojimbo* opened on 25 April of the same year: shot, cut and in the cinemas in less than four months. Kurosawa had seen many, many Westerns: John Ford was his favourite director, and he'd mentioned, on the set of *Seven Samurai*, that he wanted to make a *chambara* (samurai action picture) in the Western style.

In *Yojimbo*, Toshiro Mifune plays Sanjuro Kuwabatake, a dirty, itchy, masterless samurai with a taste for drink. Happening upon a wretched town run by two rival gangs, Sanjuro quickly observes to the bartender, 'I get paid for killing. Better if all these men were dead. Think about it.' To establish his credentials, he kills some local tough guys, then offers his services as a bodyguard to both sides.

Sanjuro's main adversary is a young gangster with a pistol, Onosuke (Tatsuya Nakadai). His mistake is to feel pity for a poor family wrecked by Onosuke, who has forced a farmer's wife to become his mistress. Sanjuro kills the woman's guards and reunites the family. Time is now short for him, his options limited. But instead of leaving town, he continues hanging around the bar, drinking. Onosuke figures out his treachery and gets the drop on him; Sanjuro is subjected to a prolonged torture beating. Escaping in a coffin, Sanjuro hides, recuperates from his wounds, and plots the violent showdown which he has, mysteriously, postponed.

It's this inexplicable delay on the part of the hero, followed by his escape and recuperation, which *Yojimbo* and *One-Eyed Jacks* have in common. The explanation isn't clear: the most obvious precedent for such a damaging delay is William Shakespeare's revenge-action-drama, *Hamlet*. Hamlet is right in thinking that his uncle Claudius is his father's murderer. But he's a fool to let Claudius know he knows, and then do nothing about it. Obviously Brando knew the story of Hamlet; and so did Kurosawa – his mafia drama, *The Bad Sleep Well*

(1960), is full of references to the play. Kurosawa and Brando were nothing if not ambitious. Did both decide, spontaneously, to borrow the key dilemma from the greatest work of English theatre? After all, if you're going to steal, steal from the best.[2]

Yojimbo became the narrative template for Sergio Leone's first Western, and One-Eyed Jacks became a visual and character reference for several of Corbucci's films. Here, in these two influential, entertaining, grandiose pictures, lie the Italian Western's most visible roots. But Kurosawa wasn't only influenced by Shakespeare and by Western films. I believe he and his screenwriter, Ryuzo Kikushima, had in mind a specific American source for their story of two warring gangs in a doomed, out-of-the-way town: Dashiell Hammett.

Hammett is best known as the author of The Maltese Falcon, adapted by John Huston into a classic film. That book was the story of a sort-of-honourable detective, Sam Spade, and his struggle to hang on to his own version of integrity; Hammett also invented a husband-and-wife detective team, Nick and Nora Charles (The Thin Man), and a memorable nameless agency detective, the Continental Op.

The Continental Op is the hero of several stories of gang warfare in rotten, out-of-the-way towns: Corkscrew and Red Harvest are two of the best. In both tales the hero is accused of pitting the gangs against each other, in order to destroy them. 'A hombre might guess,' says the sidekick in Corkscrew, 'that you was playing the Circle HAR against Bardell's crew, encouraging each side to eat up the other...' Encouraging each side to eat up the other. It's a fair description of what Mifune does. But the point of Corkscrew and Red Harvest – like Yojimbo – is that the hero doesn't have to do very much to set these gangs to eat each other. They're permanently at war; their truces are fakes; they're ready for a showdown. Just by being there, and by choice acts of manipulation, the indolent Sanjuro, or the lazy Op, can bring it on.

Corkscrew was translated into Japanese in the late 1940s. According to Katsumi Ishikuma, the writer Hideo Oguni showed Kurosawa

2 *As a director, I have borrowed/ stolen from Leone, Corbucci, Questi, Robert Aldrich, Luis Buñuel, Sam Peckinpah, Arturo Ripstein and numerous other directors. Any director who denies borrowing/stealing from other directors must be very talented indeed.*

the story. Ishikuma also recalls an interview with Kurosawa in the Japanese magazine *Cut*, in which Kurosawa said, 'I was reading many mystery novels those days. When I finished *Yojimbo*, and watched it, I found that I took many elements from Hammett's novels. I thought, it's natural, because I like Hammett very much.' Perhaps his most overt debt is to *Red Harvest*, originally titled *Poisonville*. Poisonville is another bad town, populated by rival gangs of gangsters. The Continental Op sets them against each other, and in due course they're destroyed. One scene seems to have inspired *Yojimbo* specifically: the violent showdown where Reno Starkey and his gang lob petrol bombs into Pete the Finn's headquarters, in Whiskeytown.

"We're done," a heavy voice shouted. "We're coming out. Don't shoot."

Reno called him a lousy fish-eater and shot him four times in the face and body.

Pete went down. A man behind me laughed.

This grisly and exciting scene, illuminated by the flames of the gangsters' blazing hideout, is paralleled in *Yojimbo*, when Tazaemon's premises are burned and he and his family are shot by Onosuke. It is, of course, restaged in *Fistful of Dollars*, when Ramon Rojo and his brothers burn down the Baxters' home and gun them down as they emerge.

Another clue to Hammett's influence isn't to be found in his writing, but in another American film based on one of his books – *The Glass Key*. Pessimistic even by Hammett's standards, the novel is a small epic of loyalty, love and futility set in the corrupt political environment of Albany, New York. Its anti-hero is one Ned Beaumont (called Ed Beaumont in the film), a sleazy but determined gambler whose only friend is Paul Mavdig, bootlegger-turned-pol. Ned Beaumont is a callous pathfinder; Natty Bumpo on the mean streets of upstate New York. His discovery that Mavdig is a fool, and his inevitable betrayal of his friend, give the book a tragic dimension unique in Hammett's work.

The Glass Key was first filmed in 1935, and again in 1942. The later film was directed by Stuart Heisler, whose credits are unremarkable. Heisler began his career as an editor of silent films. He ended it directing episodes of *Gunsmoke* in the sixties. He shows no affinity for the material until Beaumont (played by Alan Ladd) is kidnapped by gangsters and tortured to make him betray Mavdig (Brian Donlevy). At this point the film switches gear.

What saves *The Glass Key* – what makes it worth seeking out today – is the performance of William Bendix. 1942 was Bendix's first year as a film actor: he is stunningly good. Bendix plays Jeff, a thug who beats and *waterboards* Beaumont to make him talk. As soon as Jeff appears, we are in *Glass Key*-land as Hammett meant it. The relationship between Beaumont and the torturer-hoodlum overwhelms the latter part of the novel, as the thug, feeling increasingly sorry for himself and uncertain of his status, starts treating Beaumont as a confidant, and friend. It's all inspiringly sadistic, homoerotic, super-tense; the colourless Ladd improves immensely in the presence of a master thespian.

The torture of Beaumont isn't shown; instead there's a cut from his apprehension to a shot of his torturers, gambling. *Yojimbo* is structured the same way. But the next scene, in which Jeff and partner abandon their unconscious victim, and Beaumont escapes, is repeated in *Yojimbo* and *Fistful of Dollars*. In all three films, the badly beaten hero, eyes swollen shut, drags himself painfully around his jail. In *The Glass Key* he starts a fire; in *Yojimbo* he hides in a box; in *Fistful* he starts a fire. In the ensuing confusion, he escapes.

It's hard to read these pages in the novel, or to watch the filmed sequence, without thinking of *Yojimbo*. Did Kurosawa see *The Glass Key*? It was made during the Second World War, but Japan was flooded with American films during the Occupation – just as Italy was. A high-gloss, star-driven studio picture like *The Glass Key* would be first in line to take advantage of such newly acquired foreign markets. And both Kurosawa and Leone were fans of American movies and American thrillers.

None of this detracts from Kurosawa's vision, or his extraordinary achievement with *Yojimbo*: a cynical action film of great brilliance, which would exercise enormous influence on other filmmakers, and indeed national cinemas, as we shall shortly see.

1963

Westerns were shot in Italy as early as the silent period. During the Second World War, Giorgio Ferroni directed a comic Western, *Il Fanciullo Del West* (1943). Other Western parodies followed, including *Il Bandolero Stanco* (1952, Fernando Serchio). In the early sixties, the Italians co-produced Westerns outside Madrid, in Almería, in Yugoslavia, and in Rome. Some were Zorro movies. Others were the 'American' Westerns which bored us so: slow-moving oaters featuring waning Hollywood stars, insecurely masquerading as American films.

But it's worth a glance at some of those early co-productions, whose directors would go on making Westerns, and get better at them, and where certain cast and story elements first appeared. Two were directed in 1963 by Joaquin L Romero Marchent: *The Magnificent Three* (also know as *Tres hombres buenos* and *I tre implacabli*), and *Gunfight at High Noon* (aka *El sabor de la venganza*). *The Magnificent Three* provides the ur-plot for a number of later revenge Westerns, in which the hero's family is murdered by men who leave behind clues to their identity; transformed into an implacable revenger, he follows the clues, and dispatches the killers.

Gunfight at High Noon is also about a trio of revengers, in this case three sons who have sworn to their widowed mother to avenge their dad; the location is deliberately identified as a Mexican border town, to explain the Spanish exteriors. (There are Italian Westerns set far from the desert, in the snow, or in the woods, even in Japan – but they are rarities. Bigger-budget films could go to Almería in Spain for their exteriors; cheaper Westerns had to rely on rural beauty spots – or, worse, quarries – in Italy.)

Both films feature actors who would become familiar Italian Western players: Claudio Undari (usually portraying a tough guy, under the moniker of 'Robert Hundar') and Fernando Sancho, a big, moustachioed Spaniard who would specialise in playing Mexican bandit-generals. Marchent made several Spanish-Italian Westerns, with increasing style and sadism. Even at this early date he used his own name in the credits: the Spaniards were more insistent on this than the Italians, all of whom took 'American' pseudonyms.

Gunfight at Red Sands (aka *Gringo* and *Duello nel Texas*) is a story of racism and revenge set on the Mexican/American border. An American actor under contract to the producers, Richard Harrison, played the hero: buckskin-clad Gringo Martinez. The director was Zorro specialist Ricardo Blasco ('Richard Blasco'), the producers, Alfredo Antonini ('Albert Band'), Arrigo Colombo and Giorgio Papi. Ennio Morricone ('Dan Savio') was hired to write the score; it was his first Western. And a fine cameraman, Massimo Dallamano ('Max Dallman'), shot it. The cast included Aldo Sambrell, a broken-nosed Spanish actor who would play many Mexican bandit chiefs and henchmen over the next few years.

According to Marco Giusti, the producers weren't happy with Blasco's action sequences, and hired another Zorro veteran – Mario Caiano – to direct an additional week with Dallamano. Caiano was viewed as that boring thing, a 'safe pair of hands'. Naturally, Colombo and Papi planned to entrust him with their next Western.

The same year, their partner 'Band' produced another Western, with exteriors shot in Yugoslavia. It was directed by a youngish, gladiator-movie veteran: Sergio Corbucci.

Red Pastures

aka *I pascoli rossi, Massacro al Grande Canyon, Massacre at Grand Canyon*
(Italy/Yugoslavia)

Director: Sergio Corbucci (aka Stanley Corbett) **Producer:** Albert Band
  Screenplay: Edward C Geltman, Alfredo Antonini, Sergio Corbucci
  Director of Photography: Enzo Barboni **Art Director:** Giuseppe
Ranieri **Costumes:** Italia Scandariato **Editor:** Franco Fraticelli
Master of Arms: Benito Stefanelli **2nd Unit Director:** Franco Giraldi
  Assistant Director: Alfredo Antonini **Music:** Gianni Ferrio **Cast:**
James Mitchum (*Wes Evans*), Jill Powers aka Milla Sannoner (*Nancy*),
George Ardisson (*Tully Danzer*), Giacomo Rossi Stuart (*Sheriff Burt
Cooley*), Andrea Giordana, Burt Nelson (*Clay Danzer*), Nando Poggi (*Ace
Mason*), Edward Cianelli (*Eric Danzer*), Benito Stefanelli, Renato Terra
Caizzi (*Curly Mason*), Medar Vladimir (*Harley Whitmore*), Gavric Vlastimir
(*Bear Mason*), Attilio Severini (*Flake Mason*)

The story

Wes Evans catches up with the last two members of the Slade Gang,
who killed his pa, and shoots them. He returns to his home town of
Arriba Mesa, having been gone two years. Outside town, in Butte
Canyon, a horde of gunmen has gathered – cannon fodder for a range
war between ranchers Harley Whitmore and Eric Danzer.

Wes is offered the sheriff's badge, but declines. He wants to become a rancher. But when he discovers his beloved, Nancy, is now
married to Danzer's evil son, Tully, he decides to sell his property to
Harley, and move on.

Harley leads an army of a hundred men to attack the Danzer ranch,
but Tully ambushes them in a canyon, and a violent standoff ensues.
Wes persuades Harley and the Danzers to accept a truce, and tries to
persuade Eric Danzer not to hire a notorious gang of killers lurking in
town – the Manson brothers. He gets Eric to surrender his younger
son to Harley, as a hostage.

But Eric breaks the truce and sends Tully to give $75,000 to the
Mansons, and re-hire them to kill Harley. Tully offers the worst Manson brother, Flake, $50,000 to kill Wes, Harley and co. Flake accepts,

and sets his men to besieging the jail, and killing the sheriff. His involvement turns the tide against Harley – but in the nick of time Wes arrives at the canyon with a posse of townspeople. Many cowboys shoot each other. Wes kills Flake. Tully is shot dead by a farmer, Fred, whose leg was severed by Tully some time previously.

Harley is about to hang young Clay Danzer in front of his father, when Wes arrives, delivering Tully's corpse as an alternate peace offering. Harley spares Clay. Wes and Nancy are reunited, and Wes accepts the post of sheriff.

The film

Red Pastures is a bad film. Half-hearted and half-assed, it seeks to imitate an American cowboy picture, and fails badly at that. Right at the outset, after Wes has shot the last two Slades, there is a long tracking shot, featuring Wes's face. The actor should appear determined, or troubled, perhaps – he has finally killed all his father's killers – but Mitchum's expression changes constantly, brightening, clouding, reflecting puzzlement at the difficult task the director has set him: walk in a straight line. Mitchum has his father's looks, but no acting chops at all.

The film is lit brightly, like a TV comedy. Corbucci had been united with a great cameraman, Enzo Barboni, yet here they produced nothing of visual interest. The dark, graphic interiors of *Django* were still two films away. The exteriors – which in a Western should always be great, or at least interesting – are uniformly poor. The 'red pastures' – shot in Yugoslavia – have an unnaturally groomed appearance. Often Wes appears to be riding across a golf course. Several actors have the same, overly groomed, too-handsome, nineteenth-hole appearance: particularly orange-tanned and puppet-looking are the blonds Tully (George Ardisson) and Sheriff Cooley (GR Stuart). Corbucci has better luck with certain other characters: in particular, the rival ranchers, played enthusiastically by Eduardo Cianelli and Medar Vladimir (who looks remarkably like Roberto Camardiel, the Spanish actor).

Red Pastures' worst offence is that its characters behave unnaturally. Early on, Fred, having expounded much back-story info, abruptly says, 'See you later, Wes.' Why doesn't this Wild West homesteader, encountering his dear friend after two years' absence, invite him in? Such unexplained curtness makes no sense, and would not occur in a Ford film, where the characters act plausibly.

Few people have seen *Red Pastures*. This is a good thing. But even a bad thing can contain good elements. Despite various sources which report that the producer and Corbucci co-directed *Red Pastures*, I believe it's Corbucci's solo work. Or fault. The Italian credits favour Corbucci: the first reads, '*Un film di Albert Band*'. So, in legalese, Band/Antonini gets a possessory, not a directorial, credit. Antonini is also credited as *assistant* director, under his real name. And the final crew credit says '*Regia di Stanley Corbett*' – the pseudonym of Corbucci. So according to the credits, Corbucci directed it: it was his second feature, in fact, the other being a gladiator movie, *Maciste Against the Vampire* (1961). And most importantly, I think, there are several scenes, and themes, which recur more boldly in Corbucci's later films.

The first characteristic Corbucci element is the scene where Fred shows Wes his graveyard. The shot is ludicrous – nine crosses made out of flimsy sticks stuck in someone's lawn. But the shot is there for a reason. Corbucci wants us to dwell on this graveyard, even if it is stupid. Now Fred points to a tenth cross, and says, 'Over there... that one's mine. My leg's buried there. I brought it back and put it right there... planted it where I got it.'

The English-dubbed dialogue is confusing: apparently, the vicious Tully shot Fred's leg off, in a gundown, which claimed nine lives. This sudden focus on a cruel incident of mutilation is entirely consistent with all of Corbucci's subsequent Western work. Corbucci liked the horses, and the riders, and the big country well enough, but it was the plotting of corrupt townspeople, and subsequent opportunities for bizarre violence – often involving physical mutilation – which floated this director's boat.

Corbucci hadn't yet seen *Yojimbo*: he inherited from 'Band' the sub-plot of two powerful, warring bands. One side is led by Eric, a bed-ridden, corrupt gringo; the other by Harley, a bearded, likeable brute. Opposing factions do battle in the background of most of Corbucci's Westerns, and the status quo is always the same: gringos versus Mexicans in *Minnesota Clay* and *Django*; bankers versus bandits in

Navajo Joe and *The Big Silence*; state versus revolutionaries in his 'Mexican' films.

Red Pastures comes to life in its fight scenes, where Corbucci shows some enthusiasm, and Barboni gets his camera off the tripod. There's a well-staged brawl in a bar – Wes always fights dirty – and, during the prolonged canyon stand-off, there's a strange, stark shot of men being gunned down on a slope of boulders. All of which indicates a penchant for action, and prefigures the highly stylised shootouts of the director's later films. Corbucci always displayed an interest in the fate of corpses: during a truce in the canyon battle, the dead are arduously carried downhill.

In common with all later Spaghetti Westerns, numbers are highly inflated. In the canyon battle, those killed seems to number in the hundreds. Both factions talk of having more than a hundred armed men. Likewise, when money is mentioned, the sums are enormous: $75,000 is a lot of money to bribe saloon-dwelling lowlifes – even with a cheque!

Corbucci displays a predeliction for strong women characters. Nancy is dull, but the widow Maude, toting a shotgun, insists Wes intervene in the range war, and be sheriff like his father. His only alternative, she says, is to raise chickens. It's not a bad scene and she's a precursor of the tough women with moral voices – usually prostitutes – who populate his later films.

Though the film barely touches on it, its hero is a bounty hunter. Wes has spent two years hunting down the Slade brothers, for a $5,000 reward. No one remarks that he might have thought to bring them in alive. Corbucci just assumes a bounty hunter always kills his man. This was to be standard Italian-Western operating procedure within a couple of years.

Though bad, *Red Pastures* features several crew people who would be key Spaghetti Western personnel – among them the cameraman, Barboni, second unit director Franco Giraldi, and Benito Stefanelli, a fair-haired, gringo-looking stuntman and master-of-arms, who would become one of the form's most consistent and satisfactory heavies.

3 *As told by Christopher Frayling, in his book* Sergio Leone. Mar-co Giusti *(in his* Dizionario del western all'italiana*) says these events happened in mid-summer 1963; but I prefer Frayling's version as it presents more opportunities for the art department.*

1963 ended with visits to the cinema for Corbucci, Leone and many of their friends. The tale[3] begins one December night in Rome. Enzo Barboni emerges from the Arlecchino Cine. In the Piazza del Popolo, at the bar Canova, he runs into Mr and Mrs Sergio Leone. Barboni has just seen a samurai film, *Yojimbo*. He's completely turned on by it, and urges Sergio to see it. Leone is a young assistant director, who has directed one feature – a gladiator drama called *The Colossus of Rhodes* (1961). He's been talking with two producers, Colombo and Papi, about directing his second feature: a Western, titled *The Magnificent Stranger*.

If it's Christmas in Rome, no one's in their offices. So it's an anxious season for the young director, and he has time on his hands. Leone and Carla go to see *Yojimbo* the next day. He, too, is blown away. He's seen *Seven Samurai* of course. And countless Westerns. But *Yojimbo* is something different. Its cynicism, and its arbitrary surges of violence, are something no one has depicted so clearly, so unadornedly, before. *Yojimbo* is as much a gangster movie as a Western; Leone decides to make it the model for his upcoming cowboy film.

As soon as they get home, Leone calls his brother directors: Duccio Tessari, Sergio Corbucci, Mario Caiano. He calls his writer friend, Sergio Donati. He calls his assistant director, Tonino Delli Colli. Leone tells them all about this amazing *chambara* he's just seen.

Corbucci has already seen *Yojimbo*, on Barboni's recommendation. He has a Western in the pipeline, too, called *Minnesota Clay*. Suddenly, Leone and Corbucci, friends and rivals, are in a race to direct a Western with a *Yojimbo* edge to it. They're 34 and 36 years old.

1964

C orbucci, imagining he had raised the money for *Minnesota Clay*, hired a talented designer, Carlo Simi. They'd worked together before, in gladiator days. But Corbucci's money stalled again; his film was put on hold.

Meanwhile, Leone's producers showed him their new movie, *Gunfight at Red Sands*. Leone despised it. Papi and Colombo didn't care. Like other producers, they were filling a niche with cheap, imitation American Westerns made quickly, to be shown in Italy, Germany and Spain. They planned to shoot two Westerns, back-to-back, co-financed by Spanish and German partners. Both films would have Italian, German and Spanish actors, with an American, such as Richard Harrison, in the lead role. They liked Harrison because he was Rome based and they wouldn't have to fly him over. But his fee was high. Colombo and Papi wanted to shoot Leone's Western as soon as they finished *Bullets Don't Argue* (aka *Le pistole non discutono* or *Las pistolas no discuten*), directed by 'Mike Perkins' – Mario Caiano. Both Westerns would be filmed on the decrepit 'Zorro' set at Hojo de Manzanares, near Madrid.

Simi showed Leone the sketches he'd done for Corbucci, and Leone – who now had a start date of April 1964 – hired him as costume and set designer, in preference to the producers' art director, Alberto Roccianti. It was a wise move – but directors are sensitive beasts, and

I doubt Corbucci was happy losing 'his' designer to another film. Papi and Colombo were clearly impressed by Simi, since they hired him for *Bullets Don't Argue*, too. And Leone stuck with their other preferences: Massimo Dallamano as cinematographer, Ennio Morricone as composer. Leone and Morricone had known each other since they were schoolboys; Leone made it clear he did not like Morricone's *Gunfight at Red Sands* score.

Fistful of Dollars

aka *Per un pugno di dollari*, *The Magnificent Stranger*
(Italy/Spain/Germany)

Director: Sergio Leone   **Producer:** Arrigo Colombo, Giorgio Papi
Screenplay: Sergio Leone, Duccio Tessari, Jaime Comas Gil, Fernando Di Leo, Tonino Valerii, Victor Andres Catena   **Director of Photography:** Massimo Dallamano   **Art Director:** Carlo Simi   **Editor:** Roberto Cinquini   **2nd Unit Director:** Franco Giraldi   **Music:** Ennio Morricone
    Cast: Clint Eastwood (*Joe*), Gian Maria Volonte (*Ramon Rojo*), Marianne Koch (*Marisol*), Pepe Calvo (*Silvanito*), Wolfgang Lukschy (*John Baxter*), Sieghardt Rupp (*Esteban Rojo*), Antonio Prieto (*Benito Rojo*), Margherita Lozano (*Consuela Baxter*), Benito Stefanelli (*Rubio*), Mario Brega (*Chico*), Josef Egger (*Piripero*), Aldo Sambrell (*Manolo*)

The story

A drifter, Joe, rides his mule into the Mexican town of San Miguel. He passes a corpse, heading the other way. He sees a man and boy abused by bandits, and a beautiful woman – Marisol – held prisoner. In town, Joe is hassled by cowboys, who shoot at his mule. He visits the bar of Silvanito, who seems to know him from before. Silvanito explains the lie of the land: San Miguel has been taken over by two rival gangs of outlaws, the Rojos and the Baxters, who sell liquor and guns to the Indians. Joe observes, 'Two bosses... very interesting... There's money to be made in a place like this.'

    Joe kills four of the Baxter boys, and offers his services to Don Miguel Rojo. Miguel, impressed, hires him. Joe overhears Miguel and his brother Esteban arguing over how to deal with him. Esteban offers to kill him, but Miguel wants no trouble: the Mexican cavalry is shortly to arrive in town.

Joe and Silvanito follow the cavalry – with its closely guarded stage-coach – to the Rio Grande, where it meets a detachment of American soldiers. The Mexicans are there to exchange money for an arms shipment. But the 'Americans' are the Rojos in disguise, and the Mexican troops are machine-gunned by Miguel's brother, Ramon. Joe and Silvanito are the only witnesses to the massacre.

Ramon returns to the hacienda, and insists he wants to make peace with the Baxters. Joe, disappointed, gives Miguel back his money, and departs. That night, as the Baxters and the Rojos attempt a truce, Joe and Silvanito place two corpses from the massacre in the San Miguel cemetery. Joe tells John and Consuela Baxer that two witnesses to the massacre have escaped and are in the graveyard: this is the Baxters' chance to incriminate the Rojos, and they take it. Joe tells Ramon Rojo the same story. A gun battle in the cemetery ensues; Ramon shoots both 'witnesses' with his Winchester rifle; the truce is off.

While the Rojos are gone, Joe searches the hacienda and finds the stolen loot; he also finds Marisol – accidentally knocking her unconscious – and delivers her to the Baxters.

Next day there is an exchange of prisoners: Marisol for the Baxters' son, captured by the Rojos. For a brief moment, Marisol, her husband Julio, and her weeping child, Jesus, are reunited. But Joe, pretending to side with Ramon, breaks up the party.

That evening, Joe pretends to be drunk and – in Ramon's absence – returns to the white house where Marisol is imprisoned. He kills her five guards, and reunites her with Julio and Jesus, giving them all his money so that they can escape. But Ramon returns early and busts him; Joe is savagely beaten up. Unable to make him reveal where Marisol is, Ramon assumes she's with the Baxters. Joe escapes, the Rojos set the Baxters' house ablaze, and kill them all. Consuela dies cursing Ramon.

Joe hides in a mine shaft, slowly recovering. Out of an old metal wagon, he fashions a bullet-proof vest. When Piripero, the coffin-maker, tells him that Ramon – still hunting for Joe – is torturing Silvanito, Joe returns to San Miguel. His bullet-proof breastplate enables him to get within pistol range of the Winchester-toting Ramon. Killing the other Rojos, Joe challenges Ramon to a single-bullet, Colt-versus-Winchester duel. Joe wins.

The film

Fistful of Dollars is a really good picture. Exciting, violent, funny, cynical, and not too long, it's an excellent cowboy-south-of-the-border adventure, in the *Vera Cruz* vein. It's heavily influenced by *Yojimbo*: the characters, the plot, and most of the incidents are lifted from Kurosawa's film. Copyright doesn't seem to have been an issue in the Italian cinema of the 1960s – films were continually borrowing plots and character names from other films – so Leone's producers made no effort to contact *Yojimbo*'s producers, or to obtain the remake rights. For them, the film's inspiration was something to be ignored. The screenplay was entitled *The Magnificent Stranger* – presumably a reference to *The Magnificent Seven* (1960, John Sturges), the Hollywood Western famously based on another Kurosawa picture. It had two alternate titles, *Sputafuoco Joe* and *Texas Joe*. Though it was an Italian/German/Spanish co-production, with cast from all three countries, everyone was obliged to adopt a fake American name: the producers became Harry and George, Leone became Bob Robertson (his father, also a film director, had worked as 'Roberto Roberti').

Italian Westerns, particularly Papi's and Colombo's, still pretended to be American Westerns – so, in addition to the fake names (Peter Saint... John Speed... Frank Palance!), it was necessary to have an American actor in the lead role. Even later, when the Italians became proud of their Westerns, many native stars continued using fake American names. Very few leading actors were able to drop the fake moniker and do business with their real name: one remembers Giuliano Gemma, Franco Nero, Gian Maria Volonte as exceptions. The cinema promotes a fantasy that the 'Heroic Individual' is an American (and so must presumably be played by one). We'll see how directors like Corbucci and Sollima and Questi later subverted this. But it wasn't so easy back in 1963. Which was why Corbucci had ended up with such a modestly talented lead in *Red Pastures*: James Mitchum might be low on charisma and acting ability, but he was an American.[4] Leone had to play the game, but unlike Corbucci he genuinely cared who played the lead in his picture. So he sent the script to Henry Fonda's agent in Los Angeles, offering Hank the part of Joe.

4 *And his name was Mitchum! In Italy, in the 1960s, a famous surname was a guarantee of a career in second-rate movies, just as in today's Hollywood it guarantees you at least one TV series.*

Fonda's agent passed without showing the script to his client. Leone approached three more excellent choices: Lee Marvin and Charles Bronson (who rejected it), and James Coburn (who wanted $25,000: the producers had budgeted $15,000). Then he began approaches to the less great but possibly available: Cameron Mitchell (already signed to star in Corbucci's *Minnesota Clay*), Tony Kendall, Frank Wolff, Vassili Karis, Robert Hossein (neither of whom was American!) and finally Richard Harrison. All turned it down. Harrison had already starred in Marchent's *Gunfight at High Noon* and Papi and Colombo's *Gunfight at Red Sands*. He thought there was no real future in Spaghetti Westerns, and wanted to return to his real specialty, gladiator films. According to one version of the story, Harrison recommended another actor for *The Magnificent Stranger*: Clint Eastwood. According to another version, it was an Italian employee of Eastwood's agents, Claudia Sartori, who proposed him.

Eastwood was a TV actor who played a likeable cowpoke, 'Rowdy' Yates, in a series called *Rawhide*. He was looking for film work, and he accepted the $15,000. Eastwood's film experience was fairly minimal, though he had portrayed a sidekick to *Francis, the Talking Mule*.

Was Eastwood having a whispered joke when, to provoke a gunfight with the Baxter gang, he insisted that they apologise to his mule, for laughing at it? Both he and Lee Van Cleef remarked that the scripts they were given were incredibly verbose. The first draft of *The Magnificent Stranger*, by Leone, Duccio Tessari and Fernando di Leo, had been *358 pages long* (independent films run about a page a minute – so 358 pages equals almost six hours: *One-Eyed Jacks* territory). Eastwood knew instinctively to *cut the dialogue*. Most people on set – including the directors – spoke little or no English. According to Eastwood, the only English word Leone could say was 'goodbye'. So Clint and his stunt double, Bill Thompkins, communicated with their director via sign language, and the bilingual stunt coordinator, Stefanelli. Leone would mime the action for his cast: how to walk, how to draw a gun, how to hit someone. An intensely visual director, he paid little attention to the dialogue. With multi-national casts acting in their own languages, actors had considerable licence to misbehave. A bad actor would instinctively seek to increase the number of lines he had: it was the genius of Eastwood, and later Lee Van Cleef, to do the opposite. Faced with page after page of overwritten dialogue, they pared it down to a few words, a couple of words, a look. 'Pardon me, Ma'am.' 'Sorry, Shorty.'

The Magnificent Stranger began its six-week shoot in April, on the Zorro set. Hojo de Manzanares was a single street of wooden, anonymous buildings, dominated by a two-storey saloon, which Simi refurbished as a Spanish-style hacienda. The town was in poor shape: windows were broken, signs had fallen down, paint was bleached away. Leone and Simi relished the dilapidation, and enhanced it: San Miguel was meant to be a ghost town, inhabited only by criminal gangs, and the phantoms of those they'd killed.

These two gangs are seen in the background, from the balcony of the saloon, as Silvanito tells the stranger which side is which. These are the warring families of *Yojimbo* with an extra *Corkscrew* twist: one outlaw family is gringo, the other Mexican. The sake merchant and the silk merchant had reasons to hate each other, but they were both Japanese; in Leone's version, racism enters the frame. The Baxters – gun merchants – are mostly gringos. The Rojos – rum runners – are pure-blood Spaghetti Western Mexicans, with the one gringo henchman, Rubio (Stefanelli). This Mexican-gringo war would be the template for many, many later Italian Westerns. In Corbucci's films, the gringos – being more calculating and cynical – tend to beat the Mexicans. Here, the gringos don't have a chance against the Rojos, who – being Latins like the audiences in Italy – are depicted as infinitely more hot-blooded and effective.

The casting combines the splendid and the awful.

Awful are the stock 'cute' characters, including Piripero, the cackling coffin-maker; Silvanito, the brusque bartender; Julio and Jesus, the pathetic pair; and Juan de Dios, the town's babbling bellringer (how many towns have a professional bellringer, for God's sake? Where is the church? Where is the priest?). All are borrowed from *Yojimbo*. Piripero is played by Josef Egger, a hammy old character actor whom Leone admired for the elasticity of his face. Silvanito is Pepe Calvo, straight from central casting with a false moustache and wig. Julio and Jesus are not played by actors. There is no better moment in *Fistful* than the one where Benito Stefanelli, wearing a vest bedecked with bullets, aims his gun at the whimpering Julio and Jesus. And no bigger disappointment than the appearance of Silvanito, with shotgun, to save the pair. Hated by the audience, these cutesy characters were seemingly loved by the director. And by his co-screenwriter, Duccio Tessari, who peopled his later scripts with similar 'cute/funny' annoyances.

Cuteness aside, the supporting cast is fine. The Germans, Marianne Koch (Marisol), Wolfgang Lukschy (John Baxter) and Sieghardt Rupp (Esteban Rojo) all make a proper effort, and the 'Mexicans', played by Antonio Prieto, Stefanelli and Mario Brega, a butcher from Rome, are excellent. Koch was briefly a big star in Germany, and Leone was canny in casting her in an iconic, almost wordless role.

Leone had wanted his friend Mimmo Palmara to play Ramon, the leader of the Rojos. But Palmara was hired for *Bullets Don't Argue*, so Leone went with a stage and TV actor, Gian Maria Volonte. It was a choice of genius. Saddled with the moniker 'Johnny Wells', Volonte is one of the most *present* actors ever filmed. Soon he would become a leading man, a star, portraying Bartolomeo Vanzetti, Enrico Mattei, Lucky Luciano... But it was Leone who gave Volonte the break of his career, and Volonte returned the favour. As Ramon Rojo, he doesn't mess about, doesn't lose concentration, doesn't 'act'. Always in motion, hurrying along balconies, down stairs, stalking among his men, this actor invites a *plano secuencia*: a long, complicated tracking shot, a scene without cuts. Volonte is powerful and fascinating. He has the best part, of course: a psychotic, kidnapping mass-murderer.

Fistful of Dollars is Gian Maria Volonte's film, and Eastwood plays Joe as Ramon's foil: passive, slow, catlike in the sense that cats are lazy and, most of the time, don't do very much. He does this well.

Ramon, with his reliance on the Winchester rifle, equals Onosuke in *Yojimbo*: the deadly young punk with a pistol, so precisely played by Tatsuya Nakadai. But Volonte plays his outlaw, not as sadistic and precise, but as sadistic and outright mad. With the arrival of Ramon, Leone deviates from the *Yojimbo* narrative. In *Yojimbo*, the government inspectors keep the warring gangs in check for a while. In *Fistful*, Ramon *murders* the government inspectors – two US and Mexican army detachments – and steals their money and guns.

The hecatomb beside the Rio Bravo is the prototype for many machinegun massacres, of soldiers and civilians, in later Spaghetti Westerns. Corbucci's films have several. But in *Fistful* it's a completely original moment, not copied from *Yojimbo*. It establishes Ramon Rojo as an adversary more dangerous and powerful than Onosuke, since he is prepared to take on and defeat *the state itself*. Two states, in fact, since he has killed and robbed soldiers from Mexico and the US.

This is a crucial scene. And it wasn't directed by Leone! This whole sequence, involving Eastwood, Volonte, Pepe Calvo, and many extras, was shot by a second unit on the banks of the Rio Alberche, in Spain. The director was Franco Giraldi – hired by Papi and Colombo. I, too, have directed second unit, and the theory of it is that second unit films mere cutaways and ride-bys, and the odd shot first unit has missed. That is the theory. In reality, a second unit director is hired because the production has fallen way behind schedule and the producers need someone to direct entire scenes, with actors – quickly.

So Giraldi directed the massacre beside the river – splendidly – and also the night-time attack on the Baxters' house. This, too, is an important, memorable scene. Closely modelled on *Yojimbo*, the massacre of the Baxters is strikingly creepy and violent; it became one of the two most-censored parts of the film. What was Leone thinking of, absenting himself from these important scenes?

We know that Papi and Colombo had a penchant for throwing extra directors into the mix: in Giraldi they had picked a good one. But why did Leone let this happen? How could he fall so far behind as to miss directing these important scenes? In truth, most of the scenes in *Fistful* can be described as important: it's a tight script with only one sub-plot – Marisol. Eastwood was only briefly in the 'Rio Bravo' scene: a couple of shots, then Leone's first unit could continue using him. Giraldi would continue with Volonte – the 'supporting actor' who just happened to be stealing the film.

I get the impression Leone wasn't obsessive about *directing*. He liked setting up projects, and planning them, and he was passionate about the costumes, and the sets, and the 'historical' detail. He loved talking about these things, in grand and impressively allusive terms. But I suspect he wasn't entirely happy on the set. Perhaps he was in later films, when he was an internationally respected *auteur*... But Leone would still try to avoid directorial duties, handing entire films over to his assistants. When Eastwood first arrived in Rome, Leone had avoided him, pretending to be ill and sending Caiano to meet the actor. Perhaps Leone felt similarly intimidated by Volonte – volatile like his name, demanding, full of questions, seeing the politics in everything and *wanting to discuss it*. Some directors love talking to actors. Others do not. Like actors, directors can be complex characters. Leone included.

And most histories of *Fistful of Dollars* report that the production was running out of money by this stage. The story goes that Colombo and Papi had overspent on *Bullets Don't Argue*, and that Leone's film was paying the price. Mario Caiano insists this wasn't so: he told Marco Giusti that both films had entirely separate budgets, which – at 240 million lire each – were the highest of any Spaghetti Western to date. Others put the budget at anywhere between 40 and 200 million. A lower figure *feels* right: *Fistful of Dollars* has the air of a low-budget film, very well made.

Carlo Simi saved money by using existing sets. In Madrid, the company shot at a museum of rural life, the Casa de Campo: with the high ceilings and broad arches Simi had sketched for Corbucci, in Rome. This became the Rojos' hacienda, and it was here that Leone filmed his *Viridiana*-style 'Last Supper' – with the clan lined up behind a trestle table, while Joe and Ramon play target practice with a suit of armour (there are two suits of armour in the film: the second one is delivered, in mute, Buñuelian fashion, just in time for the Last Supper). On the Zorro set, Simi re-worked some of his *Bullets Don't Argue* sets. Both units shot in Almería: Giraldi getting the ride-bys in the canyons near Tabernas, while Leone shot Marisol's exteriors and Joe's arrival.

It seems to me that *Fistful*'s opening sequence, so striking, and so different from the beginning of *Yojimbo*, was influenced by Ed Abbey's

modern Western novel, *The Brave Cowboy*. This fine book is unfortunately out of print. But the assiduous reader can still find a copy, check
out the opening few pages, and see if he or she does not agree that
Tessari, or de Leo, or another co-author, read the scene where John W
Burns, the last anarchist cowboy, rides through the Mexican outskirts
of Duke City. We have firm evidence that Leone was aware of – and
impressed by – *The Brave Cowboy*. What evidence? I'll reveal all, in
two chapters' time.

Films have different lives with different audiences. The Italian and
Japanese audiences who watched these two films enjoyed them for
the same reasons I did: for their cynical, hard-boiled attitude, their ironic humour, their violence, their villains' villainy. But Japan and Italy had
been occupied countries; they'd seen corruption in all shapes and siz-
es, and witnessed the rise of powerful gangsters *and their political alliances*. So they were, first and foremost, appreciative of the *accuracy*
of the shady universes which Kurosawa and Leone also perceived.

Any second-rate writer-director could tell a tale of a good, upright,
masterless samurai or sheriff who saves a town from rival bandit
gangs. John Wayne starred in many such things in the 1930s, often
playing a government spy of some sort, and they were over in only
two reels. The genius of Kurosawa – and of Leone in identifying and
copying it – is his use of the anti-hero. Sanjuro is basically a drunken
tramp. His one skill is his capacity for violence. He can plan, but only a
couple of moves at a time. He scratches, burps and doesn't shave.

Joe isn't as drunk or as itchy as Sanjuro, but we believe he's drunk
when he pretends to be, because he's a character, Joe, in Leone's
movie: he isn't yet *the invincible Clint Eastwood*, whose character
couldn't possibly really be drunk, any more than he could be afraid, or
gay... Joe is the most fleshed-out of the performances Eastwood gave
Leone: relatively human, his sense of humour almost always present,
greeting every incongruous situation with the same soft, sarcastic
'hello'. Joe is more selfish than Sanjuro, who acts out of a sense of
natural justice. He saves Marisol because, 'I knew someone like you
once, and there was no one there to help.' But, overall, both Joe and
Sanjuro are pretty despicable. They stand out as 'heroes' not because
they do good things, but because they refrain from bad ones. As Don-

ald Richie put it, *Yojimbo* has 'a hero whose only virtue is a negative one: he is not actively concerned in being bad'.[5]

5 *Donald Richie*, The Films of Akira Kurosawa, *p 149*

Now this is an understandable message if you view your own society as riddled with corruption and inequity, where the bad usually win, and the good get crushed. It was natural for Japanese and Italians to feel this way. But many Brits and Americans also view their home turf as a playground of corrupt politicians, rip-off merchants and gangsters. This is why Spaghetti Westerns were so popular around the world.

But Anglo-American film critics tended to share the cultural and social assumptions of their own elite. They were uneasy around innovation, or even rigorous parody: gatekeepers with the mindset of censors. The English and American critics couldn't accept what to a teenage boy was obvious: that Spaghetti Westerns reflected, in a fractured glass, our own messed-up society. The issue of the relative goodness of the hero disturbed them greatly: Italian Westerns were often compared to *Shane*. Ignoring the similarities of art direction and costume, and the shared operatic sensibility, and the sudden outbreaks of violence, the offended critics placed *Shane* and Spaghetti Westerns on opposite sides of an untraversible cultural canyon. On one side stood 4,000 years of culture and, err, Alan Ladd. On the other, the doom of nations, and Clint Eastwood.

But Joe's low moral status wasn't *Fistful of Dollars*' worst transgression. This was its use of what the critics termed 'gratuitous violence'. Gratuitous, meaning unnecessary, or perhaps excessive, was deemed, by these respectable men, bad. A Surrealist might disagree, might defend gratuitous acts, might promote the aesthetic virtues of artificial bloodbaths. Giving bourgeois critics nightmares was a Surrealist goal! But Surrealism was in retreat, and Punk had yet to arrive. There were no Cronenburgs, no Hong Kong action seasons, no Tarantino festivals, in 1964. Spaghetti Westerns were as violent as films got. And *Fistful of Dollars* got violent in three transgressive ways:

1. *Shooter and victim in same frame*. This was a violation of the Hays Code. It seems strange today, but one of the rules of self-censorship which Hollywood had adopted via the Code was never to

show a gun fired, and its victim fall, in the same frame. This was considered too shocking for a polite, or impressionable, viewer. Two shots had to be used: first of the shooter, then of his victim falling down. Apparently, *Fistful of Dollars* was the first film to break this rule. If this is true it's remarkable. But such gatekeeper-imposed taboos still exist. I asked the head of one of the London film quangos why he thought the BBC, Channel 4 and Sky didn't show news footage of 'our' prisoners being executed in Afghanistan, or people shot and killed in Iraq. They obviously had the footage; it was screened in Latin America and the Middle East. He told me there was a general consensus in the British media not to show such footage 'as it might tend to brutalise people'.

(Such hypocrisy is far worse than anything in the Vietnam period. To embark on wars of aggression in foreign countries, to kill thousands of innocent people, to videotape it, and then censor the footage so as not to 'brutalise' homefront consumers... is there a word for this?)

2. *Mercy Killing*. Another Hays Code violation. Shooting an injured person, or any other form of euthanasia, was *verboten* under Hollywood's censorship rules. Leone breaks the rule in the scene where Joe invades Marisol's prison, and massacres her guards. It *is* a massacre: he enters with his gun drawn, while the guards are eating dinner. As he crosses the room, one of his injured victims groans. Joe shoots him again. I can't remember such a callous, throwaway killing *on screen* in a previous film.[6] Interestingly, Leone doesn't borrow it from *Yojimbo*: it is an original element. According to Frayling, Eastwood was trying to toughen up the bland image he'd acquired as 'Rowdy' Yates. Was the mercy killing Eastwood's idea? Shooting a wounded man certainly gave him an edgier image than he'd had on *Rawhide*. The scene would be repeated, like a bizarre good-luck talisman, in later Eastwood films.

6 *Much worse things took place in* The Searchers, *and in Bud Boetticher's films (where small boys are drowned in wells). But, no doubt proscribed by the Hays Code, they happened off screen.*

3. *An overall atmosphere of violence*. For the hostile critics, this, I think was *Fistful*'s greatest offence. And the death count is in-

deed both high and bloody. Joe encounters a corpse on a horse (the equivalent of *Yojimbo*'s dog carrying a human hand); then kills four men. In Giraldi's riverside scene, Ramon kills an entire troop of Mexican soldiers, having previously murdered an equivalent number of Americans. Returning from the murder of Marisol's six guards, Joe is savagely beaten by Ramon's gang. The entire Baxter family – including a woman – is burned or shot to death by laughing sadists. Finally the barman is beaten up, hung from a *strappedo* and tortured.

Numbers 1 and 2 are single issues related to Hollywood's self-imposed censorship code, and its rejection of that code during the '60s. Number 3 relates directly to *Yojimbo*. Any criticism of the film's 'gratuitous' violence can be applied equally to *Yojimbo* – which the same critics had recently reviewed respectfully, as the latest masterwork of Japan's foremost filmmaker.

The beating of the hero is brutal. It's also very well acted, particularly by Sieghardt Rupp, with his continuous, sickly laughing. The sequence ends with Mario Brega's character, Chico, stamping on Joe's gun hand. Being overtly cruel, the scene – and in particular its conclusion – was frequently cut by the censor. But the cuts damage the movie. The scene – together with its aftermath, in which Joe kills Chico, and escapes *à la The Glass Key* – only makes sense dramatically if you witness the entire thing. (The gunfighter's broken hand – from *The Naked Spur*, by way of *One-Eyed Jacks* – would be a key element of many, many later Spaghetti Westerns. So that genie was out of the box no matter what the censor did.) Censors similarly derailed the scene where the Rojos murder the Baxters. By cutting the death of Consuela Baxter, the censor denies us her prophetic curse: 'I hope you and your brothers die spitting blood!' All this stuff may be harsh, brutal, cruel, gross: but it is *not gratuitous*. It is part and parcel of the tough, exciting entertainment that is *Fistful of Dollars*: the quick of what is less a Western than a Hammett-esque action film.

Joe's bullet-proof vest is a strange turn. Arriving out of a cloud of dust, struck by Ramon's bullets, falling and rising again, Joe takes on a ghostly character. He asks, with a mocking tone, 'What's wrong?

Afraid, Ramon?' Another shot. Joe is knocked off his feet. Saved by the metal vest, he rises. 'Aim for the heart or you'll never stop me.' Joe uses Ramon's pride and faith in technology – his infallible Winchester – to get close enough to fulfil Consuela's curse.

All the elements of what we think of as a Spaghetti Western showdown – really *the Leone showdown* – are present here. There are low, wide angles from behind the Rojos, featuring their boots and spurs, big close-ups (of faces, but not yet of eyes), pistols in holsters, and the endless prolongation of the moment *before* the guns are drawn. One essential difference between Leone and Sam Peckinpah is their attitude to gunplay. For Peckinpah, the action of the gun battle is everything, to be choreographed at length, filmed from multiple angles, over several days, in slow motion; for Leone, what counts is what goes on before. It's this moment – when the gunfighters' eyes lock – which he stretches, longer and longer, in each successive movie, always accompanied by one of Morricone's biggest orchestral themes. For Leone, the action itself – the guns drawn, the bullet hits – is over in a couple of seconds. The villain, particularly if played by Volonte, may stagger around, spitting blood, causing the censor to reach again for his scissors. But *Fistful of Dollars* establishes a convention which almost all Spaghetti Westerns would observe: the showdown, not the gunfight, was the key moment of the film.

For a film which sets out, seemingly deliberately, to offend good, middle-class taste as the Surrealists did, there is a strange coda. After he's killed the Rojos, Joe saddles up his horse and remarks to the gravedigger, 'Well, guess your government will be glad to see that gold back.' What? It's hard to imagine Sanjuro, the masterless samurai, showing such concern for the property of the state. Why doesn't Joe keep that money, or at least as much as he can carry?

Morricone's music is, of course, remarkable. I won't say much more as I'm tone deaf and can't describe music in any meaningful way. Suffice to say that Morricone didn't disappoint his old school friend. His main theme bears a resemblance to Stan Jones' *Ghost Riders in the Sky*, and there's a showdown theme similar to *Deguello*, the haunting song from *Rio Bravo*. But most of Morricone's work seems completely original, both in instrumentation and in the tunes themselves. And what tunes! At this early stage in his career, Morricone wrote at least a dozen different themes *per picture*.

Corbucci claimed Leone spent the editing period 'slaving away at a Moviola machine and copying *Yojimbo*, changing only the setting and details of the dialogue'. Corbucci, of course, was gearing up to direct his own *Yojimbo*-influenced Western, so he isn't the most reliable reporter. Leone's producers simply ignored Kurosawa's film: they had their doubts about *The Magnificent Stranger*, recently retitled *Fistful of Dollars*. Disguised as an American picture, *Bullets Don't Argue* had opened in Milan on 26 August and done reasonable business. But, at the film market in Sorrento, there were no buyers at all for *Fistful*. So the film was relegated to a secondary market, Florence, where it opened on 12 September, banned to those under the age of 18.

There are several versions of what happened next. Frayling reports some of them, Giusti others. Something strange certainly took place in that one cinema near the Firenze railway station. It seems the first weekend's receipts were dismal. An employee of the distributor, Renato Bozzi, bought dozens of tickets from the box office, just so the cinema owner wouldn't pull the film. But early in the week *Fistful of Dollars* rallied and started doing business. The next weekend – according to Leone and his producers – the cinema was full. How many tickets did Bozzi buy? How many travelling salesmen did he bribe to attend screenings? His tactics worked: in November 1964 *Fistful of Dollars* opened at the Supercinema in Rome, battling American studio product like *My Fair Lady* and *Mary Poppins*. Mainstream Italian reviewers tended to look down on Leone's picture as another imitation American Western; but younger critics, including Dario Argento, responded enthusiastically. And *Variety* – the daily bible of the American industry – gave *Fistful* an excellent review: 'Crackerjack Western... with James Bondian vigour.'

By 16 December, *Fistful of Dollars* had taken 430 million lire at the box office. It was the most successful Italian-made Western, and one of the most successful Westerns generally. By comparison, *The Magnificent Seven* (1961) had earned a total of 280 million lire in all Italy. And so far *Fistful* had only played in Firenze and Rome!

Given the *Variety* review and the film's enormous box-office receipts, a letter from Mr Kurosawa was inevitable. According to Tonino Valerii, Leone's assistant, it arrived signed by Kurosawa and Ryuzo Kikushima, his co-screenwriter on *Yojimbo*. Valerii reported its contents to Frayling:

> Signor Leone – I have just had the chance to see your film. It is a very fine film, but it is my film. As Japan is a signatory to the Berne Convention on international copyright, you must pay me. – Akira Kurosawa.

Leone was thrilled to receive a letter from a Master, congratulating him on his very fine film. But Papi and Colombo were appalled, and tried to mount a defence rather than settle. Perhaps inevitably, Leone became a part of it – though they were defending the indefensible. At the start, Leone had sent all his friends and collaborators to see *Yojimbo*. He had asked Colombo and Papi to obtain the rights. Now he and they began claiming that *Yojimbo* was only one of various sources which had inspired *Fistful of Dollars*.

According to this new version of events, Leone's film was based on Carlo Goldoni's play *A Servant of Two Masters*. This was a nice try, but anyone familiar with the play will recognise it as bogus. I have acted in *A Servant of Two Masters* and – beyond the hero's titular dilemma – it has nothing in common with *Fistful of Dollars*. Leone also referred to Dashiell Hammett as a source, in particular *Red Harvest*. When the litigation delayed international sales, Papi and Colombo settled, giving Kurosawa and Kikushima Asian rights to *Fistful*, plus 15 per cent of the international box office.

Even after the lawsuit was settled, Leone continued to underplay the *Yojimbo* influence. In 1971, in a French magazine interview, he insisted, 'The film was also inspired by Shakespeare, as the prologue shows; the story goes so far as to make Clint Eastwood an incarnation of the Angel Gabriel.' Leone had a penchant, increasingly to be indulged, for grandiose statements of this kind. Sometimes he would claim Homer as his inspiration. So – was Corbucci right, and *Fistful* a scene-for-scene copy of *Yojimbo*? Or is there any truth to Leone's claims of diverse influences? Let's consider both plots, matching scenes wherever possible:

YOJIMBO	FISTFUL OF DOLLARS
Sanjuro throws a stick, follows it to town.	Joe rides into San Miguel.
Sanjuro sees farmer/son, drinks water.	Joe sees Julio/Jesus, drinks water.
Sanjuro passes dog with severed hand.	Joe passes dead man on horse.
Sanjuro instructed by town-cryer & bartender.	Joe instructed by bellringer & bartender.
Re: two-boss town; seeks credit.	Re. two-boss town, seeks credit.
Sanjuro sees undertaker next door.	Joe sees undertaker next door, places coffin order.
Sanjuro offers services, kills Ushi-Tora's men.	Joe offers services, kills Baxter's men.
Places, corrects coffin order.	Corrects coffin order.
Sanjuro joins Seibei's side.	Joe joins Rojos' side.
Overhears Seibei's clan discussing killing him.	Overhears Rojos discussing killing him.
Seibei orders noon raid against Ushi-Tora's clan.	Joe moves out.
Sanjuro sees fencing teacher run away.	
Sanjuro returns money, provokes showdown.	
County official inspectors arrive, 'all peaceful.'	Mexican cavalry arrive, 'all peaceful.'
Ushi's brother Ito & Seibei's wife compete to buy drinks.	Bartender reports re. Marisol & Ramon.
Ushi-Tora predicts officers will leave after next killing.	Departure of cavalry; followed by Joe.
Seibei & Ushi-Tora fake a peace.	Joe & bartender witness Ramon's massacre.
Appearance of Onosuke, with pistol.	Ramon announces peace; Joe returns money.
Sanjuro overhears Ushi-Tora's two killers talking.	Sundown – Ramons & Baxters peace conference.
Takes both killers (Hachi & Kuma) prisoner.	Cemetery – Joe positions corpses as if alive.
Delivers them to Seibei, tips off Ushi-Tora.	Joe tips off Baxters & Rojos, provokes showdown.
	Joe searches Baxters' place.
Onosuke and Ino kidnap Seibei's son.	Cemetery shootout – Rojos kidnap Baxters' son.

YOJIMBO	FISTFUL OF DOLLARS
	Joe rescues Marisol; takes her to Baxters'.
Onosuke proposes exchange, at 3am.	Baxter proposes exchange, next morning.
Exchange goes awry; Onosuke shoots Hachi & Kuma.	
Seibei reveals he has Onosuke's mistress prisoner.	
Exchange of Seibei's son for Onosuke's mistress.	Exchange of Baxter's son for Marisol.
Weepily observed by kid & father, Kuemon.	Weepily observed by Jesus & Julio.
Bartender tells story of Kuemon's family.	Bartender tells story of Marisol's family.
Sanjuro signs up with Ushi-Tora. Onosuke's pistol.	Joe signs up with Rojos. Ramon's Winchester.
Sanjuro tricks Ino, says guards are dead.	Joe fakes drunkenness, sneaks out.
Sanjuro kills guards, reunites Kuemon's family.	Joe kills guards, reunites Marisol's family.
Destruction of silk and sake warehouses.	Many ride-bys in Almería desert.
Next day – corpses lying in street; dereliction.	
Sanjuro, drinking, is busted by Onosuke.	Joe, returning, is busted by Ramon.
	Joe is questioned, tortured by Ramon & co.
After his beating, his guards gamble.	After his beating, his guards return.
Their orders: not to kill him.	Their orders: not to kill him.
Sanjuro is questioned, tortured by Ushi-Tora & co.	
Sanjuro hides in chest, eludes guards.	Joe kills guards, starts fire.
Sanjuro hides under boardwalks.	Joe hides under boardwalks.
Bartender questioned by Ushi-Tora & co.	Bartender beaten by Rojos.
Sanjuro leaves town in coffin, pauses to watch –	Joe leaves town in coffin, pauses to watch –
Burning of Seibei's place; massacre of his clan.	Burning of Baxters' place; massacre of Baxters.
Ito helps carry coffin out of town.	

YOJIMBO	FISTFUL OF DOLLARS
Sanjuro recuperates in temple.	Joe recuperates in mine.
Target practice; undertaker says barman is caught.	Target practice; undertaker says barman is caught.
Showdown; Sanjuro kills off Ushi-Tora's clan.	Showdown; Joe kills off Ramon's clan.
Sanjuro versus Onosuke; ruin of clan.	Joe versus Ramon.
Departure of Sanjuro.	Departure of Joe.

Looked at thus, it's pretty obvious that *Fistful of Dollars* is almost a scene-by-scene remake of *Yojimbo*, featuring similar characters. Some of Leone's scenes are better handled than the original material: for example, the prisoner exchange. There is also, in Leone's version, an overlay of Catholic symbolism: the bellringer, the cemetery scenes, Joe's 'Last Supper' with the Rojos, his departure in a coffin/burial in the mine/resurrection. But is it *Servant of Two Masters* or *Red Harvest*? Not at all. I think that Leone, when he talked to reporters, sometimes painted himself into corners. His claims to be an expert on the history of the American West quickly unravelled, as he confused Wild Bill Hickock with Wyatt Earp, and both with Buffalo Bill. When Leone said he had based *Fistful of Dollars* on Shakespeare, or Goldoni, or Hammett, or Homer, he was grasping at intellectual straws in the way that some filmmakers, who have grown up with little interest in fine art or literature, affect a high-brow demeanour in later life. He was also embarrassed by the charges of plagiarism, and wanted to set them aside.

And there *is* a twist of Hammett in Leone's work: not only are there gangsters, and corrupt policemen, there's also a propensity for dark jokes. Like the scene where Joe and Silvanito position a couple of corpses in a graveyard, so they appear to be alive. It's part of Joe's plot to trick Ramon, and it doesn't appear in *Yojimbo*. In Hammett's story, *Corkscrew*, the Continental Op does the same thing: positioning a corpse so that it appears to be alive, so as to trick the Mexican gang-boss, Big 'Nacio.

Fistful of Dollars opened internationally in 1967, and continued to do good business despite negative reviews. Here's more of Richard

Davis' anguish in *films & filming*: 'We are accustomed, however imperfectly, to a sense of poetry – from John Ford via Martin Ritt to Andrew McLaglen – bred by an ingrained tradition. In the European Western this tradition is non-existent, so that all the films produced in this genre are nothing more than cold-blooded attempts at sterile emulation.'

I sympathise with Davis up to a point: he is being very old-fashioned and operating from two long-forgotten bases on which to evaluate films or other works of art: the moral and the aesthetic. But, like contemporary critics who must pretend the current American cinema isn't complete junk, he gets confused, and equates the brilliant, the mediocre and the awful. It's one thing to call John Ford a great director of Westerns – who would disagree? Ford invented the genre. But Martin Ritt, a New Yorker, only made two Westerns, (*Hud*, 1962, and *Hombre*, 1966). Each of them was just as bleak, though not as entertaining, as *Fistful of Dollars*. And Andrew McLaglen was a fourth-rate churner out of John Wayne vehicles like *Mclintock!* (1963) and *Chisum* (1970). When Davis cites Ritt, or the absurd McLaglen, as spiritual heirs to Ford, he invalidates his argument, and reveals how barren the Western landscape really was. And just as he misrepresents Ford by claiming a pristine (and implicitly racial) continuity between him, Ritt and McLaglen, so Davis also misreads *Fistful of Dollars* as 'sterile emulation' of an American Western. It was nothing of the kind. *Fistful of Dollars* is a lively, successful emulation of a Japanese samurai film!

When it played on American television, *Fistful* was still considered too complex, or too dark, or too *something*, for the domestic audience. So a good director, Monte Hellman, was hired to shoot a five-minute 'prologue'. New footage, featuring Harry Dean Stanton as a prison governor, was intercut with close-ups of Eastwood from the film. Harry Dean tells Joe, who's now a prisoner of the federal authorities, that he'll be allowed out of jail only on condition that he 'go and clean up San Miguel'.

Thus American TV tried to turn Joe, the Magnificent Stranger, or the Man With No Name – as the posters called him – into a government agent. Like John Wayne, FBI cowboy, busting the rum runners in a two-reeler with Gabby Hayes. It was pathetic and unnecessary, and it suggests that there was something about Leone's film which still disturbed the gatekeepers at the network: something they felt obliged to explain. What was it? Even *Yojimbo*, in its first English-language release, was saddled with a lengthy set of titles explaining how Sanjuro is a masterless samurai who must live from his wits and sword. In neither case could the distributor tolerate the notion of a free-willed, anarchist protagonist. Just as John W Burns was doomed to be hunted down in *The Brave Cowboy*, so Sanjuro had to be *explained* and Joe *incorporated* into the enforcement mechanisms of the state.

It was too late. The levees of good taste and correct heroic law-making were about to be overwhelmed by a tidal wave of free-willed, violent, anarchic heroes – courtesy of the hundreds of Spaghetti Westerns made in the wake of *Fistful of Dollars*.

Minnesota Clay

aka *Le justicier du Minnesota*
(Italy/Spain/France)

Director: Sergio Corbucci   **Producer:** Ultra/Jaguar/Franco London   **Screenplay:** Adriano Bolzoni, Sergio Corbucci   **Director of Photography:** Jose Fernandez Aguayo   **Art Director:** Carlo Simi   **Music:** Piero Piccioni   **Cast:** Cameron Mitchell (*Minnesota Clay*), Georges Riviere (*Fox*), Ethel Rojo (*Estella*), Antonio Casas (*Jonathan*), Fernando Sancho (*Ortiz*), Diana Martin (*Nancy*), Alberto Cevenini (*Andy*), Joe Kamel, Julio Pena, Gino Pernice (*Scratchy*), Nando Poggi (*Tubbs*), Jose Canalejas (*Millicet*), Madeleine Dehecq, Jose Manuel Martin, Guillermo Mendez

The story

1883. Clay, a gunfighter going blind, escapes from Drunner Labour Camp determined to prove his innocence – he has been framed by Fox, now his successor as sheriff of Mesa Encantada. Fox, hired by the townspeople to protect them from a group of Mexican bandits, runs a protection racket and extorts the locals. The town continues to be terrorised by Ortiz's bandits. Clay saves Ortiz's mistress, Estella, from Fox's men. Ortiz tries to hire Clay to kill Fox.

Estella tricks Clay, telling him that Ortiz plans to kill his friend Jonathan (with whom Clay's daughter now lives). Clay rides to warn Jonathan, Ortiz attacks Jonathan's ranch, and Fox ambushes both Ortiz and Clay. Estella kills Ortiz. Back in town, realising Fox plans to ditch her, Estella helps Clay escape. Fox shoots Estella, and sends his gang out into the street to get Clay. Clay – losing his sight but taking advantage of dark stables and storehouses – decimates Fox's gang. Finally he kills Fox, and saves his daughter, Nancy.

(The English-language version ends with Clay's death in Nancy's arms. But the Italian version has an epilogue in which we learn Clay has survived, been pardoned, and recovered his sight.)

The film

The Italian version begins with big, bold titles against a red background – like *The Searchers*, or some epic, old-time American Western. This was the film which Corbucci had long planned; his tribute to *Yojimbo*. What follows is part-American, part-Italian, often bad, sometimes brilliant. The film is saddled with an elderly American lead, Cameron Mitchell, and some of the cast disguise themselves with American *noms-de-film* ('Anthony Ross', 'Joe Kamel'!), but all the crew use their real names. Corbucci was the first Italian Western director not to take an American-style screen name.

These credits suggest pride on the part of Corbucci and company, and an expectation of originality. But the script is far from original. The plot – hero breaks out of jail to clear his name – is ancient, and the dialogue dreadful: 'Don't try and follow me – I mean business!' 'I been runnin' since I was a kid.' 'Teach me to shoot, huh, Mr Clay?' Cameron Mitchell is a good rider, and a better actor than Jim Mitchum. But the character of Clay – when not engaged in acts of violence – is smug, self-pitying and dull. Having failed to persuade Jonathan and Nancy to turn him in for the reward, Clay remains terminally attached to the forces of law, order and jail. He sends Andy to the prison fort to summon the cavalry: 'The presence of the troops will stop the raids of Fox and Ortiz.'

Realising they had an older actor as their lead, the producers and/ or writers decided the film required a subplot featuring the 'love interest': Clay's daughter and the farm boy, Andy. This is terrible. Frayling observes that part of Leone's genius was his ability to think like a small boy, watching a film in the cinema. That boy hates love scenes. He especially hates love scenes when they involve two subsidiary characters. These scenes are pointless; they hold up the action, like the scenes in Marx Brothers movies which involve Zeppo. In *Minnesota Clay*, Corbucci wasn't as bold as Leone. Uncertain of his leading man, he concentrated on bland Nancy and 'likeable' Andy, a character the audience wants to see killed, *painfully*, and *soon*.

Corbucci, who was to become famous as a director of sadistic and transgressive Spaghetti Westerns, stumbled severely here. It was his second stumble, after the lifeless narrative and dolt-hero of *Red Pastures*. Yet even while making terrible mistakes, Corbucci could simultaneously surprise and innovate. He does so here, with Clay's physical affliction: blindness. This, plus the extreme suffering which Clay endures during the final gunfight, reverses the film's downhill stagger and provides us with a classic Corbucci finale – the first.

The film's debt to *Yojimbo* is small: the background action of two warring gangs. As in *Fistful of Dollars*, one gang is Mexican, the other gringo: a set-up which Corbucci would find useful in almost all his later films. But Corbucci goes one better than Kurosawa or Leone, I think, with the invention of Estella, a villainess who – like Sanjuro – continually switches sides. Estella is a great character, played by a strong and striking actor, Ethel Rojo. Rojo manages to eclipse Fernando Sancho, an extremely difficult feat. And Corbucci's old friend, Georges Riviere, is impeccable as Fox.

Fox and Estella have a complex, no-nonsense relationship: she looking for a long-term thing, he doubting he'll live long if they remain together. And Fox's gang – they, too, are more gangsters than cowboys – are simply splendid. Bad guys would be Corbucci's special area of eccentricity, and these – Gino Pernice, Guillermo Mendez, Antonio Roso – are a fine start. They're snappy dressers, dark-haired, long-nosed, skinny young character actors, bristling with leather and quirky accoutrements: bullet-holding armbands, a backwards-facing pistol belt, and a Winchester-in-a-holster. Carlo Simi's costumes for *Fistful of Dollars* were appropriate and authentic looking; his costuming for *Minnesota*

Clay is extreme, almost cartoon-like. In one scene, featuring Fox and Scratchy (Pernice), the well-dressed gangsters turn against the businessmen. It's hard to understand entirely, since it's been cut in two and presumably a preamble – the rounding up of the Rotary Club – is missing. The scene plays in wide-moving masters – *plano secuencia* – featuring as many well-dressed gangsters as possible, as Fox announces Clay's impending death, and the shakedown. When a nervous businessman reaches for his handkerchief, Scratchy shoots him dead.

As in *Red Pastures*, figures are greatly inflated. $100,000 – Fox's protection fee – was an enormous sum of money in 1883. But perhaps Fox doesn't really want the money. Scenes of mayhem follow, with fires, kidnappings, and a man hanging upside down in the street. It's all very entertaining, and, after Fox's bullying the businessmen, there's a certain class-war, political angle to the deranged action.

Not all of *Minnesota Clay* is up to this level. All the scenes involving Nancy, Andy, or Jonathan (a sometimes excellent actor, Antonio Casas) are deadly dull. Ortiz's raid on Jonathan's ranch is the epitome of dullness. Clay and his cute, white associates are virtually unscathed, gunning down dozens of Mexicans who gallop in circles around the farmhouse, waiting to be shot. This endless ride-around only ends when Jonathan, Nancy and Andy ride off in a buckboard. Even though they are circling the house, these Mexicans are apparently too stupid to chase Americans leaving via the back door.

This is Spaghetti Western action (and racism) at its worst. Still, there are flashes of a future Corbucci: director of remarkable, individualistic films. Estella has a mute, black servant. There's a short scene in a graveyard, where Clay visits his wife's grave: shot overlooking the lake at Tor Caldera, in Italy, it's a big improvement on *Red Pastures*' improbable graveyard scene. Corbucci's relationship with Simi seems to have been highly productive. 'Mesa Encantada' is the same location as 'San Miguel' and Clay rides down the same Zorro street as Joe in *Fistful*. But Corbucci films it differently, going for wide angles rather than long-lens shots, and Simi provides much dressing and foreground/background action. And his costumes! Scratchy and the boys wear leather biker jackets, confederate caps, frock coats and ruffs; Fox has a waistcoat, watch chain, cravat with jewelled pin. There are even costume changes: Fox reappears with a white hat!

Corbucci's enthusiasm for his bad guys presages greater films. Near the end, Fox waits for Estella after he's learned she's betrayed him. When she insists Clay's in the street, he makes her swear on the Bible that she's telling the truth. Then he shoots her several times, and sends Scratchy and the boys out to kill Clay. Suddenly freaked out by Estella's corpse, he orders another henchman to remove it. Then he sits down, fondling and kissing his gun. Apart from one close-up of Estella, the scene plays as a *plano secuencia*, favouring Fox. It's an unfortunate fate for Estella, the film's best character: but a wonderful, intense, insane scene.

And what follows is a top-notch shootout – entirely without music – as the blind Clay tracks, and kills, Scratchy and co *based on the sounds they make*. This is the film's big pay-off, the showy moment Corbucci had been looking forward to. It doesn't disappoint in any way. Beautifully lit – most of the scene is quite dark – it's expertly composed and paced. Mitchell plays the scene well, stumbling, falling down, freezing and listening for the sound his hunters make (a rifle click, a cork popped from a bottle). Scratchy and co, stalking Clay on the main street, are tense as piano wires, cool as cucumbers – until they shoot each other by mistake.

The absence of music is very effective. The death of Scratchy is a direct nod to *Stagecoach*, where the dying gunfighter comes looking for his drink, and falls dead on the saloon floor. And the ensuing showdown, in which Fox and Clay stalk each other through a dark warehouse, would become a staple element of many later Italian Westerns. Again, Corbucci plays it without music, and his compositions and montage are splendid.

When he's forced to confront Fox in the open – so as to save the ditzy Nancy – both Clay's hands are bloodstained, his face is a mess, he has two bloodstained bullet wounds on his torso, and one on his arm, he walks as if one leg was broken, and he is blind. *This is the first true Corbucci hero.* The American version ends with the battered Clay, having shot Fox, lying in Nancy's arms. There is a zoom out, and a freeze frame. Clay appears to be dead. This is a better ending than the original one – even if it was imposed by the American distributor.

Corbucci's original happy ending is absurd. Clay, recovered and wearing spectacles, rides off. Having reached the horizon, he takes off his glasses, throws them in the air, and shoots holes in both lenses. His sight, miraculously, has been completely restored.

It's stupid, anticlimactic, and typical of the film itself – which veers between impressive pessimism and wishy-washy mawkishness. Yet *Minnesota Clay* shows Corbucci to be a very accomplished film director, comparable to good directors of American Westerns like Aldrich, Walsh or Mann.

Much better was to come, though not immediately.

1965

'You know, I've got something in common with Hawks, and Ford, and Hathaway, and Sturges, and Walsh, and de Toth, and Lang... we're all blind in the right eye!'
– **Sergio Corbucci** interviewed, *Image et Son*

Minnesota Clay, shot in 1964, was released in 1965. By now, almost every Italian producer was planning a Western, nearly every director proposing one. Up to now, the Italian Western had been more or less in the American style. Heroes had surnames, family histories, even families. Body counts were relatively low, sadistic deeds infrequent. This was about to change. But before considering the most important and original film of the year – Leone's sequel to *Fistful of Dollars* – I'll visit a Spaghetti Western made in that old-fashioned, American style. Within a year, that imitative fashion would be extinct – but the film is a good one, with a surprising influence: *In a Colt's Shadow*.

In a Colt's Shadow

aka *All'ombra di una colt*
(Italy/Spain)

Director: Gianni Grimaldi   **Producer:** Vincenzo & Francesco Genesi **Screenplay:** Maria Del Carmen Martinez Roman   **Story:** Aldo Barni, Aldo Luxardo   **Director of Photography:** Stelvio Massi, Julio Ortiz Plaza   **Art Director:** Tadeo Villalba Ruiz, Carlo Leva   **Editor:** Franco Fraticelli (in Italy), Alfonso Santacana (in Spain)   **Music:** Nico Fidenco

Cast: Stephen Forsyth (*Steve Blaine*), Conrado San Martin (*Duke Buchanan*), Anna Maria Polani aka Anne Sherman (*Susan*), Helga Line (*Fabienne*), Franco Ressel (*Jackson*), Franco Lantieri aka Frankie Liston (*Burns*), Pepe Calvo (*Sheriff*), Andrea Scotti (*Oliver*), Aldo Sambrell (*Ramirez*), Graham Sooty (*Buck*)

The story

Two pistoleros, Steve and Duke, are paid to save a Mexican town from bandits. The older, Duke, is wounded in the shootout. He gives their money to Steve, telling him to share it with his daughter, Susan, whom Duke forbids Steve to see.

Steve takes half the money to a saloon girl, Fabienne, with whom both he and Duke have had affairs. He insults Fabienne, who tries to have a suitor kill him. Steve shoots the man dead without turning around. He picks up Susan, whom he plans to marry in defiance of Duke's threats. They ride to a town called Providence, where he attempts to buy a farm. But the town is entirely dominated by two rich gangsters, Jackson and Burns, who own every business, every store, and almost all the land.

Steve tries to buy Judge Williams' ranch; assassins attempt to kill him as he rides back. Steve and his horse play dead and get the drop on their would-be killers. Meanwhile, Fabienne arrives in town, allows herself to be seduced by Jackson, and partners up with him and Burns. She suggests hiring Duke to murder Steve.

Duke shows up and challenges Steve to a duel at dawn next day. Jackson and Burns' henchmen murder Judge Williams, but the sheriff, inspired by Steve's fearlessness, gives him the deeds to Williams' ranch. Steve and Susan move into their dream home, but Steve must return to face her father in a showdown.

The bad guys' henchmen lie in wait for both gunfighters at the appointed hour. Duke and Steve join forces and turn the tables on their foes. Duke kills Jackson; Burns tries to take Fabienne hostage, then shoots her in the back; he is wounded and arrested by the emboldened sheriff.

After the gunfight, Duke beats Steve up but lets him live. He rides off as Steve and Susan are reunited.

The film

For a Western in the American style, this is an excellent picture. It begins in the clunkiest manner, with dull conversation between two wooden heroes, riding along: a scene made all the worse by its similarity to the introduction of Ben Johnson and Harry Carey, Jr in Ford's *Wagonmaster* (1950). But as soon as Steve and Duke reach the grass-roofed, white-walled Mexican village, the film changes its tune. The gringos appear to be robbers, tying up some townspeople, hefting saddlebags full of money. But really they're there as a two-man *Seven Samurai* team, to save the village from bandits. Which they proceed to do, deftly.

In a Colt's Shadow seems to have been a true co-production: there are two cinematographers, two art directors, two editors: in each case, one Italian and one Spanish. Fortunately they managed with only one director! And what a vision this director has. Gianni Grimaldi stages his action scenes excellently, and portrays the West as already ruined by criminal capitalists, who literally own everything. The monopoly shingle of Jackson and Burns hangs over the hotel, the bank, the saloon, the livery stable, even the travel agent! When Steve enquires about buying a farm, Mr Burns tells him this won't be possible:

> BURNS: All the good land in these parts belongs to us. You see, we bought it all up because the farmers couldn't take care of it. And we'd like to see Providence develop into a rich and important city.

Stephen Forsyth is an overly handsome actor with an immobile face. But one gets used to him, as the stolid Steve. Conrado San Martin's character, Duke, is splendidly pig-headed, disagreeable and threatening. Duke hates everyone, including his surrogate son and the two women he loves. And the villains! Aldo Sambrell is briefly seen, as the bandit leader in the village, but the villainous trio in town is given plenty of entertaining screentime, including one *plano secuencia*, where they plot and flirt. Helga Line's Fabienne is aquiline and merciless. Franco Ressel is excellent as the oligarch, Jackson. He plays it like a frustrated, flustered and sadistic English public schoolmaster:

aggressively amorous with Fabienne, flogging a wooden post with his riding crop, having someone beaten up in his office (only the last portion of this scene seems to have survived – so I'm not sure who their victim is).

Best villain of all is the smooth, goateed banker, Burns (Franco Lantieri). He's super-cool, dresses all in black, and is intensely sensitive about his black-gloved right hand, which is made of wood. The original item disappeared in equally sensitive circumstances: shot off, perhaps, or cut off, because Burns is certainly a thief. Late in the film, Burns reveals his Achilles heel: he's terrified lest any harm come to his remaining hand. After Burns murders Fabienne, the sheriff and his deputies pump bullets into that very paw. A horrible, pathetic scene, worthy of Kyd's *Spanish Tragedy*, ensues:

> BURNS: The hand! My hand! They shot me in my hand! What'll I do?
>
> SHERIFF: It'll do you for the next couple of days, Burns. It's a noose for you after that.

This is an American-style picture, with added sadism on a Spaghetti scale. On the ranch there are two references to the famous door opening which begins *The Searchers*: the first time, a door opens to reveal a rifle, pointed at the hero, as he rides towards us; the second, the door admits two killers, who gun Judge Williams down. Both shots begin as identical homages to Ford, only to be subverted by violence. Grimaldi's West is packed with violent sadists. Among the assassins who think they've shot Steve and his horse with one bullet is this enthusiast:

> ASSASSIN 1: Let me go and put another bullet into 'im, Joe!

After Joe assents, another assassin explains.

> ASSASSIN 2: He was a volunteer member of one of those Mexican firing squads for over two years. And these little touches give him his biggest pleasure.

And Duke, Steve's former partner, and new father-in-law, is a total madman, loathing everyone, knowing he's been set up by Fabienne, demanding his stupid showdown anyway.

> DUKE: A pistolero is the kinda man who never fails to kill when he has to. It's our strength and our honour.

What an idiot! One is reminded of *Yojimbo*, of Sanjuro's warning to the would-be tough guys, before he kills them: 'It'll hurt.'

The showdown is beautifully staged, on the main street of the *Fistful* location. There are good stunts, and great falls. In a standard Western or action film, these falls would be covered by several cameras and repeated endlessly in the final cut. But Grimaldi and his editors are disciplined, and use each stunt only once – which makes for a tighter, better, faster sequence. Even when Duke beats Steve up, all the shots seem thoughtfully composed: the bodies, the buildings in the background, the overall geography. How often can one use the word 'composition' about a fistfight sequence?

On the basis of *In a Colt's Shadow*, one might have expected Grimaldi to direct other, distinctive Spaghetti Westerns. But he made only one: *Starblack* (1966), in which Robert Woods played a dual, Zorro-ish role, plus a couple of slapstick Westerns with the comedians Franco and Ciccio.

Given the financial success of *Fistful of Dollars*, a sequel was essential. The producers would make one, if the director didn't. Leone didn't want to make another Western, but – having seen none of the profits of his first one – he decided to make a sequel so as to spite Colombo and Papi. He'd found a new partner, a lawyer called Alberto Grimaldi. They would split the profits from this one, 50/50. It was an inspired act of revenge.

For a Few Dollars More

aka *Per qualche dollaro in piu, La muerte tenia un precio*
(Italy/Spain/Germany)

Director: Sergio Leone **Producer:** Alberto Grimaldi, Arturo Gonzales **Screenplay:** Luciano Vincenzoni, Sergio Donati, Sergio Leone **Story:** Fernando Di Leo, Enzo Dell'aquila, Fulvio Morsella, Sergio Leone **Director of Photography:** Massimo Dallamano **Art Director, Costumes:** Carlo Simi **Editor:** Eugenio Alabiso, Giorgio Serralonga **Assistant Director:** Tonino Valerii **Music:** Ennio Morricone **Cast:** Clint Eastwood (*Manco*), Lee Van Cleef (*Colonel Mortimer*), Gian Maria Volonte (*El Indio*), Klaus Kinski (*Hunchback*), Maria Krupp (*Mary*), Josef Egger (*Prophet in El Paso*), Rosemary Dexter (*Colonel's sister*), Roberto Camardiel (*Tucumcari station master*), Riccardo Palacios (*Tucumcari bartender*), Jose Marco Davo (*'Baby' Red Cavanagh*), Lorenzo Robledo (*Tomaso*), Diana Faenza (*Tomaso's wife*), Francesca Leone (*Tomaso's daughter*), Sergio Mendizabal (*Tucumcari banker*), Guillermo Mendez (*Sheriff of White Rocks*), Kurt Zipps (*Mary's husband*), Jesus Guzman (*Carpetbagger on Train*), Tomas Blanco (*Santa Cruz telegrapher*), Luis Rodriguez (*Guy Calloway*), Carlo Simi (*El Paso bank manager*), Dante Maggio (*Indio's cellmate*), Enrique Navarro (*Sheriff of Tucumcari*), Mario Brega (*Niño*), Werner Abrolat (*Slim*), Aldo Sambrell (*Cuchillo*), Luigi Pistilli (*Groggy*), Benito Stefanelli (*Huey*), Frank Braña (*Blacky*), Antonio Molino Rojo (*Frisco*), Jose Canalejas (*Chico*), Nazzareno Natale (*Paco*), Panos Papadopoulos (*Sancho Perez*), Peter Lee Lawrence (*Mortimer's brother-in-law*)

The story

In Tucumcari, New Mexico, Colonel Douglas Mortimer pulls the emergency cord and exits the train. A bounty killer, Mortimer makes short work of finding and killing his outlaw prey, Guy Calloway. Nearby, in White Rocks, Manco – another bounty killer – gets his man, Baby 'Red' Cavanagh, plus three of Red's henchmen. And, across the border, bandits break into prison to free their leader, the maniacal Indio.

El Indio holes up in a ruined church, where he gathers his gang and takes revenge on Tomaso, who turned him in for the reward. From the pulpit, he tells his gang how they will rob the legendary Bank of El Paso: he's learned from his cellmate, now dead, that the bank's money is hidden in a wooden drinks cabinet in the manager's office – not in the safe.

Pursuing El Indio, Mortimer and Manco find themselves stalking each other. Manco attempts to intimidate the Colonel and run him out of town. But Mortimer won't budge. After proving himself an equal – or better – marksman, the Colonel proposes a partnership. Still haggling over how much the gang members are worth, Manco agrees.

Pursuant to their plan, Manco frees Sancho Perez, an old friend of El Indio, from jail, and joins the gang. Sent on a distraction raid to Santa Cruz, Manco kills his partners and returns to El Paso. But Indio's bank robbery goes without a hitch, and Manco dissolves the partnership. The Colonel anticipates that El Indio will hide out in Agua Caliente, and waits for him there. After killing a hunchbacked bandit, Wild (whom he had insulted in El Paso), Mortimer sells his safecracking services to El Indio, and opens the strongbox.

El Indio orders his men to lie low. Mortimer and Manco steal the money, but are caught and beaten up. Then Indio tells his boy Niño to set the gringos free.

In a day-long gunfight on the streets of Agua Caliente, Manco and the Colonel kill off El Indio's band. Groggy – the smartest of the bandits – figures out that Indio wants his own men out of the way. He kills Niño, and attempts to steal the loot for himself. But the money is gone – replaced by a 'Wanted' poster – and Indio slips into total madness.

Manco provokes a showdown between El Indio and the Colonel – whose sister committed suicide when El Indio raped her and killed her lover years ago. Mortimer gives the entire haul of dead bandits to Manco, and rides off. Counting the take, Manco realises that he's missing $5,000 – and shoots Groggy, in the nick of time.

The film

A vast, ochre plain, with amber hills in the distance. From afar, a horseman rides slowly towards us. Money jingles, and he whistles tunelessly. The sun sears the plateau. After a long time, there is the click of a rifle, and a gunshot. In the distance, the rider falls from his horse. More gunfire, and the horse bolts. The titles appear.

This is how the film begins. One long take, lasting over a minute and a half, which does more than establish a mood. This shot, I think, is the essence of the Spaghetti Western: a harsh, desert world where human life is mercilessly exposed, and sudden violence erupts without a warning. There is no visual romanticism. The dominant sound is the hard clink of coins. Identities are unimportant: we don't know who the rider is, or where the shots come from. Or, for that matter, *why*. The killer is as anonymous as his victim. The only clue has been the jingling gold – reinforced by a post-credits caption:

> Where life had no value
> Death, sometimes, had its price.
> This is why the Bounty Killers appeared.

A grand, epic, alienating beginning, with the titles shot to pieces by rifle blasts. Now this: and note the use of 'Bounty Killer' rather than the more familiar, American-style 'Bounty Hunter'. Killer, not hunter: no sport, no fair play. The tone is set, but the setting is not. There's no reference to time or place. We are disoriented because we expected that figure riding across the range to be the hero, on his way to town. Now he's dead, we still don't know who's killed him, and the film begins again.

This opening makes an assumption no American Western had asked the viewer to make: that life is not sacred, to be protected by force of arms, but an intrinsically worthless commodity. *For a Few Dollars More* is a detached illustration of this thesis. Throughout, our expectations will continuously be denied. Those who appear villainous killers – bounty hunters – will turn out to be heroes. Here, Leone fulfilled the promise of his first Western, told an exciting and original story, and created a near-perfect example of the Spaghetti Western form.

7 *If there is a cinematic pantheon (and in idle moments film directors wonder about these things), all these marvellous films sit just one rung below the* Citizen Kane *of action pictures,* The Wages of Fear *(1951, Henri-Georges Clouzot).*

Not only is *For a Few Dollars More* a great Spaghetti Western, it's a great Western in its own right. It's as good as *Vera Cruz*. It's better than *The Magnificent Seven*. For me, it approaches the heights of *The Searchers* and *The Wild Bunch*.[7] All of its parts – cast, costumes, sets, cinematography, action, music, editing

– are correct, accomplished, hard to imagine otherwise. And first and foremost among these excellent elements is an outstanding script.

Several writers contributed to the screenplay, provisionally titled *Two Magnificent Strangers*: according to Giusti, first there was a treatment written by Fernando di Leo and Enzo Dell'Aquila; this was developed by Leone and Fulvio Morsella, his brother-in-law; then Luciano Vincenzoni was hired to write the script – his first Western – with input from Sergio Donati, Leone and di Leo.

Such a mass of writers, all picking at the carcass of an idea, would imply a flaccid, disconnected result: but the reverse is true. The script's as tightly constructed as a pocket watch; indeed, it revolves around a pair of pocket watches, worn by El Indio and the Colonel. Ah, those watches! What a great plot device – drawing us in and out of Morricone's score (they're musical watches, of course), introducing flashbacks, linking El Indio's scenes with Colonel Mortimer's.

The script's introduction of its protagonists is exemplary. The plot to rob the bank at El Paso is tautly handled. Betrayal and counter-betrayal are arranged adroitly around flashbacks, which gradually reveal El Indio's crime. Showdowns are innovative and frequent. Apparently, the formula for the James Bond films included a change of location every ten minutes: in like manner, Leone stages a classic, Western-style showdown every ten minutes, plus a bank robbery and two prison escapes. A bigger budget – 600 million lire – meant a longer shoot, new locations, a bigger cast, and an additional antagonist.

As a sequel, *For a Few Dollars More* depended on the return of its star, Clint Eastwood. Eastwood was better paid this time: $50,000. His character had a new name – Manco – and a leather wrist-strap, which he wore below his gun hand: was Manco an early sufferer of carpal tunnel syndrome? This is not explained. Otherwise, Eastwood's role was very like Joe in *Fistful of Dollars*. Less humorous, perhaps – gone were the little smiles, the cute 'hello' – but Manco, after all, must confront El Indio. As played by the magnificent Volonte, this was a devil from hell, beyond Ramon Rojo in his capacity for evil, a sadistic killer addicted to the deadly drug cannabis, fixated on a stolen pocket watch.

Manco is discovered in the White Rocks scene via two familiar items of Joe's repertoire: the half-smoked cheroot (which Eastwood detested) and the poncho (which he later claimed he brought from Western Costume in Los Angeles). Frayling observes that the poncho predates Eastwood's casting in *Fistful of Dollars*: it originates in Carlo Simi's costume sketches. Pedantically, I'd like to add that what Eastwood wore in these films isn't a poncho. A *poncho* is a large piece of material, worn as a garment in the Andes: Peru and Bolivia. The Mexican equivalent is called a *serape*. It is possible that Joe's cape was Peruvian, or Bolivian. But it looks Mexican to me.

For the rival bounty killer, Mortimer, Leone pursued his usual list of suspects: Lee Marvin, Henry Fonda, Robert Ryan. Fortunately, they turned him down a second time. Years ago, I interviewed Lee Van Cleef about his Italian experiences. He said:

> Leone came over in 1965, looking for one of two actors he had in mind for his second Western. The other one was Robert Ryan. The moment we met he made up his mind and said, that's it – that's the guy to play Colonel Mortimer in *For a Few Dollars More*.
>
> Well, I wasn't going to argue with him – hell, I couldn't pay my phone bill at the time. I went over and did the thing, I paid my phone bill, and exactly one year to the day – 12 April 1966 – I was called back to do *The Good, the Bad and the Ugly*.

Van Cleef had played a number of small roles in Hollywood movies, and Leone remembered him from *High Noon* (1952), where he played the bad guy's henchman, waiting for the train. Leone thought of Colonel Mortimer as 50-ish, and imagined Van Cleef to be the same age. In fact Van Cleef was only 40: he was blessed, as an actor, with one of those faces that seems 'always old'.

It's impossible now to imagine anyone else playing the role. Van Cleef, with his hawk-like features and mysterious air of suffering, *was* Colonel Douglas Mortimer. Italian producers, well aware of the worldwide popularity of the James Bond franchise, immediately saw the box-office value of a Mortimer-style character: the technological killer, usually clad all in black, with an arsenal of deadly, modern weapons. Later, this character would be called Django, or Sartana, or Sabata. But the prototype for all those cold, black-clad, world-weary, bounty-killer-gringo-avenger-types is Colonel Mortimer.

Klaus Kinski was another hard-working thesp whom Spaghetti Westerns made into a star. The blond, blue-eyed Polish actor had already appeared in a German Western, *Winnetou – Last of the Renegades* (1964), playing a villainous Indian (!) scout called Luke. As he makes clear in his autobiography[8], Kinski had no respect for film directors: thinking them all stupid, he worked for whoever paid him the most money, or offered the best chances to meet pretty girls. Yet it must still have been a relief, after the overt stupidity of *Winnetou*, to play a character he was actually suited for: the hunchbacked, Southern gunfighter named Wild. Kinski put his heart into the role, and reprised it, at times, in other performances – notably in *Aguirre: The Wrath Of God* (1971).

8 Kinski Uncut *by Klaus Kinski (Viking/Allen Lane, 1996)*

All the bad guys in this movie are splendid. Mario Brega, Benito Stefanelli, Aldo Sambrell and other toughs from *Fistful of Dollars* show up in Indio's gang. As Groggy, the too-clever henchman, Leone cast Luigi Pistilli – a talented, dynamic actor, equally at home in exploitation movies or the high-end political dramas of Francesco Rosi. Pistilli was like Volonte, in that regard, and one wonders whether Leone deliberately cast him as Indio's rival, to exploit that tension.

As with *Fistful*, the supporting cast is a mixture of the excellent and the 'cute/funny'. In the former category are Roberto Camardiel, in a small role as the Tucumcari station master, and Guillermo Mendez (the dandy gunfighter in *Minnesota Clay*) as the corrupt sheriff of White Rocks. In the latter fall the egregious Josef Egger, playing an old man whom Manco pumps for information about the Colonel, Kurt Zipps as the dwarfish hotelier, Maria Krup as his bosomy wife, and Antonio Ruiz as the tow-headed urchin who assists Manco. Ruiz, though irritating and uncredited, plays an important character. Watching the bounty killers square off for a fight, the kid remarks to his friends, 'Just like the games we know!' There's a little kid in the station office with Camardiel; small boys flock to every stranger who rides into El Paso; in Agua Caliente, a kid tries to pick apples. The constant presence of children as witnesses – all boys (except for the baby, played by Leone's own daughter, who is promptly killed!) – makes clear the parallel between these savage, 'adult' rituals, and children's games.

After that classic desert opening, most of the locations of *For a Few Dollars More* are urban. The first scene of the story proper takes place aboard a train, travelling through New Mexico and Texas, long after the Civil War. The place is violent and uncivilised, but there are no Cheyenne war parties on the horizon; bands of outlaws move between fixed settlements; this is no longer the frontier. All the available Western towns, in Italy and outside Madrid, were used, and a new town was built – 'El Paso' – in the desert between Tabernas and Almería.

In the middle of this clay and limestone desert labyrinth, where the road splits to Murcia or Granada, Simi built 'El Paso, Texas'. The new set was laid out as per the script. Every alley or verandah described by the screenwriters was built by Simi. On a plateau between two rows of hills, four streets converge on a broad square. Save for the huge, isolated bank (in the film, Simi plays its manager!) all the town's buildings are of wood and the occasional brick wall: chunky, authentically ugly, credible structures. To render them less hideously square – just as the Western architects had done – Simi arched or gabled the false fronts, adding trellises and balconies. The result was a crude baroque architecture: pleasingly asymmetrical. The effect of the original set (before it was blown down by the wind, re-built, and turned into a 'tourist destination') was simultaneously authentic and surreal. Simi's 'El Paso' was a superficially bustling Wild Western town, centred around two saloons and a bank, without industry, stockyards, tents, shanties, corrals, church or cemetery. A period photograph, severed at the edges.

'El Paso' is the same sand colour as the hills that rise behind it: the town is part of the desert, the desert part of the town. As with the ghost village in *Fistful*, this was the West that Leone always strove to create: an excessively gritty, fantastical, tactile environment. Depending on the camera's needs, sometimes El Paso is full of people, at other times no one inhabits it. In Leone's films, towns are not towns in any real sense: they're part of the landscape, like a rock formation or the brooding pinnacle of the triangular mountain, *El Alfaro*. They aren't places to work, raise families, or grow old – but deadly playgrounds where bank robbers and bounty killers conceal themselves, spy, plot and confront one another.

The script, with its prison breakouts and intricately planned heist, could easily be remade as a modern gangster movie. No doubt Vincenzoni and the others had seen *Rififi*, the first great heist picture; perhaps they also admired Jean-Pierre Melville's robbery thriller *Second Breath* (*Le deuxième souffle*). They wrote a clever script. Manco is given the assignment of infiltrating Indio's gang. When challenged by Indio and the other outlaws, Manco replies:

> MANCO: Well, there's such a big reward being offered on all you gentlemen that I thought I might just tag along on your next robbery. Might just turn you in to the law.
>
> INDIO: Amigo, that's the one answer that would prove you're all right.

It doesn't prove any such thing, of course, but it's a good exchange, and one of Eastwood's best moments. The gang look fantastic – the meanest-looking bunch of knife-throwing killers you ever saw – though, for such a splendid group of villains, they get to do very little. Having been told to lie low for a month, the bandits do so without a murmur: in the next scene, Kinski, Sambrell, Pistilli and co are laid out like sleepy bunnies, snoring on the floor.

A 'weakness' – or perhaps a strength – of the film's red-tinted flashbacks is that they don't convey what they're supposed to. In the first one, the younger Indio breaks into the home of a young couple (played by Rosemary Dexter and an uncredited Peter Lee Lawrence), spies on them as they admire a pair of musical watches, then murders the young man. In the second flashback, at the end of the film, Indio attempts to rape the young woman, who shoots herself with his gun.

These flashbacks are shared by El Indio and Colonel Mortimer, so when I first saw the film I assumed that the man Indio shot was the young Mortimer – i.e. Peter Lee Lawrence doubling as young Van Cleef. Presumably, young Mortimer wasn't killed by Indio's bullets, recovered, and embarked on his vengeance trail. There is no indication as to the identity of either young lover. Then, at the end of the film came the following lines, when Manco returned the Colonel's stolen watch, and saw its enclosed picture:

MANCO: Do I detect a resemblance?

COLONEL: There often is – between brother and sister.

This led me to conclude that Colonel Mortimer had been involved in an incestuous relationship with his sister, which was broken up by El Indio. This only added to the atmosphere of strangeness and perversion which made Italian Westerns so much better than American ones!

Years later, watching the film, I still read these flashbacks the same way. They are *shared* by two characters, which implies both characters participated in them.[9] This means Colonel Mortimer was having sex with his sister! Or that he was just about to. So either Leone and his writers fumbled an otherwise perfect script, or they *didn't*, in which case the film is doubly excellent.

Leone's vision of women, at least as seen through his films, is pretty bleak. In his films women are rape victims, prostitutes, or ancient crones. It might be said in his defence that these are Westerns, and that Westerns are traditionally sexist and limited in their portrayal of women. But even by the standards of Budd Boetticher, Leone's women have it pretty bleak. Contemporary Italian directors like Corbucci and Duccio Tessari were making Westerns in which women played active, aggressive roles. Leone never did. Why? Leone was married, with a daughter. Reading between the lines in Frayling's biography, I get the impression that Leone had serious problems with his mother, who lived with him throughout this period. Was she insane, as some interviewees said? Had her mental illness stricken her mute?

What a strange and hard burden to bear. You spend your days directing cowboy actors, then return at night to *mama*, to deal with her. How does this affect your art, the fantasies you unfold on film? Both these Westerns feature the destruction of families (Marisol's, the Baxters', Tomaso's): a terrible crime, but, for a Surrealist, a liberating one. This would continue.

Van Cleef enjoyed his experience on the multi-lingual, sometimes slow-moving set. 'The one area which I disagreed with in the Italian

9 *Note how film language has evolved here. Flashbacks in movies don't just 'happen': they are connected to one or more of the characters in the preceding scene. This is a rule for films in general, not just Spaghetti Westerns. For example, when a character says, 'My people suffered this indignity for centuries,' the illustrative flashback* must include the character. *It isn't sufficient for the film simply to illustrate the indignity.*

scripts was the dialogue. There was too much of it. I'd be given a god-damn half-page paragraph and say, look, I can get this across in two words. Maybe it's a difference in the languages, but I had to rewrite every damn scene I was in. I reduced the whole thing – cut it down to a "Hello" or a "Pardon me, ma'am".' I asked him if Leone spoke English. 'On *For a Few Dollars More*, no. He did the next year... But it caused no problems – I understood exactly what he wanted. It was an instinctive thing. He would demonstrate a little bit, and there was always an interpreter on the set. But I knew from the script what was expected of me.'

Technical credits throughout are excellent: Morricone's score consists of several entirely original pieces, and provides audio effects via the musical watches. Already he was being taken seriously as a composer: the same year, Morricone wrote a very different score for Pontecorvo's *Battle of Algiers*.

For a Few Dollars More was sold to 26 countries in a single day. While cinema attendances in Italy were falling, Leone's new film sold more tickets than any other film in Italian history – earning $5,000,000 between 1965 and 1968 in Italy alone. Hundreds of Italian Westerns went into production. Some clung to the Leone/Corbucci formula by importing American leads. Others used Italian actors and disguised them as Americans. One such actor – saddled with the clunky moniker of 'Montgomery Wood' – would soon become the most popular star of the Italian cinema and, before the year was out, start trading under his real name: Giuliano Gemma.

Gemma's first Westerns are routine. *One Silver Dollar* (*Un dollar bucato*) is a story of two brothers who, having fought for the Confederacy, take separate paths after the Civil War. The best scene involves Gemma's slow-witted hero being coaxed into a showdown with his outlaw brother, Blackie. But the film moves slowly, grinding to a halt long before it ends. David McGillivray, reviewing it for *films & filming*, hated it: 'I cannot see the appeal in this ultra-naive approach with its putrid colour and distinctly agitated cast, squirming to a man into postures and grimaces which they were never meant to adopt.' The violence, which McGillivray also disliked, is the most interesting part. In *Adios Gringo*, Gemma plays an honest cowpoke, Brent Landers, who must prove his innocence by tracking down the Mexican, Jack Dawson, who sold him stolen beeves. Like several of these early, minor Spaghetti Westerns, *Adios Gringo* was based on an American Western novel – in this case, *Adios* by Harry Whittington – which may account for the quirky character names: Avery Ranchester, Jake Clevinger, Tex Slaughter, *et al.* It, too, is a slow-moving film, of slight interest.

Bad these early Gemma films may have been. But they were popular! While Corbucci struggled to get another Western off the ground, Duccio Tessari – screenwriter of *Fistful*, friend of Leone – wrote a comic Western for Leone's second-unit man, Franco Giraldi: *7 Guns for the MacGregors*. And then he directed a pair of Westerns of his own, both starring Gemma/'Montgomery Wood': *A Pistol for Ringo* and *Return of Ringo*.

A Pistol for Ringo

aka *Una pistola per Ringo*
(Italy/Spain)

Director: Duccio Tessari   **Producer:** Luciano Ercoli, Alberto Pugliese   **Screenplay:** Duccio Tessari, Alfonso Balcazar, Fernando Di Leo, Enzo Dell'aquila   **Director of Photography:** Francisco Marin   **Art Director:** Juan Alberto Soler, Carlo Gentili   **Costumes:** Carlo Gentili   **Editor:** Licia Quaglia   **Music:** Ennio Morricone   **Cast:** Giuliano Gemma (*Ringo*), Fernando Sancho (*Sancho*), Nieves Navarro (*Dolores*), George Martin (*Sheriff*), Jose Manuel Martin (*Pedro*), Hally Hammond (*Ruby*), Antonio Casas (*Major Clyde*), Pajarito (*Tim*), Paco Sanz (*Colonel*)

The story

The sheriff of Quemado arrests Ringo, aka Angel Face, for shooting the Benson brothers. Ringo, who acted in self-defence and knows the sheriff and his 'cute/funny' deputy, Tim, is locked in the town jail. Then

Sancho, a Mexican bandit, robs the bank – while the sheriff is held prisoner by Sancho's girlfriend, Dolores.

Pursued by the sheriff's posse, Sancho and his gang hole up with their loot at the hacienda of Major Clyde and his daughter, Ruby (to whom the sheriff is betrothed). Surrounded, Sancho demands safe passage back to Mexico, or he will kill two people from the ranch daily, one at dawn, one at dusk.

The townspeople hope the army will descend upon the bandits and massacre them. But the sheriff, hoping to avoid the death of his girlfriend, makes a deal with Ringo. In return for 30 per cent of the stolen money, Ringo will pose as an outlaw, infiltrate the gang and free the hostages.

Ringo reaches the ranch and cuts a bullet out of the wounded Sancho. But the siege continues, with the sheriff refusing to let anyone leave, and Sancho carrying out his threat to kill the Major's servants. Meanwhile, the Major becomes enamoured of Dolores, and Pedro, one of the bandits, stalks Ruby. Ringo makes a deal with Sancho to take 40 per cent of the haul if he can get them out alive. When Pedro attempts to rape Ruby after their Christmas dinner, Ringo fights and kills him. But, when he attempts to betray Sancho, he is beaten up.

Next day, Dolores refuses to be separated from the Major, and is stabbed by one of the bandits. Sancho pays little attention. His attempted flight to Mexico is foiled by Ringo's dynamite, and the hostages are freed. Back at the hacienda, Ringo kills Sancho by deflecting his last bullet off a Christmas bell.

Ringo rides off alone, taking $15,000 with him, leaving Ruby with the sheriff, and $35,000 for the bank.

The film

Though on the surface it looks to be made in the American style (the townspeople are cute and clean; Ringo defers to the sheriff and is super-clean), *A Pistol for Ringo* seems the most postmodern of the early Italian Westerns. Cuteness and jokes are juxtaposed with graphic violence. In the opening shot, two cowboys confront each other on the main street, but instead of drawing their guns they wish each other 'Merry Christmas'. Cruel, ingenious deaths occur; bullet holes between the eyes are frequent; Sancho executes one of the servants at random, then whimsically kills the man's wife as well. Within Major Clyde's hacienda, the atmosphere is authentically Buñuelian. Clyde is Antonio Casas' best role: he plays it with all the ignorance, satisfaction and denial of Fernando Rey in *The Discreet Charm of the Bourgeoisie*. Confronted with the fact that his servants are being massacred, the Major chooses to ignore it, and romances the bandit chief's girlfriend instead. His daughter, knowing she's being stalked by the brutal Pedro, wears a décolleté white ballgown to dinner.

There is also a Godardian sequence in which Ringo and Ruby talk directly to camera as they discuss love: very sixties-modern, and a stylistic break with the rest of the film. There's even a Kurosawa moment, where Tessari parodies the Master's love of sketching out the action that is to come: Ringo lays out the gang's strategy against the sheriff on a tablecloth, using an apple, a knife and a banana.

Underlying the cutesy townspeople and hacienda romances is a refreshing groundbed of Italian Western meanness: perhaps more profound and pessimistic than Leone's. The bank robbery is marked by unnecessary killing. The sheriff, disarmed by Dolores, jumps into action as the bandits leave town, and shoots several of them in the back. Back-shooting is to be expected of the bad guys, but the sheriff? 'George Martin' (the Spanish actor Francisco Celeiro Martinez) is a strong, square-jawed performer, which makes such killings even more unsettling. When Ethan Edwards killed some would-be assailants in *The Searchers*, it was noted that he'd shot them in the back, and a warrant for his arrest was issued. The townspeople of Quemado are worse than their sheriff: the retired Colonel (Paco Sanz, who would specialise in playing crazy, violent gringos) eagerly anticipates a massacre by the army. But stranger still is the film's alleged hero, Ringo.

Ringo is an incomplete character. This isn't Giuliano Gemma's fault. Gemma plays the role impeccably: he's a great rider, he can also backflip, throw a knife and juggle a gun. (All actors pretend they can do these things. But very few really can.) Gemma has a small scar on his left cheek and the make-up team exaggerate it, enhancing this small imperfection in an otherwise eerily handsome leading man. Yet his character is beset by limitations. Ringo's strong, a deadly gunfighter, and a clever strategist, but he's also like a child. The first time we see him, he's playing hopscotch with some small boys. A Texan, he can't understand why Jesus didn't pack a six-shooter. He's indifferent to women: his interests are milk and money. He's entirely truthful with Sancho:

> RINGO: You know why I'm really here, amigo? I'm here to kill you – and all these gunslingers. You know who sent me here? The sheriff... I'm either with you at 40 per cent, or against you at 30 per cent.

For the audience, Ringo is playing an entertaining game. It's the strategy Manco employs in *For a Few Dollars More*, when he tells El Indio that he's a bounty killer out for the reward. Both films use this plot device of a gringo, disguised as a bandit, destroying the bankrobbers from within. Both share a scene in which the hero is sent with three subsidiary outlaws to create a distraction: in *For a Few*, by attacking a town with a telegraph office, in *Ringo*, by signalling with a mirror to the sheriff's men. In each scene the hero guns his partners down, and fires a final shot into a wounded man – a 'mercy killing'.

The similarities aren't coincidental. *A Pistol for Ringo* went into production first, but the filmmakers knew each other, and visited each other's cutting rooms. Tessari didn't need to see Leone's new film, anyway: two of his (uncredited) screenwriters, Fernando di Leo and Enzo Dell'Aquila, had written the original treatment for *For a Few Dollars More*.

Tessari is a fine director in terms of camera movement and choreography of actors. He and Francisco Marin fill the Techniscope frame with actors: they favour wide, moving shots in which four, five, six or more characters interact. This is the exact opposite of what we think of as the 'typical' Italian Western style of close-ups and zooms, intercut, with the camera usually locked to the tripod. Clearly Tessari isn't interested in Leone's style: he's following his instincts, and, like Buñuel's, they favour the wide shot, the multi-character set-up.

Marin's title sequence – long telephoto shots of the bandit horde, riding towards camera – is striking. Unlike his fluid camera moves, these shots were frequently emulated in later Italian Westerns. Another arresting moment – also imitated later – occurs when Ringo lights the fuse of several sticks of dynamite and threatens to blow himself and Sancho up, unless the bandit gives him a pistol. The notion of the kamikaze, or hero-as-suicide-bomber, was a mid-1960s way of show- ing the protagonist's reckless toughness. A modern Western audience might be a tad freaked out by this.

The cast is outstanding. No one is miscast, save for the child ac- tor who plays Ruby's 'cute/funny' houseboy, Chico. But no one could, or should, play that part. 'Hally Hammond' (Lorella de Luca) does her best with a nothing role as uptight, sharp-shooting Ruby. Nieves Nav- arro is brilliant as the bandit Dolores. Fernando Sancho, no slight actor, is eclipsed by Navarro's mischievous, sexy performance: clad first in a skin-tight, buckskin, bank-robbing ensemble with holster and six- shooter, Dolores falls under the Major's spell and turns up to Christ- mas dinner in a low-cut ballgown of her own. Navarro is the most compelling actor in the film, as uniquely beautiful and witty as Katy Jurado. Dolores's demise is a pity. Her flirtation with the Major, as far as we know, is unconsummated, just as it went unnoticed by Sancho: all three are as childlike as Ringo in their indifference to sex. Indeed, the only character who seems at all sexually oriented is Sancho's evil henchman, Pedro, played by Jose Manuel Martin: like Sancho, an im- port from *Minnesota Clay*.

Gemma and Sancho play entertainingly off each other. More than once the clever gringo outwits the Mexican; then the Mexican chang- es the plan and gets the better of the gringo. This Gemma/Sancho struggle was the basis for two more Westerns: *Return of Ringo* and *Arizona Colt*. At least 11 other *Ringo* films, none of them starring Gem- ma, also followed.

Return of Ringo

aka *Il ritorno di Ringo*
(Italy/Spain)

Director: Duccio Tessari   **Producer:** Alberto Pugliese, Luciano Ercoli
Screenplay: Duccio Tessari, Fernando Di Leo, Alfonso Balcazar
Director of Photography: Francisco Marin . **Art Director:** Juan Alberto

Soler **Costumes:** Rafael Borque **Editor:** Licia Quaglia **Assistant Director:** May Velasco, Fernando Di Leo **Music:** Ennio Morricone **Cast:** Giuliano Gemma (*Montgomery Brown*), Fernando Sancho (*Esteban Fuentes*), Hally Hammond aka Lorella De Luca (*Hally*), Nieves Navarro (*Rosita*), Antonio Casas (*Sheriff Carson*), Pajarito (*Morning Glory*), George Martin (*Paco Fuentes*), Juan Torres (*Barman*), Victor Bayo (*Jeremiah*), Tunet Vila (*Medicine Man*), Monica Sugranes (*Elizabeth*)

The story

Ringo, aka Captain Montgomery Brown, returns home after the Civil War. In a bar off the tumbleweed-strewn prairie, two men are waiting to kill him. Ringo shoots his would-be assassins, and the bartender, Jeremiah, tells him that, since gold was discovered, the Fuentes brothers have taken over his hometown of Mimbres, declaring it part of Mexico. Ringo drinks himself into a stupor after learning that his home and his wife, Hally, have been expropriated by Paco Fuentes. Jeremiah obtains herbs from a local medicine man. Using these, Ringo dyes his skin brown.

Disguised as a Mexican peon, Ringo rides into Mimbres. He sees an old gringo, the Judge, shot by a hidden assassin; the sheriff looks the other way. Ringo has some run-ins with the Fuentes brothers, and finds work as an assistant to the local florist. He discovers his father, a US Senator, was murdered by the Fuentes. Ringo decides to murder his wife, but is confounded when he sees Hally with their daughter, Elizabeth, born after he left for the war.

Rosita, a fortune-telling prostitute and Esteban's lover, is fascinated by this nameless Indian. Yet no one who knew Montgomery Brown recognises him. Paco and Esteban fake Montgomery's funeral, and Paco proposes marriage to Hally, via the priest, in the cemetery. The florist and his assistant deliver flowers to the Brown/Fuentes mansion. Ringo, sneaking around upstairs, finds Elizabeth and encounters Hally face-to-face. She, of course, recognises him. Apprehended by Esteban, Ringo pretends to be a thief. As a punishment, Paco stabs him in his hand.

Ringo recuperates at the florist's. Hally visits him and he tries to persuade her to run away with him and Elizabeth. But Hally insists that he face the Fuentes, on behalf of all the cowardly gringos. Afraid,

Ringo lets Rosita read his cards. He goes back to the bar, removes his make-up and challenges Paco, in church, on his wedding day. The sheriff dies in the ensuing shootout, which concludes, with dynamite explosions and machinegun fire, at the mansion. The Fuentes are killed, Rosita rides off, and Ringo, Hally and Elizabeth are reunited.

The film

Marco Giusti writes that Tessari wanted to call this film *The Odyssey of the Long Rifles*. Howard Hughes lists the many parallels with Homer's epic. Ringo is Odysseus, Hally is Penelope, their daughter Elizabeth is Telemachus. Tessari began work on this outrageously ambitious project as soon as *A Pistol for Ringo* was finished. When *Ringo* was a huge success, a sequel was called for. But – despite its title and a near-identical cast – *Return* isn't a sequel at all.

The first Ringo was a loquacious, dark-haired, gunfighter dandy who drank only milk, had no personal attachments, and, as far as we know, possessed only one name. Montgomery Brown is the son of the US Senator for New Mexico. His family owns (or used to own) a substantial mansion outside Mimbres, New Mexico. He's married, has a daughter and was, until a couple of months ago, a captain in the US Cavalry. He's taciturn and frequently drowns his sorrows in drink. And he's a blond!

Tessari makes Montgomery Brown a different character; the only dialogue calling him 'Ringo' is off-camera or when the speaker's back is to us: in other words, it may have been added later, when the dialogue was created in 'post'.[10] The other thing which makes the character unique – not only different from Ringo, but from almost all other Spaghetti Western heroes – is his capacity for fear. As the *Monthly Film Bulletin* put it, 'When Ringo realises that he must destroy Fuentes and his gang, he is afraid; this is the film's core, and it is treated with an imagination unequalled in other Italian Westerns.'

Gone is the jokey quality of Tessari's earlier scripts: in its place is an operatic seriousness. 'Cute/funny' characters are kept to a minimum:

10 *All the dialogue in these films was recorded in post-production. On set, a guide track was usually recorded, with the actors speaking their native languages: Italian, Spanish, English, German. Corbucci claimed his actors would simply count in different languages, and he created their dialogue later. So it was possible to rechristen characters, if the market preferred: 'Walter of the West' to be called 'Django', or 'Montgomery' to be 'Ringo'.*

Pajarito, as the florist, is less annoying than previously; only the child who plays Elizabeth is unbearable. At one moment the winsome tyke offers Ringo – disguised as a Mexican – a bunch of flowers, and one is reminded of the moment in *Frankenstein* (1931) where the Monster accepts flowers from a child, then drowns her. Surely this is the association we are meant to make, in a film full of allusions to classical literature and to other films. Tessari's decision to play it straight only makes things funnier on the grander scale. And the better actors respond wonderfully. Antonio Casas does a creditable job as the alcoholic sheriff, Carson. Nieves Navarro, as the fortune-teller, Rosita, is magnificent. Again, she plays a gangster's moll who changes sides; this time she survives and rides away, heroically sidesaddle. The scene where she asks for a drink, then slides Ringo's glass all the way along the bar, is diabolically sexy. Apparently Navarro was married to one of the producers, Luciano Ercoli, a rare instance of beneficial industry nepotism.

Fernando Sancho is remarkably restrained as Esteban, the elder Fuentes brother. Clearly he was capable of more than the standard Mexican bandit general he usually portrayed. But the film's real stand-out is George Martin, the Spanish actor who played the back-shooting sheriff in *A Pistol*, cast here as the younger, and more deadly, brother: Paco. The two roles couldn't be more different: a gringo in the Duke Wayne mould and a racist Mexican aristocrat. Martin manages both parts impeccably; a proper actor! He and Sancho are supposed to be the bad guys, but more than once the viewer (or at least this viewer) tends to side with them – as in the funeral procession scene, where three gringos surprise the two brothers, with pistols and a shotgun. These gringos are stupid. Having got the drop on the Mexicans, the gringos lose the advantage and are cut down by Paco's knife and Esteban's sixgun.

As one might hope from a Tessari script, there is considerable violence, though the body count is lower than usual. Esteban rides gringos down, shoots a wounded man, and fires his gun at corpses: all in a non-too-successful attempt to make Sancho more villainous (he remains entirely charming in his aristocratic role). Ringo is stabbed in the hand (à la *One-Eyed Jacks*). A Mexican is shot out of his boots (this incident, along with other violent scenes, is missing from the English *and* the Italian versions, which are six minutes shorter than the French and Spanish ones). Dying, drenched in blood, Sheriff Carson shoots several Mexicans in the back. Ringo wounds Paco repeatedly before killing him. The final battle at the mansion involves a machinegun, emblazoned with a wrought-iron brand name, 'Butterfly'.

The film's premise – that Mexicans have taken over an American town, reducing the gringos to a conquered people – is absurd, the stuff of Ku Klux Klan and Minuteman daydreams. But Tessari plays this straight as well. It helps that Sancho and Martin are blue-eyed boys, who display racism not only towards gringos but to their own, darker-skinned compatriots. The scene where Ringo decides to 'become' a Mexican is played without dialogue as a *plano secuencia*, with the most epic Morricone score. Music wells up as Ringo fingers the coarse Mexican peasant garments he must henceforth wear. The blond, white hero masquerading as an *indio* – for the darker-skinned, working-class southern Italians who flocked to Giuliano Gemma Westerns, it must have been a tremendous kick: like the sign outside the saloon, reading, 'No Entry for Dogs, Gringos and Beggars' in English and Spanish. And Ringo, playing to the Fuentes' notion of the lazy *indio*, declines an offer of work, because he's already eaten today.

Gemma's character is as complex as a Gemma character can be. Montgomery Brown – the son of Senator Brown – is reduced to the status of an alcoholic *peon*, sleeping in horse troughs. As in Homer, or a Jacobean tragedy, disguise is 100 per cent effective. No one – other than his wife – recognises Ringo once he's dyed his skin and donned a straw hat. Ringo, understanding nothing about women, assumes his wife has willingly betrayed him, and plans to murder her. Only the discovery of his daughter makes him reconsider the assassination scheme. Uncertain what to do, Ringo delays. A guest at his wife's engagement party, Ringo wanders the house – and a strange interlude occurs. He crosses his wife's bedroom with his eyes closed. On her desk, he finds everything in its place, including a music box – which plays the film's main theme – and a riding crop. Clearly these spark fond memories. Ringo fondles them.

A music box? A whip? There is potential for something Buñuelian here – along the lines of the music-box-obsessed, would-be wife-murderer in *The Criminal Life of Archibaldo De La Cruz*. Tessari clearly knows, and admires, the Master, Don Luis. But he only hints at the fetish, then moves on.

Hally is the film's moral voice – though Ringo certainly has a point. If the gringos of Mimbres won't stick up for themselves, why should he sort things out for them? But Ringo loses sympathy when he whines, 'It's too much for just one man – and I've got a broken gun-hand!' Please. Hally agrees to run away, but, after she's gone, Ringo's distraught. He knows he's just played the bounder; now he's afraid *and* ashamed. Tessari emphasises this with the image of a door – blown by the wind – opening and closing, opening and closing in the background.

Unable to decide, Ringo takes a hallucinogenic walk across town – framed, in medium shot, by stained-glass windows. He arrives at Rosita's room. She reads his cards. 'A man who hopes, fears.' She shows him a card. 'You see? Now you're afraid.'

But having acknowledged his fear, Ringo can confront it. The inevitable, fumbling target practice follows. And unlike Joe in *Fistful of Dollars*, or Sanjuro in *Yojimbo*, Ringo doesn't have to go it alone. As Sheriff Chance discovered in *Rio Bravo*, Western communities often contained eccentrics who thirst for justice with a sixgun.[11]

Ringo's return is magnificent. Arriving at church for his wedding, Paco is confronted by coffins containing the corpses of his men. He insists on going ahead with the wedding. When Hally hesitates at the altar, he reminds her that Elizabeth is waiting at home. Then, just as Hally's obliged to say 'I do', Ringo appears – a white man again, in his spotless US Cavalry attire – at the vortex of a dust storm, calling out Paco's name. Is this fantastical scene racist? Maybe. But it's mitigated by the blue eyes versus brown eyes issue, by the fact that Paco is a low-down child-threatener, and by the Rainbow-of-Diversity Coalition which Ringo has assembled to defeat the foe: a Native American, a woman sex-worker, an alcoholic, a bar owner and a florist.

11 Rio Bravo *was intended as a response to* High Noon *(1952), a liberal parable about McCarthyism, in which the honest sheriff cannot find anyone to back him against an outlaw gang. Howard Hawks,* Rio Bravo*'s director, and John Wayne, its star, took issue both with* High Noon*'s politics, and with its depiction of the frontier populace as cowardly and pacific. Spaghetti Westerns generally took the* High Noon *route, depicting entire towns of disarmed, corrupt and cowardly urbanites, whom bandits rob, kill and banish at will, and whom only a lone, armed hero can save.*

It's also worthy of note that Ringo's uniform is a blue one. Monty Ford fought for the North, not for the South. As a rule, Spaghetti Western heroes fought for the Union. Whereas, in American Westerns, the hero was generally a Southerner. Why is this so? I think it has to do with the near-mythical official story of the War Between the States. Outside the United States, the world's children are taught that the American Civil War was fought to free the slaves. In America, too, most children are fed this bogus line. In fact, the War Between the States was fought over the right of individual states to secede from the Union. The vile institution of slavery helped provoke the conflict, but secession, not slavery, caused the War. And to help ensure a Union victory, *President Lincoln permitted slavery to continue in the northern states, which bordered the Confederacy*. Slavery was only abolished in the North after the South surrendered.

Knowing this, and perhaps wishing their massive country could indeed be broken into smaller, less powerful units, some Americans mythologised the South for non-racist reasons. Most white Southerners fought not for ideological reasons, but out of local loyalty. The original American Western directors – particularly John Ford – were highly knowledgeable about the West, and about American history. *The Searchers* is a fairly accurate portrayal of events which might have occurred on the Texas frontier in the years after the Civil War. Ford made his hero, Ethan Edwards, an ex-Confederate. There are diverse reasons: an actual affinity for the South on Ford's part, his Irish-American love of 'lost causes', and the fact that being a Johnny Reb in possession of freshly minted federal gold only added to Edwards' outlaw glory, and mystique.

Almost all American Westerns followed this pattern. Sure, the Union won, but the South was a lost and therefore noble cause, and they had way cooler capes and uniforms. Gary Cooper plays a former Confederate officer in *Vera Cruz* (1954). Peckinpah's *Major Dundee* (1964) is the story of a Union major forced to lead a brigade of Confederate prisoners against the Apache. Some of the rebels are scurvy dogs (step forward, greatest American actor Warren Oates!) but their leader is a dashing Irishman, Captain Tyree. Tyree is more the hero than Dundee: handsomer, braver, better-uniformed. But Tyree is killed leading a gallant charge; Dundee has to soldier on, finish the mission, pick up the pieces. Peckinpah, as we might expect, subverts the traditional vision of the glorious rebel Southerner. Later American Westerns such as *The Outlaw Josey Wales* (1976) simply traded in its counterfeit currency.

Spaghetti Westerns had a different genesis. Their directors, veterans of quickly made, popular action films, picked their icons differently. This was popular cinema, yes, but for some filmmakers it was also radical cinema: a chance to tell an allegorical story, or to comment on white racism, or on the wickedness of US foreign policy. For such politically engaged directors, the hero couldn't march around in a Confederate uniform, any more than he could wear a Gestapo outfit. There are exceptions, like Gemma's character in *One Silver Dollar*, or Anthony Steffen's in *Django the Bastard*, and there are bad Unionists, for sure. But in general, in Spaghetti Westerns, the good guys wore blue.

Return of Ringo has a two-part showdown: on the streets of Mimbres, ending with the sheriff's death, then back at the Brown/Fuentes hacienda. This is too much showdown, particularly as the two sequences are linked by an eggy scene in which Ringo urges the gringos to resist their oppressors. The Brown mansion isn't a particularly interesting location, and the film visits it too often. An Italian friend joked to me that Tessari shot the film at the producer's house; maybe he wasn't joking.

Like the first *Ringo* film, this one is often beautifully constructed, with long dollies and tracking shots. When Ringo enters the saloon, there's a 360-degree pan-and-track around the room, following the barman to Sancho, to a henchman, to a guitarist, to another henchman, who throws a knife, which lands in the wall near Ringo's head. Ringo smiles and strolls into a two-shot with the barman, at the bar. Over their shoulders, Esteban appears in the mirror. The solo guitar and song, which accompanies the scene until the knife is thrown – an uncredited Mexican ballad – is delightful. It's a pleasing scene on the eye: and an inspirational display of skill, for any filmmaker.

Even more striking is a *plano secuencia* in the producer's house, when the Fuentes are celebrating Paco and Hally's engagement. It begins with Rosita, on the patio, singing a song called 'Guitarra'. We dolly left with her to some appreciative henchmen, then Ringo and the florist enter frame. We follow them to the right, and meet Rosita in a medium-close-up, with a rose pressed to her lips (to hide her mouth and help with synch – she's still singing!). In the background, behind Rosita, Hally and the Fuentes clan descend the stairs. We follow this group, joined by the sheriff and the priest, and enter the dining room. The camera rests while the priest says grace (and off-screen the crew gets ready for the second half of the shot). Then all are seated, and we continue to dolly right, behind the seated guests, looking back into the patio beyond the dining room. From the end of the table we follow a waiter to the window. He opens it, to reveal Rosita, singing. We dolly around the far side of the table, following Ringo and the florist. The shot ends in a close-up of Hally, thanking the florist for such splendid bouquets.

The shot lasts just two minutes, but any filmmaker will appreciate the hours of planning, group effort and repeated takes which such a complex camera move demands. Other than the gorgeous Nieves Navarro, nothing in the scene is very interesting: the *plano secuencia* is thus a good way of filling in some minor plot points while stimulating the eye.

Return of Ringo was hugely successful. More ambitious than *A Pistol for Ringo*, it was less imitated, and the Ringo franchise was soon diluted in the Spaghetti Western mainstream. It's noteworthy how everyone's skills developed while making the two films. The direction gets more assured, the camerawork more adventurous, the acting, overall, much better. Apart from too many visits to the producer's house, *Return of Ringo* is a pretty flawless, freestanding film.

Three unofficial sequels sprang up the same year. *$100,000 for Ringo/100,000 Dollari per Ringo* starred Richard Harrison: it was his most successful Western to date. Tessari's collaborator Alfonso Balcazar contributed to the script; Fernando Sancho played the Mexican bandit chief. *Ringo del Nebraska*, also known as *Savage Gringo*, was credited to a noted director of horror films, Mario Bava. The actual director was an elderly Spaniard, Antonio Roman: Bava directed second unit. The hero, played by Ken Clark, was named Nebraska; he became *Ringo* in post-production. Other films imitated the Ringo style and plot elements without borrowing the title or the hero's name. One of these was a new Western by Sergio Corbucci. Seeing it for what it was, the US distributor changed its title to *Ringo and His Golden Pistol...*

Johnny Oro

aka *Ringo & His Golden Pistol*
(Italy)

Director: Sergio Corbucci **Producer:** Joseph Fryd **Screenplay:** Adriano Bolzoni, Franco Rossetti **Director of Photography:** Riccardo Pallottini **Art Director:** Carlo Simi **Costumes:** Berenice Sparano, Marcella de Machis **Editor:** Otello Colangeli **Assistant Director:** Ruggero Deodato, Gaetanino Froscella **Music:** Carlo Savina **Cast:** Mark Damon (*Johnny Oro*), Valeria Fabrizi (*Margie*), Ettore Manni (*Sheriff Norton*), Giulia Rubini (*Norton's wife*) Franco de Rosa (*Juanito*), Andrea Aureli (*Gilmore, the bar owner*), Pippo Starnazza (*Matt*), Loris Loddi (*Stan Norton*), Nino Vingelli, John Bartha, Vittorio Bonos, Bruno Scipioni, Giulio Maculani Silvana Bacci, Giovanni Cianfriglia (*Sebastian, the Indian*), Evaristo Signorini, Amerigo Castrichella, Figlia Francesco, Giovanni Cariffi, Ivan Basta, Lucio de Santis, Mauro Mannatrizio

The story

Johnny ('Jefferson Gonzales... born in a gold mine'), a bounty hunter, kills all the Perez brothers, save the youngest, Juanito – who has no price on his head. Johnny collects his money; Juanito murders the bride, priest and altar boy from his brother's shotgun wedding, and swears revenge against Johnny. By now Johnny's in the town of Coldstone, where his old pal Sheriff Norton no longer permits the carrying of guns. Having handed his golden pistol over to the sheriff, Johnny kills three of Juanito's Mexicans with a bomb disguised as a canteen. The sheriff jails him; outside town, Juanito teams up with renegade Indians, led by an angry, alcoholic chief, Sebastian. They demand that

Johnny be turned over to them. Fearing a raid by Juanito's men and the Indians, the townsfolk all leave town. Only Sheriff Norton, his wife, the town drunk, and a few plotting businessmen (secretly in league with the Indians) remain – plus Johnny, who is still in jail.

While the sheriff patrols the empty street, Gilmore, the corrupt barman, and his cronies let themselves into the jail to seize Johnny: but he overpowers them, locks them up and quickly plants dynamite aboard the town's aerial goods hoist. Then he returns to jail. Juanito and co sneak into town. Sebastian plants his tomahawk in Gilmore's head. Next morning, he demands the sheriff surrender Johnny. Norton refuses.

The Mexicans and Indians take up exposed positions, or ride up and down the main street. They're shot by the sheriff and co. None of their arrows or bullets find their mark. By the time Norton lets Johnny out of jail to lend a hand, almost all are dead. Johnny dynamites the survivors. Brooding on Coldstone's destruction, the sheriff is shot and wounded by Juanito, who takes the sheriff's son, Stan, hostage. Johnny must face Juanito in a showdown on the burning street. Though disarmed, he is able to blind Juanito with his gold cigarette lighter, and shoot him dead.

Johnny bequeaths a quantity of gold to rebuild the town.

The film

Johnny Oro is worse, in some ways, than *Red Pastures*. For most of the film, Corbucci's talent – visible in the best scenes of *Minnesota Clay* – has deserted him. Though the film has an American lead, Alan Harris (aka 'Mark Damon'), it seems intended for the domestic market: the Italian crew and cast all use their real names. Many Italian Westerns featured some kind of pop song, which – even if not included in the film itself – could be offered to radio stations and record stores as a .45. Inevitably, these songs were sung in English. *Johnny Oro*, by contrast, is sung in Italian and plays over the opening credits.

Johnny Oro is a very protracted nod to the first *Ringo* film, without the hero's capacity for strategy, or ability to manipulate the action. Johnny spends 22 minutes (two reels of film) in jail. Briefly released, he returns voluntarily and spends another 17 minutes there. And it doesn't make any difference! Johnny Oro is like a supporting actor – the kid gunfighter – in someone else's movie. Indeed, the film plays like a succession of subplots: the sheriff and his family; revenge-bent Juanito; the bartender and his corrupt business pals. Johnny shows up now and then, but even for a post-Brando, Spaghetti Western hero, he's unusually lethargic.

The film was shot in the *Minnesota Clay* locations: beside the lake and rock formations of Tor Caldara, and at the Elios Films set, outside Rome. Carlo Simi, the designer, created an impressive overhead pulley system for transporting dynamite. He left the saloon interior almost bare; and dressed the sheriff's office like the *Rio Bravo* set. The Italian credits say Simi also designed the costumes, but Marco Giusti and others credit Bernice Sparano and Marcella de Machis with the designs. Either way, they're good. Johnny dresses stylishly, in black with gold trimmings. Damon has beautiful grey eyes, which match his outift. He wears a bolero jacket – the first of many Corbucci characters to do so – with gold spurs, gold gun, and gold cigarette holder.

Ettore Manni plays a stolid sheriff. Valeria Fabrizi is outstandingly sexy as the saloon girl, Margie, but Corbucci shows little interest in her character. The bad guys are unconvincing: Franco de Rosa is too sweet-faced to play a believable killer, and Giovanni Cianfriglia, a grey-eyed muscleman, is an unlikely Indian named Sebastian.

Johnny Oro is one of the worst Spaghetti Westerns. Even its action is bad. Indeed, the film's main offence is that Corbucci suppresses his own natural inclination for cruelty and innovative violence. Early on, Juanito's men shoot his brother's wife; they then murder the priest and altar boy who participated in the ceremony. For Corbucci, this should have been an opportunity for on-screen killing, twitching bodies and smears of blood. Instead, the priest and choirboy are shot off-camera. Since this director would later pride himself on his ingeniously violent, anti-clerical scenes, this is very strange. And the killing of the spunky bargirl, Margie, is simply pointless. She's the only attractive, interesting person in a stupid film; there's no reason to kill her, especially as she's shot off-screen, like Estella in *Minnesota Clay*. Was this some early notion of politeness, or propriety, on Corbucci's part – shooting his priests and his female characters off-camera? There's just one instance of what will become characteristic Corbucci sadism: when Sebastian hurls his axe at Gilmore, we're treated to two shots of the actor with the special effect attached to his head. It comes out of nowhere, like the priest killing. And it's at odds with the underpowered, jokey finale.

Up till now, the body count has been low. Then comes a prolonged final shootout, in which every ride-by, every fall from a building or a horse is repeated several times; and every explosion occurs at least twice. There is also fisticuffs, of a jokey, you-missed-me variety. Johnny's a bit of an acrobat, hiding in the rafters, swinging from beams. After the dark, obsessive showdown of *Minnesota Clay*, Corbucci is being self-consciously 'funny'. It doesn't matter that the result *isn't* funny, or even that it's excruciating, flat and tedious. Corbucci tried, and failed, to cut a funny, wacky, out-there, sixties movie out of Western cloth. *Johnny Oro* was the dire, yet prescient, result.

This was something new: a largely comic Western pitched at a domestic audience which included children (Sheriff Norton's kid is chased by Indians in another tedious scene). It wasn't necessarily an experiment Corbucci liked. On set, he and Damon discussed making another film: a Western far more pessimistic and violent. Damon told me that he and Corbucci wrote the story together, and that he was Corbucci's first choice to play the title role – *Django*.

Django would be the prototype of the angst-ridden, tragic Italian Western. In the same way, *Johnny Oro* was the ur-*Trinity* film, the inspiration for the acrobatic *Sabata* and *Sartana* movies. It's the first Italian Western to attempt self-parody, to treat the Western as pop art, an acrobatic comedy medium. While making a bad film, Corbucci was becoming a more confident filmmaker; more capable than when he made *Red Pastures*. In *Johnny Oro* he experiments relentlessly with the zoom lens: crash zooming to establish a character; zooming to bookend sequences or at either end of a transition; playing whole scenes in single zooms or zooms combined with camera moves. Often he and Riccardo Pallotini will shoot with a long lens through out-of-focus foreground objects: a technique Corbucci would pursue in later films. Here it's overdone and pointless: he's trying out styles, and, after all, nothing much is at stake. Corbucci would make two masterpieces: films as good as almost any Western, Italian or American. How could he also direct such dross as this? Later he'd say he didn't care; he didn't like Westerns. Yet he could swoop, as we'll now see, steeply and swiftly, from the ludicrous to the sublime.

Django

(Italy/Spain)

Director: Sergio Corbucci   **Producer:** Manolo Bolognini, Sergio Corbucci   **Screenplay:** Sergio Corbucci, Franco Rossetti, Piero Vivarelli, Jose Gutierrez Maeso, Bruno Corbucci, Fernando Di Leo   **Story:** Franco Rossetti, Sergio Corbucci, Bruno Corbucci   **Director of Photography:** Enzo Barboni   **Art Director, Costumes:** Carlo Simi   **Editor:** Nino Baragli, Sergio Montanari   **Assistant Director:** Ruggero Deodato   **Music:** Luis Enriquez Bacalov   **Cast:** Franco Nero (*Django*), Loredana Nusciak (*Maria*), Jose Bodalo (*General Hugo Rodriguez*), Eduardo Fajardo (*Major Jackson*), Angel Alvarez (*Nathaniel*), Jimmy Douglas aka Gino Pernice (*Brother Jonathan*), Simon Arriaga (*Miguel*), Erik Schippers aka Remo De Angelis (*Riccardo*), Chris Huerta (*Mexican officer*), Raphael Albaicin, Jose Canalejas, Ivan Scratuglia, Silvana Bacci, Guillermo Mendez, Rafael Vaquero

The story

A man in Union blue, Django, drags a coffin across a muddy landscape. He carries his saddle. A runaway prostitute, Maria, is captured by Mexican bandits, who tie her to a wooden bridge and whip her. Red-hooded Klansmen gun the Mexicans down. They plan to crucify and burn Maria, but Django intervenes. Django and Maria arrive in an unnamed, muddy town. Against the wishes of the barman, Nathaniel, Django hides Maria in the saloon. The barman explains that this ghost town is the war zone of two rival gangs: General Hugo Rodriguez and his Mexicans, and Major Jackson, a white racist with a large gang.

Jackson shows up with six of his men, including a protestant evangelist, Brother Jonathan, and a wild-eyed killer, Ringo. They try to extract protection money from Nathaniel; Django shoots five, but spares Jonathan and Jackson. He challenges Jackson to return with his 48 surviving men. When Jackson reappears, with his men in red hoods, carrying burning crosses, Django mows them down with the machine-gun inside his coffin. Only Jackson and a handful of Klansmen escape.

Django visits the grave of his wife, or girlfriend – murdered by Jackson. General Hugo arrives in town and cuts off Brother Jonathan's ear. He makes the preacher eat his ear; then shoots him. Django, returning, is intercepted by Hugo's men and taken to Hugo, an old friend whose life he saved in prison. Django proposes to Hugo that they steal Major Jackson's gold, currently lodged in the Mexican army's Fort Charriba. Following Django's plan, Hugo and co gain access to the fort, kill many soldiers and steal the gold. Jackson survives and gives chase; but the Mexican army won't pursue Hugo across the border.

When Hugo is slow in sharing the booty, Django steals the gold. Maria insists on leaving with him. But, at the bridge, the coffin containing the loot falls into quicksand, and is lost. Hugo arrives; Maria is shot; and Django's hands are crushed by horses' hooves. Heading south, Rodriguez and his men are massacred by Jackson and the Mexican army. Django returns Maria, who is still alive, to the saloon. Jackson comes looking for him, and kills Nathaniel. In the cemetery, Django waits for Jackson and his five surviving men. By biting off his pistol's trigger guard, and resting the gun on a cross, Django is able to eradicate the racists.

The film

The opening – a medium shot on the back of Django's head as he walks away from camera – is the opening shot of *Yojimbo*.

And the ending could be *Fistful of Dollars*, or *A Pistol for Ringo*, or *Return of Ringo*, or any of the Spaghetti Westerns in which the hero's gun-hand is injured. Except that this is *Django*, and while the idea may be the same, Corbucci takes it to some weirder, crueler level of Surrealist violence; amplifies the sacrificial religious symbolism of the hero-with-damaged-hands by staging the showdown in a cemetery; and, in case we still don't get the joke, naming his lead character after the jazz guitarist Django Reinhardt, famous as a brilliant musician despite a serious deformity of one hand.

Almost everything in *Django* is similarly overstated: acting, music, cinematography, art department. And at the same time the film is highly disciplined. *Django* is the first of Corbucci's Western scripts to drop the subplots: apart from brief scenes with Nathaniel and the prostitutes, and short cutaways to Jackson and the Mexicans, all the scenes involve Django. There's no sheriff; no 'cute/funny' character. Nathaniel comes close to being cute, but he's credibly afraid of the ever-presence of death, and brave in spite of himself, concealing Maria's whereabouts when he dies ('cute/funny' characters are unfortunately immortal, reborn in other films).

Django is a huge step forward. Corbucci's earlier Westerns suffered from unsteady, often boring narratives, bad transitions, 'cute/funny' characters, and tedious horse-riding-through-landscape scenes. All this is gone. *Django* doesn't have any horses for the first half hour (Django, Maria, the Mexican bandits and Jackson's men all arrive on foot). Nathaniel and the prostitutes are quickly established as the town's only inhabitants. The ghastly prelate, Brother Jonathan, Major Jackson and General Hugo are monsters, with no characteristics other than meanness.

The film is marvellously contained. There are four principal locations: the bridge, where Django and Maria meet, and where their plan unravels; the saloon in town; the graveyard; and Fort Charriba, which appears in only one scene. All takes place within a couple of days. Django has a revenge motive but – like his prior history with Hugo – it's very unclear. We're told his girlfriend was killed by Jackson – yet Jackson doesn't appear to know Django. Revenge wasn't the strongest motivation for a Corbucci hero: his goal was either justice or money. This alleged murder of Django's girlfriend seems like an afterthought, an unnecessary addition: Django has motivation enough to kill the Major and his men, as they've ruined his game of solitaire. Much of the dialogue is poor. Lines like, 'Listen, Maria, love is something I can never feel again. The girl I once loved was killed and I can never forget that,' should never be spoken, in any language. But *Django* is so precisely constructed that it doesn't matter. The action is non-stop. A machinegun demonstration by Django demolishes Nathaniel's bar; the Mexicans raid the fort and steal Jackson's gold; Django and Hugo's henchman Ricardo get into a savage fistfight which ends with Ricardo's death by pickaxe; Django tells a prostitute to undress. Thrilling and bloody events follow one another in quick succession – as in a James Bond film.

Casting is excellent. Legend has it that Corbucci discovered Franco Nero pumping gas at a petrol station. In fact, the 23-year-old actor had played several small film roles, including Abel in *The Bible... In the Beginning*, directed by John Huston the same year. Though it's hard to believe, Corbucci initially wanted Mark Damon to play Django. Manolo Bolognini, the producer, persuaded him to look at other actors, claiming Damon was unavailable. Corbucci considered Fabio Testi, but went with the 23-year-old with striking grey eyes; impossible now to imagine any other actor in the role. Loredana Nusciak is a beautiful, enigmatic Maria. Eduardo Fajardo and Jose Bodalo are fine villains, in the style of Georges Riviere and Fernando Sancho, and Luis Rodriguez ('Guy Calloway' from *For a Few Dollars More*) appears uncredited as the short-lived henchman, Ringo.

Gino Pernice, Scratchy from *Minnesota Clay*, is memorable as Brother Jonathan. This is a perfect Corbucci cleric: hypocritical and confrontational, thin-faced with a strap beard, he rants at prostitutes, serves as chaplain to the Ku Klux Klan and collects protection money. His fate at the hands of General Hugo – trapped, forced to eat his own severed ear, then shot in the back – is the high point of this, the bloodiest Spaghetti Western to date.

In the documentary *The Spaghetti West* (2005), Bolognini says Corbucci wanted to shoot *Django* in midwinter snow. The budget was limited, and Bolognini preferred to use the Elios Films set, so they compromised on mud. It was an inspired choice. Carlo Simi's colour scheme is almost entirely brown, grey and scarlet. Having built a magnificent set on virgin turf in Spain for Sergio Leone, Simi returned to Italy to renovate the Elios location. This was a long street of irregular, plain-faced buildings with imperfect sightlines, east of Rome. It wasn't an inspiring location, though many of the better low-budget Westerns were shot there. Simi's work here is a masterpiece of low-budget art direction – a town at the end of its tether, windows smashed, doors boarded, awash with mud, the road littered with fallen trees and broken timbers. A strange criterion for excellence, perhaps, but the designer's job is to convey in visual terms the 'message' of the film. *Django* is a tale of xenophobia, banditry and violence. For it, Simi built nowhere: a town with no name, a battleground where there is literally nothing worth fighting for.

Within, the bar is like a junk shop, its chairs invariably upended. Everything and everyone is dirty, its hero and his coffin most of all. Bolognini reports that the Italian censors gave *Django* an 18 certificate *and* requested that he cut out the ear-severing scene. The producer's solution was to 'forget' to remove the scene from certain review copies. Once the scene was described by the press – adding to the controversy – it was easier to leave it in.

Django was banned by the British censor until its video release in 1993. It seems to have received a limited theatrical release in the United States. Fragments of Django's massacre of Klansmen, in a sea of mud, made it to Britain via *The Harder They Come* (1973). *Django* is the film which Ivan (Jimmy Cliff) goes to see at the Rialto Cinema; flashbacks from the scene occur during Ivan's final shootout with the police. Perhaps it was the anti-clericalism, in addition to the violence, which upset the British. Reviewing the film for *Monthly Film Bulletin*, Chris Frayling observed:

> A clear streak of anti-clericalism… was to become one of the trade-marks of Italian Westerns aimed at the home market (as distinct from Leone's more sentimental presentation[s] of the priesthood, which were pitched at the international market).

Django was definitely a film for the domestic market. There were no American pseudonyms in the credits; for the first time, Corbucci had an Italian leading man.[12] Did the lack of money oblige the director to make a tighter, leaner film? Aesthetically, the minimal nature of Simi's settings – Elios a mud bath, Fort Charriba a few shacks – is a tremendous virtue. Two other collaborators are key: the cinematographer, Enzo Barboni, and the composer, Luis Enriquez Bacalov. Barboni's work on *Red Pastures* was uneven, even bad. In two years his style had improved immensely. Barboni adopts a brutal, uncompromising style at the outset: a zoom-out from the back of Django's head

12 *An Italian leading man who, like many of his contemporaries, suffered the indignity of hearing his voice replaced for the domestic as well as the foreign version of the film. Bolognini, considering Nero's voice 'too young', hired another actor, Sergio Graziano, to dub the voice of Django. Graziano also replaced Nero's voice in* Texas Goodbye *and* Massacre Time.

reveals a sea of mud, an undistinguished landscape and a coffin. There are zooms, but the film is not zoom-crazy. Instead, the lens helps the story, isolating Maria in the saloon; crashing in on Django as he opens fire on the Klansmen in the muddy street. Barboni's lighting and camera moves are elegant. There are some striking wide-angle establishing shots, and a good hand-held fight scene. *Django* is noteworthy as one of the very few Spaghetti Westerns shot in the 'standard' European widescreen format (1:1.66), as opposed to the super-wide Techniscope frame (1:2.35). Obviously, the tighter frame is more appropriate for such a claustrophobic, enclosed film.

Bacalov's score is big, with emphasis on the trumpets. It seems less influenced by Morricone than by the Argentinian composer's own notions of how an epic Western score should sound. There's a full orchestra throughout and little in the way of 'modern' touches: no boings, no whistling solos, no screeches. The titles are bold and red – Corbucci loved red credits – superimposed over images of boots, coffin and mud. Thus do composer, cameraman, director and designer – working in unison – prepare us for the tale of Django's fall.

The film is influenced by *Yojimbo* and *Fistful*. But *Django* is more than this: an impressionistic, cruel, anti-clerical, pop-cultural stew. It's a film where everyone is dirty and despicable: where gangsters mutilate each other, and hookers wrestle in mud. Corbucci made Franco Nero an international star, and created a character who appeared (in name, at least) in 31 sequels. Django, even more than Ringo, had something uniquely Italian about him. As Frayling wrote:

> In his Sunday-best soldier's trousers, worn-out boots and working man's vest, with his saddle carried over his shoulder, [Django] seems less like an archetypal Western hero than one of the *contadini* on his way back from the fields, with working tools on his back, dragging his belongings behind him. With its direct points of contact with the Southern Italian audiences, and above all its huge success on the home market (city and country), *Django* probably had more impact on the Italian Western… than any other.

It would be Django, not Joe or Ringo, who became the model for the Spaghetti Western hero: sometimes an avenger, always after the money, cool and doomed, often dead or barely alive, as the end titles rolled... Nero's Django is almost entirely taciturn: vulnerable, angelic, strangely robotic. Loredana Nusciak plays Maria the same way: emotionless, inert, and – once she gets hold of a rifle – merciless. Nero and Nusciak are the only cast members who don't overact. Yet each character's silence seems not to be innate, but learned, a result of endless proximity to mindless violence. Consider their situations. Maria is a prostitute who has fled from the gringos to the Mexicans, and been threatened with death by both. Django has returned her to her oppressors' hangout. Her situation couldn't be much worse. Django, meanwhile, is a veteran of the Civil War, where we assume he saw much violence and stole a machinegun. General Hugo says Django saved his life in jail: presumably he was a prisoner, not a warder. Now he's an arms dealer and thief, a killer without remorse. Naturally, such a damaged individual can watch a woman whipped; the marvel is that he intervenes, to save her from a burning cross.

If Maria and Django were real people, we'd call them victims of post-traumatic stress syndrome, with the trauma ongoing. So they are perfect for each other! And, though *Django* may seem pessimistic, it is by Spaghetti Western standards quite an upbeat film. The bad guys are all killed, the hero and the heroine survive, and, as Maria predicts, they'll meet again. This is rare in an Italian Western, and it tells us something of Corbucci's fondness for women, and for personal bonds.

The coffin which contains a machinegun is one of the most iconic, memorable images of the Spaghetti Western. Beyond its anarchic entertainment value, was there a political message in this image? In 2001, the Italian Prime Minister, Giulio Andreotti, admitted the existence of a NATO-sponsored terrorist group within Italy. Called the 'Gladio' Network, this was intended as a 'stay behind' network, to be activated in the event of a Soviet invasion. Inevitably, its ranks filled up with fascists, who, trained by MI6 and the CIA, engaged in terrorist attacks on their own countrymen.

'Gladio' terrorists set off bombs in Milan (1969), on the Italicus Express (1974) and in Bologna Railway Station (the *second-class* waiting room!) in 1980. Their purpose – NATO's purpose – was to create a climate of fear and tension in which the Communists would not be allowed to join the government. During the sixties, according to Andreotti's report, the terrorist group buried 138 secret arms caches, most often in cemeteries.

Corbucci was a 'political' director. Had he heard of this fascist network, with its arms caches in graveyards? Corbucci's Westerns would increasingly feature corrupt networks of rich people: bankers in league with businessmen, paying off the sheriff *and* the bandits. In their merger of corporate power and state power, their racism and use of physical violence, Corbucci villains like Major Jackson are *de facto fascists*. And scenes in cemeteries, where arms or money are hidden in coffins, were already becoming Corbucci's stock-in-trade.

Presumably Italian newspaper reports or books hinted at this 'Gladio' business. A criminal network burying guns and dynamite in churchyards could hardly do it unobserved. If rumours surfaced in 1965, this may explain why both *Django* and *The Good, the Bad and the Ugly* revolve around guns or money hidden in coffins: while entertaining its audience, the Spaghetti Western was commenting on the contemporary political situation, at one remove.

Beyond Django Reinhardt, there is political resonance in the title and the hero's name. Joao Goulart, the democratically elected President of Brazil, had been overthrown by a US-sponsored coup the previous year. Goulart's nickname was 'Jango'. And one of *Django*'s more extreme scenes – where Major Jackson guns down fleeing Mexicans for sport – has historical precedents. Brazilian Indians had been enslaved by whites, and used for target practice in this manner, as late as the 1950s.[13] So Corbucci wasn't simply inventing an outrageous action sequence; he was depicting colonialist atrocities which had happened in his lifetime, transposed to his Italian Wild West.

13 *Norman Lewis,* Sunday Times, *23 Feb 1969, quoted in Gerald Colby & Charlotte Dennett,* Thy Will Be Done, *Harper Collins, 1995, p 623.*

A pedant writes, regarding dates: *Django* was filmed in late 1965 (as Hughes observes, the actors' breath condenses in the winter air on the Elios set). According to Giusti and others, *Arizona Colt* – the third part of Gemma's *Ringo* trilogy – was shot in 1965 as well. *Django* and *Arizona Colt* were released in 1966, as was *Johnny Oro*. But *Django* and *Arizona* probably weren't shot at the same time, since they have three actors in common: Lucio De Santis, Jose Terron and Valentino Macchi. Terron appears throughout *Arizona Colt*, as a member of Fernando Sancho's gang, in both Italian and Spanish footage. There's snow on the Sierra Nevada in some of those Spanish exteriors. And there are leaves on the trees in the Cinecittà Western town set. So we reckon *Arizona Colt* was shot in spring 1966.

1966

'Back-to-back with *The Good, the Bad and the Ugly*, I made *The Big Gundown*. But now, instead of making seventeen thousand dollars, I was making a hundred-and-something: which was Leone's doing, not mine.' **– Lee Van Cleef**

Spaghetti Westerns still received no foreign recognition. *Fistful of Dollars*, beset by legal problems, had not yet opened abroad. But there was much buzz about what Leone would do next. He was reputed to be working on a remake of *Gone with the Wind*; he was also said to be preparing a movie version of Céline's great, pessimistic novel *Voyage au Bout de la Nuit*. United Artists had acquired the rights to Leone's second Western, and they were keen for him to make a third. While Leone considered his options, Michele Lupo directed a big-budget Western in Spain and Italy. His previous Western, *For a Fist in the Eye* (*Per un pugno nell'occhio*), was one of many quick and crude 'Franco and Ciccio' parodies. His new film also had parodic elements; it was also the last authentic *Ringo* sequel, and a compendium of Spaghetti Western clichés, to date.

Arizona Colt

aka *The Man from Nowhere, Minami Kara Kita Yojimbo*
(Italy/Spain)

Director: Michele Lupo **Producer:** Elio Scardamaglia **Story:** Ernesto Gastaldi, Luciano Martino **Screenplay:** Ernesto Gastaldi, Michele Lupo, Luciano Martino, Lewis E Ciannelli **Director of Photography:**

Guglielmo Mancori, Francisco Marin   **Art Director:** Walter Patriarca
Editor: Antonietta Zita   **Assistant Editor:** Anna Maria Roca   **Assistant Director:** Roberto Pariante, Valere Tantini   **Music:** Francesco De Masi
    Cast: Giuliano Gemma (*Arizona Colt*), Fernando Sancho (*Gordo Watch*), Nello Pazzafini (*Kay*), Corinne Marchand (*Jane*), Roberto Camardiel (*Double Whiskey*), Rosalba Neri (*Dolores*), Pietro Tordi (*Priest*), Andrea Bosic (*Pedro*), Mirko Ellis (*Sheriff*), Gerard Lartigau (*John*), Tom Felleghy, Renato Chiantoni, Valentino Macchi, Gianni Solaro, Jose Manuel Martin, Emma Baron

The story

To obtain more men, the bandit Gordo Watch, aka Gordon Wacht, raids a Mexican jail and frees the prisoners. A dandy gunfighter is the first to break out, but he avoids Gordon's press gang. The dandy gives a ride to Double Whiskey, one of Gordo's men, who has accidentally been left behind.

In the badlands, Gordo offers the escapees a choice: they can join his band, the Sidewinders, or be killed. Only one chooses the latter. Whiskey and his benefactor catch up with the bandits. When Gordo asks who he is, the gunfighter – since they're now in Arizona – says his name is Arizona. And his second name is Colt... Faster on the draw than Gordo and his men, Arizona Colt declines the invitation to be branded with an 'S' on his arm, and leaves.

Piqued by this rejection, and by Whiskey's evident amusement, Gordo sends his main henchman, Kay, and five other Sidewinders to kill Arizona. But they fall into a trap. Arizona sends Kay back to Gordo in his long johns. Gordo sends Kay, dressed as a dude, to reconnoitre the town of Blackstone Hill and its bank. Waiting at the stage station, Kay runs into Arizona. The two take the stage to town. Arizona pretends to be a naïf and interrupts a poker game, while Kay learns that the toughest guys in town are leaving to do some gold mining: Blackstone Hill will be defenceless till they return. Arizona pursues a blonde saloon girl, Jane. Kay makes love to Jane's sister, Dolores – but when she sees his Sidewinder brand, he kills her and flees.

Next day, after Dolores's funeral, Arizona cheats at cards while Gordo and the Sidewinders rob the bank. He offers to hunt down Kay if

Dolores's father will let him sleep with Jane, in addition to the reward. The deal is made. The Sidewinders ambush the miners and rob them. When Gordo uses them for target practice, Whiskey is perturbed. Arizona pursues Kay and kills him. But Gordo shoots Arizona in the hands and legs, and leaves him for dead.

Whiskey steals the Sidewinders' loot and carries Kay's body and the wounded Colt to Blackstone Hill. Jane nurses him back to health. But her father and the indignant citizens run Arizona out of town before he and Jane can consummate their deal. Arizona and Whiskey hole up in an abandoned church; Jane comes and tells them that Gordo has returned to town; he's threatening to kill everyone if his money is not returned. Arizona declines to help, but Whiskey is moved, and returns to Blackstone Hill to fight Gordo. Arizona follows to support his friend. Wearing a coat with fake hands wrapped in bandages, Arizona gets the drop on the Sidewinders and wipes them out. He pursues Gordo into an undertaker's warehouse, where the bandit is betrayed by his musical watch. Arizona cripples Gordo and delivers him, alive, to the townspeople. He departs without claiming his promised night with Jane.

The film

Arizona Colt is a fine, opportunist amalgam of *Django*, *For a Few Dollars More* and the *Ringo* films. The *Monthly Film Bulletin* loathed it for its 'unbridled violence and gratuitous sadism': these things, plus some good characterisations, are its virtues. The film was blessed with a big budget, which purchased some fabulous waistcoats, many extras, horses, explosions, and a strong cast. It's decidedly a *Ringo* film: Gemma's character, a dandy pistolero who drinks milk and loves money, is more of a ladies' man than Ringo was, but equally selfish and – if possible – even more childish. As previously, Gemma is pitted against Fernando Sancho – who adorns this Mexican bandit chieftain with two embellishments: a perm and a musical watch. The watch, of course, is lifted from *For a Few Dollars More* – as are the prison break, the preparations for the bank robbery and the scene in which Gordo produces Colonel Mortimer's long-barrelled revolver to shoot a running, human target. *Django* also provides the theft of the Mexican bandits' loot, the strong heroine and the crippling of the hero. Lupo was primarily a director of comedies, and *Arizona Colt* is never entirely serious, even at its most sadistic.

The principal screenwriter, Ernesto Gastaldi, would write several notable Westerns, including *$1,000 on the Black* and *My Name is Nobody*. Larger budgets brought a new element to the Spaghetti Western mix: an American or dialogue editor. Previously, as Eastwood and Van Cleef recalled, the American actors had edited their own dialogue. Now Leone could afford to hire a blacklisted Hollywood writer, Mickey Knox. And one Lewis E Cianelli was employed, to give *Arizona Colt* a more authentic 'American' sound (on the set, the actors were still speaking Italian and Spanish). Cianelli was an itinerant American with one Hollywood credit – associate producer of *Heller in Pink Tights* (1960). Later he played small roles in Italian action films, and provided dialogue services for Corbucci on *The Big Silence*. He did good work on *Arizona Colt*. In the scene where Gemma's character invents his name, the Italian dialogue is minimal: '*Arizona Colt. Una tierra... una pistola.*' Cianelli embellishes it: 'Arizona Colt. A great state... and a great gun.' He's at his best with Gordo's dialogue, especially in the scene where the bandit leader gathers the newly released prisoners, and displays the many 'Wanted' posters with his face on them, offering ever-increasing sums for his delivery, dead or alive.

> GORDO: When I began I was a poor *peon* like you. Before I explain why I saved you, let me tell you how I started. My father had a musical gold watch. I always wanted to hear that music. He told me, "Gordo, you'll have this watch when I am dead." So five seconds after, it was mine!

Gordo is, not surprisingly, offended that the Americans spell his name wrong on their posters: 'Gordon Wacht'. At the same time, he promises the prisoners a good life if they ride with him: 'I'm always looking for new muchachos – to replace the ones who are killed!' These scenes, including a *plano secuencia* where the Sidewinders make camp, show Sancho to be a fine actor – and comedian. Nello Pazzafini perspires well as Gordo's inept henchman, Kay. The women of the film are beautiful, the townspeople grotesque, the bad guys evil-looking. Giuliano Gemma is perfect. But the most interesting character in the film is Roberto Camardiel's: the alcoholic Whiskey, aka Double Whiskey.

It would be impossible to write a character like this today, whose addiction to alcohol is portrayed as entirely benign, an endearing character trait. A contemporary screenwriter would be obliged to make Camardiel's character confront his demons, realise he's harmed himself and others, and get off the stuff, or die in the attempt. In a good American Western like *Yellow Sky* (1948), the dangers of filling your canteen with whiskey, and embarking on a desert trek, are vividly displayed. So Camardiel's is a fantastical personage, like Jay C Flippen's whiskey-drinking Sioux in *Broken Arrow* (1957). And – like Flippen's character – he's very important in the film's moral scheme. Whiskey, not Arizona, is our moral compass. Django and Joe, in *Fistful*, knew the right thing to do, and did it. Arizona makes excuses: when Jane comes to plead for the townspeople, he scoffs, 'Those kind men who threw me out, when I couldn't defend myself?' Ringo II was afraid; Ringo III is simply selfish. For most of the film Arizona Colt has been invulnerable; when he's wounded the game ceases to be fun. But Whiskey is moved by Jane's story, and decides to return to Blackstone Hill – even though he knows he'll die there, and Arizona will keep the gold.

Arizona follows Whiskey, and saves the day, of course. But this is out of buddy-loyalty. Whereas Whiskey returns out of a sense of duty, to rescue people he doesn't know, and doesn't like. So Whiskey is really the hero of the film. Roberto Camardiel isn't obvious hero material: he's round, short, balding and limps, while Giuliano Gemma is textbook handsome, and an athlete. Yet our sympathies go with the fat little drunk in the Johnny-Rotten chequered suit and fur coat. In the end, neither man gets the girl. Arizona rides off alone, and Whiskey, his Sidewinder brand erased by an explosion, seems set up for a life of ease.

Whiskey is the first example of what Leone was about to call the 'Ugly' character: dark skinned, not good-looking, not tall, who would exhibit heroic and empathetic tendencies, while the 'Good', white hero remained aloof. The 'Ugly' character differs from subsidiary good guys such as the barmen in *Fistful* and *Django*, or Sheriff Carson, because he *isn't* good. Whiskey is a bandit, a switcher-of-allegiances, and a murderer. Popular cinema had come to favour invulnerable, ice-cool, technologically adept heroes, like James Bond and Flint. The Westerns swung in that direction, too – but with a counterbalance. Italian directors as different as Lupo and Leone both saw a need for an additional heroic character – darker, shorter, livelier than the gringo – with whom a shorter, darker, livelier filmgoer might more readily identify.

The shoot began with the Almería locations – the desert canyons and the prison exterior. These two weeks were blessed by perfect weather: crisp winter sunlight. The Italian shoot followed, at Anzio, where *Django*'s mud-wastes were filmed, and on the rather boring Western backlot at Cinecittà. The credits suggest two different crews, one Spanish, one Italian. But Sergio D'Offizi, who was the camera operator, says this wasn't the case. He told Giusti:

> The only director of photography was Memmo Mancori, and his only operator was me.

Offizi recalled that a Spanish director of photography, Paco Marin, became nominally involved because the producers needed to comply with a co-production treaty. The rules of the treaty changed while they were shooting, and Marin was dropped from the credits. Offizi refers to Mancori as 'a saint'. Mancori favoured wide shots with sharp focus – every distant mountain and rock formation in the Almería desert; every extra, with his exaggerated Victorian pompadour, in the saloon. There are no out-of-focus backgrounds, almost no long-lens shots until the final showdown. Then a series of jump cuts – in the manner of *The Birds* – enclose the defenceless townspeople, corralled in the street. Mancori's style is like successive panels of a very detailed comic book. One *plano secuencia*, in particular, stands out. It takes place on the Cinecittà street set, after Whiskey's brought Arizona back to town. Mancori tracks with a funeral procession to people taking off their hats, and finds the guilty and remorseful Whiskey, watched by various townsmen, doffing his Davy Crocket cap. As the suspicious townsmen start to surround Whiskey, the track reverses direction, following him as he tries to exit, confronting him with yet more glaring locals. It's a well-executed piece of camerawork and choreography.

At other times, the film moves slowly, with several irrelevant sub-plots (one of them includes a cockney-dubbed, 'cute/funny' protestant preacher, who should be killed immediately, but isn't). Worth noting is the excellent psychedelic credit sequence: despite these films' violence, Gemma was always playing a proto-hippy, I think. In *Return of Ringo* he puts a flower in the barrel of Sancho's gun – and for the first third of *The Long Days of Revenge* he is invisible beneath a huge mop of hair and beard. *Arizona Colt* also features a decent score by Francesco de Masi (guitar and whistling by Alessandro Alessandroni) and – always welcome – a scene with genuine singing cowboys, riding to their doom.

The Bounty Killer

aka *The Ugly Ones, El precio de un hombre*
(Italy/Spain)

Director: Eugenio Martin   **Producer:** Jose Gutierrez Maesso (Discobolo/Tecisa)   **Screenplay:** Don Prindle, Jose Gutierrez Maesso, Eugenio Martin   **Director of Photography:** Enzo Barboni   **Art Director:** Francisco Canet   **Editor:** Jose Antonio Rojo   **Assistant Director:** Sinesio Isla   **Music:** Stelvio Cipriani   **Cast:** Tomas Milian (*Jose Gomez*), Richard Wyler (*Luke Chilson*), Ilya Karin (*Eden*), Mario Brega (*Miguel*), Ricardo Canales (*Blaine Novak*), Hugo Blanco, Luis Barboo, Manolo Zarzo, Frank Brana, Jose Canalejas

The story

A bounty killer, Luke Chilson, pursues two outlaws through the desert. He kills one and apprehends the other in the tiny settlement of New Charcos. The locals refuse to help him; unknown to Chilson, one of them – the beautiful Eden – is in love with the outlaws' leader, Jose Gomez.

Eden slips Jose a pistol at a nearby stagecoach stop. She leaves before Jose and his gang massacre the lawmen who are attempting to take him to jail. Chilson, hearing of Jose's escape, returns to New Charcos to look for him. Jose shows up and Chilson tries to arrest him – only to be betrayed by an alcoholic former sheriff, Novak, and a simple blacksmith, Miguel, both of whom admire Jose. When Jose's gang arrive, they torture Chilson and kill an innocent cowpoke, Heffner. Delaying their escape to Mexico, Jose turns on his former friends and orders his men to loot the town.

Jose gets increasingly drunk and crazy as the settlement is wrecked. He shows no romantic interest in Eden. When she asks him to leave, he orders her to come with him to Mexico. She responds by freeing Chilson, who escapes, then returns in disguise. Aided by Novak and Eden, Chilson wipes out Jose's gang and, in a showdown, shoots Jose – who dies, drooling in the dust.

The film

A Spanish-Italian co-production, *The Bounty Killer* was offered to Sergio Leone prior to *Fistful of Dollars*. Leone wrote his own screenplay, based on an American Western novel Jose Gutierrez Masseo had optioned. As often happens, the producer didn't like the director's script, and Leone left the project. Masseo offered a new version to a Spanish director, Eugenio Martin.

In the US, *The Bounty Killer* was retitled *The Ugly Ones*, to cash in on the success of Leone's latest. It's admirably cynical and distanced: a concise *Noir* Western, shot almost entirely in one Almería location, with a strong female lead. There is much callous killing and torture; an unlikeable hero is pitted against an even less likeable villain, in a settlement populated by idiots and dupes. The locals, including the former sheriff, admire Jose Gomez, who they think of as a victim of racism and an unhappy childhood. Inevitably, they discover he's a psycho killer. Richard Wyler is suitably taciturn as the bounty killer. Milian, in his first Spaghetti Western, is annoying – smirking, laughing, weeping, fingering guns and bolts of cloth. If this were his only Western one might dismiss the young Cuban-American as the wretched refuse of the New York Actors' Studio. But it's not all Milian's fault: the part of Jose Gomez is minimally drawn, and, unlike Gian Maria Volonte, Milian couldn't yet weave gold out of straw. With better roles he'd soon become a proper leading man. Milian remained in Spain after the shoot to act in a second Western, where his co-star would be Roberto Camardiel: *Django Kill.*

The best element of the film, besides its tight narrative, is Enzo Barboni's lighting and camerawork – not as dramatically stylised as *Django*, but equally impressive, with fluid tracks and cranes. Martin was an efficient director who made three other Westerns of no great note, including *Bad Man's River* (1971) and *Pancho Villa* (1972).

When I read that Leone was going to adapt *Voyage au bout de la nuit* (*Journey to the End of the Night*), I got hold of an English translation and read it. Would that Sergio Leone had made Céline's novel into a film! Anti-war, ferociously cynical, teetering on the edge of despair, there is something very appropriate to Leone in the way the doctor hero, over a period of many years, encounters the criminal Robinson. But Frayling's interviews with Leone's associates suggest he never read the book: instead, his brother-in-law, Fulvio Morsella, may have read extracts aloud to him. Leone, like many other directors, wasn't very book-oriented. It was Luciano Vincenzoni who wanted him to make Céline's novel into a film. Vincenzoni reported, with some glee, how Leone had carted Céline's novel to a TV interview with French critics, and discussed it earnestly, even though he hadn't read it!

Another Western was inevitable. Somehow Vincenzoni had become involved in foreign sales; in this capacity, he took the UA reps to a sold-out screening of *For a Few Dollars More* in Rome. They loved the film (their marketing department quickly re-christened Eastwood the 'Man With No Name'). They wanted another Leone Western right away, and asked Vincenzoni for the plot outline. Vincenzoni made something up on the spur of the moment. 'It's a film about three rogues who are looking for some treasure, at the time of the American Civil War.' Fine, said the Americans, who bought the picture for a million dollars, on the spot.

For a Spaghetti Western, this was an enormous budget. Leone, Vincenzoni, Eastwood, and all concerned should have been very happy. But, as Frayling recounts, this third picture made enemies of all three men. Eastwood and Leone had never really liked each other; each man thought himself responsible for the other's success. I'm with Leone here; Eastwood was a limited, solid actor, who required a stunt double just to ride a horse. Many other actors (Richard Harrison, Robert Woods, Franco Nero, Fabio Testi) could have played Joe/Manco/the Man With No Name. But no other director could have made *Fistful of Dollars* or *For a Few Dollars More*, films with extraordinary confidence and verve. Leone was a genius; Eastwood was lucky. And now the lucky actor demanded a huge fee – $250,000 – plus a percentage. UA raised the budget to $1.3 million to accommodate Eastwood's salary, but Leone didn't forgive him. Leone also fell out with Vincenzoni. Frayling thinks the director was jealous of his writer, who certainly wielded a lot of power, having brought UA to the table. Leone hired two other writers, who contributed little, in an attempt to cut Vincenzoni down to size. In post-production, he hired Sergio Donati to work on the script; then he fell out with Donati as well.

Thus it often is. Money is the lifeblood of the cinema, but it's also the medium's curse. Friends don't fall out over creative differences; they fall out over money, and over the status they think it brings. Leone, with an unhappy home dominated by a mad, mute mother, had formerly been in his element on set, and in the cutting room. But, editing his latest, biggest Western, he became uncertain, fearful and close to despair.

The Good, the Bad and the Ugly

aka *Il buono, il brutto, il cattivo, El bueno, el feo, y el malo,*
Le bon, la brute et le truand
(Italy)

Director: Sergio Leone   **Producer:** Alberto Grimaldi   **Screenplay:** Age-Scarpelli, Luciano Vincenzoni, Sergio Donati   **Story:** Luciano Vincenzoni, Sergio Leone   **Director of Photography:** Tonino Delli Colli   **Art Director, Costumes:** Carlo Simi   **Editor:** Nino Baragli, Eugenio Alabiso   **Special Effects:** Eros Bacciucchi   **Assistant Director:** Giancarlo Santi   **Music:** Ennio Morricone   **Cast:** Clint Eastwood (*Blondie/Joe*), Eli Wallach (*Tuco*), Lee Van Cleef (*Angel Eyes/Sentenza*) Aldo Guiffre (*Capt Clinton*), Mario Brega (*Corp Wallace*), Luigi Pistilli (*Father Ramirez*), Al

Mulock (*Elam*), Antonio Casas (*Stevens*), Livio Lorenzon (*Baker*), Antonio
Casale (*Jackson*, aka *Bill Carson*), Rada Rassimov (*Maria*), Angelo Novi
(*Young Monk*), Frank Braña (*Bounty hunter*), Claudio Scarchelli (*Bounty
hunter*), Sergio Mendizabal (*Blond bounty hunter*), Nazareno Natale (*Mexican
bounty hunter*), John Bartha (*Sheriff*), Sandro Scarchelli (*Deputy*), Antonio
Molino Rojo (*Capt Harper*), Jesus Guzman (*Pardue, hotelier*), Chelo Alonso
(*Stevens' wife*), Antonio Ruiz (*Stevens' son*), Enzo Petito (*Milton*), Victor
Israel (*Southern sergeant*), Silvana Bacci (*Mexican prostitute*), Aysanoa
Runachuagua (*Mexican pistolero*), Lorenzo Robledo (*Clem*), Romano Puppo
(*Slim*) Benito Stefanelli, Luigi Chiavarro, Aldo Sambrell (*Members of
Sentenza's gang*)

The story

Sentenza, a hired killer, learns from one of his victims of a hidden cache of army gold worth $200,000. Having killed the man who hired him, he sets out to look for the loot. Joe, a bounty hunter, makes money turning Tuco Ramirez, a Mexican outlaw, over to the law, then freeing him from the gallows. But, bored with Tuco's constant complaints, Joe abandons him in the desert. Tuco survives and swears revenge.

Sentenza searches for Jackson, aka Bill Carson, who knows where the money is hidden, among the disheveled ranks of the Confederate army. Tuco pursues Joe and – catching him in a similar scam with another outlaw, Shorty – drives Joe into the desert without water. In the desert they encounter a coach full of dead Confederates, and the dying Carson. Carson tells Tuco of the gold buried in Sad Hill Cemetery; separately, he tells Joe in which grave the money is stashed.

Forced into a partnership with Joe, Tuco takes him to the San Antonio mission, run by his brother, Pablo. But, after Joe has recovered, he and Tuco – disguised as Confederates – are captured by Union troops. They are imprisoned in the Battleville prison camp, where they encounter Sentenza, impersonating a Union sergeant. Tuco makes the mistake of using the name Bill Carson: Sentenza has him tortured to learn the location of the loot. He sends Tuco, in the company of his torturer, Corporal Wallace, to be hanged; and invites Joe to help him find the gold.

Tuco escapes and kills Wallace. In a bombed-out town, he runs into Joe and the two team up to gun down Sentenza's gang. But Sentenza

106

escapes, and the partners' path is blocked by Union and Confederate forces fighting over a bridge. Tuco and Joe blow up the bridge and arrive, at last, at Sad Hill, a huge military cemetery where Sentenza awaits them. Here, accounts are settled, and the gold unearthed. Joe subjects Tuco to a final bout of torture before riding off with his share.

The film

Vincenzoni told Frayling that the title came to him in a dream. This may be so, but it isn't the whole story. The three words, in English, hail from the dedication to Ed Abbey's book *The Brave Cowboy*. This reads as follows:

> *To the outlaws: the good and the bad, the ugly and the pretty, the live and the dead.*

Leone and his collaborators had a wonderfully fractured view of US culture. Leone really believed that 'duck, you sucker' was an expression frequently used by Americans. He apparently believed that 'Blondie' was an appropriate name for a male protagonist (or perhaps he didn't, given his feelings about Eastwood). So likewise he may have imagined 'the Good, the Bad and the Ugly' was also a commonly used phrase. It wasn't. Abbey's conjunction is his invention. I'd guess Vincenzoni read the book and forgot about the dedication till his dream; or that Morsella read *The Brave Cowboy* aloud to Leone, translating it from English, and the dedication stuck in Leone's head.

The first title Vincenzoni gave United Artists was *The Magnificent Rogues*; in keeping with Leone's tradition of paying homage to Kurosawa and Sturges (*Fistful* having started life as *The Magnificent Stranger*, *For a Few...* as *Two Magnificent Strangers*). The film was planned as a three-hander: a tale of escalating rivalry between the aloof, unbeatable gringo, a pitiless, implacable villain, and a subsidiary hero, funnier and more fallible, who – like Whiskey in *Arizona Colt* – would appeal to the wider audience. As Frayling reports, Eastwood didn't like the idea of an additional hero-figure. Leone, lying as directors unfortunately must, told him the character of Tuco was merely an assistant, Joe's 'water-boy'. Of course, he was anything but: a short, increasingly fat guy himself, Leone identified with the anti-social bandit, Tuco, and with the actor who was to play him. In an interview with a young journalist, Dario Argento, Leone said Gian Maria Volonte would play the 'Ugly' character, Eastwood the 'Good', and Enrico Maria Salerno the 'Bad'. (Salerno was a talented and respected actor whose voice had replaced Eastwood's in the Italian versions of the *Dollars* films.) But Leone quickly dropped Volonte in favour of an American actor: Eli Wallach. This was a somewhat boring choice: Wallach had played a very similar role, the Mexican bandit chief, in *The Magnificent Seven*. But Wallach was an excellent actor, and Leone – whose English had much improved – quickly bonded with him.

Leone offered the role of Sentenza to Charles Bronson, who was interested, but had signed up for *The Dirty Dozen*. So the part went to Lee Van Cleef, who assumed that it had always been his. Thus began a string of jobs, and a steady income at last, for one of the Spaghetti Western's most memorable actors.

Though filled with gunfights and exciting action, the long version of *The Good, the Bad and the Ugly* isn't much of a Western. It's too picaresque by far, let down by sequences in which characters ask for directions, or assemble their disposable gangs. Some scenes are magnificent – for instance, the opening sequence, played without music, in which Al Mulock and two other tough guys attempt to ambush Tuco in a tiny frontier settlement. But other scenes are repetitive, slow and flat. Joe and Tuco's fixation on petty revenge and hangings seems very childish – was such childishness enjoyed, or *endured*, by the audience? The lengthy torture of Tuco by Wallace (Mario Brega) is boring; the cutaways to an orchestra of weeping soldiers are cloyingly sentimental.

Morricone's main theme is still his most famous composition – perhaps to the composer's frustration, given his vast body of work. The film has a fine, exuberant score, though it relies on variations of the same piece, 'Story of a Soldier'. Hugo Montenegro's version of the main theme became a worldwide hit; but the film's greatest quality, I think, is its visual aspect. Working with a new cinematographer, Tonino Delli Colli, Leone developed the shot for which he'll always be remembered: starting small, with a forest path or a single gravestone, then tracking and craning up and out to reveal a massive Civil War battlefield, or a cemetery filled with thousands of graves. Delli Colli does fine work; Carlo Simi's design is magnificent. Trains, wrecked towns and buildings, the battlefield, the prison camp: every element is finely detailed and seemingly authentic, from the Navy Colt revolvers to the long-haired Union scouts, from the Confederate spy chained to a cattle-catcher, to the cannon, gattling guns and spiked wooden ramparts. Simi's work recalls Matthew Brady's famous photographs of this first, utterly modern war.

In fact, there was very little fighting in the South West during the American Civil War. Columns of soldiers, clad in blue and grey, riding through desert canyons and over sand dunes are a fantasy: thanks to Simi, they are entirely believable. Even the rare mistakes – Joe loading his Navy Colt with finished cartridges rather than caps-and-balls; Tuco praying to a portrait of Jesus in a nation whose goddess is the Virgin of Guadalupe – seem 'authentic'. Simi's costume design is equally impressive. For him, the War was an improvisational affair: most of his soldiers have uniforms, but many don't. Mulock and Eastwood both wear duster-like long coats.

The Good, the Bad and the Ugly refers to other Westerns, and non-Westerns: the scene where Stevens (Antonio Casas) offers Sentenza a thousand dollars not to murder him recalls From Russia With Love (1963), where James Bond offers a hired assassin double his salary, not to be killed. The driverless coach with a dead man on board hails from Ford's She Wore a Yellow Ribbon (1949): in that film it's the pay-master's wagon. And the film reminds me, quite strikingly, of It's a Mad, Mad, Mad, Mad World (1963), Stanley Kramer's Cinerama comedy in which a diverse gang of greedy and debased citizens race each other to find a cache of stolen money, buried underground.

The film has aural shortcomings. Morricone's score is great, but the sound design is deficient. One ker-thunk sound is used repeatedly, to represent everything from a falling body to a closing door. Gunshots aren't properly synched to the action. There are some good, whistling, bomb-falls, but a glorious opportunity is missed: flies crawling on hats and faces cry out for a sound effect. Yet no buzz is heard. On the set of Straight to Hell, in Almería, the actors daubed themselves with sugar water to attract flies. How we prized those flies! Every insect that landed on an actor's face was rewarded with a unique buzz by the sound designer, Justin Krish. Films made in the sixties didn't have sound designers as such, but they *did* have sound effects *editors*, and such a lame job of effects cutting suggests that Leone and his staff were simply running out of time.

The film had two excellent editors, Nino Baragli and Eugenio Alabiso. Did they struggle with the volume of material Leone shot? Leone was increasingly anxious because his film was more than an hour longer than the one Vincenzoni had promised United Artists. It was the first time Leone had worked directly for the Americans, and they wanted a picture no more than two hours long. This was simple economics for them: a shorter running time meant fewer reels of film to buy and process, and more daily screenings. Also, in certain countries, features were screened in double-bills, which implied a certain maximum length. But Leone was having his *One-Eyed Jacks* moment. *The Good, the Bad and the Ugly* is a big film, with three main characters and many incidents; three hours, he felt, was a good length for it.

In fact, he might have preferred an even longer film. In addition to that brilliant, characteristic shot, Leone was developing his especially slow style of storytelling, to be perfected in his *Once Upon a Time* films. He was stretching scenes of tension to the breaking point, if not beyond. *The Good, the Bad and the Ugly*, in its longest version, runs 182 minutes. When the film opened in France, it was 166 minutes long. In the US, its running time was 161 minutes. In England, it first showed as a 148-minute solo feature, and was then cut down to under two hours, to fit a double-bill. Three hours is long for an action movie, and – now that I've seen the film at various lengths – it seems to me that there are, in fact, two different films, both going by the same name.

One is Leone's preferred version: a long, rambling, picaresque tale which Vincenzoni wrought as an homage to Céline, and which Leone later claimed was influenced by Chaplin's *Monsieur Verdoux* (1947) and also by Cervantes. Let's call this film *The Magnificent Rogues*.

The other is much, much shorter – something like the British re-release version of the seventies, which the distributor cut drastically. Gone was the scene where Sentenza beats up a prostitute; gone the scene after it where Tuco crosses the bridge and steals a pistol; gone was the scene with Tuco's brother, the priest, and most of the prison camp. Non-action scenes were shortened or entirely eliminated. This was the pure action version of *The Good, the Bad and the Ugly*: racing as fast as it could for Sad Hill Cemetery.

Such different films!

There's a tendency among critics to think that 'longer is better' and that the director always wants/deserves/should get the longest possible version of his film. But that isn't always true. Directors of very long films can sometimes be accused of losing the plot. In this instance, what is the point of the (rediscovered) scene where Tuco visits a cave and his gang slide down on ropes to meet him? It's cartoonish, not very well lit or shot. The scene where Sentenza visits a ruined fort is beautifully photographed, but it's irrelevant, and its dormitories of wounded soldiers reappear in later scenes. The long 'restored' sequence in the desert, where Tuco further tortures Blondie, is embarrassing, childish and slow.

Only one of the restored clips has real value. It takes place just before the last Civil War battle, where Tuco pretends he and Joe are Union volunteers. The drunken Captain Clinton (Aldo Guiffre) doesn't believe them, and asks who they are.

CAPTAIN: What did you say your name was?

TUCO: Ah, I, eh...

For a splendid moment, Tuco gives up. He can't be bothered to think of a new fake name, nor to repeat the name of Bill Carson, his previous alias. In the face of so much carnage and madness, and no end in sight, his mind has packed up. As has the mind of Joe.

CAPTAIN: And you?

Joe looks discomforted. He can't think of a name either.

CAPTAIN: No, ha ha ha! Names don't matter...

This seems to me an important part of the film, and of Leone's work in general, where even the Magnificent Rogues are reduced to silence, in the face of the infinite reach of man's perfected killing machine. It makes the same point as Joe's remark, 'Never seen so many men wasted so badly,' regarding the battlefield, and rings less false.

Even as war is treated – entirely correctly – as a hideous meat-grinder, Vincenzoni and Leone are generous to the Union officer class. Captain Clinton is a humane man, drowning himself in liquor, who, twice daily, must lead a pointless assault on the bridge. And the commandant of the prison camp, despite a ludicrous make-up job, is incensed by 'Sergeant' Sentenza's brutality and thievery. Dying of gangrene, he still hopes to 'courtmartial all who dishonour and discredit the Union'. Sentenza, a most postmodern hero/villain, smiles: 'I wish you luck.'

Mickey Knox, the American writer, has been credited with the English dialogue. But my English-language script says on its title page,

MELTON S DAVIS, ENGLISH DIALOGUE
'IL BUONO IL BRUTTO IL CATTIVO'

Who was Davis? An Internet search reveals Melton S Davis as the author of *Who Defends Rome?* and *All Rome Trembled*, books about the Second World War; in 1983 he wrote an article for the *New York Times* with the by-line 'Melton S Davis reports frequently on the arts in Italy'. Knox was originally an actor: he played one of the train robbers in the classic *noir* thriller *White Heat* (1948). Blacklisted by the studios, he moved to Europe, and was Orson Welles' assistant director on *Chimes at Midnight* (1965). Knox certainly supervised the dialogue re-recording (where Wallach seems to have improvised prodigiously). Did Knox work with the actors, using an English script by Davis? Or was Davis hired to transcribe the 'dialogue continuity' after the film was locked?

The Good, the Bad and the Ugly features another Hays-busting 'mercy killing'. As in the previous *Dollars* films, it's done by Eastwood. For some reason, these 'mercy killings' became an obsession with Clint. Dirty Harry pulls the trigger on a wounded bank robber who says 'he gots to know' whether Eastwood's gun is empty or not. His gun is empty on this occasion, but when he plays the same game with the villain, played by Andy Robinson, it's loaded. As a director,

Eastwood got into a fight with the Pentagon over his insistence on including a 'mercy killing' in his 1986 war movie, *Heartbreak Ridge*. This magnificent work (detailing the glorious victory of the American military over a handful of Cuban construction workers in Grenada) had the initial support of the Pentagon: free troops, tanks, helicopters, the use of Camp Pendleton – the largest Marine base in California – as a location. Of course, in return for such taxpayer-funded *largesse*, directors must submit their scripts to the military, and make a variety of changes. Among the changes the Pentagon required was the removal of a 'mercy killing', which, they assured him, had not occurred. Even though the event was fictitious, Eastwood insisted on including it, at an enormous cost to his financiers.

As a director, Eastwood has proved uniquely uninspired. His directorial chops seem borrowed from Leone, or from his other mentor, Don Siegel. He has little to say, beyond revisiting this one obsession. Late in his career, Eastwood directed a film which justified the 'mercy killing' of beautiful, crippled women by old men: *Million Dollar Baby*. But enough of Eastwood for now. *The Good, the Bad and the Ugly* was his last Spaghetti Western. He ended it on bad terms with Leone. Yet, from afar, he would continue to exert an influence – as we shall see.

Militarism in Spaghetti Westerns is portrayed as a psychotic disorder, akin to racism. Wars are depicted as utterly destructive, of benefit only to profiteers. This is a very European viewpoint, of course. Not all Americans, and very few American Westerns, are opposed to militarism and war. But *Django* is unambiguous: what is Franco Nero's character but a damaged, gold-hungry arms dealer? And *The Good, the Bad and the Ugly* makes the point repeatedly, as armies retreat through shelled towns, and thieves, forced to carry their own coffins, are shot by firing squads. In the Spaghetti Western world, anyone covered in medals or wearing a natty uniform is to be avoided. They are invariably: 1) a Mexican bandit chief, 2) an ex-Confederate patriarch trying to restart the Civil War, or 3) a fetishistic sadist (Jackson, in *Django*, is both 2 and 3). Of course, 'anti-war' films tend to be hypocritical: we, the audience, enjoy the battle scene, with its explosions and its falling extras, just as we enjoy the coach full of corpses, and the gunfights and showdowns. But *The Good, the Bad and the Ugly* never suggests that war is glorious: unlike the Hollywood cinema, at its worst in war-loving epics like *Glory* (1989). For its historical and political truthfulness, and the authenticity of its design, I think *The Good, the Bad and the Ugly* is the best film yet made about the American Civil War.

There are almost no women in the film: just Stevens' handsome, mute wife, a couple of prostitutes, and some old ladies. Westerns are notoriously macho, of course, and not many have decent roles for women. But Ford often made decent roles for women, and Corbucci did, too. Corbucci could be very cruel to the women characters in his films, just as Ford could be cruel to his actresses. But one senses both directors valued them. In a Corbucci Western, a family's destruction is a significant event: in *Hellbenders*, it would be the subject of the film. For Leone, the destruction of the family is a pretext to show the villainy of the bad guy; Leone gets it over with early on, then jumps to the exciting stuff. In his preference for a world without women, Leone more resembles the last great American Western director, Sam Peckinpah.

Near the end of *The Good, the Bad and the Ugly*, Eastwood's *serape* shows up. In a rare act of unremunerated kindness, Blondie gives his coat and a smoke to a dying soldier, then picks up the iconic 'poncho' in exchange. This suggests an interesting twist: that the *Dollars* trilogy operates in reverse: beginning with the Civil War adventure and the acquisition of the cape; heading West with the railroad and the bounty killers in the 1880s; and concluding, near the turn of the century, in a small town on the Mexican border, San Miguel.

The Big Gundown

aka *La resa dei conti, El halcon y la presa, Colorado*
(Italy/Spain)

Director: Sergio Sollima   **Producer:** Alberto Grimaldi   **Screenplay:** Sergio Sollima, Sergio Donati, Tullio Demicheli   **Story:** Franco Solinas, Fernando Morandi   **Director of Photography:** Carlo Carlini   **Art Director:** Carlo Simi, Rafael Ferri, Enrique Alarcon   **Costumes:** Carlo Simi   **Editor:** Gaby Penalba   **Special Effects:** Eros Bacciucchi

Assistant Director: Nino Zanchin   **Music:** Ennio Morricone   **Music Director:** Bruno Nicolai   **Cast:** Lee Van Cleef (*Jonathan Corbett*), Tomas Milian (*Cuchillo*), Walter Barnes (*Brokston*), Luisa Rivelli (*Lizzie*), Fernando Sancho (*Capt Segura*), Nieves Navarro (*The widow*), Benito Stefanelli (*Jess*), Maria Granada (*Rosita*), Lanfranco Ceccarelli (*Jack*), Roberto Camardiel (*Jellicoe*), Nello Pazzafini (*Hondo*), Spartaco Conversi (*Mitchell*), Romano Puppo (*Rocky*), Tom Felleghi (*Chet*), Calisto Calisti (*Miller*), Antonio Casas (*Brother Smith & Wesson*), Jose Torres (*Nathan*), Gerard Herter, Angel Del Pozo (*Shep*), Antonio Molino Rojo

The story

A Texas bounty hunter, Jonathan Corbett, kills four escaping outlaws, then attends the wedding party of the daughter of a powerful railroad speculator, Brokston. Brokston offers Corbett financial help with his political ambitions; in return, Corbett offers to track down a Mexican, Cuchillo, accused of raping and murdering a little girl. The sheriff is on hand to give Corbett a badge.

Corbett follows Cuchillo across the border, and catches up with him in a small town, and again in a Mormon camp. Each time, Cuchillo escapes. Corbett tracks Cuchillo down on a bizarre ranch, inhabited by a sexually super-charged widow and a gang of killers. The Widow has seduced Cuchillo and attempts to seduce Corbett; Cuchillo sets the killers against the alpha-male sheriff, and escapes again. After a long chase, hunter and prey are both thrown into Captain Segura's jail. Corbett doesn't raise the alarm when Cuchillo escapes. Before he goes, Cuchillo insists that he is innocent. Brokston, his daughter, son-in-law Shep, and bodyguard ('Baron Von Schulenburg, a genuine Austrian baron') arrive. Brokston has organised a manhunt. A big-game hunter, he revels in the prospect of human prey. Itching for a fight, the Baron needles Corbett. Shep tries to assault a young girl, and Corbett realises Cuchillo is right.

In a desert showdown, instigated by Corbett, Cuchillo's knife proves faster than Shep's pistol. The Baron gets his gunfight, and loses it; Corbett, wounded, shoots Brokston out of his saddle. Brokston's Mexican allies desert him. Corbett and Cuchillo ride together across the desert; then head north and south.

The film

Lee Van Cleef and several other actors followed producer Alberto Grimaldi from one big-budget Western to another. As with *The Good, the Bad and the Ugly*, the money came from an American studio: but studios act in mysterious ways, and though UA put up the cash, Columbia released the film. Van Cleef was joined by Antonio Casas and a host of Leone tough guys, including Benito Stefanelli, Antonio Molino Rojo, Brank Braña, Lorenzo Robledo, Spartaco Conversi, and Romano Puppo (a tall, sharp-featured stunt man who usually doubled Van Cleef in riding scenes). From the *Ringo* films came staunch Fernando Sancho and the delectable Nieves Navarro. An American actor, Walter Barnes, portrayed the villainous capitalist; Gerard Herter was his Austrian bodyguard, caped and crewcut; a Spaniard, Angel del Pozo, played the querulous rapist, Shep. They are a perfect Axis of Evil.

The original script was by Franco Solinas, co-author of *Battle of Algiers*, and Fernando Morandi, an assistant director on that film. One presumes their original intent was to make a political Western, and that Grimaldi was aware of this when he hired Sergio Sollima to direct it. Solinas, having written *Salvatore Giuliano* (1962) for Francesco Rosi, had a pedigree in political films. He wrote all or part of four different pictures, each with the theme of an uneasy alliance between a cynical gringo and a revolutionary peasant (*¿Quien Sabe?*, *Tepepa*, *A Professional Gun*, and *Burn!*); he also wrote *State of Siege* (for Costa-Gavras, 1972), *The Assassination of Trotsky*, and the remarkable *Mr Klein* (both for Joseph Losey, 1972 and 1976). *The Big Gundown* is the story of an American intervention in Latin America: unusually, it ends well; both for the American, and for the Mexican whom he was supposed to kill or capture.

Sollima, like Solinas and Morandi, wanted to make a political Western. They did this in two ways: the events of the narrative, and the nature of the second lead, Cuchillo. Solinas and Morandi's first draft was called *Il Falco e la Presa – The Falcon and the Prey*. The Falcon was a young, cynical American sheriff; the Prey a wiser, older Mexican. Sollima and Sergio Donati revised the script, retitling it *La Resa dei Conti – The Settlement of Accounts*. In their new version, the Falcon is an older gringo, seeking to trade bounty hunting for a career in politics, and the Prey is a spry young outlaw who won't submit. Sollima said of the Cuchillo character, 'Young people could see him as one of them, not a cold superhero like Clint Eastwood, but someone really human, who stole when he had to, who lied continually, who had all the human failings of a social class of which the Western rarely spoke.' Leone and Lupo had established the 'Ugly' hero: but, for Sollima, an ugly, fat guy wasn't the solution. His 'Ugly' character was young, good-looking, someone who could challenge the 'Good' gringo for full, heroic status. So the actor who played that part was crucial. Sollima cast the young star of *The Bounty Killer*, Tomas Milian.

Cuchillo Sanchez isn't just a thief, he's a *social bandit*. The corrupt army Captain, Segura (Fernando Sancho), identifies him as one of the 'dogs of Juarez'. So we know Cuchillo is a revolutionary. And Milian, the hip, young Cuban-American, was perfect for the role – one which he played many times thereafter. The hunt of the falcon for his prey is well told, with genuine reversals rather than the contrivances of *The Good, the Bad and the Ugly*. Of course, *The Big Gundown* is quite different, and a lot shorter; as with *Battle of Algiers*, its politics are crucial to its success. But it's also a very good movie: a classic battle-of-wills Western in the style and territory of *Vera Cruz*. Corbett's conversion from cynical bounty hunter to revolutionary ally is nicely done: after a night in a Mexican jail, he's turned loose, and discovers what it's like to be poor, hungry, and without a gun. In a marketplace, he considers stealing some bread – and is promptly spotted by the Austrian proto-fascist, who offers to buy it for him. Brokston insults Corbett and looks forward to liquidating Cuchillo personally – 'You didn't know that hunting was my passion, did you?... after making money.' Shep tries to rape another little girl. And the Baron plays 'Fur Elise' on the piano, expounds his theory of gunfights to Corbett, and shows him his spring-loaded metal holster – specially designed in Europe.

These are great characters, and great dialogue, down to Brokston's last line before Corbett shoots him: 'You're too smart to be a senator.' Carlo Simi's design and costumes are excellent; and Morricone contributes one of his finest scores (if we exclude the hideous, screeching vocals of Edda Dell'Orso, and the diabolical song, 'Run Man Run').

Marco Giusti reports two Italian versions of *The Big Gundown*, one 135 mintues, one 108 minutes long, plus various shorter foreign versions. Howard Hughes compares three different versions: one, released in Italy in March 1967, 105 minutes long; one an 85-minute version made by Columbia Pictures, which removed all references to the rape; and one a 95-minute 'compromise' version.

Hughes describes the longer version, in which an entirely different opening scene unfolds. Corbett gives the three robbers the chance of a fair shootout, or the certainty of a hanging. It's still pretty cold-blooded, but not as callous as he appears in the short version, killing them without a qualm. Other gunfights are missing from the short version, and some scenes with Nieves Navarro are seriously cut. Scenes with Antonio Casas, as a priest who attempts to convert Cuchillo, are also missing. From Hughes' description, I think we can live without these scenes. This may be a case like *Minnesota Clay*, where the American distributor, acting from the basest of commercial motives, improved a film.

Lee Van Cleef is tremendous. For the first time in his career, he plays an action hero, and does the job to perfection. Ironically, the producer, Grimaldi, wasn't keen on him, and had offered the lead to James Coburn. Only when Coburn turned it down was Sollima able to offer Van Cleef the role.

Such a good film has really only two failings:

1) The level of violence against women, even for a Spaghetti Western, is excessive. Women are shot and slapped in Leone's films, but *The Big Gundown*, despite its claim to progressive politics, is more brutal. Two Mexican thugs beat up Cuchillo's wife for at least a minute – punching her, kicking her in the stomach, grabbing her breasts – before Cuchillo, who's been hiding in the rafters, jumps down and knifes them both. Why did he wait?

2) The perfunctory death of the Austrian Baron. With his cape, jackboots, marine buzz-cut, waxed moustache, and monacle, Von Schulenburg is one of the Spaghetti Western's greatest creations to date, endlessly polite and quizzical, itching for a big gundown. Precisely played by Herter, the Baron says he's killed 23 men in

duels, and modestly insists he's sure Corbett has killed more. Regarding duels, he always looks at the adversary's eyes, not their hands. The eyes, he says, always betray the gunfighter. This is an obvious set-up for a tremendous showdown, featuring extreme close-ups of both men's eyes and the inevitable moment where Von Schulenburg falters and draws first – what Leone had just done, so marvellously, in *The Good, the Bad and the Ugly*. But Sollima doesn't take advantage of it. The showdown between Van Cleef and Herter – which should be the *pièce de resistance, the* big gundown – isn't. Compared to the knife-versus-gun fight which precedes it, it's perfunctory: a few medium shots. Undoubtedly director and crew were running out of time, and had to shoot it quickly and move on. But it's a shame.

14 *There is a similarity between* The Big Gundown *and my own film*, Walker. *Brokston's conversation with Corbett – he will support Corbett's political ambitions since he has plans to build a railroad across Texas – is very like Vanderbilt's conversation with Walker. And the relationship is similar – Brokston is fat, powerful, with a cynical sense of humour; Corbett is straight-backed, priggish and sincere. His line, 'I'm interested in progress, not your personal profit,' could be one of Rudy Wurlitzer's. I'd certainly seen the* The Big Gundown, *but Rudy hadn't, and the scene is his, not mine. We were all obviously on the same page, Solinas first of all: he named his manipulative gringo adventurer in* Burn! *'Sir William Walker'.*

Aside from these complaints, *The Big Gundown* holds up extremely well, and remains one of the exemplary Spaghetti Westerns.[14] And Solinas, its author, was not idle. The same year he adapted a Western screenplay by another writer, Salvatore Laurani: turning it from a conventional cowboys-versus-indians tale into an even more overtly political statement, and an excellent mini-epic of the Mexican Revolution – *¿Quien Sabe?*

¿Quien Sabe?

aka *A Bullet for the General*
(Italy)

Director: Damiano Damiani **Producer:** Bianco Manini **Screenplay:** Franco Solinas **Story:** Salvatore Laurani **Director of Photography:** Antonio Secchi **Art Director:** Sergio Canevari **Costumes:** Marilu Carteny **Editor:** Renato Cinquini **Assistant Director:** Enrico Bergier **Music:** Luis Enriquez Bacalov **Music Supervisor:** Ennio Morricone

Cast: Gian Maria Volonte (*El Chuncho*), Lou Castel (*Bill Tate*), Klaus Kinski (*El Santo*), Martine Beswick (*Adelita*), Jaime Fernandez (*Gen Elias*), Andrea Checchi (*Don Felipe*), Carla Gravina (*Rosario*), Spartaco Conversi (*Cirillo*), Joaquin Parra (*Picaro*), Jose Manuel Martin (*Raimundo*), Santiago Santos (*Guapo*), Valentino Macchi (*Pedrito*), Antonio Ruiz (*Chico*), Aldo Sambrell (*Lieut Ferella*)

The story

During the Mexican Revolution, a government munitions train is forced to stop by the presence of a crucified army officer on the tracks. El Chuncho, a bandit loyal to the *Juaristas* suffers heavy casualties in his assault on the train – which stops only after Bill Tate, a gringo, murders the engineer. Tate pretends to be a prisoner and joins Chuncho and his small band of revolutionaries after they execute the surviving soldiers. Tate, whom Chuncho christens 'Niño', soon becomes a useful member of the gang, helping them acquire more army weapons, to be sold to Chuncho's hero, General Elias.

In the newly liberated town of San Miguel, Chuncho meets his old friend Raimundo, and the former town boss, Don Felipe. Don Felipe is terrified, his beautiful wife spirited in his defence. When Chuncho's men assault her, Tate gets into a fight with them. Chuncho kills one of his own men, Guapo, for threating Tate. Don Felipe is made to drive Chuncho and his followers back to San Miguel, then killed. Next day, Chuncho prepares to drill the villagers and be a proper general. His gang, in disagreement, ride out with their share of the weapons. Chuncho and his brother, Santo, a liberation priest, remain. But Chuncho quickly misses the bandit life and abandons San Miguel on the pretext of recovering a machinegun from his former gang. Having killed one of them, Picaro, Chuncho resumes leadership of the others, and decides to sell the weapons to General Elias first, before returning to San Miguel.

General Elias's emissary arrives, pursued by army troops. Thanks to the machinegun, Chuncho and Tate decimate the army. But Chuncho's last pair of loyal men is killed, and the woman gang member, Adelita, takes Tate's money and rides away. Unseen by Chuncho, Tate kills Elias's emissary, and throws his money away. Chuncho decides they must ride to Elias's camp – something Tate has wanted from the beginning. When Tate falls victim to a malaria attack, Chuncho discovers a golden bullet in Tate's valise.

In General Elias's camp, Chuncho's weapons are welcome – even though the revolutionaries are starving. Elias pays Chuncho, then tells him San Miguel has been the scene of a massacre by the army: almost everyone Chuncho abandoned there is dead. Aghast, Chuncho sentences himself to death for cowardice. His brother, El Santo, volunteers to shoot him.

But Tate, from a high vantage point, assassinates Elias, and then kills El Santo – before Chuncho's sentence can be carried out. Tate escapes, seen only by Chuncho, as Elias's doctors announce to the crowd that he is dead: killed by a golden bullet.

Some weeks later, Chuncho, now an impoverished beggar, tracks Tate down at the Morelos Hotel in Ciudad Juarez. He tries to shoot him, but Tate insists he has been waiting for Chuncho. He gives Chuncho half of the bounty money he received from the Mexican government, for killing Elias: $100,000. Chuncho, the bandit, is astonished at Tate's loyalty and generosity. He allows himself to be shaved, dressed in a suit, and taken to a whorehouse by the gringo. Next day, the two prepare to leave for a new life together in the United States.

But when Chuncho sees Tate push Mexicans aside at the railroad station, he remembers his roots and kills Tate as he boards the train. Tate asks him why he's done this; Chuncho replies, '*¿Quien Sabe?*' – 'Who knows?' Tate's body heads for the United States, as Chuncho, tearing off his shoes and clothes, flees down a corridor of boxcars, exhorting the poor to buy dynamite.

The film

This is the first Spaghetti Western with a voiceover narration! And, luckily, one of the only ones. It's at the beginning of the film. We see, as a crowd protests, four citizens shot by firing squad. About to die, one of them calls out, *¡Que viva Mexico!* Cut to a close-up of Bill Tate, the gringo, in his business suit and grey fedora hat, and The Voice is heard:

NARRATOR: From 1910 to 1920, Mexico was torn by internal strife. During the entire decade, the vast territory was devastated by bands of marauding bandits. Scenes of this kind were commonplace, as the various factions tried to dominate the others, and bring order out of chaos.

What gobbledy-gook is this? Who on earth thought it necessary to tell us such a thing? What we've just seen is as good a set-up as any; the ensuing film will illustrate all this info as a matter of course. Such a stupid, sententious voiceover – present in both English and Italian versions – suggests a bad film. But what follows is excellent. ¿Quien Sabe? is so good, it seems like an authentic document of the Mexican Revolution, a long war in which both sides acted with extreme cruelty to the enemy and callous disregard for their own people's suffering.

The art director, Sergio Canevari, had worked on *Battle of Algiers*. He brought a rigorous attention to detail – from small items like paper amulets and straw-mat coffins, to *Nacionales de Mexico* rolling stock, and huge, fake organ-pipe cacti, planted in the Almería desert. The result of Canevari's work, together with Marilu Carteny's costumes and the mobile camera of Tony Secchi, is a Spaghetti Western which *seems* 100 per cent authentic. Nothing is out of place in ¿Quien Sabe?, a fully realised political allegory about US involvement in Latin American politics which is simultaneously an entertaining action film, and a painful meditation on heroes, and their heroics.

Gian Maria Volonte and Lou Castel (this *supergringo* was, in fact, a Colombian named Luigi Castellato) are both excellent. The one element which might seem out of place is Klaus Kinski's character: a blond, blue-eyed, brown-robed priest who is allegedly Chuncho's half-brother. But all the scenes involving El Santo are fine: Kinski was still giving his best efforts to the roles he played, and his scenes with Gian Maria Volonte are the best in the film. Both actors were famously intense, so Damiano Damiani, the director, had his work cut out for him. Volonte's wife, the striking, red-headed Carla Gravina, had been hired to play an aristocratic enemy of the Revolution (and, one imagines, to keep Volonte occupied). Still, on one occasion the director came to blows with his actor, knocking him off his horse. Volonte, disliking his costume, had turned up naked on set. Yet their work was excellent, and I imagine Damiani was grateful for the constant presence of Solinas, his celebrated script-rewriter. Solinas could engage with Volonte and Castel about their roles, or their shared leftist politics, he could talk to Kinski about women, he could chat to his friends in the art department about the authentic details of the set. Such a writer can be of great benefit to the director, freeing him/her up for other directorial things.

Given the terrible cruelty of the Mexican Revolutionary War, it's not surprising that the most striking moments of *¿Quien Sabe?* are violent ones: the officer crucified on the railroad tracks; the rebels' execution of the *Rurales*; the shooting of the wounded. So it was a problem when these moments – important for the film – were all cut for the film's UK release: a massive lurch from 135 to 77 minutes, leaving behind an unintelligible film, retitled *A Bullet for the General*. Longer versions exist (in France, the film was called *El Chuncho*) but the complete one seems to be lost. But what remains of *¿Quien Sabe?* – the 102-minute version, say – is excellent.

¿Quien Sabe? seems to have influenced *The Wild Bunch*: Peckinpah's masterpiece, shot the following year. Both films share the same sympathy for the followers of Juarez versus the murderous crew who control the army (Solinas and Damiani are less idealistic overall than Peckinpah, as we shall see). Both feature a bandit leader with an entourage of young peasant boys: the style is the same, as are the costumes. The *caudillo* – the big guy – is the same, whether it's our hero, Chuncho, or Peckinpah's villain, Mapache. Chuncho and Mapache are childishly obsessed with technology: automobiles and machineguns. Both directors focus on the presence of children. And both cast the same actor as an 'iconic' Mexican character: the Puerto Rican, Jaime Fernandez, who played the Revolutionary general, Elias, in *¿Quien Sabe?*, and the Revolutionary kid, Angel, in *The Wild Bunch*. Peckinpah usually pretended ignorance of foreign films, or any influences upon his work. But I find it impossible to believe Sam didn't see *¿Quien Sabe?*

These Italians had a more complex view of the Revolution than Peckinpah and his screenwriters. All saw it in allegorical terms: for Peckinpah, it was an allegory of Vietnam, for Solinas, of US interventions in Latin

America. But Peckinpah, in his depiction of the *Juarista* rebels and their village life, is entirely positive: the scenes in Angel's village are among the only entirely optimistic moments in his usually dark oeuvre. Solinas and Damiani take a more jaundiced view. After the liberation of San Miguel, Secchi shoots a two-minute *plano secuencia* in which we're introduced to Chuncho's old friend Raimundo, now lacking an arm, and learn that it's time to deal with the local aristocrat, Don Felipe. Chuncho is in favour of killing him, but, after dallying with the Don's wife, Rosario (Gravina), Chuncho shoots one of his own men, and conscripts Don Felipe as his chauffeur. The film forgets him for a while; then, at the end of a night-time fiesta in the newly liberated village, the camera cranes down to reveal Don Felipe's corpse, lying in the street. How, the film asks, can a Revolution so cruel to its enemies, and so careless of its own, survive? This is a good question, which later 'Tortilla Westerns' (as these Revolution-themed pictures became known) sometimes forgot to ask.

Chuncho kills his henchman, Guapo, because Guapo has threatened the gringo, Tate. Chuncho has fallen in love with the mysterious gringo, whom he has named 'Niño'.

EUFEMIO: Chuncho! Why'd you kill Guapo?

CHUNCHO: Because Guapo... was about to kill Niño. And Niño... is a friend of mine.

PICARO: Wasn't Guapo a friend of yours, too?

CHUNCHO: He's no more. Don't worry about him.

Guapo means 'beautiful', and *niño* in Spanish means 'little boy'. It's the same nickname Volonte's character gave to his enormous henchman in *For a Few Dollars More*. Chuncho's infatuation with Tate, and Tate's desire to reform and tame the savage Chuncho, give us the first overtly gay bond, I think, in any Western. Certainly there were implicit male affairs in many Westerns, American and Italian, before this one. But this is the first time the love affair was clearly on the table. Not that it's portrayed as a good thing: Chuncho's love for Tate causes a catastrophe for the *Juaristas*; Tate's obsession with Chuncho brings about his death. For all that, *¿Quien Sabe?* is still a love story.

I once thought *¿Quien Sabe?* to be critical of General Elias, the well-dressed *Juarista* leader who Bill Tate kills. Elias is, indeed, attired like an aristocratic gentleman; he's clean-shaven, unlike most of the revolutionaries. But he is playing a part: the *caudillo's caudillo*, the leader of a Revolutionary Division, like Villa, or Zapata. When we first see him, in his headquarters, he offers the hand of friendship to a gringo, or a well-dressed guy, whose support he clearly needs. Elias is a politician, and revolutions need politicians. His endorsement of Chuncho's self-judgement, as a traitor who must be executed, is entirely sound. Tate's assassination of Elias is a disaster, which will only prolong the war and raise the body count. It is an outrage; yet it recalls the murder of Don Felipe, an ineffectual aristocrat, who, stripped of his power, threatened no one. Solinas and Damiani provide no answers. Everyone in the film is trapped in an impossible situation: the lieutenant on the train, unable to give the order to proceed and crush his captain, crucified on the tracks; Don Felipe and Rosario, awaiting their death sentence; Santo and the army priest, who condemn each other, and die on the battlefield; Adelita, who loses her lover and abandons the cause; Chuncho and Niño, narcissists destined to destroy each other. *¿Quien Sabe?* seems like an immediate riposte to Solinas's own *The Big Gundown*. In that film, Corbett and Cuchillo could resolve their differences and coexist, as equals; none of the characters here can do this. Both societies – primeval South, Machiavellian North – are destined to go down in flames.

Such is the pessimistic conclusion of the first, and best, of these Tortilla Westerns. None of the later ones, not even Sergio Leone's, came near to *¿Quien Sabe?* in intelligence, narrative or insight. Its allegory is pertinent and sustained, but never intrudes. The 'Good' gringo is morally inferior to the 'Ugly' Mexican; in fact, he is not good at all – but neither is the Mexican. And who is the 'Bad'? Is it the crucified officer? Is it Don Felipe, quaking with fear? Is it Chuncho's gang, who care more for money than ideas? Or is it the Mexican generals, in their office with pictures of sailing ships, paying Bill Tate 100,000 pesos to kill their countryman, then asking for a receipt?

Even someone as ignorant of music as I can recognise a great score by Luis Enriquez Bacalov: it's an excellent orchestral soundtrack, which, at times, entirely recycles some of Bacalov's original music for *Django*. Ennio Morricone received a credit as Music Supervisor, but this seems to have been a device of the producer to profit from Morricone's growing repuation.

Massacre Time

aka *Le colt cantarono la morte e fu..., Tempo di massacro,
The Brute & the Beast, Colt Concert, Le temps du massacre*
(Italy)

Director: Lucio Fulci **Producer:** Terry Vanteli, Oreste Coltellacci **Screenplay:** Fernando Di Leo, Vincenzo Dell'aquila **Director of Photography:** Riccardo Pallottini **Art Director:** Sergio Canevari **Editor:** Ornella Micheli **Assistant Director:** Giovanni Fago **Music:** Lallo Gori **Cast:** Franco Nero (*Tom*), George Hilton (*Jeff*), John McDouglas (*Scott*), Nino Castelnuovo (*Jonah*, aka *Junior*), Lynn Shane, Tchang Yu (*Undertaker*), Janos Bartha (*Carradine*), Aysanoa Runachagua (*Souko*), Rina Franchetti (*Prostitute*), Tom Felleghy, Franco MoriCi, Yu Tckang, Attilio Severini, Mario Dionisi, Romano Puppo, Roberto Alessandri

The story

Jonah, a mad, corrupt, whip-wielding young man in a white suit, leads a hunting party after a man his minions have just freed from a box. His dogs track the man down and kill him in a river. Under the credits we follow the bloody river downstream, to a camp where Tom Corbett is panning for gold. A man from his home town appears and tells Tom that Carradine, a local worthy, wants him to return home at once. Tom does so.

He finds Laramie Town to be under the commercial and physical domination of one man, Scott. Tom's home, a substantial hacienda, has been taken over by Scott's henchmen. Tom searches for his brother, Jeff, who has become an alcoholic, and his mother, Mercedes. Both encourage him to leave at once. When Tom goes to visit Carradine, the man and his family are all gunned down.

Mysteriously, Scott's brutal henchmen are under orders not to kill Tom. Tom insists on going to see Scott himself, aided by Jeff who, though a drunk, is an ace gunfighter. Jeff shoots nine of Scott's men to ease Tom's passage to Scott's ranch. At the ranch, a white-suited party is in progress. When Tom attempts to speak to Scott, Jonah intervenes and flogs him. Scott, beaten and bloody, staggers back to his family's shack, where Mercedes is shot down by passing gunmen.

Next day, Tom and Jeff go to take revenge. But Scott's Indian henchman requests a parley. Scott appears, and tells Tom that he is Tom's real father: it was he who sent the message, via Carradine. Scott says Tom is his heir; he warns him that Junior is mad. Then he's shot dead by Jonah. Tom and Jeff descend upon the Scott ranch and wipe out the surviving henchmen. Jeff raids the liquor cabinet; Tom does away with Jonah.

The film

Fernando di Leo directed a series of police films while working on numerous Western scripts: this was his first solo credit, though Giusti reports that Vincenzo Dell'Aquila also worked on it, and the director, Lucio Fulci, says he finished it. It's very in the di Leo mould: hyper-macho – there are no women characters of any real significance – and super-heroic. The pairing of Franco Nero and George Hilton is inspired. Nero does his usual, solid stuff; Hilton plays it as if Dean Martin's character from *Rio Bravo* were the real hero. It was a great break for Hilton, a Uruguayan actor who had just arrived in Rome. In a film without women, he is the nearest thing to a love interest: di Leo's script contains much sexual ambivalence. The villainous Jonah appears to have a blond boyfriend (who sadly disappears) and an incestuous relationship with his dad. Nino Castelnuovo is splendidly manic as Jonah, and 'John McDouglas' (Giuseppe Addobbati) is a tremulous and ineffectual patriarch, in the Antonio Casas mould.

The film was originally titled *Tempo di massacre*, a title di Leo borrowed from a book by Franco Enna: hence the clunky title change to *The Colt Sang Death... and it was Massacre Time*. The film was also meant to be a co-production with Spain, featuring that fine actor George Martin – hero and villain of the *Ringo* films. But the Spanish producers objected to the script's violence, and when Fulci, previously a director of comedies, refused to reduce it, the deal fell apart. So *Massacre Time* was made more cheaply, in Italy, in a manner faithful to a screenplay which Fulci called '*assolutamente artaudiana*' – absolutely in the style of Artaud's Theatre of Cruelty. The film is very violent. Women and young girls are shot and their staring corpses lingered over; explosive bullet hits – rare in Spaghetti Westerns – are used. Nero's character is mercilessly whipped, and, one assumes, left permanently scarred. In the final struggle, his hands are stamped on as they were in *Django* (Fulci's assistant director, Giovanni Fago, had brought Nero to his attention, after the Spanish deal faded). All is done stylishly. The murder of Carradine's wife and daughters comes as an antidote to the scene of pious grace-saying which precedes it. And the flogging takes place in the middle of a gracious garden party, in which hosts and guests are dressed from head to toe in white, like Medellin coke dealers at play, in the carefree 1980s. To call the scene Buñuelian doesn't do it justice. And the sequel is weirdly funny. Bleeding from face and hands, Tom staggers home to Mercedes and Jeff. A horrific mess, he falls across the table where Jeff is torturing a bug.

TOM: I'm seeing Mr Scott tomorrow. He had some guests today.

JEFF: Junior's good with a whip, ain't he?

TOM: Yes!

Mercedes (who Tom still imagines is his mother) tries to tend to his wounds, but is shot by Junior's passing gunsels. It's absurd, but played straight. And the result is very entertaining. The film was a big hit, earning more at the domestic box office than the highly popular *Arizona Colt*. Both films, rather menacingly, feature the hero doing somersaults. Gemma backflips out of a tree, while Nero – or his stunt double – performs the first 360-degree somersault in a Spaghetti Western. There would be more of these. But not just yet. More interesting is the seriously gay subtext between heroes, and between villains. In the best of these scenes, Scott tries to discipline his son, as Jonah plays the organ in the family music room.

JONAH (playing the organ): Your favourite piece, isn't it? You taught it to me, sitting on your lap, remember?

SCOTT: Son, I want to talk to you.

JONAH: You want me to finish the piece. You always used to ask me for it, until a few years ago.

SCOTT: You're grown up now, Junior.

JONAH: You love me, Daddy? Aren't we still one? Remember, you and me – not you, not me, both of us – (he tries to strangle SCOTT) You pushed me away from you!

And so it goes. One dreads to think what's gone on with this pair, as the perverse Jonah/Junior, clearly the stronger character, gets the upper hand once again. The scene ends with Scott, defeated, playing a duet with his deranged, triumphant son.

The same year, Nero starred in a less interesting Western, *Texas, Goodbye* (aka *The Avenger*), in which his character also turned out to be the villain's abandoned son. But he didn't make a habit of such roles. The theme of town and countryside dominated by one commercial monopoly seems borrowed from *In a Colt's Shadow*. Like the Masonic pyramid in *El Topo*, a sinister logo overhangs all of Scott's businesses. Scott's henchmen are hoisting this logo onto the facade of Tom's old hacienda (an early appearance by Mussolini's villa as a film location), when he returns. Huge holes in the narrative are refreshingly ignored. (Why did the wealthy Scott abandon baby Tom in the first place? Why has Tom grown up in ignorance with Mercedes and Jeff? Who is the prisoner Jonah and co release from a cage and chase to death?) Well-choreographed action, intense performances, and a fine score by Lallo Gori make *Massacre Time* a splendid entertainment, a great attempt to *épater les bourgeois*, and a taste of greater Spaghetti Westerns still to be made.

Massacre Time was a lower-budget Spaghetti Western, intended for the national market, which achieved a genuine, demented status on its own terms. But some less interesting westerns, made with bigger budgets, share *Massacre Time*'s concerns. *The Hills Run Red* (aka *Un fiume di dollari*), Carlo Lizzani's first Western, was a deliberate homage to the dark American Westerns of Anthony Mann. The film was intended to showcase Dino de Laurentiis's newly built Western town, but Lizzani – a radical, intellectual director – was otherwise left to his own devices. The result is a good-looking film (it was shot by Tony Secchi, just before *¿Quien Sabe?*), somewhat boring and old-fashioned. Its most notable element is the hero, Jerry Brewster, played by Thomas Hunter. Having learned of his wife's death, Brewster is in a paroxysm of grief, rage and over-acting for the remainder of the film. It's very entertaining, so over-the-top as to make James Stewart in *The Naked Spur* seem positively restrained.

In *Massacre Time*, the villains are a degenerate aristocratic clan. In *Texas, Goodbye* and *The Hills Run Red*, the bad guys are bandits and killers who, having acquired money, adopt aristocratic airs. Segal, villain of *Hills*, lives in a mansion with servants and calls himself 'Milton', while Cisco Delgado, the former bandit in *Texas, Goodbye*, plays a vast organ in a baronial hall, and cohabits with an Englishman who inhales vapours in a bath-chair. All three films make clear the class divide between their heroes and villains: in this way they're closer to *In a Colt's Shadow* than to Sergio Leone. Of course, Spaghetti Westerns in the Leone style continued to be made. One of them was *A Stranger in Town*.

A Stranger in Town

aka *For a Dollar in the Teeth*, *Un dollaro tra i denti*
(Italy/USA)

Director: Luigi Vanzi   **Producer:** Roberto Infascelli, Massimo Gualdi, James Hager, Allen Klein   **Screenplay:** Giuseppe Mangione, Warren Garfield   **Director of Photography:** Marcello Masciocchi   **Art Director, Costumes:** Carmelo Patrono   **Editor:** Maurizio Lucidi   **Assistant Director:** Antonio Segurini   **Music:** Benedetto Ghiglia   **Cast:** Tony Anthony (*The Stranger*), Frank Wolff (*El Aguila*), Gia Sandri (*Maruka*), Jolanda Modio (*Cica*) Raf Baldassare (*Corgo*), Aldo Berti (*Marinero*), Enrico Capoleoni, Arturo Corso, Loris Bazzocchi, Antonio Marsina, Ivan

Scratuglia, Salvatore Puntilla, Angella Minervini, Rosella Berga-Monti, Fortunato Arena, Ugo Carbone, Lars Bloch (*Capt Ted*)

The story

A gringo, known only as the Stranger, rides into an apparently deserted border town. He witnesses a massacre of Mexican soldiers by bandits disguised as a procession of black-robed priests. These are the bandits of El Aguila, with whom the Stranger plots the robbery of a consignment of US gold, intended for the Mexican government. Aguila betrays the Stranger, giving him only a dollar for his trouble.

Inevitably the Stranger steals the gold; is tracked down by the gang, and tortured. Left to the sadistic attentions of a female bandit, Maruka, the Stranger kills her, recovers the gold, and saves a Mexican girl, Cica, who has been abused by El Aguila.

El Aguila recaptures Cica and threatens her and her baby. But the Stranger, armed with a shotgun, eliminates the entire gang, finally placing a dollar between Aguila's teeth. When US troops return to recover their gold, the Stranger claims half of it as bounty.

The film

An entirely routine and derivative Spaghetti Western. Somehow it acquired a reputation of sadistic violence which is undeserved: the film is stupid, rather than cruel. It seems to be the first Spaghetti Western with American producers, James Hager and Allen Klein (of Beatles infamy). At a time when heroes still had names, *A Stranger in Town* borrowed from the United Artists campaign for the *Dollars* films, and gave us a protagonist without one.

Tony Anthony was an unappealing hero, but a somewhat durable one. There were three sequels, all just as brain-dead, one set in Japan, one made in 3-D. These films are unique in that they have *nothing at all to recommend them*. In Britain, the *Monthly Film Bulletin* pursued the notion that there was something peculiarly wicked or subversive about them when it wrote of *Stranger*, 'The only departure from the formula [is] an entirely gratuitous hint of lesbianism... there is one interminable and particularly unpleasant sequence in which the hero, having smashed a woman's skull on a stone floor and with blood streaming from his eyes, crawls round the town to no apparent purpose until he finally ends up where he started.'

If only it was as good as that! In Italy, the film was given an 18-and-over certificate. But there is little to shock or to corrupt in the version I've seen. The scene where the Stranger is left alone with the supposedly lesbian sadist is pitiful, badly acted, and boring. The pace is slow. There is violence against men, violence against women, threatened violence against babies, all of it dull. Anthony, poncho-clad, chubby, bouffant, double-chinned, was talented at nothing beyond sticking around for sequels. Frank Wolff, an American actor who had just arrived in Rome, tried to be Gian Maria Volonte, and failed completely. You'd think that, threatening a crying baby with a knife, he could have pulled it off, but he just seems winded and uncomfortable. I haven't seen a performance where Wolff played a bad guy or sadist convincingly: a good actor of good guys, he didn't seem to have this in him. El Aguila's gang are better at being bad. 'They call me Marinero,' one of them (Aldo Berti) tells a priest, 'because I like the water.' He then drowns the priest in a horse trough. Another gang member obsessively combs his hair and moustache. But that's about it.

A subplot, involving the US Army gold, suggests that the Stranger is some kind of secret agent for the army. It isn't developed, though it leads to a tedious joke in which the Stranger calls a Union captain (Lars Bloch) George though his name is Ted. The idea of hero-as-army-spy is inglorious and seems out of place in an anarchic medium like the Spaghetti Western; it's the stuff of John Wayne two-reelers from the 1930s. But Vanzi wasn't the only director exploring the possibility. 'Winnie' Getz, the sub-hero of *The Hills Run Red* (played by a superannuated Dan Duryea), was also a secret agent for the military authorities.

The final showdown – machinegun versus shotgun with a narrow-gauge railroad running in between – was shot on the *Fistful of Dollars* street, and is a little livelier than anything that's gone before. Vanzi and cameraman Masciocchi occasionally manage a decent light-dark composition: there's a shootout entirely in darkness, lit only by gunshots, and a good moment where the bad guys all reveal themselves by lighting matches in a pitch-black room. Otherwise the camerawork is unimpressive, the sets look freshly painted and relatively new, and the pace is way beyond tedious. The score, by Benedetto Ghiglia, is very poor, and endlessly repeated.

(I don't like *A Stranger in Town* or any of its sequels. But I feel obliged to include it because its very existence shows how seriously the Americans had begun to take Spaghetti Westerns. They weren't just investing in 'high-end' ones like *The Good, the Bad and the Ugly* and *The Big Gundown*. They were financing bad, low-budget ones as well. And while *Stranger* didn't do good business in Italy, it was a big success in the United States. For a positive view of this film, see Giusti, pp 157–8.)

Meanwhile, Sergio Corbucci had not been idle. *Django* and *Johnny Oro*, made in 1965, were not released until 1966. In the meantime, he had conceived, shot, and released another revenge Western. Pre-sold, by the producer, Dino de Laurentiis, to an American studio, this one required an American lead. Corbucci's choice was a young actor whose only film experience was as a *Playgirl* centrefold: Burt Reynolds.

Navajo Joe

aka *Un dollar a testa*
(Italy/Spain)

Director: Sergio Corbucci   **Producer:** Ermanno Donati, Luigi Carpentieri   **Screenplay:** Dean Craig, Fernando Di Leo   **Story:** Ugo Pirro **Director of Photography:** Silvano Ippoliti   **Art Director:** Aurelio Crugnola   **Music:** Ennio Morricone   **Cast:** Burt Reynolds (*Joe*), Aldo Sambrell (*Mervin 'Vee' Duncan*), Nicoletta Machiavelli (*Estella*), Tanya Lopert (*Maria*), Fernando Rey (*Rattigan*), Franca Polesello (*Barbara*), Lucia Modugno (*Geraldine*), Pierre Cressoy (*Dr Chester Lynne*), Nino Imparato (*Chuck Holloway*) Alvaro De Luna (*Sancho*), Valeria Sabel (*Honor*), Mario Lanfranchi (*Clay*), Lucio Rosato (*Jeffrey*), Simon Arriaga (*Monkey*), Chris Huerta (*El Gordo*), Angel Ortiz (*El Cojo*), Gianni Di Stolfo (*Reagan*), Angel Alvarez (*Blackwood*), Rafael Albaicin (*Bandit*)

The story

Duncan and his large band of scalphunters massacre the inhabitants of a peaceful Indian village. Riding to collect the bounty, Duncan's men fall victim to a solitary rider, Navajo Joe. In the town of Piute, the sheriff refuses to pay Duncan for any more scalps: those days, he says, are over. Duncan kills him, then runs into an old associate, Lynne – a former crook who has become the doctor and banker in a nearby town, Esperanza. Lynne tells the bandits that a train carrying half a million dollars is on its way to Esperanza. Navajo Joe intervenes when Duncan's men pursue three saloon girls and their pimp: one of the prostitutes having overheard Lynne and Duncan plotting.

Duncan and the bandits attack the train, killing all the guards and passengers. But, that night, Joe liberates it, and delivers it to Esperanza. Lynne kills the wounded witness, Geraldine, on his makeshift operating table. Joe offers to protect the townspeople of Esperanza from Duncan: he wants a dollar a head from every man in town, plus the rewards for Duncan and his half-brother Jeffrey. Despite their priest's objections, they reject him on racist grounds ('We don't make bargains with Indians'). But, after Lynne pretends to ride to fetch the rangers, Lynne's wife, Honor, persuades the townsmen to hire Joe. When the safe turns out to be empty, Duncan and his men kill Dr and Mrs Lynne. Then they are caught in a one-man, dynamite-and-rifle ambush, courtesy of Joe. Duncan foils this by dragging an Indian maiden, Estella, into the street by her hair.

Joe surrenders and is beaten up and hung by his feet. When the funny/cute old pimp frees him, Duncan goes on the rampage, encouraging his men to kill townspeople until Joe and the money are returned. Estella finds Joe and persuades him to return and save the town. Duncan departs in pursuit of Joe, pausing only to kill the preacher, Rattigan. Joe decimates the remainder of Duncan's men, and, in an old Indian cemetery, reclaims the pendant Duncan stole from his wife. He and Duncan are both mortally wounded in the cemetery showdown. His horse returns to Esperanza with the missing money, to the townspeople's delight.

The film

With a bigger budget than *Django*, and a guaranteed worldwide release care of United Artists, was it inevitable that *Navajo Joe* not be as good? The film is commendably cynical: the townspeople are racist, money-grubbing grotesques who deserve to die. But, while full of incidents, it lacks energy.

The *Monthly Film Bulletin* admired Silvio Ippolito's photography, but I don't like it. His zooms are juddery and uncertain. He relies too much on day-for-night scenes. These are difficult to pull off, and Leone and Dallamano – when they used them in *Fistful of Dollars* – paid attention to the lighting and kept the skies to a minimum. Corbucci and Ippolito do neither. Long sequences, shot in daylight, are played as night-time scenes with burningly bright white skies. Likewise the action – usually the strong point of a Corbucci film – is thrown away. The scalping of Joe's wife – the kind of thing Corbucci delighted in – is decorously played off-screen. Aldo Sambrell and his bandits ride in circles around the army train, yet still manage to shoot everybody on board. There's an attempt to turn *Navajo Joe* into a mystery thriller: Lynne's face is partially hidden via the placement of set items and props, during his first conference with Duncan. Corbucci was pursuing his interest in long-lens shots framed *through things*: that is, with out-of-focus elements in the foreground. Here he was trying to put the effect to some narrative purpose: we're supposed to wonder, who is the traitor to the town? But Corbucci drops the subplot, and the device, the next time Dr Lynne appears. So what's the point of it?

Later, Corbucci was to complain about being obliged to direct Westerns. There's a certain deliberate irony in this; no one (other than the Korean director kidnapped by Kim Jong Il) is really forced to direct films. But he certainly lacked inspiration on the set of *Navajo Joe*. The film's best elements are in its script: written by Fernando di Leo and 'Dean Craig' (either Mario Pierotti or Piero Regnoli), from an original story by Ugo Piro. Some of the script is terrible, yet at times the dialogue is priceless, especially when spoken by the priest, Rattigan.

RATTIGAN: Citizens of Esperanza, we have assembled here to expect a very special train which will be arriving with its precious load. I hope you know how precious. You are all quite aware what it means to us all to receive this grant of $500,000 from our state. This gift offers all of us definite advantages. And all this will mean a great deal to our town. And may we now all acknowledge the efforts of our distinguished mayor, Mr Jefferson Clay, to whom we sincerely offer our thanks...

And so on, and on, the Reverend goes. He name-checks all the local dignitaries present, ending with the one who's in the process of betraying them to the scalphunters, Dr Chester Lynne. Rattigan is perfectly portrayed by Fernando Rey: his speech is irrelevant, and mind-blowingly pompous, like one of the Ambassador of Miranda's homilies, in *The Discreet Charm of the Bourgeoisie* (1972). Of all Spaghetti Western directors, Corbucci reminds me most consistently of Buñuel. And the whole scene becomes even more surreal when we learn that no one in town has a gun, or knows how to shoot one. Rattigan explains, 'We here in Esperanza, thank God, are a peaceful community. There isn't a gun in town.' In the real Wild West, this would be highly unlikely. There were a lot of guns around, and while it might be easy to set the place on fire, sacking a town filled with armed, two-fisted pioneers was very hard. In American Westerns, outlaws tended to inhabit the ranges and wild country, outside towns. But in the Italian West, especially as depicted by Corbucci and Tessari, the townspeople – having surrendered their weapons to the sheriff or the bad guys – are often powerless: feckless urbanites, at the mercy of savages and grandees.

Mervin 'Vee' Duncan is uncommon in that he has a substantial army of outlaws – what looks, at the outset, like 50 men. The guerrilla war with Joe and the raid on the train must account for half of these outlaws, but the credit scenes – featuring the entire horde riding across a river, towards camera – are most impressive. This image, of a gang of bandits riding straight towards a long lens, would become a staple of Corbucci movies, and every other Spaghetti Western which could afford an outlaw horde. Such telephoto shots are used by Peckinpah in *The Wild Bunch* and his later pictures; and by Valerii and Leone in *My Name is Nobody*. Yet this iconic shot was borrowed from another film: the introduction of the outlaws in *A Pistol for Ringo*.

Duncan's gang is believably large, because, for many years in the nineteenth century, there was a brisk trade in Indian scalps. Bands of scalphunters raided against hostile war parties and peaceful Indian camps, with little distinction. This is the stuff of Cormac McCarthy's novel, *Blood Meridian*, the story of a band of scalphunters and killers not dissimilar to Duncan's. *Blood Meridian, or, The Evening Redness in the West*, was published in 1985, 18 years after *Navajo Joe*'s US release. Did young McCarthy see it, at the drive-in or some second-run cinema in Texas? The horde, its contempt for savage and civilisation both, and the powerlessness of 'civilised' men to resist it, are the subject matter both of *Navajo Joe*, and of McCarthy's great book.

As in *Minnesota Clay*, there is an evil alliance between an urbane town-dweller and a savage bandit. But Corbucci is clearly more interested in his principal villain, the anguished half-breed, Duncan.

> DUNCAN: Nobody ever had mercy on me. When I was a boy they beat me. Even called me... bastard! I didn't cry and I couldn't fight back. So that began my revenge to get back at them. Brought out my hatred for the Indians, like my mother, and to kill white people like my father. My father was a preacher like you, a minister. Bred by mercy. But I got a bad break when somebody killed him and beat me to the punch!

Corbucci gives Aldo Sambrell plenty of screen time, and Ippoliti affords him the best lighting. Duncan is clearly the director's favourite character – but Joe is a good one, too. Later Burt Reynolds remarked that making *Navajo Joe* was 'the worst experience of my life'. But he is good in it, if not particularly like a Navajo. Unlike most Corbucci heroes, Joe has a long speech, in which he points out that *he*, not the white racists of Esperanza, is the *real* American. 'And my father, and his father before him, and his father before him, and his father before him. You. Where was your father born?' he asks the sheriff. 'Scotland,' is the reply.

Joe's surrender – after Estella, the Indian maid, lets herself be captured – is pathetic. A genius who channelled Buñuel, Corbucci was also the Bud Boetticher of Italian Western directors: inventive but repetitive, letting potentially strong women characters trip on their skirts. His supporting bad guys have a good time; his 'cute/funny' pimp is an annoying character. All unfolds in a routine fashion. Corbucci doesn't really get up to speed until it's time to kill Rattigan. Having herded the townspeople into the church, Duncan threatens to burn it down. Then, striking a deal with Joe, he prepares to leave. The good Reverend steps forward, extending a hand.

    RATTIGAN: Thank you, Duncan... for mercy and sparing our lives.

    DUNCAN: Their lives. Not yours.

And Duncan kills him. This is the best moment of the film, together with its graveyard showdown and deeply cynical coda. While Joe is looking for an axe with which to hack Duncan to death, the battered outlaw draws a hidden pistol, and shoots Joe in the back. Joe hurls his tomahawk, which pierces Duncan's skull. Both men are mortally wounded.

CU Joe. Shaky zoom in on his horse. CU Joe.

Dissolve to the town of Esperanza. Unfortunately, Mayor Jefferson Clay and most of the other characters have survived, and are lamenting the loss of their money. Joe's horse gallops straight to the saloon, riderless. In Joe's saddlebags, the citizens find the cash.

They are overjoyed. 'Where is he?' 'Who cares? The money's all that counts!' 'Take his horse to the corral.' Here Estella, the Indian maiden, intervenes. She sends the horse galloping back out of *Dinocitta*, by way of the El Paso set, into the desert of Tabernas...

It's a noble ending, for the horse. But the good human is dead, and the survivors, whose only god is money, neither know nor care. These are perfectly expressed Corbucci sentiments. Though a minor work, *Navajo Joe* isn't shameful. It continues to shape the Corbucci world of racist villains, kindly whores, sentimental pimps, dead bodies (to be zoomed in on), bandidos (to be overdressed), priests (to be shot), a powerless civilian populace (to be threatened with annihilation), and a showdown in the graveyard.

By the end of 1966, the Italian Western was making conventional use of Christian symbolism in very specific ways. In the manner of a mainstream Hollywood film, churches and priests might be presented as symbols of 'the Good' (Tuco's brother, the Mormons in *The Big Gundown*), and the hero's suffering depicted in a manner analogous to Christ's (Django's broken hands, the stigmata of Arizona Colt). But, in the style of Buñuel, some directors made increasingly subversive use of Christian symbols – graves, cemeteries, crosses – as props in violent dances of death. These more radical Westerns might feature priests shot for entertainment (*Django* and *Navajo Joe*) or priests shooting other priests, for failing to exercise the preferential option for the poor (*¿Quien Sabe?*).

No matter how derivative its origins, the Spaghetti Western had slipped the traces. It was racing into new, uncharted, dangerous territory.

1967

'I never liked Italian Westerns. I made one, and to tell the truth, I only like one; the one I did myself.' – **Giulio Questi**, interviewed, *Spaghetti Cinema* #67

Sergio Leone was busy working with two young writers – Bernardo Bertolucci and Dario Argento – on the treatment of his next Western, *Once Upon a Time in the West*. Sergio Corbucci was engaged in a spasm of filmmaking – directing two Westerns and a spy thriller in one year. But 1967 is noteworthy for the release of a Spaghetti Western made in the summer of '66: Giulio Questi's *Django Kill*. Apologies in advance to Don Giulio, for using a title he hates. The film is also known as *Oro Maldito*, and *Oro Hondo*, and *If You Live, Shoot!* It is a famous film maudit, an authentic filmmaker's statement, which requires no prior knowledge of, or interest in, Westerns. The film is complex, mysterious, and personal. Its dense structure demanded extra time in the cutting room, and it ran into immediate problems when it was done. There were difficulties with the censors, and also with distributors, who – struggling for something 'marketable' – branded it as a *Django* sequel. *Django Kill* is as perfect a statement of the director's intention as Corbucci's *Django* – but a very different film.

Django Kill

aka *Se sei vivo, spara!, Gringo uccidi, If You Live, Shoot!,
Oro hondo, oro maldito, Tire encore si tu peux*
(Italy/Spain)

140

Director: Giulio Questi   **Producer:** Alessandro Jacovoni   **Screenplay:** Giulio Questi, Franco Arcalli, Benedetto Benedetti   **Director of Photography:** Franco Delli Colli   **Art Director:** Enzo Bulgarelli, Jose Luis Galicia, Jaime Perez Cubero   **Editor:** Franco Arcalli   **Sound Designer, Assistant Director:** Gianni Amelio   **Music:** Ivan Vandor   **Cast:** Tomas Milian (*The Stranger*), Piero Lulli (*Oaks*), Milo Quesada (*Tembler*), Paco Sanz (*Alderman Ackerman*), Roberto Camardiel (*Sorro*), Marilu Tolo (*Flory*), Raymond Lovelock (*Evan*), Patrizia Valturri (*Elizabeth*), Daniel Martin, Edoardo De Santis, Miguel Serrano, Angel Silva, Sancho Gracia, Mirella Panfili

The story

Two Indians encounter a wounded bandit, crawling from his grave. They nurse him back to health. In flashbacks, he recalls an assault on a 'Wells Fargo' covered wagon, guarded by the US Army. The Stranger and his partner, Oaks, massacre the guards, caught swimming in a river, and steal a strongbox full of gold. Oaks doublecrosses the Stranger and his fellow Mexicans, making them dig their own mass grave, then gunning them down. The Indians believe the Stranger can tell them about the Happy Hunting Ground, so they stick with him. Recovered, the Stranger follows Oaks to town.

Oaks and his men have shown up in the saloon and tried to buy horses. He is recognised from a 'Wanted' poster. An armed mob, driven by the saloon keeper, Tembler, and the pastor, Alderman Ackerman, lynches the bandits. Oaks escapes, and holes up in a store. The Stranger arrives and accepts a bounty of $500 to capture the bandit. He shoots Oaks, who is carried to the saloon and operated upon. When they discover the Stranger has shot Oaks with gold bullets, the locals tear the living bandit apart, and extract the gold.

The Stranger spends the night in the saloon, haunted by bad dreams. Tembler's mistress, Flory, spies on her husband and Ackerman as they argue over the bandits' gold, which they have piled on Tembler's desk. Tembler's son, Evan, slashes Flory's finery with a knife. Sorro, an eccentric rancher who wears white and dresses his henchmen in black, rides into town. He orders Tembler to surrender the bandit's gold.

When the Stranger and the Indians cut down the hanging corpses of his former partners, the townspeople order them to leave. Horse hunting, the Stranger encounters Sorro and his men – kidnapping Evan. All repair to his ranch where Sorro offers the Stranger work, throws a pork-eating party for his men, and sends a messenger to town. Told of the kidnapping, Tembler lies and insists that Ackerman has all the gold. Sorro orders the boy killed. The Stranger intervenes and saves his life, via a drunken shooting game. Sorro has the boy cut loose, the Stranger becomes oblivious through whiskey, and Evan is surrounded by increasingly amorous *muchachos*. In the morning, while Sorro and his men sleep, Evan takes a gun and commits suicide.

The Stranger returns Evan's body to town. Furious over the boy's death, he slugs Tembler, and gets in a savage fight with several locals. Tembler and Flory, knowing that Sorro's men will search the saloon, stash their gold in Evan's coffin. Ackerman invites the Stranger to live in his house. He encourages him in an affair with his half-mad wife, Elizabeth, who is usually kept locked in her bedroom. Turning against the Stranger, Ackerman steals his gun and shoots Tembler with it. The townspeople, hunting for the presumed killer, scalp one of the Indians; Ackerman shoots Flory with a borrowed rifle; Sorro's men capture the Stranger and torture him by crucifixion and ordeal-by-bats. The Stranger swears he'll never tell; but, terrified by bats, iguanas and a mole, he cracks and reveals that the gold is in the cemetery. Sorro's *muchachos* uproot the entire graveyard but find nothing: Ackerman has already dug the money up. The surviving Indian frees the Stranger, who kills Sorro's henchmen, and their mounts, via a horse laden with dynamite. He then shoots Sorro, in his boudoir.

The Stranger returns to town. Ackerman's house is ablaze. Elizabeth, locked in her room again, has set it on fire. Ackerman opens the cabinet to retrieve his gold; molten gold pours out onto his hands and face. The Stranger and the townspeople watch Elizabeth, and Ackerman, covered in boiling gold, die in the flames. The Stranger rides off, passing two kids making distorted faces – insisting 'I'm uglier than you'.

The film

Django Kill happened by chance. Westerns were a big business by the mid-1960s; there were large audiences for them; there were financial incentives to make Italian films; also to shoot co-productions. A producer, Alessandro Jacovoni, had made a deal with a distributor to supply several Westerns. Having no Westerns at all, he needed to shoot some – fast. He knew a director named Giulio Questi, who had co-directed several films and was preparing a comedic horror film, *Death Laid an Egg*. Jacovoni asked Questi if he had any Western scripts. Questi didn't; he wasn't particularly interested in Westerns, but this was also a chance to do something he wanted, cloaked in a Western guise. So Questi and his partner, Kim Arcali – co-writer and later editor of *Death Laid an Egg* – quickly wrote a screenplay (falsely credited to a Spaniard, Maria del Carmen Marinez Román, in order to qualify for co-production status). Though set in the Wild West, it was based on Questi's experiences as an anti-Fascist partisan in World War Two.

Questi was born in Bergamo, a small town near Milan. He joined the partisans at the age of 18, and fought with them for two years, in the mountains, until the collapse of Fascism. The bizarre events of *Django Kill*, the specificity of the killings, the ongoing attention to the disposition of corpses, and the homoerotic behaviour of the villains, suggest that those two years of Questi's life were pretty intense. But he doesn't discuss them much in interviews: what he wants to say is in the film. Questi did explain why he rejected invitations to direct other Western scripts:

> For me, the Italian Western was only a way to tell stories that I had more than in the head – in the heart... I didn't use the movie Western formula, only the look; but I wanted to recount all of the things, the cruelty, the comradeship with friends, the death, all the experiences I had of war, in combat, in the mountains.

Questi called *Django Kill* 'a unique experiment that I can't repeat mechanically'. It's certainly a film where all the elements are in synch. Tomas Milian, who seemed mannered in *The Bounty Killer*, is relaxed and confident in this more complex role. So Questi was a good influence on Milian, reducing his tendency to emote without meaning. Still, the actor, interviewed in *Westerns all'italiana* #25, felt ambiguous about the director:

It was like working with Antonioni in a way because Giulio Questi is an intellectual revolutionary... Giulio's a very creative, crazy man... it's like working with Antonioni because he likes the images more than the acting. I tried to do my best.

I find the acting in *Django Kill* excellent. But it's a certain kind of acting. There's a ludicrous, 'coarse actor' quality to some of the supporting characters: the 'mystical' Indians and the subsidiary townspeople who look like they've been shot from a cannon, through a jumble sale. All this is in keeping with the film's state of extremes. There are two strong women, played by Marliu Tolu and Patrizia Valturri, and four fine villains – Oaks (Piero Lulli), Ackerman (Paco Sanz), Tembler (Milo Quesada), and Sorro (Roberto Camardiel). Sanz, as the black-clad Alderman, has some outstanding villainous moments, particularly when he argues with Quesada about sharing the money:

> ALDERMAN: No man can say I was anything but honest. I've defended the morals of the folk here, always. I've never been afraid to teach the way of justice and the fear of God. (caressing the bags of gold) I taught half of them to pray. Now we must divide this gold. Split it equally – or do you want to cause trouble that will attract the attention of Sorro?

But it's Roberto Camardiel who steals the show. Sorro, as written by Questi and Arcali, and played by Camardiel, is a big, hairy-bear aesthete. He plays with toy soldiers, converses with his pet parrot, and operates a hand-cranked barrel organ. He dresses his henchmen in all-black cowboy outfits with white piping; himself in a white dress shirt, black vest, and long white planter's coat. He's like the aristocratic villains of *In a Colt's Shadow* – but more terrible, more dangerous, more personally *involved*. Sorro tortures his victims with lizards and what he claims are vampire bats. He's shocked that Tembler could stoop so low as to lie, in order to keep the money, risking his own son's life. He's also a heartless killer, instantly ordering Evan's death. Sorro has the best dialogue, especially when he's trying to recruit the Stranger to his gang.

SORRO: You see what a good time my boys have, here? Why don't you join them in their entertainments?

Cut to shots of the *muchachos* tearing at a roasted pig: the image recalls an earlier one of Oaks, on the operating table, torn open by townsmen digging for golden bullets. Delighted by the scene, Sorro continues:

SORRO: The best of everything! I taught them well to enjoy good things.

CUs of the *muchachos* stuffing their faces with pig. Cut to ECU of blond, expectant Evan, their prisoner.

The Stranger is utterly uninterested in joining Sorro's gang. But Sorro has interesting things to say about the importance of food, drink, and the refined pleasures of crime. Milian does a good job with his strangely passive character. After the initial robbery, the Stranger takes revenge on Oaks, then falls into a mysterious lassitude – spending a night with each of three strange families: Tembler's, where the son harbours homicidal hatred of the mistress; Sorro's all-male clan of black-clad *fascisti*; and Ackerman's horror-movie household, with its kabuki-white madwoman.

Django Kill strongly resembles a horror movie: the lighting in the saloon when the bandits first arrive is intensely moody: Oaks' henchman remarks how dark it is. The sets – all of whose interior walls seem *painfully* distressed – recall the depressing, peeling sets of one of Corman's Poe movies. Ivan Vandor's music adds to the horror-movie tone, as does Questi's focus on corpses: as they are moved from place to place, the camera *lingers* on them, at a length which makes Corbucci's morbid preoccupations seem mainstream. Tembler, with his avarice, piety and sadism, his wife locked behind a heavily barred door, is straight from a horror film – and so is she. Though her scenes with the Stranger are tender, Elizabeth really *is* insane. Let out of her cell to seduce him, she acquires matches and the means, finally, to burn down her happy home.

So, including the Oaks gang, this Stranger is given a choice of four evil 'families', all of them mad, all apt to betray him. Plagued by

145

nightmares, he suffers from horrific flashbacks. His return from the dead (his hand, emerging from the grave, recalls the dream moment in Buñuel's *Los Olvidados*), invokes numerous religious symbols and parables – particularly when the Stranger is stripped almost-naked, and crucified; and when his adversaries despoil a graveyard, throwing the crosses on the ground. But it's hard to know what it all means. Asked about the Christian symbolism, Questi denied that it was there. 'I never thought of Christ, and this is not the first time that someone was shot and didn't die,' he said.

'But he is crucified,' his interviewer persisted.

'Me, I put him on a cross? I don't remember... but anyway the cross had no Christian significance; the cross is a combination of wooden pieces the more practical for tying a man...'

Now, this is hard to believe! Tomas Milian, skinny, unshaven, muscular, wearing only a loin-cloth, tied to a cross, looks like the Christ above the altar in every church in Italy. Questi knew this. This director, too, reminds me of Luis Buñuel, denying any religious overtones in his film, just as he also insisted there was no homosexual element whatever.

'I don't know where that idea came from,' Questi said, when someone called *Django Kill* a gay Western. 'I don't particularly like homosexuality... I know that where there are men there is always homosexuality and so in a West made up essentially of men, the homosexual dimension was logical.' What? Earlier in the same interview, he spoke of *Django Kill* as a film made from the heart: logic and the heart are different things. The violent, homoerotic undercurrent of Questi's film has little to do with logic: more, perhaps, with the director's extreme, unspecified, wartime experiences.

Questi was fortunate to be able to make, out of the blue, an entirely personal work. Various features were later made in homage to *Django Kill*, among them the Mexican Westerns of Alberto Mariscal, Tinto Brass's *Yankee* (1967), Cesare Canevari's *Matalo* (1970), and my own *Straight to Hell* (1986).

The evil town in which most of the film takes place is the *Fistful of Dollars* set, at Hoja de Manzanares. The arrival of the bandits in town is a fine sequence, in which various forms of child abuse, spousal abuse, and cruelty to animals, are suggested. A naked boy plays with his dick. A drunk sits with his boot on a little girl. Through a window, we see a man menacing a woman; she threatens to bite him. This is surreal stuff, unnerving for bandits and audience alike, but it also gives the impression of having been abruptly trimmed. Most of the film, aside from the deliberate flash-cuts of the flashbacks and final massacre, is evenly paced and carefully edited. The ragged edges of this arrival scene suggest the scissors of the censor.

When *Django Kill* opened (as *Se sei vivo spara!*) in Italy, in February 1967, it played peacefully for about a month, for adults only. Then, in Milan, there were complaints, and an Italian court banned the film on 18 March. Two cuts were made – the scene where the townspeople fall upon Oaks to remove the gold bullets; and the scalping of the Indian. *Se Sei Vivo Spara!* was back in the cinemas within a week. But, for foreign distribution, many other scenes were trimmed or lost, as Questi and Arcali's 120-minute film was reduced to 115, and then to 95 minutes.

These cuts were dreadful: there no longer seems to be a complete version of the film, in any form. This may have given rise to the reports of animal butchery and humans being roasted on spits: scenes which seem not to exist (though there is certainly some offal lying on the ground in the last montage of corpses). The English-language dubbing has been criticised. In it, one of the mystic Indians exclaims, 'It's the voice of the dead,' when he hears the buried Stranger groan. The line isn't in the original Italian version – nor is the paroxysm of moaning and grunting as the Stranger drags himself out of the grave. But it isn't a bad line. Given these fake Native Americans, with their blowpipes and their Goodwill garments, why shouldn't they have English accents, as well?

I think that some of *Django Kill*'s particular strangeness – so marked, even in a sea of weirdness like the Spaghetti Western – comes from this demented English dubbing. I'm quite sure its practitioners, in some low-end recording studio in Soho, were drunk when they did it. And the result is good. In the Italian version, some of this weird spirit is missing. Also, the characters have shifting names. The Alderman is sometimes Ackerman, sometimes Hagerman. Sorro is often Zorro. And though there's no version in which the Stranger's actually called Django, there *is* one, somewhere, where he's known as Barney.

When I first met Carlo Lizzani, in 1985, he said, of Questi, 'Damiano Damiani and I always said he would be a very great filmmaker. But he was very shy.' *Django Kill*, the first Spaghetti Art Western, has many enthusiasts. I was aghast when I first saw it, even in a censored version: it was so perverse and strange, so unlike the Leone films I'd previously enjoyed. But the memory of it stayed with me, and I very much admire *Django Kill*, so extreme in every way – its costumes, its sets, its characters, its plot, its pessimistic end.

Giulio Questi's is one of the handful of great Italian Westerns so far produced, along with Leone's films, *Django*, and *¿Quien Sabe?* Now another Western – almost as personal and strange as Questi's – was about to join this small, extraordinary band: Lizzani's *Requiescant*.

Requiescant

aka *Kill & Pray, Let Them Rest, Tue et fais ta prière*
(Italy/Germany)

Director: Carlo Lizzani   **Producer:** Carlo Lizzani, Alvaro Mancori, Anna Maria Chretien, Ernest Von Theumer   **Screenplay:** Adriano Bolzoni, Armando Crispino, Luccio Battistrada, Karl-Heinz Vogelmann **Story:** Renato Izzo, Franco Bucceri   **Director of Photography:** Sandro Mancori   **Art Director:** Enzo Bulgarelli   **Costumes:** Lina Nerli Taviani   **Editor:** Franco Fraticelli   **Music:** Riz Ortolani   **Cast:** Lou Castel (*Requiescant*), Mark Damon (*George Bellow Fergusson*), Pier Paolo Pasolini (*Don Juan*), Ninetto Davoli (*El Nino*), Franco Citti (*Burt*), Barbara Frey (*Princy*), Feruccio Viotti (*Dean Light*), Rossana Martini, Mirella Maravidi, Carlo Palmucci, Frank Braña, Ivan G Scratuglia, Spartaco Conversi

The story

A community of Mexicans is invited to a parley by the Confederates who have invaded their lands after the Civil War. But the peace conference is a trap, and the gringos, led by the racist Fergusson, massacre their guests. Only a small boy escapes. He is found wandering in the desert by an itinerant preacher, who adopts him and names him 'Jeremy'.

Though raised as pacifist and vegetarian, the young man discovers he has the innate skills of a gunfighter when he shoots two stagecoach robbers. When his adoptive sister, Princy, runs away, Jeremy promises to find her. Because of his habit of praying for those he's killed, he quickly earns the nickname 'Requiescant' ('Let they rest...'). In San Antonio, where Fergusson owns all the stores, his henchman Dean Light has won Princy in a poker game, and is keeping her drugged. Requiescant goes to Fergusson, and asks for Princy back.

Intrigued by the innocent young killer, Fergusson invites him to a drunken party in his white-supremacist enclave. When Light threatens to skin Princy alive, Requiescant rescues her. The two are led by a crazy, mute flute player to a ruined fort with ancient, Toltec statues. Here Requiescant's memories flood back. Remembering the massacre for the first time, he rages madly amid his family's unburied bones.

Princy and Requiescant are caught and tried by Fergusson and his cohorts. Requiescant is tortured; Princy is killed. Fergusson murders his own wife. Requiescant joins forces with a revolutionary priest, Don Juan, and his team of black-clad killer-priests. He kills Dean Light; hides in a church which Fergusson's men burn; and escapes death by sheltering beneath the church's iron bell. Mexican servants leave the local haciendas in droves – taking the gringos' guns with them. His empire crumbling, Fergusson is abandoned by his wealthy supporters. He loses in a showdown with Requiescant, and falls bleeding into an open grave, full of his Mexican victims' bones.

The film

Carlo Lizzani's previous feature, *The Hills Run Red*, was a modest Western in the American style, with an insane, revenge-fixated hero. *Requiescant* is a grandiose, pretentious, political Western *all'Italiana*, also with a mad, revenge-fixated hero. I find *The Hills Run Red* uninteresting, *Requiescant* brilliant and compelling. But various threads tie both films together – as if Lizzani was developing ideas in one, simply in order to make the second. Both films begin in the aftermath of the Civil War, with an act of military violence. In both, the villain is a Confederate renegade who has broken his word, and become rich and pretentious.

Each villain has a violent, black-clad enforcer. In *Hills*, it's Garcia Mendez, wonderfully over-egged by Henry Silva; in *Requiescant*, it's the ironically named Dean Light (Ferruccio Viotti). Both films track their half-mad hero through abnormal sufferings, and end with his revenge.

In 1967, Lizzani was a well-regarded, active, politically engaged, mainstream Italian director. He still is. At the Venice Retrospective in 2007, only two of the Spaghetti Western *maestri* present were currently making films: Giulio Questi, directing personal art on digital video, and Carlo Lizzani, presenting his new World War Two drama, *Hotel Meina*. Lizzani wrote, '*Hotel Meina* is another chapter of that ideal story (fascist and antifascist images) that I have been constructing over the decades with films based on real events or literature.' While not based on either, *Requiescant* certainly fits the same bill, with its dramatic juxtaposition of racist, hierarchical images (Fergusson's ranch and private army, the padded cell in which he keeps his wife, the graveyard filled with his unburied victims' bones) and radical ones (Requiescant: polyglot, pacifist shootist, allied with an outraged populace and radical priests).

Yet it limits *Requiescant* to describe it, simply, as 'political'. It *is* political, in that it deals with male-female relationships, racism and the vices of unrestrained power. But it's more than that: it's a deeply weird, unconventional Western with remarkable imagery and intense performances. The political aspect is given extra weight by the presence of Pier Paolo Pasolini, as the revolutionary priest Don Juan, and several members of that director's repertory company in supporting roles. Bizarrely, Pasolini was viewed by the financiers as a 'popular' element, who would counterbalance some of the lesser-known actors. This was good news for Lizzani, who still had to struggle to persuade Pasolini to act in his film: he ended up paying him, not in cash, but with a Ferrari.[15]

The politics of *Requiescant* aren't especially complex: rich people (and their henchmen) are evil, treacherous perverts, and poor people (especially poor people who follow the revolutionary path) are good. The film's religious tone might seem a contradiction: leftists, socialists, communists and

15 *Fellini's episode*, Toby Dammit, *of the Poe portmanteau* Histoires Extraordinaires, *concerns a decadent movie actor who comes to Rome to star in a Spaghetti Western, funded by the Vatican. The actor, played by Terence Stamp, is paid not with money, but with a Ferrari. It's a great short film.*

the like are presumed to oppose the church, with its exploitative, imperial history and its fondness for *fascisti*. Lizzani squares this circle, just as Vatican II did: by espousing the preferential option for the poor. Don Juan and his men are 'good' in Spaghetti Western terms because, like El Santo in *¿Quien Sabe?*, they have taken revolutionary vows of poverty and solidarity with the oppressed *peones*; and since vows and solidarity alone do nothing, these priests have taken up arms. Requiescant's mysticism goes beyond this revolutionary Christianity into other territory. As played by Lou Castel, he is a simpleton, constantly engaged in a profound, mystifying experience: praying fervently for those he's killed, turning the other cheek, mortified to discover the remains of his family. To rescue Princy, he walks straight into the lion's den, calling himself Fergusson's brother. Like Christ, Requiescant returns from the dead; he undertakes a series of tests and sufferings; however, his catharsis is not crucifixion and forgiveness, but a revenge crusade. Raised by a protestant pastor, yet praying in Latin, he follows a peculiar religion. Adding to the miraculous tone, Requiescant's life is saved by the same artefact – a church bell – which crushes Fergusson.

Morbid, strange, frequently funny, *Requiescant* recalls *Django Kill*, which also teems with religious symbols and characters beyond the verge of madness. The script, principally written by Armando Crispino and Lucio Battistrada, is both picaresque *and* tightly constructed. Requiescant is a fine character, hovering between idiot comedy and vengeful sadism. He rides his horse facing backwards, reading a bible; spurs it with frying pan; and ties his gun to his waist with string. Yet his hanging game with Light is worthy of a Jacobean madman. Viotti, one of Pasolini's crew, is excellent as Light. Franco Citti plays a twisted killer who carries a Barbie doll to massacres, for luck. But top acting honours must go to Mark Damon, who plays the maximum villain, Fergusson. Damon, never satisfactory as a hero, does his best work as the demonic grandee who owns the town, has murdered Requiescant's pa, locked his wife in a cell, and seeks to bring back slavery. Damon's fragility and puppet-like aspect, liabilities when he played Johnny Oro, become assets as the basilisk-like Fergusson selects senators, patronises his black butler, and intones, 'The old South has much to say yet.' It helps that the screenwriters give him all the film's best lines.

As he degenerates into madness, Fergusson drives all the female whores out of his mansion. Tearing their 'frills and furbelows' from a closet, he unburdens himself to his flunky, Light:

FERGUSSON: You're a good boy and you've been faithful to me. Forget about women... inferior beings... Morons... Animals whose main purpose is to reproduce. One day everything here will be yours... I'm not as good lookin' as I used to be, am I?

Fergusson tells his wife Edith to be dignified, then strangles her with a rope. He reports back to his henchman, 'She died well, Dean. It was a beautiful moment for her.' After Requiescant has hanged Dean, Fergusson defends the memory of his drug-addicted gunsel. And as Fergusson's slave state comes apart around him, he chides his fellow aristocrats for their cowardice. 'Your honour is only an escucheon – while mine's a way of life.' Indeed! Fergusson dons a black Dracula cape in later scenes, and favours white pancake and black eye shadow. At the end he tries to shoot himself.

FERGUSSON: Let me die like a gentleman.

REQUIESCANT: I don't know how a gentleman dies.

Requiescant shoots him several times, then the church bell falls on him. Amen.

Lizzani told me he had worked with Pasolini on the script of *Requiescant*. 'This was the late sixties – a time of much upheaval – and we wanted to say something... revolutionary. Damiano, also, with *¿Quien Sabe?* With a Western, it was possible to say things you could not otherwise say. We did try, through the Spaghetti Western, to say something up to date... something polemical... something about *justice*.'

Ephraim Katz was – like most American critics – suspicious of a director with leftist politics. In the *Film Encyclopaedia*, he wrote: 'Many of Lizzani's well-intentioned social dramas have been marred... by the director's overly dogmatic Marxist ideology on the one hand, and by commercial requirements on the other.' Neither consideration seems to have dominated here: the result is a tight, concise, original Spaghetti

Western – at once political and surreal. *Requiescant* is a film of bizarre images that remain with the viewer: Fergusson shooting candle flames off servants' heads; his death beneath the bell which sheltered Requiescant; Don Juan cradling a machinegun in swaddling clothes; Requiescant raging through the massacre-ground, tearing up bones and ribcages from the red earth...

Requiescant opened in Italy in March 1967. The censor made cuts in several of the violent scenes, including the tortures of Requiescant and Edith, and gave the film a 14+ certificate. The film was popular in Italy and Germany, but made few inroads elsewhere. The French distributor had great hopes for it, planning to open the film in one of Paris's most prestigious cinemas. Unfortunately she booked the cinema where *Once Upon a Time in the West* had just opened. But Leone's film enjoyed a two-year run, relegating *Requiescant* to minor Paris cinemas. The French censor required cuts; the censored, French-dubbed prints were titled *Tue... et fais ta priere* (*Kill and Pray*). In 1970, the distributor offered me an uncensored, English-language print, subtitled in French, for 150 pounds. I didn't take her up on it. Now I wonder: would that 35mm print be vinegar today? Or would the uncut, English-speaking version have survived?

$1,000 on the Black

aka *$1,000 sul nero, Blood at Sundown, Sartana sangue e la penna,*
Les colts de la violence
(Italy/Germany)

Director: Alberto Cardone   **Producer:** Mario Siciliano, Karl Spiehs
Screenplay: Ernesto Gastaldi, Vittorio Salerno, Rolf Olsen, Giorgio Stegani   **Director of Photography:** Gino Santini   **Art Director:** Amedeo Mellone   **Costumes:** Maria Baroni, Rosalba Menichelli   **Editor:** Romeo Ciatti   **Music:** Michele Lacerenza   **Cast:** Anthony Steffen (*Johnny Liston*), Gianni Garko (*Sartana*), Erika Blanc (*Joselita*), Carlo D'Angelo (*Judge Wood*), Daniela Igliozzi (*Mary*), Gianni Solaro, Gino Marturano (*Forrester*), Sieghardt Rupp (*Ralph*), Carrol Brown (*Rhonda*), Angelica Ott (*Manuela*), Franco Fantasia (*Sheriff*)

The story

Two hired killers attempt to shoot Johnny Liston, walking below them in a canyon, with rifles. But they miss and he plays dead, then overpowers them in hand-to-hand combat, and confiscates their boots. Johnny is out of jail after serving 12 years for a murder he didn't commit. He goes to see his brother, Sartana, who lives in an Aztec fort, and calls himself a general. But Sartana is cohabiting with Manuela, Johnny's beloved. Johnny rides on. Sartana slaps Manuela, and whips and abuses her mute brother, Jerry. The bootless killers show up at the fort: Sartana, their employer, shoots them.

Johnny saves the life of Joselita Rogers, whose father he is supposed to have killed. She disdains him. He visits his mother, Rhonda, in the town of Campos: she lives in a big, white mansion whose owners Sartana has killed ('I'm the mistress of this house where I used to work as a servant'). But Rhonda, deeply unhappy, has become an alcoholic. Johnny watches as the 'general' and his gang demand money and valuables from the frightened townspeople.

Johnny and Sartana fight; Sartana ride through the desert canyons to another town, Blackstone Hill, and extracts tribute there. He robs the townspeople and humiliates Jerry further – but Johnny appears on a rooftop, shoots several of his men, and forces Sartana to leave. When Sartana attempts to rob the town of Wishville, Johnny is there first and – helped by Jerry's dynamite-throwing skills – decimates Sartana's 'troops'. Back in Campos, Rhonda horsewhips Sartana for allowing Johnny to beat him. Johnny tries to persuade the men of Campos to join up with Wishville against Sartana – but they beat him up instead. Joselita offers to recruit supporters from Blackstone Hill. But her confidant, Judge Wood, delivers her to Sartana. Sartana and the Judge have been in league for 12 years, since they framed Johnny for murder. Johnny, taking the Judge as a hostage, heads into Sartana's trap. He's able to free Joselita, and escape from Sartana's execution-party.

In Blackstone Hill, the townsfolk believe the Judge's word against Johnny's. Rejected by Joselita and the townspeople, Johnny rides away. Sartana raids Campos, looking for Johnny. He kills the sheriff and sets the town ablaze. A delegation of local matrons visits Rhonda, pleading for her help. She forces them to beg on their knees, then persuades Sartana to leave town – but she is mortally wounded in the crossfire. Rhonda dies in her good son's arms. In the final showdown, Sartana is killed by Johnny and Manuela.

The film

Alberto Cardone shot two Westerns back-to-back in 1966. Both were revenge stories with complex family ties. In *$7 on the Red* (*Sette dollari sul rosso*) the hero's quest for revenge is complicated by his wife's killers having kidnapped his son – and raised the boy as their own. 'Jerry' grows up to be a callous, vicious killer who tries to provoke his true father into a gunfight, and shoots his adoptive mother dead. He dies, stabbed by his own knife, in his father's arms. The film begins weakly, and is much improved by the conflict between the hero, Johnny, and his hideous progeny. *$1,000 on the Black*, completed and released in 1967, is a Cain and Abel story in reverse, in which a good, principled brother must kill a sociopathic one. There is no father figure; only an angry, dominating, alcoholic matriarch, whose death – as in *$7 on the Red* – provokes the final cataclysm.

$7 on the Red is an okay picture with a couple of great sequences. *$1,000 on the Black* is a Western of a high order. It's visually stylish, bursting with effort, almost. Sartana is a new character, a blond white guy masquerading as a Mexican general (*alla* Santa Anna, conqueror of the Alamo), sadistic, childish and insecure. He writes a 'W' on a wanted poster which bears his face (does he think it is an 'S'?) and makes the sheriff shout an oath of loyalty. After he kills a would-be bounty hunter, he asks, 'Well sheriff, how many is this?' 'Twenty-six,' the quaking lawman replies. Sartana then steps into the street and addresses the lined-up populace.

SARTANA: Take a look at what I did for you! I freed you of a man who kills for the dollar! (sneers) Folks, seek into your hearts, and be generous to a general who has to keep soldiers to defend you. No obligation to give: I leave it to your conscience.

He passes his hat around, relieving them of their money, jewellery and watches. When he returns a gold nugget to a miner, mother – watching from her window – declares, 'Good boy, Sartana! He never forgets that we were once poor, like that old man.' When Sartana executes a businessman, while kissing his lucky-death amulet, Johnny is shocked, but Rhonda defends her son: 'If Sartana killed him, he had a reason.' Gianni Garko relishes his role: he said he thought of Richard Widmark; his white teeth and square jaw recall Kirk Douglas: clearly, he's also chanelling Klaus Kinski. For most of the picture, Sartana dotes on his mother, kneeling at her feet and kissing her hands, plying her with stolen necklaces; but in the end he's more violent and mysogynistic than any Widmark character. He kicks, beats and scratches his hostage-girlfriend, and shoots a townswoman in the back; one assumes, automatically but wrongly, that he will murder mom.

Anthony Steffen is not particularly strong or engaging. He's good in fistfights, boring the rest of the time. He's literally wooden: in shoot 'em ups, he makes no effort to take cover or change position – just stands stock still and fully upright, in plain sight of his enemies, blasting away with his Winchester. This is an untenable approach to gunfighting: either the character is suicidal, or he knows he's invulnerable (which makes his predicament uninteresting). But Steffen was on to something, perhaps: other Spaghetti Western actors, including Garko, were soon to adopt this zen-like indifference to bullets. Presciently, Johnny frees Joselita from the bandits' fort by sporting a dynamite-packed kamikaze belt – the second instance of a potential suicide bomber in a Spaghetti Western.

The women in this film all dress like Tyrolean milkmaids. Rhonda is a powerful character, Joselita a faller-downer of the Boetticher school, who believes, wrongly, that Johnny killed her pa. 'What a terrible thing for our town,' Joselita declares, 'that nobody dare touch the brother of Sartana.' Immediately, a bounty hunter steps up, insults Johnny, and promises Joselita, 'There isn't a price on his head, but I'll kill him if you want me to.' Manuela is another victim/whiner – but she too takes action at the end. Three active women is a record for any Italian Western (otherwise the record would be two, in the *Ringo* movies, *Django Kill*, and some Corbucci films). And even miserable Manuela has her actor's moment, when, surrounded by *chac mools* and other 'Aztec' artefacts in Sartana's fort, she staggers about, then faints. Presumably she's been overcome by the ancient horror of the place, recently rekindled by Sartana's crimes. Gino Santini's photography is generally good, and, when the camera is on a dolly following the action, or when he plays a scene in *plano secuencia*, it can be excellent. The staging is striking, and bizarre: all characters, on and off horseback, invariably line up like chess pieces. In a night-time scene, a circle of torches, held by the gang, flares up in perfect unison. Rhonda's house and Sartana's fort are equally overdone – her place dark with dust and decay, his ablaze with Aztec and Toltec death-god statuary. Sartana and Rhonda, similarly, are the biggest, and best, characters in the film. Like them, we loathe the tedious townsfolk. Mother and son are glorious, godlike, doomed. A child's savage innocence (the maid who becomes queen of a mansion; the fatherless brat who becomes a Mexican *generalissimo*) inhabits them, as it does the film – visually fantastical, with no concession to that dull and deadly notion, 'realism'.

The toy-like atmosphere of the Western towns and Sartana's fort is reinforced by Cardone's use of matte shots. The first (used several times for the arrival and departure of different riders) is an exterior of the fort, with big *chac mools* and other idols rising out of the stone walls. The background – a horizon with jagged mountains – is either a model, or a painting. The second shot appears once, late in the film, as an establisher for one of the towns. There are hills in the foreground, mountains in the distance – all models – and, in between them, a cloud of dust overhangs the painted buildings of a Western town. This is the first instance I know of a matte being used in a Spaghetti Western. Of course, Italian credit sequences were visually very inventive, with complex mattes and superimpositions, often designed by Luigi Lardini. And Leone would later use a matte, in *Duck, You Sucker!* (1971). But Cardone was the first (and only) director to use such an effects shot to establish a location. I think these shots serve the same purpose as those Tyrolean dresses, or the torches flaring *en masse* in a perfect circle, or the bandits' horses backing up in unison: they heighten the toy-like nature of Cardone's strange and clever artifice.

There's one attempt at comic relief, involving a pacifist storekeeper who sells bullets and dynamite. But the rest of the film is played as melodrama, would-be tragedy. When Sartana returns to Campos for the final battle, there's a strange scene, played in what seems a hastily composed wide shot with no coverage, in which the storekeeper warns Sartana that he's in trouble, because there's someone in town who's not afraid of him. Sartana laughs and rides on. This scene must mean something to Cardone, or he would have got rid of it. Later the pacifist draws a gun, and dies in battle. A local businessman, mortally wounded, groans, 'I hope we can make it.' Such dialogue is pathetic: Cardone must want us to side with Sartana, against the townsfolk, in these robberies and shootouts. And yet Cardone's womenfolk are unique, in that they actually fire rifles at the bandits, rather than reloading the rifles of their husbands (see *The Searchers*; see *Minnesota Clay*).

Both *$7 on the Red* and *$1,000 on the Black* end with the deaths of mother and bad son. Rhonda and Sartana are pretty base characters, so it's hard to call their fates tragic; there's no fall from high estate. Yet we pity them. Unlike Rosa, Rhonda succeeds as a peacemaker, only to fall victim to a stray bullet. On the action front, there's a fight – with fists, bottle, pitchfork and axe – as brutal and well staged as one could wish for: the protagonists are Sartana's black-clad lieutenant, Ralph (Sieghard Rupp, from *Fistful*), and the mute Jerry (Gianni Solaro). In the final showdown, Johnny plays it straight, and his brother cheats. But Manuela blasts Sartana with her Winchester, before he can wield his concealed gun. Cut to the sun, obscured by clouds. Cut to a high angle, looking straight down – *God's POV* – on Sartana's corpse. Johnny enters the frame, and kneels beside the brother he has killed. He yells for the others to keep away. Cut to Johnny leaving town alone, with Sartana's body slung over a horse. In the English-language version, there's an ill-matched freeze frame with a title:

'Thou Shalt Not Hate Thy Brother in Thine Heart'
Leviticus XIX

There is enormous striving-after-something here, as throughout the film – but what? Significance? Meaning? Camp overload? Parts of

$1,000 on the Black are quite bad (the fake horse-riding shots; some of the editing choices) and much of the plot – the mute boy's tale, Joselita versus Judge Wood – is tedious. It's possible the entire thing is a tongue-in cheek gag (another *Arizona Colt*, which also took place in the town of 'Blackstone Hill'), enlivened by some good fights, bold cinematography and a wonderful performance by Garko. It's also possible that *$1,000 on the Black* is the first self-consciously mythological Western since *Shane*.

It wasn't long before another producer wanted to make a film about Sartana, starring Gianni Garko: Aldo Addobbati, who planned a bigger-budget, all-action, all-star movie. *$1,000 on the Black*'s producer, Mario Siciliano, quickly sued Addobbati. But the real power lay with the actor: Garko voted with his feet, by going to work for Addobbati. This was one of those rare cases, like *Terminator 1* and *2*, when the dead villain of the first film – thanks to his rising star power – is reborn as the hero of its sequel.[16]

16 $1,000 on the Black *is often dated as 1969, presumably because it was re-released to capitalise on the success of Addobbati's* Sartana *film. According to Marco Giusti,* $1,000 on the Black *was made in 1966 and released in 1967. For the same reasons as* Django Kill, *I've treated it as a '67 film.*

Hellbenders

aka *I crudeli*

(Italy/Spain)

Director: Sergio Corbucci   **Producer:** Alfredo Antonini   **Screenplay:** Ugo Liberatore, Jose Gutierrez Maesso, Lewis Garfinkle, Virgil Gerlach   **Story:** Alfredo Antonini, Ugo Liberatore   **Director of Photography:** Enzo Barboni   **Art Director:** Jaime Perez Cubero   **Costumes:** Nori Bonicelli   **Editor:** Nino Baragli, Alberto Gallitti   **Assistant Director:** Ruggero Deodato, Maria Berrutia   **Music:** Ennio Morricone   **Cast:** Joseph Cotten (*Jonas*), Norma Bengell (*Claire*), Julian Mateos (*Ben*), Gino Pernice (*Jeff*), Angel Aranda (*Nat*), Maria Martin (*Kitty*), Al Mulock (*The beggar*), Aldo Sambrell (*Pedro*), Enzo Girolami (*Commander of Fort Brent*), Jose Nieto (*Sheriff*), Claudio Gora (*Rev Pierce*), Julio Pena (*Sgt Tolt*), Benito Stefanelli (*Slim*), Claudio Scarchilli (*Indian Chief*), Alvaro De Luna, Rafael Vaquero, Ivan Scratuglia, Simon Arriaga, Jose Canalejas

The story

Jonas, a fanatical Confederate general, is determined to rekindle the Civil War and defeat the Union. With his sons Ben, Nat, and Jeff – the 'Hellbenders' – he prays, then massacres a division of Union soldiers transporting a consignment of used banknotes. Killing two additional henchmen ('They weren't kin – only joined us for the money'), Jonas conceals the money in a coffin. His mistress, Kitty, is to play the 'widow' of a dead Confederate officer, Captain Ambrose Allen, whose remains Jonas and sons pretend to be transporting home. The deception gets them past the first party of Union troops. But Jonas and Kitty detest each other, and when she attempts to steal the loot, Nat kills her. Ben is sent to find a replacement: he tricks Claire, a saloon gambler, into taking Kitty's place. Claire saves the Hellbenders from discovery by a sheriff's posse by pretending to faint over the coffin. When Jeff tries to rape her, he and Ben come to blows.

By chance, their little convoy passes through Sundog, a town Captain Ambrose Allen frequently visited. The preacher insists on having a service for him, and on reintroducing the 'widow' Allen to her old friend, Sergeant Tolt. Fortunately, Tolt is blind; when he promises to produce photographs, Nat murders him. In the desert, they are attacked by Mexican bandits; Jonas shoots their leader, Pedro, under a flag of truce. Another Union detachment, searching for the thieves, intervenes and saves the Hellbenders.

Claire insists on visiting the fort where her 'husband' was to have served. Here they see Pedro and his fellow outlaws hanged: since the robbery, the territory is under martial law. Claire, sick of the whole mission, requests that the coffin be buried in the military cemetery at the fort. They leave, and Jonas sends his sons back at night, to dig it up. With the coffin disinterred, the group moves on, Jonas single-minded as ever, Claire shuddering with pneumonia. But their horses are killed by a mad beggar, and they are overtaken by a tribe of Indians: the Indians want Jeff, who has raped and killed the chief's daughter. Nat and Jeff draw down on each other; Ben tries to intervene; all are shot.

Jonas, mortally wounded, tries to drag the coffin away – it falls and breaks open, revealing the corpse of Pedro. His sons have desecrated the wrong grave. Ben and Claire watch as the dying Jonas drags the Hellbenders' standard across the parched mud of the riverbank, in a last, doomed effort to reach his Confederate promised land.

The film

Alberto Antonini ('Albert Band'), the producer of *Red Pastures*, had acquired the rights to a book, *Guns of North Texas*, by Will Cook. For some reason, Antonini felt compelled to make not one, but two films, out of Cook's book – both of them starring Joseph Cotten. Why does a producer do such things? Why does a dog lick his balls? Because he can.

The first of these pictures was titled *The Tramplers* (*Gli uomini del paso pasante*, 1965). Cotten – venerable star of *Citizen Kane* and *The Magnificent Ambersons* – played a Southern patriarch, Temple Cordeen, who refused to believe the Civil War was over. The cast included Jim Mitchum (of *Red Pastures* fame) and a pre-*Django* Franco Nero. *The Tramplers* ended with four of Cordeen's five sons dead, and the patriarch deranged. *Hellbenders* is a variation on the same story. Like *The Tramplers*, it was adapted by Antonini and Ugo Liberatore from *Guns of North Texas*, and featured Joseph Cotten. There the relationship between the two films ends.

Having co-directed *The Tramplers* with one Mario Sequi, Antonini realised that a good Western needs only one, talented, director. He picked a great one: Sergio Corbucci. And Corbucci brought his team on board. Jose Gutierrez Maesso, who had written parts of *Django* and *Minnesota Clay*, and produced *The Bounty Killer*, was contracted to rework the script. Corbucci hired Enzo Barboni, *Django*'s cinematographer, and Nino Baragli, *Django*'s editor; Jaime Perez Cubero as art director; Morricone as composer. All were masters of the Spaghetti Western trade: each was a major step up from the crew of *The Tramplers*.

Corbucci and Maesso focused on the character of Jonas – leader of the Hellbenders. Jonas is, obviously, another version of Major Jackson, the Klan leader and principal villain of *Django*. Both men are obtuse, monomaniacal racists who can't accept the Civil War is over. Both are violent, treacherous hypocrites. Jackson is worse than Jonas, more of a sadist, but Jonas's plan – 'a new Confederation of

States, united under God' – is considerably more threatening. Jackson collects and hoards money; Jonas wants to put money to work. Like Django, he drags what is most precious to him around the West in a coffin. And, like Django, his dream is shattered when the coffin breaks open – revealing the corpse of a bandit who has vowed to see Jonas in hell. Like Django's gold, the flag of the Hellbenders is sucked beneath the rapids. Antonini's surreal notion – to make two different films based on the same book, with the same actor – paid off, because he picked a Surrealist director. Corbucci had experienced a shaky year since *Django*. *Navajo Joe* was a poor film, but it had helped him define what was important to him: what themes and images he would persist with. *Django* is mainly urban, a film of dark interiors. Almost all of *Hellbenders* happens outdoors, in daylight, as the convoy heads south. Yet the films seem like companion pieces: the continuing story of the Jackson/Jonas character, played well by Eduardo Fajardo, but portrayed brilliantly by Joseph Cotten.

After Jonas, the most compelling presence is the gambler, Claire (played by a fine Brazilian actor, Norma Bengell). Claire is the most developed Corbucci woman to date: tough, strikingly but unusually beautiful, amoral up to a point, ultimately principled. She is strong, even by Corbucci standards. Kitty (Maria Martin), the first 'widow', drunk and avaricious, is murdered by the loathsome Jeff (Gino Pernice, from *Django* and *Minnesota Clay*). But Claire isn't apt to be killed by any of these boys. She is as strong-willed as Jonas, and her determination reminds us how important the relationship of husband and wife was in Corbucci's Westerns: even when the husband doesn't really exist, and the 'widow' is trying to bury a coffin stuffed with a million dollars. I think we can witness Corbucci becoming a self-aware *auteur* in *Hellbenders*, consciously deciding which of the elements of his films are really important to him. A strong woman character is essential. A coffin full of guns, or dollars, he cannot resist: likewise the shots of corpses after the ambush, lying in the river, a-swirl with blood. Yet he ignores another instinct (kill the priest!) when the Hellbenders are forced to attend a church service. The priest survives; the gang ride out of town. *Django* was, I think, an entirely instinctive work – like Questi's *Django Kill*. Now, Corbucci was subordinating his instincts to the need for a strong, credible story. Not coincidentally, *Hellbenders* features the first credible romance in any of his films: the love of Claire and Ben, united not by passion, but by their basic decency, and shared victimhood.

Shooting a year after *The Good, the Bad and the Ugly*, Corbucci inherited various props and costumes from Leone: notably, the Confederate Army hearse, which previously carried the dying Bill Carson to his meeting with Tuco and Blondie. But Corbucci's depiction of the Civil War is quite different from the other Sergio's. Leone refused to make any real distinction between North and South: in one memorable scene, Confederate troops 'became' Unionists as grey dust blew off their uniforms. For him, the Civil War was a massive killing machine, something his heroes had to avoid, to reach their goal. For Corbucci, there's a real distinction between North and South. His Northerners are courteous to women and to their defeated adversaries, and attempt to play by the rules (though the rules are broad, and allow for the lynching of Mexicans without trial). By contrast, Corbucci's Southerners are avaricious, fanatical, dishonest, and (in the case of Jeff) rapists. When Pedro raises a white flag, Jonas shoots him; the sheer dishonour of this infuriates the bandit, who vows to see Jonas in hell. So, in Corbucci's West, the Civil War still evokes a clear opposition of *good and bad sides* (with both against the Mexicans). Nori Bonicelli, Corbucci's wife, was costume designer, and she made little attempt to 'age' the Hellbenders' or the Union troops' uniforms. The war may be over, but its conflicts are as fresh as the colours both sides wear. In one ironic sequence, underscored by Morricone's horns, the adversaries are finally united: Corbucci depicts the Union cavalry dragging Mexican prisoners with ropes around their necks, while escorting the Confederate hearse to a safe haven.

Note the presence of a Canadian actor who was to make a handful of striking appearances in Spaghetti Westerns – Al Mulock. Mulock had a career of small roles in film and television, starting in 1955 as one of the assassins in a British Shakespearean gangster movie, *Joe Macbeth*. Like other North Americans, he made the pilgrimage to Rome in the sixties, and his pitted, cadaverous face appears – in huge close-up – at the very start of *The Good, the Bad and the Ugly*. Other

Italian directors began using Mulock's stark features and intense presence to good advantage: but he would not be around for long. In *Hellbenders*, Mulock plays an unexplained character, who appears near the end of the film: a mad, nameless beggar who, having pleaded for charity, slaughters the Hellbenders' horses, and forces the brothers, at gunpoint, into sadistic fighting games. What does this individual's presence signify? His killing of their horses dooms Jonas's little army, but they are doomed anyway: the Indian war party is on its way, the prized coffin contains no money, but only Pedro's corpse. This beggar, played by Mulock, is like the scalphunters in *Navajo Joe*: a symbol of Corbucci's pessimistic vision of the West, and another prototype for McCarthy's *Blood Meridian*. Both filmmaker and novelist exposed a similarly grisly personal frontier: no paradise or place of possibilities, but a parched hideout for malevolent loners, driven by demons, on the run from hideous pasts.

Face to Face

aka *Faccia a faccia, Le dernier face à face, Cara a cara*
(Italy/Spain)

Director: Sergio Sollima   **Producer:** Alberto Grimaldi   **Screenplay:** Sergio Sollima, Sergio Donati, Tulio Demichelli   **Director of Photography:** Rafael Pacheco, Emilio Foriscot   **Art Director, Costumes:** Carlo Simi   **Editor:** Eugenio Alabiso   **Assistant Director:** Maurizio Mein, Mariano Canales   **Music:** Ennio Morricone   **Cast:** Gian Maria Volonte (*Brad Fletcher*), Tomas Milian (*Solomon 'Beauregard' Bennett*), William Berger (*Charlie Siringo*), Jolanda Modio (*Marie*), Carole Andre (*Cattle Annie*), Gianni Rizzo (*Williams*), Lidia Alfonsi (*Belle De Winton*), Angel Del Pozo (*Maximilian De Winton*), Aldo Sambrell (*Zachary Shot*), Nello Pazzafini (*Vance*), Jose Torres (*Aaron*), Frank Braña (*Jason*), Antonio Casas, Rico Boido (*Sheriff*), Lorenzo Robledo (*Fallace*), Francisco Sanz (*Rusty Roberts*), Manlio Busoni, Linda Veras, Rosella D'Aquino

The story

Brad Fletcher, a consumptive, resigns his post as a history teacher in New England, and heads West. There, he gives water to an arrested bandit, Beauregard Bennett; Beau escapes, taking Brad hostage. That night, Brad saves Beau's life by removing a bullet. Brad becomes fascinated by Beau, and witnesses a Pinkerton agent, Charlie Sirringo, attempt – and fail – to join Beau's gang. Williams, a businessman, hires Beau to kill a rival, Sam Taylor. An unlikely friendship develops between Beau and Brad. Beau re-constructs his outlaw band, signing up his old partner, Maximilian de Winton, on the de Winton plantation. He introduces Brad to Puerto de Fuego, an anarchist community in the high desert, where there is no law.

Here Brad rapes Maria, girlfriend of Vance, one of Beau's men. In the inevitable fight which follows, Brad kills Vance by bashing his head against a rock. Brad attempts to lead the others on a bank robbery, and Beau challenges him to a duel. Brad faces Beau with an empty pistol. Having tested Brad and found him worthy, Beau tells the professor to lead the bank robbery. But the robbery turns into a massacre when Sirringo, now a member of the gang, attempts to thwart it. Beau – stung by Brad's observations on his cruel lifestyle – fails to stab a kid who alerts the sheriff. As a result, Beau is captured by Sirringo, and most of Bennett's Raiders, including Maximilian, are killed. Brad and Maria make it back to Puerto de Fuego where – shot in the back by Sirringo – Maria dies.

Brad rallies the people of the former anarchist community to become outlaws, and follow his orders. A gathering of cattlemen and bankers concludes that Brad and his outlaws are cutting a swathe through their profits. They offer Beau his freedom, if he will lead a vigilante horde against Brad and co. Beau refuses; instead his friend Zachary leads the mob on a bounty hunt: $100 per man, $50 per woman, $25 per child. The vigilantes attack Puerto de Fuego at night, surprising and killing almost all the outlaws. Brad leads the survivors – mainly women and children – out into the desert. They're joined by Beau, who has escaped. When Sirringo intervenes to save Brad and Beau from the vigilantes, he is shot by Brad. Beau, having discovered his good self, shoots Brad. Sirringo, wounded, fakes Beau's death so that he can start a new life with the handful of survivors.

The film

Sergio Sollima made political Westerns. With Milian, in *The Big Gun-down*, he had created the character of Cuchillo, who both viewed as a working-class hero. So Milian was inclined to trust Sollima, and play a very different, less-obviously heroic role, while they prepared an official 'Cuchillo' sequel. As an actor, Milian was now being described as 'difficult': like John Wayne, he had come to identify with the idealised character he played; like 'Che' Guevara, he was young, bearded, photographed in a way that made him look like Christ. Milian had studied in the Actors' Studio. In LA, his best friend was Dennis Hopper. Both Hopper and Milian worshipped at the shrine of the late James Dean. Of course he was going to be difficult!

And Sollima had his work cut out for him, because Milian's co-star was the actor for whom the word 'difficult' had been invented: Gian Maria Volonte. Volonte, whom Leone had pointedly *not* invited back for *The Good, the Bad and the Ugly*, was famously political and intense. Francesco Rosi worked with him several times and Volonte gave him extraordinary performances: just as Klaus Kinski did Werner Herzog. But there were actors, and directors, who didn't like Volonte, among them Jean-Pierre Melville who swore publicly, after *Le cercle rouge*, that he'd never work with him again.

As a director, I think it's better not to slag off your actors. Even if you can't stand them personally, or you think they acted badly, so what? Actors aren't cast just for being lovely people; if an actor acts badly it's the director's fault – for miscasting him, or failing to elicit a performance. Melville's complaints about Volonte were basically three-fold: 1) he didn't hit his marks perfectly, the way Alain Delon or Yves Montand did; 2) he talked a lot about politics; 3) he flew home to Italy every chance he got, rather than staying in France.

1) is a small problem for a good cinematographer, and not really the director's business; 2) and 3) are not crimes, especially as *Le cercle rouge* is a weak picture, inferior to Melville's great thrillers, and Gian Maria Volonte is the best thing in it! The other actors are quite stiff by comparison: of course, they are striving to please the boss, by hitting their marks to within an inch.

So *Face to Face* was blessed with potentially electric casting chemistry: Volonte, the radical who sometimes missed his marks and liked to argue, and Milian, the radical who thought he was God, or at least Her representative.

Face to Face has the simplicity of a fairy story: a bad man (the outlaw) becomes good, while a good man (the academic) becomes bad. But the script questions the conventional distinctions, Italian and American, between Good and Bad. Its white characters – including the initial protagonist and the Pinkerton Detective – might be the heroes of other films. Here, they are uniformly bad. As in *The Big Gundown*, the script – by Sollima and Sergio Donati – pits the 'Good' gringo against the 'Ugly' Mexican. Cuchillo and Beauregard Bennett have vitality and capacity for change. Jonathan Corbett was stuck in the rut of his conventional approach to justice. Brad Fletcher is the opposite: like a postmodern academic, he is entirely flexible. Having witnessed Beau's fearlessness and vitality, he falls in love: not with Beau, but with Beau's easy exercise of power. Like a banker or industrialist attracted to the rituals of fascism, Brad can't wait to receive his uniform. With Beau in prison and the rest of the gang dead, Brad confronts the proto-hippies who have made Puerto de Fuego an anarchist paradise, without rules. Henceforth, he announces, it will be his personal outlaw headquarters, and all will obey him.

> BRAD: I was right! Here's the loot, to prove it! Don't say I made an error. Don't say I lost my head. The bullets were whistling all around me... and yet they didn't touch me. My plan succeeded because it was the perfect one! But the men weren't, and the men failed you. However, men can be replaced.

Amazingly, most of the Puerto de Fuegans sign up to work for Fletcher – just as they did in the service of William Walker, another memorable madman who also dressed in black, instituted slavery, and claimed to be able to walk through swarms of bullets, while all around him his men died. Did Sollima or Donati think about Walker while creating the character of Brad? Most likely they knew about him, just as Franco Solinas did.

Arch and uncomfortable at the beginning, Brad Fletcher becomes increasingly magnetic as the film progresses. Late in the day, the cabal of bankers and cattlemen hires another Pinkerton spy. Brad recognises another eastern university graduate like himself, and orders the man tortured. Then he straightens his collar, and mops his brow.

> BRAD: The philosophy of violence, do you recall it? One violent soul is just an outlaw, one hundred a gang. But they're an army at 100 thousand. That is the point: beyond the confines that limit the individual criminal, violence by masses of men is called *history*.

So Brad Fletcher has become a connoisseur of evil, even beyond Sorro in *Django Kill*. This makes him a fascinating character, a sort of super-fascist – offering his fellow citizens a choice between armed thuggery and slave labour. Outside Puerto de Fuego, the 'civilised' community is depicted as unredeemable. All are thieves, slaveowners, and dry-gulching capitalists (Gianni Rizzo defrauds his shareholders for the first of many times): a mob of torch-bearing vigilantes, bent on plunder and revenge.

It's all so weird, original and entertaining – a dual-hero film, like *Performance*, with similar gay undertones – that I want to like the picture more, and to forgive it for being slow-moving, and silly, and having ludicrous haircuts. But I haven't seen a complete version, and based on what I have seen there are real problems with *Face to Face* – areas in which the film just doesn't deliver on its excellent premise. Tomas Milian put his finger on one of them in his interview in *Westerns all'italiana*: he found it difficult to work with Volonte, he said, but what really bothered him was that:

> My character, who was supposed to be very violent before the movie starts, begins the movie when he's wounded. So Volonte's character has an arc and mine becomes flat. Mine starts already wounded and so became almost passive for the rest of the film. They just said I was a very famous bandit, etc, etc, but you never *see* the bandit.

Milian is right. Beauregard Bennett, saddled with a ridiculous name, gets kicked and shot, but there is no scene to establish him as a seriously powerful or dangerous character. So his 'reform' isn't very interesting, and the balance between him and Brad Fletcher is off. *Face to Face* repeats this error by omission several times: sometimes it may be censorship cuts, as with Brad's rape of Maria. But more often it seems to have been a conscious decision by the director to play important scenes off-camera. Thus, just as there's no scene establishing Beau as a violent bandit leader, there are no scenes depicting Brad as a serious outlaw (the bankers and ranchers just complain about him afterwards), and only the aftermath of the vigilante raid on Puerto de Fuego is seen.

Now, for a Western to avoid three potential action sequences seems strange. For a Spaghetti Western to avoid them (along with numerous other potential moments for gratuitous violence, such as the death of Vance) seems actually culpable. What was Sollima thinking?

There's a fine, Leone-style showdown in the anarchist camp, where Beau challenges Brad to a duel. This is well staged, strikingly photographed. It's followed by an excellent scene – almost a complete *plano secuencia* in which Brad's voiceover describes the preparations for the bank robbery and the robbers individually arrive in town. The bank robbery itself is great. But these are the action sequences. The rest is talking, often about things we never see; worst of all, there's an ineptly staged, faux-Ford dancing sequence. It's all so strange, so interesting, so incomplete. Many big themes – betrayal, justice, racial intolerance, a marginal hero versus a corrupt society, the relativity of good and bad, the nature of violence – are touched on, then ignored.

Face to Face opened in Italy in November; it was a big hit. Domestically, Milian and Volonte were now stars: in the same league as Franco Nero, hovering just below Giuliano Gemma. But in 1967, the top international star of Spaghetti Westerns was still an American: Lee Van Cleef. As the actor whom the US distributors relied on, Van Cleef made three Italian Westerns that year, the best being *Death Rides a Horse*.

Death Rides a Horse

aka *Da uomo a uomo*
(Italy/Spain)

Director: Giulio Petroni   **Producer:** Alfonso Sansone, Enrico Chroscicki
Screenplay: Luciano Vincenzoni   **Director of Photography:** Carlo

Carlini **Art Director:** Franco Bottari **Costumes:** Luciano Sagoni
Editor: Eraldo Da Roma **Special Effects:** Eros Bacciucchi **Assistant Director:** Giancarlo Santi, Mario Molli **Music:** Ennio Morricone
Cast: John Phillip Law (*Bill*), Lee Van Cleef (*Ryan*), Luigi Pistilli (*Walcott*), Anthony Dawson (*Cavanagh*), Jose Torres (*Pedro*), Mario Brega (*One-Eye*), Carla Cassola (*Betsy*), Archie Savage (*Vigro*) Guglielmo Spoletini (*Manuel*), Felicita Fanny, Ignazio Leone, Elena Hall, Carlo Pisacane, Nino Vingelli, Romano Puppo, Giovanni Petrucci, Franco Balducci, Natale Nazareno

The story

A small boy, Bill, witnesses the murder of his father, and the rape and murder of his mother and sister, at the hands of bandits. Each killer has distinguishing features: a spur, a scar, a tattoo, an earring, a skull pendant. Fifteen years later, Bill is a young man, practising his marksmanship when a stranger, Ryan, arrives to visit the victims' graves. Ryan has just spent 15 years in jail, framed by outlaw partners. Now he seeks revenge.

Next day, the sheriff tells Bill that Ryan has killed two men in town: one was clearly a murderer of Bill's parents, given his distinctive spurs. Bill declines an invitation to become deputy sheriff. Instead he follows Ryan and attempts to team up with him, since they both have a score to settle with the same men. But Ryan steals his horse, and turns him down. In a nearby town, Ryan tracks down the saloon keeper Cavanagh, and demands $15,000 from his former partner – a thousand for each year he spent in jail. Cavanagh tries to hire Bill to kill Ryan, but when Bill sees the four aces tattooed on Cavanagh's chest, he shoots him dead.

Ryan confronts another former gangster, Walcott, who has become the banker and 'First Citizen of Lyndon City': he demands a $30,000 bribe. But Walcott traps him and frames him for the theft of a million dollars from Walcott's own bank. Bill busts Ryan out of jail and the two make their way separately to Walcott's desert hideout. Here Bill kills another of the murderers, but is captured by the remaining bandits, and buried up to his neck in sand. Bill is rescued by Ryan, who marshalls the Mexicans of the settlement to defend themselves against the outlaw band.

Walcott's gang returns and puts the Mexicans to flight. Ryan and Bill are trapped overnight in an abandoned house. In the morning, as Ryan shaves, Bill sees his skeleton medallion – and realises that Ryan was with the murderers that night. Ryan admits to arriving after the killings, and to saving young Bill from the flames.

No matter. Bill is determined to kill all those who induce his red-tinted flashbacks. But Walcott's men attack, and they renew their temporary truce. As a dust storm blows, Walcott's gang is decimated, and Walcott is killed. Ryan turns his back on Bill, refusing to participate in a showdown. Bill fires – but only to kill the last gangster, Cavanagh's bartender. The two men part, no longer enemies, not yet friends.

The film

Though Giulio Petroni directed it, *Death Rides a Horse* feels to me like the work of a different *auteur* – it is Luciano Vincenzoni's film. Vincenzoni had already written one great tale of revenge and shifting allegiances, *For a Few Dollars More*, plus a more complex saga of interpersonal treachery, *The Good, the Bad and the Ugly*. On the latter film, he had been forced to share his credit with writers who contributed little or nothing. This time, story and screenplay credits were Vincenzoni's alone. As it stars Lee Van Cleef as an ageing gunfighter; uses the same red-tinted flashbacks to link avenger and murderers; and revolves around jailbreaks and a bank robbery, *Death Rides a Horse* invites comparison with *For a Few Dollars More*. It survives this. *Death Rides a Horse* is a lighter-weight variant on Vincenzoni's earlier script: unapologetic, entirely successful on its own terms.

The opening scenes, of a downpour at night, followed by murder and rapine, are well done. Even the rape scene, potentially a minefield of bad taste and lousy sexual politics, is reasonably restrained: it justifies the obsessive, monomaniacal nature of Bill, and, in the case of John Phillip Law, it's a good explanation for some powerful non-acting. Lee Van Cleef takes up the heroic slack. The bad guys – including Leone stalwarts Luigi Pistilli and Mario Brega – play their parts appropriately, the Almería landscapes never looked better, and a new location makes its appearance: a freshly built Western town right outside

Tabernas, known then as the *Estudios Decorados* (and today as 'Texas Hoolywod'). '*El Viento*' – where the dust-blown shootout occurs – is the old set of *The Bounty Killer*, on the Llano del Duque in Almería. The art department is inventive (outside a saloon, a poster advertises the display of the head of Joaquin Murietta), and there's a strong Morricone score. Sometimes, *Death Rides a Horse* veers into the territory of a cartoon, or a Saturday morning serial, as when Ryan falls through a well-placed trapdoor into Walcott's torture chamber. The script comments on the actors' traits in a self-aware, postmodern way: Ryan is told he hasn't smiled in 15 years (scowling was Van Cleef's trademark thespian 'schtick'); he tells Walcott he has a mean, villainous face (Luigi Pistilli's striking features secured him countless bad-guy roles); Walcott informs Bill, 'You've got a handsome face,' (Of course he does! He's the young American lead!) and so on. Yet Petroni keeps *Death Rides a Horse* on the straight and narrow trail. Either it was Petroni's call, or the art and costume budget didn't stretch to Vincenzoni's original vision of Cavanagh's saloon:

> Abundance of luxury and bad taste in this spot which is strange for the West. Velvet drapes, flowered upholstery, and baroque mirrors and doors.

> A small stage with a drawn curtain, a chandelier that seems to have belonged to an opera house, game tables, a long bar, few customers, a few women wrapped in large ostrich feather boas; and among the clients two or three brutes in strange, eighteenth-century costumes who hide their pistols poorly beneath their embroidered doublets, and their killers' faces under their powdered wigs.

But all moves smoothly, and well. The script ignores the intervening 15 years. Obviously Ryan has been in jail, and two of his treacherous former partners have become rich. But why are his other partners still hanging around, as lowly bandit henchmen? And what has Bill been doing for the last decade-and-a-half? Shooting at bottles and tin cans? Why does he wait so many years to take off after the family's murderers: is there a minimum legal age for revengers in this state? No matter – for Vincenzoni, one and 15 were prime numbers: one screenwriter, 15 years, 15 thousand dollars, maybe a 15-picture deal with UA... Clearly he was having fun. Vincenzoni refers not only to his own scripts, but some classic Westerns: Raoul Walsh's *Pursued* (the massacre and flashback set-up), *The Magnificent Seven* (the marshalling of the townspeople to defend themselves), *Rio Bravo* (the '*DeGuello*' played by the villains, in anticipation of the heroes' deaths), and *Fistful of Dollars*, with Van Cleef – dressed in a *serape* and leading a mule – walking into the outlaws' lair. There's even a nod to Robert Aldrich's dark nuclear thriller *Kiss Me Deadly* when Ryan traps the hand of his betrayer, Cavanagh (Anthony Dawson), in his desk drawer.

It's interesting to see how Van Cleef departed from the script. Near the end, Vincenzoni had Ryan wax sentimental, telling the younger gunfighter:

> RYAN: I was thinkin' I would have liked to have had a son like you... because I'll probably end up some day with a bullet in my back... and there won't be any son to avenge me.

Now this is a tough nut for any actor to crack. Van Cleef gets through the first three lines as scripted, then drops the fourth line – impossible to say without wincing. Instead, he plays it as if his character's become embarrassed, and throws the speech away with a simple, 'Ah, forget it.' This was Van Cleef's genius.

Petroni's direction is fast-paced, and his action scenes are excellent. For most of the film, he and his cameraman, Carlo Carlini, place their protagonists in the dead centre of the frame, a waste of the magnificent widescreen panorama which Techniscope provided. Compare the widescreen compositions of Leone and Massimo Dallamano in *For a Few Dollars More*: Petroni and Carlini's are more constrained, as if they were framing everything centrally for television, as American features tend to. It's noticeable because when numerous characters are involved – townspeople, or bandits – the compositions take advantage of the 1:2.35 aspect ratio, only to revert to a square-box, middle-of-the-frame aesthetic as soon as the American leads appear. These widescreen moments – featuring mostly extras – may be the work of another director: Giancarlo Santi, who had been Leone's assistant director on *The Good, the Bad and the Ugly*, and who was Petroni's assistant now.

Death Rides a Horse did boffo box office, and Van Cleef made two more Westerns for its producers, *Day of Anger* (1967) and *Beyond the Law* (1968). *Day of Anger* partnered him with Giuliano Gemma in a similar set-up: in one of his frequent 'transformations' Gemma's character goes from town bum to deadly gunfighter, trained by Van Cleef. Inevitably, a showdown ensues. Directed by another of Leone's assistants, Tonino Valerii, it features two fine villainous cameos – by Benito Stefanelli and Al Mulock. Plodding and slack beside *Death Rides a Horse*, it's still better than *Beyond the Law*. Both films suffer from the perceived need to 'pair' Van Cleef with a 'sexy' younger man. The teaming works with John Phillip Law, oddly enough, because Law is so wooden, and so strange. But it falls flat with Gemma and is disastrous in *Beyond the Law*, where Van Cleef is reduced to playing a strike-breaker for an Eastern European mine manager (Antonio Sabato).

1967 was also a year of sequels. The dire team of Vanzi, Klein and Anthony made a follow-up to *A Stranger in Town: A Man, a Horse and a Gun*, aka *The Stranger Returns*. 'Tony Tony', as his fellow actors knew him, was still a pudgy shadow-boxer, devoid of charisma. As a director, Vanzi was equally devoid of skill. And Klein's most profound achievement was still the break-up of The Beatles. Not surprisingly, *The Stranger Returns* is worse than its predecessor. *Run Man Run* was intended by Sergio Sollima and Tomas Milian as the further adventures of Cuchillo Sanchez, peasant hero of *The Big Gundown*. Sequels made by the film's original director are sometimes better than the original (*For a Few Dollars More*, *Mad Max II*), and the first 30 minutes of *Run Man Run* are entirely entertaining, as Cuchillo witnesses gun-fights and the horrors of war, and is fought over by beautiful women. Thereafter, the film collapses into repetition and feeble jokery. The problem is two-fold: script, and cast. Sollima was a talented director,

174

but he wasn't a talented screenwriter: in the absence of Solinas and Donati, Sollima's script just peters out. Meanwhile, where once was Lee Van Cleef, Sollima gives us Donald O'Brien – a cardboardy, unlikeable American-in-black; instead of Walter Barnes, enter a duo of ham actors with bad wigs, pretending to be French. Sollima's hostility to capitalism, and love of the common man, are unchanged, but – as in *Face to Face* – he fails to deliver the exciting action scenes on which a good Western depends.

Bandidos

aka *Crepa tu... Che vivo io*
(Italy/Spain)

Director: Massimo Dallamano   **Producer:** Solly V Bianco   **Screenplay:** Romano Migliorini, Gianbattista Mussetto, Juan Cobos   **Director of Photography:** Emilio Foriscot   **Art Director:** Jaime Perez Cubero   **Costumes:** Carlo Gentili   **Editor:** Gianmaria Messeri   **Assistant Director:** Stefano Rolla, Luigi Perelli   **Music:** Egisto Macchi   **Cast:** Enrico Maria Salerno (*Richard Martin*), Terry Jenkins (*Ricky Shot*), Venantino Veantini (*Billy Kane*), Maria Martin (*Betty Starr*), Marco Guglielmi (*Al Kramer*), Chris Huerta (*Vigonza*), Massimo Sarhielli, Jesus Puente, Antonio Pica

The story

Bandits, led by Billy Kane, attack a train. They kill all the crew and passengers except for a celebrated sharpshooter, Richard Martin. Kane beats Martin – his former mentor – to the draw, and puts him out of business via a bullet in each hand.

Martin becomes the proprietor of a sharpshooting road show. When his protegé, young Ricky Shot, is killed by drunks, Martin insists on fighting them. He's backed up by a tough young stranger, who adopts the 'Ricky Shot' moniker, and role. Martin trains the new Ricky to shoot, while tracking Billy Kane. Vigonza, Billy's former partner in the train robbery, tells Martin he's afraid to go up against Ricky. Kramer, another former gang member, wants to team up with Vigonza, or Martin, or anyone, against Billy. Billy shoots him in the saloon.

Vigonza pays Ricky, who now has a reputation as a gunfighter, to help lay a trap for the gang boss in the bar. But Ricky tips Billy off: Vigonza and his men are all killed. Ricky reveals that he's been unjustly convicted of participating in the train robbery; he asks Billy to hand over one of his gang – to testify as to Ricky's innocence. Billy terrorises his own men – paid by Vigonza to sit the assassination attempt out – kills two, and turns a third over to Ricky.

Betrayed, Richard Martin saws the barrel off a shotgun and lies in wait for Billy Kane at dawn in the dark saloon. But he shoots the wrong man, and loses his nerve when his former pupil challenges him to a straight duel. Billy shoots Martin in the back, and sets off with his surviving henchmen to raid the bank. Ricky learns from saloon girl Betty of Martin's death, and that Billy – like him – was Martin's pupil. He returns to gun down the robbers, and kills Billy after a protracted prowl through the barn.

The film

Bandidos, like the Lee Van Cleef movies just discussed, is a Western in which an old gunfighter teaches a young one his deadly trade. *Bandidos* is the best of these films: the deepest, and the best looking. In its psychological slant it's close to its original prototype, *The Tin Star* (1957) – Anthony Mann's *Noir* Western, in which Henry Fonda taught Tony Perkins to shoot. Its visual aspect incorporates cast and place – these are actors and landscapes we haven't seen before, at least not in Westerns – and some particularly accomplished cinematography.

According to the credits, *Bandidos* was shot by a Spaniard, Emilio Foriscot. But the camera operator, Sergio D'Offizi, says this wasn't so: according to D'Offizi, the director, Massimo Dallamano, lit and shot the entire film. This makes sense. Foriscot seems to have received a 'co-production' camera credit on *Face to Face* as well, even though Rafael Pacheco photographed that film. Dallamano (aka 'Max Dallman') had shot *Fistful* and *For a Few Dollars More* – both unusually well-composed films. *Bandidos* displays, if anything, a higher standard. There's always deep focus, with multiple planes of view. Set-ups often contrast exterior light and interior shadow. The word *bravura* was invented to describe some of these camera moves: dollying the length of a train surrounded by corpses, ending on dead lovers' interlinked hands; tracking along a bar counter behind a sliding bottle; following the hero up a flight of stairs into a dark interior, in mid-gunfight.

Bandidos is the first Italian Western to qualify as a tragedy, in the original sense of the word. Like Hamlet, its hero suffers a fall from high estate. Richard Martin, impeccably dressed, sporting a pencil moustache, is a celebrity sharpshooter. Outgunned and crippled by his former student, Martin seeks revenge. But he does this in the slowest, most humiliating manner possible, running a low-rent medicine show out of a beaten-up wagon, trying to groom young men as surrogate killers. Betrayed by his latest protegé, who has no interest in killing Billy Kane, Martin sinks lower still. He lies in wait with a sawn-off shotgun to ambush Billy – and fails at this, as well. Richard Martin is a good, beefy role – but it's also a tough one, involving a good deal of humiliation and self-abasement. The part was played by Enrico Maria Salerno, a classically trained thespian who'd dubbed Eastwood's voice into Italian in the *Dollars* films. Salerno pulled all the stops out: his portrayal of Martin, beating his broken hands against his adversaries, or the wall, is painful to watch. It's over the top even for a Spaghetti Western. Martin's demise – shot in the back, he sinks, grimacing fiercely, to the floor – is perhaps the longest death-while-clinging-to-the-bar-rail scene ever filmed.

By contrast, the other actors are notably cool. Venantino Venantini is chilling as the handsome killer, Billy Kane. A young American, Terry Jenkins, is fine as Martin's idealised doppelganger, Ricky: good-looking in the same square-jawed way as Venantini – stoic, yet more animated than the doll-like John Phillip Law of *Death Rides a Horse*. Subsidiary bad guys are given names and character traits. There are surprisingly few Spaghetti Western regulars – only Chris Huerta, blue-eyed and baby-faced, playing a particularly mean and classist Mexican bandit, Vigonza. Having invaded a poor peasant's house to use as a hideout, Vigonza enslaves the man, then kills him. (Marco Giusti lists Luigi Pistilli, also from the *Dollars* films, in the cast – but I haven't spotted him.) Just as the cast was unusual, so were the exterior locations, which Dallamano shot not in the familiar desert of Tabernas, but in northern Spain.

This is a film with many good scenes, and two great ones. Both take place in saloons – at Elios Films (the *Django* set), and at the *Dinocitta* location. In the first, the outlaw, Kramer (Marco Guglielmi), visits the bar. Crossing the street, he sees a hearse pass. It's a clear sign, yet he goes through the batwing doors – to find his feared and hated enemy, Billy Kane, waiting for him. Dying from two of Billy's bullets, Kramer terrorises the sheriff, patrons and dancing girls. He becomes obsessed with a dusty oil painting hanging on the wall: *The Death of Sardanapalus*. When he demands to know who Sardanapalus is, the sheriff, whom Kramer has pinned to the stairs, supposes he was an old king.

KRAMER: What'd he want to go killing all those women?

SHERIFF: They say he didn't want to die alone.

KRAMER: You know, he had the right idea... If I'm gonna hell I want some company!

Kramer decides to murder the saloon girls one by one, at which point their brave boss, Betty, intervenes, and Ricky shoots him dead. Word gets back to Vigonza that Ricky is an ace gunfighter, and an enemy of Billy Kane. Vigonza thinks he can hire Ricky to spring a trap on Kane; just as Martin assumes he has trained Ricky to kill Kane. Both are wrong. There are only two constants in *Bandidos*: Richard Martin's desire for revenge against Billy, and the unreliable and shifting loyalties of everyone else. Vigonza's mistaken trust in Ricky leads to the film's second great scene.

In the bar, Vigonza and six of his men set up a crossfire to assassinate Billy. Ricky's part in the plot is to distract Billy, then light a match – this will be the Mexicans' signal to open fire. Ricky and Billy face each other off in an excellent, sexy scene. Acting, dialogue, compositions, editing, music, all are of a high order, working in unison.

RICKY: There are six of 'em. When I light a match they'll shoot ya. There's one sitting by the table. The rest are over there. Vigonza's hiding behind the piano. I can see the tip of his boot.

BILLY: Which end of the keyboard?

RICKY: The one where the high notes are.

BILLY: Can you get one of them?

RICKY: Two...

Chill, off-hand manliness like this enhances any Western, no matter what its nationality. Apart from some strangely unsuccessful day-for-night photography, *Bandidos* shines visually. It has a great art department, and an epic, trumpet-led score by Egisto Macchi. Almost every scene is one of action. Even the weaker scenes entertain, and the film ends with a state-of-the-art showdown-in-a-darkened-warehouse.

Outstanding cinematographers who became great directors are rare: the most notable being perhaps Nic Roeg, who graduated from shooting *Masque of the Red Death* to co-directing – and shooting – *Performance*. I find *Bandidos* as impressive and stimulating an *opera primo* as Roeg's. Yet, after this film, Massimo Dallamano never directed another Western. It was as if, in a Western context, he had only one thing to say. The theme he chose was revenge: obsessive, long-term revenge by an older professional, directed against his student.

What follows is pop psychology, idle speculation. But I'm a director, too, damnit, and this stuff is fun. After two Spaghetti Westerns in which he did spectacular work – establishing the visual conventions of the form – Massimo Dallamano had been dumped by his director. Instead of hiring Dallamano to shoot the final film of the trilogy, Sergio Leone went with a new cinematographer, Tonino Delli Colli, instead. How did Dallamano feel about that? Not good: it never feels good to be dropped from something that you've been a vital part of creating. In such circumstances, the mind broods on betrayal; idle thoughts of revenge may even occur. A year or so after being dumped by Leone, Dallamano directed his first dramatic feature: a Western, visually striking, whose cast, story and locations owed nothing at all to Sergio. *Look at the Western I am capable of*, its director was saying: *With a tenth of Leone's budget, I have made* Bandidos*!*

So what if Emilio Foriscot received the camera credit, for co-pro-duction reasons? What did that matter to Dallamano? Sergio Leone knew who had made *Bandidos* – directed it, lit it, and shot it, too.

A convention is safely established when it's parodied. Someone who dislikes the Spaghetti Western might say it's a parody in itself: but I don't think that's true – any more than *Yojimbo* or *One-Eyed Jacks* are parodies. Films like *Django* and *Requiescant* and *Django Kill* take themselves quite seriously, on their own moral and aesthetic terms. But as the sub-genre grew, and became increasingly popular, 'comic' Spaghetti Westerns were an inevitable part of it. First came the slap-stick Westerns of Franco and Ciccio – Franco Franchi and Ciccio In-grassia – a team of comics who allegedly made 150 different movie parodies during their joint career, including *Two Mafiosi in the Wild West* (1965, Giorgio Simonelli) and *The Handsome, the Ugly and the Stupid* (1967, Giovanni Grimaldi).

These were fairly predictable parodies, enlivened by familiar actors like Fernando Sancho and Mario Brega. But in '67, as the form expand-ed, it became crazier, and more varied, and some truly bizarre hybrid Spaghetti Westerns appeared. Armando Crispino directed a Western version of *Don Giovanni* – *John the Bastard*, starring an English actor, John Richardson. This was an idea with great possibilities (Crispino was one of the screenwriters of *Requiescant*), none of them realised. And how to explain *The Bang-Bang Kid*, an Italian-American co-produc-tion with three directors, American, Italian, and Spanish? Like *¿Quien Sabe?* it was saddled with a voiceover narration: telling of a Western town whose beleaguered inhabitants 'began to think of themselves as peasants or serfs'. Cut to the extras clad in mediaeval costumes; cut to the castle, outside town, where the villain, Bear Bullock, wears a crown and kingly robes. Into this *melange* rides Merryweather T Newbury (Tom Bosley), a travelling salesman from Chicago, seeking to demonstrate his robot gunfighter, CXA 107, aka 'The Bang-Bang Kid'. Many years ago I must have watched *The Bang-Bang Kid*, since I have written two pages of notes about it. Where did I see it? In France, in the cinema? In the US, on late-night TV? As I can't remember anything about it, I conclude it wasn't very good. Another 'comic' Spaghetti Western of the same eccentric school was *Rita of the West*. This film has a bad reputation, even among enthusiastic critics. Let me try and defend *Rita* here.

Rita of the West

aka *Little Rita Nell'west, Rita prendi la colt, Crazy Westerners*
(Italy)

Director: Ferdinando Baldi   **Producer:** Manolo Bolognini   **Screenplay:** Ferdinando Baldi, Franco Rossetti   **Director of Photography:** Enzo Barboni   **Art Director:** Giorgio Giovannini   **Costumes:** Franco Antonelli   **Editor:** Nino Baragli   **Music:** Robby Poitevin   **Cast:** Rita Pavone (*Rita/Jane*), Terence Hill (*Black Star/Texas Joe*), Lucio Dalla (*Fritz*), Teddy Reno (*Sheriff*), Adriano Bellini (*Ringo*), Gordon Mitchell (*Chief Sitting Buffalo*), Fernando Sancho (*Sancho*), Nini Rosso, Gino Pernice (*Tribunal president*), Nina Larker, Enzo Di Natale (*Django*), Franco Gulay (*Lawyer*), Livio Lorenzon (*Outlaw*), Romano Puppo

The story

Little Rita is a famous gunfighter whose mission is to rid the West of gold, which she believes to be the root of all evil. She and her musical friend, Fritz, gun down the James Gang, who are robbing a stagecoach. They take the stolen loot to Chief Sitting Buffalo's camp, in time for hookah smoking and a dance routine. Then the money is added to a mound of gold in a cave – loot which Rita and Sitting Buffalo have acquired, and plan to destroy. But they discover that the boxes are empty, their contents having been stolen by Ringo.

In a dusty, near-deserted town, Ringo confronts a gambler and demands his gold. The gambler and his three men are all killed in the ensuing gunfight. Rita arrives but she and Ringo are so evenly matched that their bullets collide in mid-air. Rita proves a better fistfighter than Ringo. When he tries to shoot her from a distance, with a collapsible carbine, Rita blows him up with a pistol-launched hand grenade.

Rita confronts Django, dragging his coffin. His hands are broken and bloody, so when Rita demands his gold he gives it up. Django lies in wait in a graveyard and attempts to bushwhack Rita. Her bullet-proof vest saves her. When Django insists she remove it, she agrees. He tries to cheat in the ensuing gunfight, and Rita kills him.

Rita meets a handsome man, Black Star, and becomes infatuated with him. She and Fritz are kidnapped by Sancho and his Mexicans, who dance whenever their leader's name is spoken. They're saved by Black Star and Rita's arsenal. Rita takes Black Star to the Indians' camp, and – while she dreams of their wedding – he tries to steal the gold. Rita saves him from execution and Black Star tries to reform: shooting Sancho and two other Mexicans in the back after they rob the bank. Sitting Buffalo and his tribe blow up the mountain, forever burying the gold. As a big dance number takes place in the saloon, Sitting Buffalo tells Rita she must 'return to the void'. Black Star, arriving after she has left, vows to follow her. The last shot is of one cowboy constellation pursuing another, across a cartoon sky.

The film

Bolognini was the producer of *Django*, Franco Rossetti one of its screenwriters. Enzo Barboni was *Django*'s cameraman, Nino Baragli its editor. The male lead was Terence Hill, cast for his resemblance to Franco Nero. And Baldi, the director, was a veteran of violent Spanish and Italian Westerns. If anyone was capable of pulling off a hardcore, portentous Spaghetti Western – something better than Mario Lanfranchi's overblown *Death Sentence* (*Sentenza di morte*) – these were the guys. So why would they make a musical instead? Why not? Rita Pavone was a pop idol with a big fan base in Italy. Naturally, she should be a movie star. And there was an insatiable market for Italian Westerns. Sometimes the worst, or weirdest, ideas become unstoppable.

The result is so odd as to be worth watching – if one is in the mood for something odd. After dispensing a couple of poor pop songs, the two 'cute/funny' characters, Rita and Fritz, are obliged to confront real Spaghetti Western heroes – in the roles of villains – and kill them. Django is Django, wearing Franco Nero's coat and hat, and dragging his familiar coffin. 'Ringo' is Clint Eastwood's character from the *Dollars* films, complete with stubble, *serape*, and cheroot stub. Since Barboni shot and lit *Django*, the Django scenes are livelier – particularly when Django, mortally wounded, expresses his wish to 'die American-style'. As the expiring icon explains, Italian and Japanese movie characters tend to die quickly, whereas in American films the characters make a long speech first. Django then begins to reminisce about his childhood (ironically, the version I've seen cuts before we hear his long, sad tale).

Terence Hill's character is nebulous: he's supposed to be a bad guy who reforms and falls in love with Rita. But his face is largely immobile and one never gets an idea of what he's doing there – other than as a serving of beefcake. There's something artificial about Hill – even given the context of these Spaghetti Westerns. The name was invented by an actors' agent, Giuseppe Perrone, for his client Mario Girotti. But Mario provided only the face and physical accoutrements. The voice of 'Terence Hill' was provided by various other actors, in the dubbing stage. Most Italian actors – serious ones, or those who thought they were serious – would eventually insist on dubbing their own characters. But Girotti never did, and 'Hill' remained this strangely uninteresting, distant, multiple persona.

Rita of the West is interesting because of what it attempts: it tries to be a film with a female protagonist; it tries to be a musical. It succeeds at the first, though the meaning of the last scene is unclear. Is Rita a goddess? Is she an alien? Does Black Star share her stellar stuff? As a musical, it begins terribly, with a dire rock 'n' roll duet by Pavone and Lucio Dalla; improves with the involvement of professional dancers in the Indian camp and the saloon, choreographed by Gino Landi; overall it's a fair attempt at a great idea. The Americans managed this genre-breaking fusion much better: compare *Oklahoma!*, or *Paint Your Wagon*. That *Rita* isn't better is down to the director, I think. Ferdinando Baldi directed many Westerns, but few good ones. With Duccio Tessari or Richard Lester at its helm, *Rita of the West* might have been remarkable, memorable, even amazing. In the hands of Baldi, it hovers around the quality level, and the aspiration, of a Monkees TV episode.

Despite the producer's hopes, *Rita* fared badly. This was apparently due to the news – broken just before the film's release – that Rita Pavone was getting married. The groom was another Italian pop star, Ferruccio Ricordi, who went by the moniker of 'Teddy Reno'. Reno had played another 'cute/funny' role in *Rita*, the nervous sheriff. He was not a strong actor. Nor was his new role, as Rita's husband, well received. Rita's teenage fans deserted her, and boycotted her film. 'As soon as word got out about the wedding, it was all over,' Bolognini recalled. 'I just broke even, thanks to the foreign sales.'

Franco Rossetti directed his first, and only, Western the same year: *Desperado*. This looks like an attempt to repeat what Rossetti thought was *Django*'s formula: extreme violence in a muddy ghost town. The violence – which includes torture, the shooting of a blind man, and the hero kicked and riddled with bullets in a sea of mud – is very entertaining. But Rossetti blows the other important stuff: the casting. Corbucci usually picked solid, interesting actors for his heroes and villains; whereas Rossetti's lead, Andrea Giordana, looks like a teenager in his cynical, tough-guy role. A good *Django* rip-off should have great villains, and here *Desperado* founders too, with mediocre performances all round.

And Corbucci? The co-founder of the Italian Western had completed the excellent *Hellbenders*, gone to Greece to shoot an anti-communist spy thriller, *Death on the Run* (*Bersaglio mobile*), and returned to Rome. He was a little tired of Westerns. Interviewed for the documentary *Westerns Italian Style*, Corbucci allowed a comment on dialogue recording to cascade into a startling revelation:

CORBUCCI: Speech usually in my Westerns isn't important because we use every nationality. French. Mexican. American. It's often better for all the actors to count than to speak. For example, the Frenchman would say, 'Un, deux, trois,' and the American would say, 'One,' that means, 'Yes,' or it could mean anything. It's unimportant. That's why I hate Westerns.

INTERVIEWER: After this, Mr Corbucci, what film will you do?

CORBUCCI: A Western, naturally!

And why shouldn't Corbucci feel a little tired, a tad cynical? His best film, *Django*, had run into trouble with the censors: it was still stuck in Italy, where it was being ripped off by Franco Rossetti and others, not to mention mercilessly parodied – by its co-creators – in *Rita of the West*. The trip to Greece had been a change of scenery. So, when Italian and French producers proposed a Western with Jean-Louis Trintignant, Corbucci insisted that they shoot it in the snow. This was his original plan for *Django* – but, according to Lars Bloch, producer of *Westerns Italian Style*, Corbucci also wanted to go skiing. So he chose locations surrounding the exclusive ski resort of Cortina, in Northern Italy.

Against his instincts, Corbucci was about to make another Western: to be shot quickly, as these films were, and finished by the end of the year. The budget didn't stretch to building a Western town in the Dolomites – this would be Elios Films, covered in shaving foam – but there was money for a top-notch international cast, a good crew, and ski lodges at Cortina. When Trintignant confided that he couldn't speak English, Corbucci remembered an idea Marcello Mastroianni had shared with him.

'I'd like to make a Western, but I don't speak English,' the Italian actor had said, 'so why not make a story about a *mute pistolero*?' At the close of 1967, Corbucci decided to recycle Mastroianni's idea.[17]

17 *I have relied on Howard Hughes' chronology of Corbucci's films. His source is a series called* The Glittering Images: Westerns all'italiana, Book 1 - The Specialists, *which gives* The Big Silence *an Italian release date of Christmas 1967. Marco Giusti confirms that* The Big Silence *was a 1967 production, but thinks of it as a 1968 film when he writes, '1968's Westerns are disturbing, visionary. This is the richest and most beautiful moment of the genre.'*

The Big Silence

aka *Il grande silenzio, Le grand silence, The Great Silence, Levend ov dood*
(Italy/France)

Director: Sergio Corbucci   **Producer:** Atilio Riccio for Adelphia/Les Films Corona   **Screenplay:** Sergio Corbucci, Bruno Corbucci, Vittoriano Petrilli, Mario Amendola   **Director of Photography:** Silvano Ippoliti

Art Director: Riccardo Domenici   **Costumes:** Enrico Job   **Editor:** Amedeo Salfa   **Assistant Director:** Filiberto Fiaschi   **Music:** Ennio Morricone   **Cast:** Jean-Louis Trintignant (*Silence*), Klaus Kinski (*Tigrero/ Loco*), Frank Wolff (*Sheriff Burnett*), Vonetta McGee (*Pauline*), Luigi Pistilli (*Policutt*), Mario Brega (*Martin*), Carlo D'Angelo (*Governor*), Marisa Merlini (*Regina*), Maria Mizar (*Miguel's mother*), Raf Baldassare (*Schultz*), Bruno Corazzari (*Charley*), Spartaco Conversi (*Walter*), Remo De Angelis (*Fake Sheriff*)

The story

In the mountains of Utah, a mute bounty hunter, Silence, kills four men lying in ambush for him and shoots the thumbs off a fifth. A group of impoverished types appear from the snowy wastes and kill the fifth man; their leader, Walter, pays Silence and thanks him for their delivery.

At the Governor's mansion, the Governor dispatches a cynical but kindly sheriff, Burnett, to bring order to the area around Snow Hill. If the voters pass an amnesty bill, the Governor insists there will be no more killing of the dispossessed or the impoverished. Meanwhile, bounty killers, Tigrero and Charley, kill two outlaws who have attempted to return to town. On the stage to Snow Hill, Burnett meets Silence and Tigrero, who is transporting the corpses to town for the rewards. Tigrero, always polite and chatty, remarks that it's their patriotic duty to exterminate the renegades. Silence accepts a horse from a dead man's mother, in return for killing Charley. This is easy, because Charley is readily provoked.

Tigrero shoots James Middleton, another accused outlaw. Middleton's widow, Pauline, buries his body and promises Silence $1,000 to kill Tigrero. The local banker and justice of the peace, Policutt, offers Pauline $1,000, but only in return for sex. Pauline refuses, and offers Silence her body instead. Silence immediately appears in the saloon, where he attempts to goad Tigrero into a gunfight. But Tigrero won't draw his gun. Instead he insists on a fistfight – one which he is likely to win, till Silence clubs him with a log. Tigrero's men draw on Silence, who kills them all. Sheriff Burnett intervenes and arrests Tigrero.

Pauline tends to Silence's wounds, and they make love. Flashbacks reveal that Silence's parents were killed by bounty hunters – including

Policutt – when he was a kid: one of these cut the boy's throat to silence him. As a young man, Silence tracked down the killers and killed them, shooting off Policutt's thumb. Next day, Policutt attempts to bail Tigrero out; Burnett says he's going to take Tigrero to the Tonopah jail. On the trail, the sheriff invites the homeless outcasts to return to Snow Hill for food and shelter. But he is bushwhacked by Tigrero, who rallies his fellow bounty killers to attack Snow Hill.

Policutt tries to rape Pauline; his sidekick Martin sticks Silence's hand in a red-hot brazier. Silence, belatedly, kills them both.

Tigrero arrives looking for Silence. He takes the 'bandits' hostage, and shoots Regina, the saloon madam who has opposed him and Policutt. Tigrero threatens to murder all his hostages. Pauline proposes that, since Silence is crippled, they should both run away. But Silence insists on returning for his final showdown with Tigrero at the saloon.

Silence, Pauline and the hostages are all killed. Leaving town next morning, Tigrero steals Silence's pistol from his corpse.

The film

The Big Silence is Corbucci's tightest, most relentless Western; his best and his bleakest. It's shot in his trademark messy, over-edited, jerky-zoom style, and its telephoto 'close-ups' are frequently out of focus. Yet it is incredibly beautiful. Corbucci was never particularly interested in the deserts of Almería: it was here, in the Dolomites, that he found his Monument Valley. There are striking scenes of men riding through the snow, while the interior illumination – especially the dark scenes at the end – is very fine. Many shots are filtered by smoke, or falling snow, or windows. Indeed, there are so many rippling images through glass that the film at times resembles a ship inside a bottle, or a snowscene – fair metaphors for the enclosed, cruel world herein displayed. The cameraman was Silvio Ippoliti, whose work on *Navajo Joe* was average, at best. Some unique chemistry was at work to make *The Big Silence* special, to make their strategy of *shooting through things* work at last: the chemistry started with a lean, tight script by Corbucci and his colleagues, and the director's refusal to deviate from it.

There are no subplots, no 'cute/funny' characters. The sheriff (Frank Wolff) and Regina (Marisa Merlini) are bearable because they have a dark sense of humour, and a moral sense. The English-dubbed version suggests that the 'bandits' led by Walter (Spartaco Conversi) are religious outcasts: in the first scene he declares, 'The new Governor will declare an amnesty. And we'll be able to think as we like.' And Tigrero, in the English dialogue, asks, 'What if one of them had his day in court and got acquitted? Then they'd all be using the courts to spread... whachamacallit!' None of this is in the Italian dialogue. Perhaps it's the work of Lewis Cianelli, meant to suggest that these Utah outlaws are Mormons. If so, Corbucci ignored the religious angle. Instead, *The Big Silence* is the purest distillation of the corrupt, capitalist West yet committed to film. Only Robert Altman's *McCabe & Mrs Miller* (1971) portrayed the gangster West this well. Both films, interestingly, depict snowbound communities; both are as ironic as they are pessimistic. Policutt hopes Sheriff Burnett will defer to him, as he's not only a banker and storekeeper, but a justice of the peace. But Burnett has never heard of him. There are no Confederate ideologues raising millions to resurrect the South here, no trains bringing in a million dollars' worth of gold. Instead, there's just one small, mean, snowbound town – run by a bitter crook, desperate to exterminate the people he's impoverished.

Against this grubby, enclosed, frozen backdrop, Silence and Tigrero are beings of a different order. Silence appears like an angel, whenever he's needed. He only kills bounty killers, only draws his gun in self-defence. But he still gets paid, in money, horses or sex. As another sheriff remarks, 'It's a pretty good way to kill someone. The law can do nothing about it.'

Tigrero seems more like a devil than an angel of light. Yet how different are they? Tigrero is a killer for money, but so is Silence. He can control his temper; unlike the stupider outlaws who surround him, he has no intention of being provoked into a 'fair' fight. He's a little guy, smaller than Silence, but surprisingly tough. In one-on-one fisticuffs, this 'Little Tiger' looks set to eradicate his opponent, till Silence whacks him with a log. Silence may be the champion of widows and bereaved mothers, but he doesn't play fair either. He just operates according to a strategy which works for him, in this Corbucci world. As killers,

Silence and Tigrero are evenly matched. When Silence abandons the cynical rules they live by, when he becomes a hero facing impossible odds, he's doomed to die.

Such heroics had worked for Django, and for Minnesota Clay, both of whom survived. But no longer. Corbucci's widow, Nori, told Katsumi Ishikuma that her husband had the deaths of Che Guevara and Malcolm X in mind when he conceived *The Big Silence*. Malcolm was assassinated on 21 February 1965; Che captured and killed on 8 October 1967. For the radical, for the revolutionary, both deaths were terrible news. You could only take on the powerful and the wicked for a short while, it seemed, before they crushed you. Whatever set of rules you played by, in the end you lost. What is most marvellous about *The Big Silence* – more so than the fine script, or the superb images – is the way the two main performers communicate this. Tigrero ('Loco' he's called in the English version, but he isn't mad) is Klaus Kinski's finest role in any Western. Polite, patient, always laughing to himself at the absurdity of it all, he keeps a little book, wets his pencil and adds up his tally of souls. This is great acting – as is the work of Jean-Louis Trintignant, who has the more difficult role. Unable to speak, Trintignant has to convey everything via action or expression. It's a near-impossible assignment. Many an actor – Terence Hill, John Phillip Law, Franco Nero – would have seemed doll-like, robotic, in the role. Trintignant later said that Silence was 'his favourite part'. He pulls it off *flawlessly*. His character's moral quandary, and decision to sacrifice himself, are perfectly conveyed.

The Big Silence's pessimism was born in a decade where young and inspirational leaders were regularly snuffed out by hidden gunmen 'acting alone'. Corbucci felt the pain of such killings, yet he professed to scorn the resignation which his hero, Silence, showed. 'It was right that Kinski won,' he said in conversation with Duccio Tessari, on RAI. 'He was braver, he shot straighter, he kept his cool.' But this doesn't sound genuine to me: Tigrero isn't braver or better than Silence. He's a cheat and a liar, and his henchmen shoot the hero through the saloon window, in a low-down, cowardly ambush. It's the moral baseness of Tigrero and his ilk, and the decency and cool of Silence, that make the ending so shocking; it makes *The Big Silence* a great film.

The message of *The Big Silence*, which Corbucci ignored on the RAI talk show, but which he really knew, is that *sometimes, even though you know you'll fail, you still do the right thing.* Classical drama may have dealt in tragedy, but the cinema, for the most part, doesn't. Movies are capitalism's first 100 per cent-owned art form, and capitalism isn't about sacrifice or doing without or losing; it's about expanding, winning, and kicking ass. Even Christianity, for all its passion and suffering, doesn't involve such a total sacrifice as the one Corbucci depicts: Jesus dies but is reborn within a couple of days, and goes to sit at Dad's right hand, forever. Silence faces his death with no expectation of anything, and gets nothing. It's an atheist's sacrifice – done regardless of the consequences, without anticipation of reward. As Corbucci saw so clearly, back in 1967, this was the sacrifice of Che – murdered just before filming began. And it was Malcolm's sacrifice, as well.

Both men walked into the lion's den, knowing they would most likely die, knowing they would not see their dreams realised, doing it anyway, because it was the right thing. *The Big Silence* depicts nobility and heroism of a high and spiritual order. Sure, Silence is killed. He loses the game. And in so doing, he becomes the *noblest* hero of any Western film since *Shane*.

Because, all else being equal, in any other movie, Silence could have killed Tigrero and his men. It's his affair with Pauline that pits him against Policutt, that gets his hand stuck in a brazier, that causes him to become a real hero, and seals his fate.

Fine material brought out the best in everyone involved. The score is one of Morricone's finest: light, restrained, affecting, entirely different from his other Western work. The performances of Vonetta McGee as Pauline, Luigi Pistilli as Policutt, and Mario Brega as Martin, are excellent. And the costumes – by Enrico Job – are quite unexpected: showing considerable hippy influence in the many shawls, stitched leather jackets, and ankle-length fur coats.

The Big Silence presents three powerful women characters: Miguel's mother, who contracts Silence to avenge her son, Pauline, and Regina. Though they don't wrestle in mud, they're still 'Corbucci' women: all three seek justice via the pistol; two of them die with gun in hand. What little humour there is, is actually funny – primarily the scene where Silence provokes Tigrero's colleague, Charley, by leaving the bar door open and letting the wind blow in. Charley (Bruno Corazzari) is tearing apart a chicken while explaining, to anyone who will listen, how 'I keep eating and eating, and still I'm miserable'. Seconds later he notices the draught, reaches for his pistol, and is dead. Blood seeps into the barroom floor, just as it does into the snow. Given such marketable elements – the violence, the action, the ironic humour – and the top-notch cast, *The Big Silence* should have been Corbucci's breakthrough film: the one which gained him an international reputation – as *Django* might have, had it not fallen beneath the censors' knives.

But *The Big Silence* did not do well. It would be 30 years before it appeared, in the home-video market, in England or the United States. This time, it wasn't the censor who wrecked its chances: it was an American studio.

Somehow, during the making of *The Big Silence*, 20th Century Fox became involved. This was potentially good news. Vincenzoni's relationship with UA had resulted in half a dozen Italian Westerns – including Leone's films – breaking into the American market. In theory, studio participation guarantees an American release and more lucrative foreign sales. In fact, this is not always so. The studio boss, Daryl F Zanuck, took against the picture: according to Corbucci, he swallowed his cigarette while watching it. Zanuck wanted an alternative ending, to be used in territories where the pessimistic conclusion 'wouldn't play'. Corbucci, ever cynical and efficient, had already shot one: the sheriff gallops into town to rescue Silence and the farmers, Pauline also gets in on the gunplay, and Silence shoots Tigrero in the saloon.[18] Silence shows up with a metal glove apparently filched from a suit of armour. He's thus able to deflect bullets and use his burned gun hand. Where did the glove come from? A suit of armour doesn't appear in the film. Is it a reference to *Fistful of Dollars*, where the Rojos shoot holes in a suit of armour and Joe wears a bullet-proof metal breastplate? Presumably Corbucci didn't give a damn about the alternate ending. Hadn't the Americans re-cut *Minnesota Clay* to make it appear that Clay was killed? Surely they would get the infinitely darker, stronger, deeper *Silence*... right?

18 *The picture negative for this strange scene has happily been preserved, though the sound is lost – it can be seen, mute, on the Fantoma Region 1 DVD, titled* The Great Silence. *This is a better-looking, more complete version of the film than the Imagica Region 2 DVD.*

Clint Eastwood was in Italy in 1967, doing publicity duties for the *Dollars* films. So it's possible he saw *The Big Silence* when it opened in December. Certainly the distributors thought he had. In 1973, while working in Paris, I visited the distributor of *Le Grand Silence*. This company had ties to 20th Century Fox. I asked its manager if he thought the film would ever be shown in Britain or the United States. He told me that the studio was planning to do an English-language remake, starring Clint Eastwood. This – not the film censor – was the reason Corbucci's masterpiece was being withheld.

Did Eastwood really want to remake *The Big Silence*? Is this why Fox became involved: to secure the property for their rising star? It's possible. But the studio never did that remake. Instead, they made a similar-looking, snowbound Western called *Joe Kidd* (1972). Its hero – played by Clint Eastwood – carries a Mauser Bolo automatic pistol, identical to Jean-Louis Trintignant's. When *Joe Kidd* flopped, this may have increased the pressure within the studio to suppress Corbucci's film.

Since *The Big Silence* is probably the best of all Spaghetti Westerns, this was something of a pity – especially as Corbucci had tried so hard to stretch himself, including not only a pessimistic ending but a romantic love scene, between Trintignant and McGee. Talking about the film a few years later, Corbucci recalled Luis Buñuel:

I am opposed to the happy ending. Remember the end of *The Big Silence*! ... People don't go to the cinema to see love scenes. Buñuel was right when he said the most embarrassing thing, for a filmmaker, is to point the camera at a couple kissing. Nothing is more banal than a kiss. Generally you can't have love scenes in stories which are action-based – though in *The Big Silence* I shot quite a beautiful love scene between a black woman and a mute. There was something very beautiful and very morbid about it. This was the only love scene I ever included in a film of this genre, where the women are generally bizarre.

It sounds as if Corbucci was proud of *The Big Silence*. And well he should have been. It's a great work, a great Spaghetti Western, a great Western, a classic of transgressive cinema. Do any films end so bleakly as this one? Other Italian Westerns would end with the hero killed by bounty hunters: *Escondido* (Franco Giraldi, 1967, released in 1968),

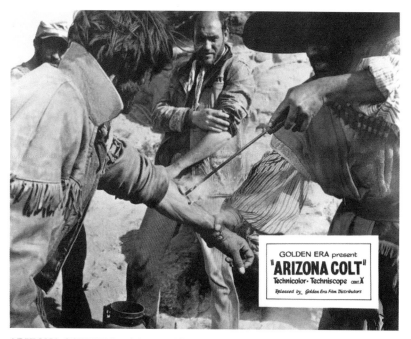

ARIZONA COLT El Gordo's new Sidewinders are tagged.

THE BIG SILENCE Two Bad Men: Klaus Kinski as Loco, Luigi Pistilli as Policutt.

DJANGO Unhappy couple: Loredana Nusciak as Maria, Franco Nero as Django.

CEMETERY WITHOUT CROSSES Jean Mondaroux' remarkable ghost town.

FOR A FEW DOLLARS MORE Gian Maria Volonte as El Indio, archetypal 'Mexican' villain.

FOR A FEW DOLLARS MORE Peter Lee Lawrence and Rosemary Dexter: she plays the Colonel's sister, but who is he?

FOR A FEW DOLLARS MORE Lee Van Cleef as Colonel Mortimer, prototypical gringo techno–bounty-killer.

FISTFUL OF DOLLARS Last Supper at the Rojos'.

THE GOOD, THE BAD AND THE UGLY The Civil War visits Carlo Simi's 'El Paso' set.

The same set, wrecked by a storm a decade later. Rebuilt and paved over, it's now 'Mini Hollywood'.

¿QUIEN SABE? Crucifixion on the tracks.

JOHNNY HAMLET Gilbert Roland: great actor, real Mexican!

ONCE UPON A TIME IN THE WEST In his element, Sergio Leone directs
Claudia Cardinale and Charles Bronson.

ONCE UPON A TIME IN THE WEST In a pickle, Henry Fonda and Bronson
deliver the daftest Western dialogue ever written.

SABATA Stengel, ultimate grandee-villain (Franco Ressel), meets Sabata (Lee Van Cleef) - suicide bomber and ghost.

TODAY IT'S ME... TOMORROW YOU! Brett Halsey and Tatsuya Nakadai: showdown between *Yojimbo* and the Italian West.

is a good, dark, pessimistic story whose outlaw hero – played by Alex Cord – receives an amnesty from the governor, and is immediately gunned down; Robert Woods, in *El Puro* (1969, Edoardo Mulgaria), meets a similar fate. These are good films, but they lack the density, the intensity of Corbucci's masterpiece. *The Big Silence* is a unique work of art: it should have confirmed Corbucci's reputation, as a talent equal to Sergio Leone.

But no one saw it. The Italian opening – Christmas, 1967 – was inauspicious: a film given a Christmas opening is one the distributor wants to get off his hands. *The Big Silence* did badly in Italy, better in France, and excellently in Germany. Beyond that... nothing. 20th Century Fox sat on it, promoting instead their pallid imitation, *Joe Kidd*. While mediocre Corbucci movies like *Minnesota Clay* and *Johnny Oro* played in the US, *The Big Silence* remained invisible.

Corbucci had made a great film – another great film, better than *Django*. Again, it was ignored. Is this why, hereafter, he became so cynical, so dismissive of his own work; is it why, by the 1970s, he seemed tired, his features second-rate? Corbucci had striven to be original, to try some radical new things. He had succeeded, quite remarkably. Now his two great Westerns were being suppressed, for stupid reasons, while his bad ones were widely seen.

By the end of 1967, the Spaghetti Western was both an established, commercial phenomenon, and a creative tornado with no clear direction, nor visible end in sight. Revenge plots tended to predominate – or to be more successful at the box office. The primary villain was no longer the Mexican *bandido* (though there was still plenty of work for Fernando Sancho), but a white businessman – usually a saloon owner, or a banker. Heroes still tended to be white men, but there was a growing minority of darker-skinned protagonists; and even women heroes, and heroes who didn't win. Tomas Milian was patenting the role of the heroic, revolutionary Mexican. And any jail was likely to contain the soulful Jose Torres, best friend of the hero, unjustly incarcerated.

1968

One can forgive the *Maestro*, Ford, for not having seen any Spaghetti Westerns – born in 1895, the great American director was 74 when he gave this interview. Burt Kennedy's hypocrisy, on the other hand, is appalling – within a year, he was himself directing a mediocre Spaghetti Western, *The Deserter*; and, in 1970, he distinguished himself with a rape-themed, British Spaghetti rip-off, *Hannie Caulder*.

But in 1968, Kennedy was stating the party line on Italian Westerns: that there was something inherently wrong with them, and, implicitly, with the people who acted in them or made them. Notwithstanding the popularity of *The Good, the Bad and the Ugly* or *For a Few Dollars More*, or the fact that reputable Americans such as Joseph Cotten, Eli Wallach, Woody Strode, Robert Ryan and Orson Welles, starred in them. No matter how much money they made, or who appeared in them, Italian Westerns were judged entirely bad by American filmmakers and by the American critical fraternity – and thus by their English colleagues who, then as now, rarely disagreed.

French critics had already picked up on the Italian Western as something of artistic and cultural importance. In English-language publications, a fistful of writers expressed enthusiasm for the medium: David Austen and David McGillivray, in *films & filming*, Mike Wallington and Christopher Frayling in *Cinema*, and Ernest Callenbach in *The Velvet Light Trap*.

And though most English-speaking critics still loathed them, the public and the studio/distributors were more enthusiastic. Sergio Leone was regarded as one of the most interesting and bankable new directors: hence the many exciting rumours as to his next project (that remake of *Gone with the Wind? Journey to the End of the Night, enfin?*). But success, as good tales so often tell us, is a double-edged sword. At the height of his powers, viewed as the top director of action Westerns, Leone wanted to be thought of as something more. Like certain other makers of popular spectacles, he aspired to be considered an intellectual, an *auteur* of more than oaters. Unlike Corbucci, he retained his fanatical enthusiasm for cowboy films. Pushed by American studio backers – Paramount, this time – for more of the same, Leone decided to make something quite different. Working with two new writers – Argento and Bertolucci – and Sergio Sollima's collaborator, Sergio Donati, he crafted a long, slow, self-consciously significant, self-important, *art Western*.

Leone aimed to succeed where Brando had failed with *One-Eyed Jacks*.

Once Upon a Time in the West

aka *C'era una volta il west, Il était une fois dans l'ouest*
(Italy/Spain/USA)

Director: Sergio Leone   **Producer:** Fulvio Morsella   **Executive Producer:** Bino Cocogna   **Screenplay:** Sergio Leone, Sergio Donati **Story:** Dario Argento, Bernardo Bertolucci, Sergio Leone   **Director of Photography:** Tonino Delli Colli   **Art Director, Costumes:** Carlo Simi   **Editor:** Nino Baragli   **Assistant Director:** Giancarlo Santi   **Music:** Ennio Morricone   **Cast:** Henry Fonda (*Frank*), Claudia Cardinale (*Jill McBain*), Jason Robards (*Cheyenne*), Charles Bronson (*Harmonica*), Frank Wolff (*McBain*), Gabriele Ferzetti (*Morton*), Keenan Wynn (*Sheriff*), Paolo Stoppa (*Sam*), Marco Zuanelli (*Wobbles*), Lionel Stander (*Barman*), Jack

Elam (*Snakey*), Woody Strode (*Stony*), John Frederick (*Member of Frank's gang*), Enzio Stantianello (*Timmy*), Al Mulock (*Knuckles*), Aldo Sambrell, Spartaco Conversi, Benito Stefanelli

The story

Three gunfighters wait at a lonely railroad station. They've been sent by Frank to meet a man with a harmonica. They try to shoot him; he shoots them. At a lonely farmhouse in the desert, the McBain family, preparing for a wedding party, are massacred by Frank and his gang. Jill McBain arrives by train in the local settlement, Flagstone, and hires a driver to take her to her husband's ranch. In a *posada* en route, she meets the man with the harmonica, and an escaped outlaw, Cheyenne. She arrives at the farmhouse in time for her family's funeral. A scrap of clothing found at the farm convinces the sheriff and his men that Cheyenne is the killer. A posse takes off after him; Jill remains, and searches the farmhouse – trying to find an explanation for the massacre.

Next morning, Cheyenne visits Jill, and protests his innocence. After he leaves, Harmonica shows up and tears up Jill's dress. Two more of Frank's men attack the ranch; he kills them. In town, Jill insists that Wobbles, Frank's henchman, get a message to Frank. Harmonica follows Wobbles to a private train. Here, Frank and his partner, Morton, a railroad magnate, hold court. Frank takes Harmonica prisoner, kills Wobbles, and rides off to deal with the McBain widow himself. Cheyenne, who has hidden aboard the train, rescues Harmonica.

In Flagstone, Jill takes delivery of a load of lumber and tools: her late husband apparently planned to build a railroad station on their property. Frank kidnaps Jill, and humiliates his partner, Morton. Harmonica tells Cheyenne he has seen documents which will make McBain's property, Sweetwater, hugely valuable if the station is built by the time the railroad arrives. The outlaws set about building the station. But Frank convinces Jill to sell the property to him at auction: his men rig the bidding, only to be outbid by Harmonica, offering Cheyenne – for whom there is a $5,000 reward – as surety.

Aboard the train, Morton bribes some of Frank's men to kill him. They attempt to assassinate their boss on the streets of Flagstone; he's saved by Harmonica's intervention. Frank finds the rest of his gang, and Cheyenne's, dead in and around the private train: they have shot each other in an attempt to spring Cheyenne. Morton, who dreamed of seeing the Pacific Ocean, dies in a ditch beside the tracks. Frank returns to McBain's, to face Harmonica, and learn why he's been pursuing him. He loses the gunfight, and in a final flashback remembers who Harmonica is: the younger brother of a man he murdered, years ago. Cheyenne and Harmonica say goodbye to Jill, and ride out. Cheyenne dies just out of sight of the McBain ranch, gut-shot by Morton during his escape. Harmonica carries his body into the hills.

The film

As befits an art Western, the film is the designer's triumph: it was, I think, the high point of Carlo Simi's illustrious career. Never, before or after, did he create so much, so quickly. Leone had been on a location scout to the United States in 1967. He proclaimed himself underwhelmed: there were too many freeways, too many visible power lines, he said. So he would shoot the majority of his film in Spain. But this time there was to be no recycling of old Zorro sets. At La Calahora, an entire town, with railroad station and stockyards, was built. In Monument Valley, USA, Simi raised an inn and a hanging arch. And, near Tabernas, he built a huge ranch house – a Swiss chalet in the desert – using logs left over from Orson Welles's production, *Chimes at Midnight*.

The symbolism of this is important. The McBain house is completely out of place, out of proportion. Where, in a desert like this, did McBain get the wood? A real farmhouse, or ranch house, would have been one storey high, sunk in the earth, covered in sod. And what is McBain's business here? Is he a rancher – if so, where are his cows? If he's a farmer, what are his crops? McBain is a fantasy figure: a professional frontiersman, making a living out of nothing, with a hostile desert, full of killers, all around. So his house *has to be impressive*. It must stand out, like *2001*'s monolith: one lone, valiant redoubt of humanity, in a hostile land. The film's last big location is the railhead, where the train reaches the ranch. Frame buildings are going up, hundreds of extras are working on the rails. And Simi peppers the desert landscape with wooden warehouses, or barns, or locomotive sheds

– which, in their unnatural size and shape, resemble McBain's chalet. McBain may be dead, but his house, in Simi's grand design, is multiplying. Civilisation (or, at least, the buzzing, smoking helltown of the railhead) has arrived.

Construction on a big scale enabled a new type of filmmaking. Gone was the old strategy of 'shoot 'em going through the door, and film the interiors at Elios'. These were all sets with practical interiors. We see the life of the town through the saloon doors; the desert, and then the railroad workers, through McBain's windows; the band of outlaws beyond the train. The only studio work was the *posada* interior, the bedroom scenes, and some of the train interiors (those with obvious rear projection outside the windows).

Simi goes to town on Morton's Pullman car, with its elaborate dressing and furnishing, and its retractable, grippable gantry – for the crippled magnate to haul himself around. Frank and Morton are not much different from the bad guys of *In a Colt's Shadow*: two more killers with refined tastes and aristocratic airs. But Spaghetti Western grandees and bankers had previously been rooted in their mansions or their townhouses: wicked but static. The private train, conceived by Leone and his co-writers, executed by Simi, freed the villains and – by making them mobile – extended their evil range.

Much has been written about *Once Upon a Time in the West* as a compendium of references to other Westerns. Frayling, Hughes, and others discuss the film's many references to other Westerns, including *The Searchers*, *High Noon*, *The Iron Horse*, and even Tinto Brass's *Yankee* (1966). The film is extremely allusive, and most of its allusions are to American films, but there is one very specific to the Italian cinema, which I think has been ignored. It's a reference to Fellini's *8½*, in which the hero, played by Marcello Mastroianni, goes to the railway station to meet a train. The person he's waiting for hasn't shown up, he thinks – but then the train pulls out, revealing Claudia Cardinale awaiting him, on the far side of the tracks. It's a striking moment in a famous Italian film, and it's hard to imagine Leone wasn't thinking of it when he staged Charles Bronson's arrival.

But, beyond its many allusions, *Once Upon a Time in the West* is uniquely original and ambitious. What he'd toyed with in the past, Leone made concrete now: a vision of men like gods. In the *Dollars* films, the heroes were compared to children, playing kids' games. But now Leone had the cast he wanted, the actors who'd previously rejected him: Henry Fonda, a movie god himself, star of *Fort Apache* and *My Darling Clementine*; Charles Bronson, epitome of taciturnity; Jason Robards, the, uh, proper actor, from New York; Claudia Cardinale, goddess and icon in her own right. This cast could play gods. Not only could they wear that pretentious mantle: for the most part, they wore it well.

No wonder Leone wanted Wallach, Van Cleef and Eastwood to play the killers waiting for the train. To establish them in tight close-ups (as he does Jack Elam, and Woody Strode, and Al Mulock), with all the history of the three previous films, and then to kill them! It's a great director's joke; it also says, *I'm breaking with what I've done before – this film will be different*. Van Cleef told me he was willing to make the guest appearance: Eastwood, more protective of his image, wasn't.

Tonino Delli Colli's cinematography contributes to the Olympian feel. Visually the film is on a par with John Ford's Westerns – especially the colour ones, *The Searchers* and *She Wore a Yellow Ribbon*. It's one of the most beautiful Westerns ever made. Many images – a landscape, a big vista of the town, a dark interior, Claudia Cardinale's face in a mirror, long-coated, dusty men – are breathtaking. Much of the action is bathed in mythic, golden light. The wide shots are generally striking, but Leone and Delli Colli play their compositions 'safe' in medium and close shots – usually placing the character at the dead centre of the frame, in the manner of Petroni in *Death Rides a Horse*. This is not the way Kurosawa composed *Yojimbo*. Since both *Death Rides a Horse* and *Once Upon a Time in the West* were made with American money, one wonders if conservative framing, with an eye to US TV broadcast, was part of the deal.

The other great, epic aspect of *Once Upon a Time in the West* is, of course, the music. For the first time, Morricone delivered a score in which each principal character has his or her theme. Jill's music is appropriately lush and orchestral; Cheyenne is accompanied by a hopalong banjo; Harmonica, well, he gets the harmonica, usually segueing into Frank's big guitar murder theme; and Morton receives strings and piano. It works extremely well. It's a diffferent approach from his early

Leone scores, in which a variety of thrilling music was applied almost haphazardly to thrilling scenes. It isn't necessarily better, but it's quite professional, and different. Leone often remarked, in interviews, that he got the best of Morricone's scores, and that Corbucci and co received the music he rejected. I don't think that was always so: Morricone's music for *The Big Silence* is different from all his other Western work, and perhaps his best score of all. But there was certainly a rare affinity between Leone and Morricone, and their collaboration was at its high point here.

Despite these rich, complex creative elements, *Once Upon a Time in the West* is, at heart, a simple film. And this is due to the script.

At the time, several critics remarked that this is the story of many an old Western, about land over which the railroad must pass, and who owns it. Such films invariably feature a straight-shooting hero, a widow woman, and a gang of bad guys, working for the Santa Fe Ring. This is the stuff of an AC Lyles two-reeler, or a TV episode: to be made into a feature, it would usually require various subplots, and subsidiary characters. Consider another old-fashioned premise, the wagon train. When Ford made *Wagonmaster*, he filled it with supporting characters, all involved in interrelated subplots. There are two cowboys, one cool, the other goofy, hired to guide a Mormon wagon train through dangerous country. There's a foul-mouthed Mormon leader and several other Mormon characters. There's the hoochie-coochie show of Dr A Loxely-Hall, employing two men and two women, one of them drop-dead gorgeous. There's a rough-riding sheriff. And there's a gang of five outlaws, four of whom have personalities and names. In the first two reels of *Wagonmaster*, we're introduced to 13 different characters, all of whom participate in the action for the duration of the film. And the film is only 86 minutes long.

Leone takes things entirely in the opposite direction. *Once Upon a Time in the West*, in its longest version, lasts 167 minutes. Only five characters participate in the principal action: Jill, the widow; Harmonica, the revenger; Cheyenne, the outlaw; and Frank and Morton, the bad guys. A sheriff, played by Keenan Wynn, appears in a couple of scenes. An Italian character actor, Paolo Stoppa, has the nothing part of Sam, a wagon driver. Lionel Stander appears once, as a saloon keeper. Frank Wolff's character, McBain, has one scene, and is killed. Some familiar supporting actors, including Strode, Elam, Mulock, Stefanelli, Conversi, and Sambrell look mighty fine in their long coats (borrowed by Simi from Western Costume in Los Angeles!). But none of them has a name, nor much to do, other than look tough, then die.

So it's left to the five main actors to carry a very long, slow-moving picture, most of whose spartan dialogue is about coffee, or heroism, or railroad land grants. A great film depends on great actors. So how do they do? Very well indeed, for the most part. Cardinale is perfect, though little is asked of her beyond strength and beauty. Henry Fonda showed up in Rome with a false moustache and brown contact lenses, determined to make a break with his familiar, blue-eyed image. Leone persuaded him to drop the lenses and the 'tash: it was, of course, that granite-hewn, steel-eyed look which he'd always wanted. And Fonda could play an excellent villain: remember his ambitious, racist army officer in *Fort Apache*. Now, at last, the symbol of American goodness and purity – *Young Mister Lincoln* – was playing a hired assassin, child-murderer, kidnapper and rapist, and doing it excellently. Fonda is so strong that he manages to overshadow Gabriele Ferzetti, a fine actor in his own right. And Bronson is spot-on as the taciturn revenger. Amazingly, Paramount didn't want him at first, and Leone approached James Coburn (who turned the part down), and also considered Terence Stamp, Rock Hudson and Warren Beatty for the revenger. It's hard to imagine that, now.

My only doubt is about Jason Robards' character, Cheyenne. Robards is a very good actor, and he does the best he can. But, other than wear a long coat, talk about coffee, and participate in a stunt-double shootout aboard the train, he doesn't do very much. Most of Cheyenne's important actions – his two escapes from his guards, his outlaw activities – happen off-screen. So why is he here? I think that, although Leone was trying to make a break with his previous Westerns, he was still hung up on them, structurally and thematically. Leone's two great Westerns both had three protagonists: Monco, El Indio and the Colonel; then Blondie, Tuco and Angel Eyes. In the latter film, Leone codified his three character types, as 'Good', 'Ugly', and 'Bad'. One of the most original aspects of *Once Upon a Time in the*

West was, supposedly, its woman protagonist, Jill. But Jill isn't an active protagonist. She arrives, stays at the ranch, fetches water, is kidnapped by Frank, and falls haplessly in love with the revenger. Little Rita of the West had a somewhat busier schedule. Instead of making Jill a part of his characteristic *triello*, Leone just grafted her onto a different trio – that of Harmonica, Cheyenne and Frank.

This doesn't make story sense. The *triello* structure, created by Leone and Vincenzoni, was already perfect. If Leone still wanted a simple, ideal confrontation, it was Harmonica versus Jill versus Frank. Harmonica was the cool, indifferent 'good' character that Eastwood had played; Frank was the callous killer in the Van Cleef mould; Jill is fabulously beautiful, but with the same, reality-based survival instincts as Tuco. Perhaps this was too much of a stretch for Leone (especially in Vincenzoni's absence[19]): fully incorporating a woman into the intimate, manly world he had created. Hence his inclusion of the 'Ugly' character of Cheyenne – in the original script, Manuel 'Cheyenne' Gutierrez. Wisely, Robards made no attempt to play his character with a Mexican accent. But it's still hard to tell why he's there. Cheyenne has little or nothing to do in this picture, other than wax sentimental about his mother, and insist on his own nobility.

19 *Marco Giusti lists Luciano Vincenzoni as one of the screenwriters of* Once Upon a Time in the West. *But he isn't credited, and Frayling reports that he didn't work on it.*

> CHEYENNE: I'd kill anybody... but never a kid. Be like killing a priest. A Catholic priest, that is.

In this short speech (part, unfortunately, of a longer one), Cheyenne sums up two things: 1) his irrelevance in a Spaghetti Western and 2) Leone's relatively craven attitude to the church. Frayling has pointed out that Corbucci could be fiercely anti-clerical, killing priests and cutting off pastors' ears, because his primary audience – working-class Italians – shared his cynicism about organised religion. Whereas Leone was spending American money and aiming for an international (i.e. American) audience; and Hollywood, like all Mafia enterprises, is sentimental about piety, and priests.

It might be argued that Cheyenne is necessary, if only for his death scene: that this is symbolic, and makes his character worthwhile. I don't buy it. Whatever Leone wished to convey about the death of the West, he had already done: in killing off Frank and all his men, and in the emotional emptiness and asexuality of Harmonica, who, once Frank is dead, rejects Jill also.

I've only one other criticism of *Once Upon a Time in the West*: the quality of some of the dialogue. Jill has a horrible speech in which she anticipates being raped by Cheyenne and his men, but for sheer show-stopping embarrassment and clunkiness, no Western has ever featured dialogue as bad as that of Fonda and Bronson, when they meet for the last time, and discuss the nature of manliness:

HARMONICA: So you decided you aren't a businessman after all.

FRANK: Just a man.

HARMONICA: An ancient race.

Who wrote this rubbish? It's hard to believe Bertolucci or Argento or Donati could have been responsible for it, or for the drivel which follows. But someone was to blame. In the bigger picture of the film itself, this matters less, perhaps: the visually and aurally amazing flashback which follows it makes one forget. And *Once Upon a Time in the West* also contains one of the best lines ever spoken in a Western, when Aldo Sambrell and another outlaw follow their arrested boss to the railroad station.

SAMBRELL: Two tickets, amigo. To the next station. One way only.

The line implies a lot: what they plan to do, and how it's likely to turn out. What makes it a great piece of dialogue is that what it's about – matters of life and death; loyalty to one's outlaw chief – is unspoken. (And that's how great art, as opposed to self-conscious Art, operates.)

Sergio Donati remarked that Leone had reached a crisis while editing his previous film: wanting everything bigger, and bigger. Now he had made a film that was bigger in every possible way: the most expensive Italian Western yet, with the finest line-up of American and Italian stars, the most elaborate design and costumes, the most original locations – even a week's shoot in Monument Valley! Donati also said that, for both him and Leone, the film was about the death of the West 'because when the railroad comes, the adventure is over'. So it's a more pessimistic film than the violent treasure hunts that went before.

Once Upon a Time in the West is a masterpiece. A long, slow-moving Cowboy Art Movie, it was destined to be misunderstood by its distributors. But it confirmed Leone's status as perhaps the most exciting young director in the world. Yet, instead of being happy and fulfilled, Leone seems to have become increasingly troubled as the film progressed. When they'd worked together, Eastwood had been amused by Leone, acting out scenes for his cast; he'd compared him to a cartoon character, and teased him for wearing a belt *and* suspenders. Directors tend to be intensely sensitive and paranoid, and I suspect Leone took this all to heart: so, as he grew fatter and more like a cartoon caricature of a bearded backwoodsman, he avenged himself on one of his film's characters.

The character is Wobbles, a frontier laundryman played by Marco Zuanelli. Wobbles is an unpleasant, minor character who acts as a go-between for Harmonica and Frank. He is clearly mean to his laundresses, but his main crimes are 1) being fat and 2) wearing a belt *and* braces. Early in *Once Upon a Time in the West*, Wobbles is tortured by Harmonica, who beats him up, throws him around, and traps his head in a clothes wringer. It's an odd scene, since we don't know who Wobbles is, and it doesn't advance the plot much. Later Wobbles is killed by Frank, who shoots him three times, in his belt buckle and suspenders. Ha, ha, ha! I remember, as a teenager, digging the rampant sadism of Italian Westerns, including Frank's massacre of the McBain family, but feeling there was something wrong and unnecessary in the torturing of Wobbles. Wobbles isn't an important character. His scenes are boring. There's no need to torture him, no need to focus on him at all. By emphasising Wobbles' suffering, I think Leone was trying to shake free some suffering of his own. But what? His sense of having been humiliated by Eastwood? A terrible home life, with a mad, mute mother? Something more?

It wasn't necessary. All Leone needed to do, when his actor upset him with the belt-and-braces remark, was to invite Eastwood to a screening of John Ford's *Wagonmaster*, and to point out how Ben Johnson and Harry Carey, Jr both wore belt *and* suspenders (in addition to their gunbelts). Ben and Dobe Carey were better cowboys, better riders and better actors than Clint would ever be. Thus educated, Eastwood might have calmed down. Perhaps, realising that he had much to learn as an actor, he would have agreed to be killed, for the opening of *Once Upon a Time in the West*.

Leone's Art Western had a chequered distribution. With the producers worried about the narrative, Leone was first encouraged to make *Once Upon a Time in the West* even longer, by adding a scene in which Charles Bronson's character recovered from his bullet wound. Inserted after the opening sequence, it added a couple of minutes to the picture. Then, in Britain and the US, the film was decimated – not by the censor, but by Paramount. Italian Westerns had been trimmed by distributors before: in some cases, distributors' cuts tightened up and, arguably, improved the films. But the cuts to *Once Upon a Time in the West* were disastrous. This is a very long film. Unlike Leone's earlier Westerns, it must be seen in its complete form, if only to be understood. Despite a modest premise and a linear plot, it's far from a conventional action Western. Any attempt to 'cut out the boring bits' makes that plot incomprehensible. Thus the English-language version of Leone's film remained gutted and incomprehensible for many years.

C'era una volta il West opened in Italy a few days before Christmas. As with *The Big Silence*, the distributor was having doubts: Christmas is a graveyard for anything but family films. The film did little business at first, but built an audience, and kept playing in certain cinemas: Frayling likens the 'build' in its reception to the response to *2001*. In France, the reviews were very favourable, and Leone was lauded as a new master of *le septième art*. *Il etait une fois dans l'ouest* played, uncut, in one Parisian cinema for two years.

1968 was a good year for revolutionaries, and for the Italian Western. In addition to Leone's film, several other fine pictures – and some interesting ones – were made. One was Giulio Petroni's follow-up to *Death Rides a Horse*: a story of the Mexican Revolution, *Tepepa*.

Tepepa

aka *Blood & Guns, Tepepa... Viva la revolucion!*
(Italy/Spain)

Director: Giulio Petroni   **Producer:** Franco Clementi, Alfredo Cuomo, Nicolo Pomilia, Richard A Herland   **Screenplay:** Giulio Petroni, Franco Solinas, Ivan Della Mea   **Director of Photography:** Francisco Marin   **Art Director:** Guido Josia   **Costumes:** Gaia Rossetti Romanini   **Editor:** Eraldo Da Roma   **Music:** Ennio Morricone   **Cast:** Tomas Milian (*Tepepa*), Orson Welles (*Colonel Cascorro*), John Steiner (*Dr Henry Price*), Annamaria Lanciaprima (*Maria Virgen Escalande*), Paloma Cela (*Consuelo*), Jose Torres (*El Piojo*), Luciano Casamonica (*Paquito*), Angel Ortiz, Gorge Wang (*Chu*), Giancarlo Badessi (*Sergeant*), Paco Sanz

The story

Henry Price, an English doctor, rescues the revolutionary bandit Tepepa from a firing squad run by Colonel Cascorro. He intends to kill Tepepa himself, but the bandit escapes and Price is arrested by the army. Tepepa frees Price, and the two become allies. Price tries to convince himself that Tepepa did not rape and murder his beloved, Consuelo. Tepepa is invited to a meeting with the president, but it is a trap organised by his friend El Piojo, whose hands have been cut off by the authorities. Tepepa kills El Piojo, and Price decides to take El Piojo's young son, Paquito, clad in a sailor suit, to California by train. Colonel Cascorro intervenes and presents evidence that Tepepa *is* the rapist/killer of Consuelo.

Price agrees to help Cascorro find Tepepa, but they are led into a trap in the canyons. A battle ensues, in which the government troops are decimated. Colonel Cascorro shoots Tepepa with a concealed weapon, and is killed by the revolutionaries. Price operates on Tepepa to save his life, but Tepepa admits his guilt on the operating table: he is the murderer of Consuelo. Tepepa insists that women don't matter when the Revolution is at stake. Price kills him.

Attempting to leave the rebel camp, Price is shot by Paquito.

The film

Tepepa is another long Italian Western – originally 136 minutes – which suffers in its shorter incarnations (96 minutes in the US, 80 minutes in Germany). The story is strong, the narrative complex. There are multiple flashbacks, showing, in slow motion, the girl whom Price loved and Tepepa murdered; and depicting Madero and Huerta's betrayal of the Revolution, as seen through Tepepa's eyes. Tepepa is more than the humble Cuchillo Sanchez: he's like El Chuncho in *¿Quien Sabe?*, a peasant general, a witness to great events, a man with revolutionary responsibilities. *Tepepa* borrows a fair amount from *¿Quien Sabe?* (it has the same screenwriter, Franco Solinas, though Solinas modestly claimed his co-writer, Ivan Della Mea, was responsible for it all). Both films depict the same gay ambivalence between the gringo and the Mexican; the same little boy asking the gringo, 'Do you like Mexico?' And the same answer, from Doctor Price, as from Bill Tate, the mercenary: 'No.' In both films, the gringo attempts to adopt a Mexican as a pet and take him back to the US. Both films end with the pet killing the master.

Tepepa's message is both revolutionary – the Revolution is righteous; Madero, Huerta and Cascorro are traitors to it; it *can* be won – and at the same time cynical: what does it matter if the Revolution succeeds, if the revolutionaries are sexist pigs, opportunists, killers, traitors themselves? There's no way out of the quandary the film presents: certainly the last shot, of a galloping horde, with Tepepa's image superimposed, doesn't provide a solution. The Revolution is worthwhile, and terminally fucked. A depressing message, back in those heady days – but the basis for a rattling good story.

The opening was shot in Guadix, a city between Almería and Granada, with a hilly aspect similar to Mexican towns like Guanajuato, and San Luis Potosi. Tomas Milian – Tepepa – was fresh from a big role in Dennis Hopper's *The Last Movie* (shot the same year but not completed until 1971). John Steiner – Price – was a young British theatre actor, who had just appeared in Peter Brook's *Marat Sade*. For the role of the Mexican colonel, Cascorro, one would have expected Eduardo Fajardo, or Fernando Sancho. But there was an American producer in the mix, Richard Herland, and he got the script to Orson Welles.

Welles, blacklisted by the studios, was forced to raise money independently, in order to eat and to direct his films. This usually translated into acting work, often in films (or commercials) in which he had no interest at all. In 1968, Welles was already in Spain, directing *Chimes at Midnight*. He accepted the role.

On their first day on set, Milian got into an argument with Welles. 'Orson Welles obviously didn't give a damn about going to Spain to do Westerns with this young actor Tomas Milian,' Milian told *Westerns All'Italiana*. 'Obviously he was doing it for the money. But for my dignity I wanted him to behave like he was doing it because he liked the script and the movie. So he started being very difficult and I just grabbed him by the balls, not literally, and had a talk with him.'

Tepepa doesn't feature in *any* of the biographies of Welles. This is strange, and suggests that Welles himself didn't rate it much, or mention it in interviews. Yet his performance in *Tepepa* is remarkably good. With the addition of a little brown-face make-up, and a wispy, Fu Manchu moustache, Welles looks surprisingly Mexican; and he brings real conviction, and literal weight, to the role. Orson Welles's acting in *Tepepa* has been unjustly neglected, I think. When I first saw the film, it was dubbed in French, and I failed to appreciate what Welles was doing. In English, he gives a fine performance.

John Steiner told Westerns *All'Italiana* that, after his last day's work, Welles made off with 6,000 feet of colour negative, with which to shoot a film of his own. Petroni liked Welles, and doesn't mention this. Steiner was quite dismissive of the film's political inclination:

> ...there was a time in Italy when the Communist Party was rising to power and becoming very popular. Everybody in the film industry was paying lip service to social justice, of which there was very little in Italy, so it was pretty natural...

> Solinas, who had written the script for *Tepepa*, was your classic product of those times, and would write things about the injustice to the peons and how the military were sucking the country dry, and they loved that sort of story. I think in Giulio Petroni's case, I think he was just making a Western. It was popular to have those sorts of undertones to your movie and that's why they were there.

Steiner wasn't the first actor to underestimate his director. I saw Petroni introduce *Tepepa* in Venice in 2007 – a long version of the film. Interviewed by Marco Giusti, he told the audience it was his intention to make a political film. And a director doesn't include long scenes featuring Madero and Huerta – Mexican presidents – unless he intends to make a film that deals with politics! While still happy with his more traditional Western, *Death Rides a Horse*, Petroni seemed prouder of *Tepepa*. The film remains a favourite of Tomas Milian, who was told that, when the film played in Mexico, the audience stood up and applauded.

Perhaps they did. *Tepepa* is a fine film, well shot, well acted, well art-directed, original in its use of Andalucian locations, with great action and a splendid score. The first meeting between Price and Cascorro features the colonel drunk, surrounded by cronies and women; a revolutionary shoeshine boy attempts to kill him and is shot. It's almost identical to the scene in *The Wild Bunch* (1969) where Angel sees General Mapache with his ex, and tries to kill him. As in *The Wild Bunch*, an automobile makes frequent appearances. One wonders whether Peckinpah saw *Tepepa*. Did it play in Mexico while Sam was shooting there?

The script is very strong, whoever wrote it. Welles and Milian have intelligent debates about power and revolutionary politics. Despite its traditional/leftist depiction of valiant peasants fighting cruel oppressors, the film makes Tepepa an ambiguous character: selfish, a liar, a rapist – but actually on the side of the poor, unlike the English doctor, the Mexican colonel, or the 'reformist' president, Madero.

Milian's last scene is both powerful, and depressing. Tepepa, having just sent four women and many men to their deaths in battle, lies on the operating table. Feverish, he exults, anticipating their triumph, and tells the Doctor, 'All women are alike... God has made them all the same way... And then what is a girl compared to the Revolution, Doctor? Just imagine, Doctor, if you would have killed me because of a *señorita*!'

And the Doc kills him.

1968 was a busy and fruitful year for the Spaghetti Western. The biggest-budget, highest-profile films were *Once Upon a Time in the West*, *Tepepa*, and Corbucci's new Tortilla Western, *A Professional Gun* – also set in Mexico during the Revolution. The canvas was expanding, as Leone, Petroni and Corbucci worked with bigger budgets, international casts, and longer shooting schedules. Yet some of the most interesting Westerns made this year were low-budget films, often transgressive even by Spaghetti Western standards. I'll deal with Corbucci's film, then turn to these smaller, stranger films.

A Professional Gun

aka *Il mercenario, The Mercenary, Salario para matar*
(Italy/Spain)

Director: Sergio Corbucci   **Producer:** Alberto Grimaldi   **Screenplay:** Luciano Vincenzoni, Sergio Spina, Sergio Corbucci   **Story:** Franco Solinas, Giorgio Arlorio   **Director of Photography:** Alejandro Ulloa **Art Director:** Luis Vasquez, Piero Filippone   **Editor:** Eugenio Alabiso **Assistant Director:** Filiberto Fiaschi, Ricardo Huertas   **Music:** Ennio Morricone, Bruno Nicolai   **Cast:** Franco Nero (*Sergei Kowalski*), Tony Musante (*Paco Roman*), Jack Palance (*Curly*), Giovanna Ralli (*Columba*), Eduardo Fajardo (*Col Alfonso Garcia*), Bruno Corazzari (*Studs*), Remo De Angelis (*Hudo*), Joe Kamel (*Larkin*), Franco Giacobini (*Pepote*), Vincente Roca (*Elias Garcia*), Jose Riesgo (*2nd Mexican*), Angel Ortiz (*3rd Mexican*), Fernando Villena (*Sergeant*), Tito Garcia (*Vigilante*), Angel Alvarez (*Notary*), Juan Cazalilla (*Mayor*), Guillermo Mendez (*Captain*), Jose Zalde (*Innkeeper*), Alvaro De Luna (*Ramon*), Jose Antonio Lopez (*Juan*), Milo Quesada (*Marco*), Raf Baldassarre (*Mateo*), Jose Canalejas (*Pablo*), Simon Arriaga (*Simon*), Paco Nieto (*Antonio*)

The story

Sergei Kowalski, aka the Polack, finds Paco Roman in a bullring, working as a rodeo clown. In a flashback, Kowalski recalls Paco's beginnings as a poor miner who rebels against the overseers and owners of his local mine. Paco is sentenced to be executed, but escapes and becomes a full-time revolutionary. Sergei, meanwhile, is hired by the mine owners – the Garcia brothers – to escort several shipments of silver to the United States. Sergei heads for the mine. The Garcia brothers are waylaid by Curly and Sebastian, gay killers and gamblers, who murder them after extracting the news of Kowalski's assignment.

At the mine, Kowalski finds only dead men, lynched by Paco and his 'twelve apostles'. Colonel Garcia, a friend of the dead mine owners, arrives and begins an artillery bombardment. Paco hires Kowalski to set up a machinegun, which – together with a car laden with dynamite – turns the cavalry charge into a rout. When Kowalski leaves the rebels' camp, he falls foul of Curly, who proposes to torture him in pursuit of the silver. But Paco's rebels show up and gun down Curly's men. Curly weeps over Sebastian's corpse, swears he will kill Paco, and departs, naked.

Paco robs a bank and frees the prisoners from jail. But only one person volunteers to join his rebel band: Columba, whose father was hanged by the authorities. Increasingly convinced of his own importance, Paco stays behind to defend the town. Kowalski leaves, and meets up with Paco, Columba, and the survivors later: the town has been destroyed by Garcia's artillery. Columba, increasingly disappointed by Paco, sets up a fight between him and the gringo. Kowalski becomes more selfish and intransigent – insisting on a signed contract, taking showers with the rebels' drinking water. Dogged by Curly, Paco pursues the Revolution, paying Kowalski cash all the while. The rebels occupy a church and Columba becomes Paco's adviser; Paco orders an old friend, who has betrayed the cause, castrated.

When Kowalski tries to depart with his money, Paco puts him on trial for abusing Mexicans, and imprisons him. He marries Columba. Next morning Garcia arrives and shells the town. His military adviser, Curly, has commissioned a plane to strafe the rebels from the air. Kowalski, freed, shoots the aircraft down. Six months later, Curly and Kowalski track Paco down in the bullring. Curly intends to kill him, on principle, and for a reward of 1,000 pesos, but Kowalski obliges him to make it a fair fight.

In a duel, Paco kills Curly. Kowalski takes the wounded Paco back to Mexico to collect the 1,000 pesos. But he discovers there's a reward for him, too, and Garcia puts both men against the wall. Columba intervenes to save them, and Paco and Kowalski part company in the desert. Kowalski intervenes once more, to shoot Garcia and his men, as they lie in ambush for Paco.

The film

When Corbucci told reporters that he hated Westerns, and that his next picture would be a Western, he was talking about *A Professional Gun*. Corbucci was, of course, an ironist, since when he gave that interview he was creating *The Big Silence*, one of the best Westerns of them all. So he must have retained some residual love of the form, I think – no matter how equivocal he was beginning to feel about it. The titles say it all. *The Big Silence* is a profound, visionary piece of art. *A Professional Gun* (also called *The Mercenary*) seems like a work for hire: payday. And nothing wrong with that. Corbucci and his collabora-tors were workers in the commercial, popular cinema – why shouldn't they be well paid? Especially as Vincenzoni and Grimaldi had cultivated their relationship with a Hollywood studio, and the Americans were prepared to invest more money – in salaries, and in the shoot – than their compatriots.

In one way this is a traditional Vincenzoni script: like the Leone films, and *Death Rides a Horse*, it's the tale of an uneasy partnership, with long, enforced desert treks. But it's also clearly Franco Solinas's work. Solinas wrote the original treatment with Giorgio Arlorio, who valiantly struggled to pretend there was something original in it:

> The encounter and parallel portraits of two opposing men... An infallible American pistolero, and a poor Mexican rebel peasant. The most extreme conscious individualism and the maximum revolutionary ignorance... A chance meeting, a problematic alli-ance imposed by circumstances, the ephemeral, reciprocal illu-sion that each man can change the other one, and after a vital game, the inevitable conclusion of death.

This, or something like it, was Arlorio's pitch to Grimaldi. It's also (with the exception of the chance meeting) a description of *¿Quien Sabe?*, *Tepepa*, *The Big Gundown*, and (nationalities aside) Solinas's script for *Burn!* In late 1967, Grimaldi described *A Professional Gun* to *Cinema d'Oggi* as a similarly high-end picture, to be directed by Gillo Pontecorvo, and to star Peter O'Toole, Burt Lancaster and Antonella Lualdi.

By 1968, Pontecorvo had moved on to *Burn!*, and *A Professional Gun* was in the hands of Sergio Corbucci. Corbucci's first casting choices were bizarre: James Coburn for the American, and Franco Nero as the Mexican. It's certainly true that there are blond, grey-eyed Mexicans. But there aren't many, especially among the poorer *mestizos* and *indios* who tend to be the revolutionary heroes of these films. Nero wasn't happy about the idea: he was now a movie star, so he had some say in which part he was going to play. And he wanted to play the American. Hence the problem: as a star, Nero would be dubbing himself in English, and his Italian accent was very strong. Corbucci – who preferred his actors to count, not speak – decided that his white protagonist would be Polish. That way Nero's accent wasn't an issue. Dialogue was particularly important because *A Professional Gun* contains a voiceover narration, by Nero's character, of the 'how did we get here?' variety. It doesn't seem particularly necessary, and may have been added at the eleventh hour, by the studio. Studio concerns were also present in the casting of the Mexican. Jack Palance and Eli Wallach were both considered; eventually another refugee from the New York Actors' Studio, Tony Musante, was hired.

What a lot of stodge! Not a foot of film had been shot, and Corbucci's movie was already boring. *The Big Silence* had been liberated, had taken wing, thanks to its mute hero, its absence of unnecessary dialogue. *A Professional Gun* was already sinking beneath the dead weight of another multi-lingual, international co-production. And one must ask: why did Mexicans never get cast as Mexicans in these films? Other than the marvellous Gilbert Roland, no Mexican actors of any note appeared in Spaghetti Westerns. Of course, it made economic sense for Aragonese actors and Almería gypsies to play Mexicans in these films – but why did the producers import Cubans, and Puerto Ricans, and New Yorkers to impersonate *Mexicanos*, often badly, when there were (and are) so many good Mexican actors?

Having considered Palance for the 'Ugly', Corbucci cast him as the 'Bad': a gay gambler and assassin, improbably called Curly, with fine-tuned, Grecian locks to match. It was a perfect choice. Palance was a consummate actor, fluent in four languages, who got along with everyone on set, especially the director. Musante, on the other hand, annoyed the director by being 'Methody' – always demanding motivations, and taking too much time to prepare. But what did Corbucci expect? Did it surprise him that a graduate of the Actors' Studio behaved this way?

Nero and Corbucci understood each other. Kowalski, like Django, is a gringo arms dealer who massacres his enemies wholesale with a machinegun. This wasn't much of a stretch for Nero, who wanted to break with his previous, iconic role. So Corbucci's costume designer, Jurgen Henze, organised him a new wardrobe – light colours, straw hats, dusters, and 'bush ranger' jackets – and Nero grew a big, drooping moustache, in the Stefanelli style. He looked most fine: the moustache made him seem older, and fiercer, than before.

The art direction is very good. Though some familiar locations are used, Corbucci and the designer, Luis Vasquez, made an effort to find dusty squares and tile-roofed ranch buildings which looked convincingly Mexican. Much care went into the detail, from the signage and the cars, to the gramophones and the characters' celluloid collars. Alejandro Ulloa, the Spanish cinematographer, shot a good-looking film: unlike Ippolito in *Navajo Joe*, Ulloa had an eye for dramatic desert skies; like Ippolito in *The Big Silence*, his restless camera followed impromptu flocks of crows. There are enough zooms and long-lens shots to keep Corbucci happy; the framing is precise, but less conservative than Leone's or Petroni's, with wide two-shots, multiple-character compositions, and close-ups which push the edge of the frame. When the lead actor is centred, other actors are placed to the left and right of him: Ulloa and Corbucci never forgot they had a Techniscope frame to fill.

The score is by Morricone and his arranger, Bruno Nicolai. It's a good one, particularly the whistling theme – performed by the inevitable Alessandro Alessandroni – which accompanies Kowalski. These are excellent production credits – music, cinematography, design, costume – so why is the film so *plodding*?

Partially, it's the script. Solinas's original story for *A Professional Gun* ends with the gringo killing his Mexican partner, for the reward. This is a much better conclusion: a variant on *¿Quien Sabe?* and *Tepepa*, in which the Mexican kills the gringo. But it's also very dark, in the pessimistic vein of *The Big Silence*. Perhaps mindful that he was working for Grimaldi and the Americans, Corbucci went with a new, 'upbeat' ending, in which gringo and Mexican ride off with displays of mutual respect, as in *The Big Gundown*. As a result, *A Professional Gun* – Corbucci's biggest-budget, largest-scale Western to date – feels strangely underpowered: like a big car with a little engine, or missing cylinders. The body count is high, but the violence is underplayed. From Corbucci, one expected acts of extreme cruelty, mutilation and sadism – plus the murder of a priest or two. But Corbucci plus United Artists equalled Corbucci 'lite'. Instead of sadism, he resorted to low comedy – as when the general, played by Eduardo Fajardo, is forced to eat a dead lizard. This is just gross, and childish; the demonic dimension of *Django* and *The Big Silence* is entirely absent. In a way, Vincenzoni had become the man who knew too much. His script for *For a Few Dollars More* compares the adults to children playing games; a thesis which worked perfectly there, and partially in *The Good, the Bad and the Ugly*. However, it has gone sour here. Instead of insight into adult rituals, Vincenzoni's contribution to the script seems to be childishness.

So, Kowalski is childishly greedy – insisting on handfuls of money when he's under fire; demanding showers with the rebels' water. And Paco is childishly jealous – imagining Columba (Giovanna Ralli) is having sex with the gringo – and childishly stupid. Howard Hughes reckons *A Professional Gun* is mainly influenced by Louis Malle's *Viva Maria* (1965), but it seems to me to be a remake of *¿Quien Sabe?* with the complexities removed, and a happy ending imposed. In all these Tortilla Westerns, there is a traitor who was once the hero's dearest friend: in *Tepepa* it's El Piojo, whose hands have been cut off by the *Federales*; here it's Pepote (Franco Giacobini), who Paco condemns to be castrated. This is the closest the film gets to Corbucci's ironic mutilation kick (Pepote, a womaniser, has spent the Revolution's money on girls). Marco Giusti recalls seeing a graphic castration when

A Professional Gun was first released in Italy: but it's gone from the 'international' versions.

The only character of any real worth, in these reduced circumstances, is Curly. Palance doesn't simper or make a big thing out of Curly's gayness; he's just a precise and deadly dandy, who weeps when his lover is killed. Kowalski's attempt to humiliate Curly by stripping him naked and making him walk out into the desert completely fails: Palance is so strong, so dignified, so unfazed by acting in the nude. What a marvellous, willing thespian! It's a pity Curly is reduced to being Eduardo Fajardo's sidekick in the second half, since he's the most interesting personage in the picture.

A Professional Gun develops Corbucci's interest in strong women characters – in this case Columba, the freed prisoner who becomes Paco's revolutionary conscience. She has a powerful voice, like the women in *The Big Silence*, or Estella in *Minnesota Clay*. This is something Corbucci and Solinas brought to the table: strong women don't feature in Vincenzoni's other Western scripts. *¿Quien Sabe?*, of course, had a similar woman character, Adelita (Martine Beswick). Otherwise *A Professional Gun* is of slight interest: a watchable, recycled Tortilla Western with obvious politics and too much comedy. Compared to *The Big Silence*, the sets are certainly bigger, but the grandeur is gone. Big budgets never guarantee a great film. Nor do small budgets, either. But within the lower-budget realm, there is usually more freedom to experiment, and to innovate – as the following Spaghetti Westerns make clear.

Black Jack

aka *I dannati della violenza, Un uomo per cinque vendette, Black Joe*
(Italy/Israel)

Director: Gianfranco Baldanello **Producer:** Fernando Franchi, Alexander Hakohen **Screenplay:** Luigi Ambrosini, Gianfranco Baldanello, Mario Maffei **Story:** Giuseppe Andreoli, Luigi Ambrosini **Director of Photography:** Mario Fioretti **Art Director:** Nicola Tamburro **Costumes:** Maria Luisa Panaro **Editor:** Mario Gargiulo

Assistant Director: Federico Chentrens   **Music:** Lallo Gori   **Cast:** Robert Woods (*Jack Murphy*, aka *Black Jack*), Lucienne Bridou (*Susan*), Rik Battaglia (*Sanchez*), Mimmo Palmara (*Indian Joe*), Larry Dolgin (*Reb*), Nino Fuscagni (*Peter*), Dalia Lahvi (*Lola Sanchez*), Sascia Krusciarska (*Estelle*), Ivan G Scratuglia (*Rodrigo*), Giovanni Bonadonna, Romano Magnino, Federico Chentrens (*Gordon*), Fredy Unger (*Billy*)

The story

Jack Murphy, an outlaw known as Black Jack, is hiding out in an abandoned ghost town with his sister, Estelle, and her husband, Peter. Jack plans to rob the bank of New Tuscos City with his gang of outlaws. The robbery goes smoothly, and Jack stashes the loot, then makes love to his girlfriend, Susan, in the New Tuscos livery stable. When he shows up to share out the money, the gang want more than their customary 75/25 split. Jack refuses, shoots a couple of them, and makes off with the money. Jack's Indian sidekick, Joe, provides him with a fresh mount; then betrays him to the bandits, leading them to the ghost town. The gang breaks into the saloon, where Jack, Susan and Peter sleep. One of the gang, Sanchez, discovers Estelle and takes her hostage. Jack surrenders, and is hanged and beaten up by his former partners. He reveals where the loot is when Sancho threatens to turn Estelle over to Joe.

All for nothing. Sancho rapes Estelle, and Joe scalps her. Reb, another old friend, stabs Jack in the hand, and Gordon shoots him in both legs. The bandits ride off, leaving him hanging. But Susan appears and saves Jack's life. Jack recovers, but is horribly crippled, able to walk only with a stick. Having practised sufficiently with his guns, he abandons Susan and promises he will bring Sanchez back to Peter, alive.

Black Jack's revenge is speedily accomplished. He pays the local townspeople $10,000 to kill one bandit, Miguel. He ambushes Gordon, and his brother Billy, at their gold mine. He kills Reb with his own knife, in a gambling joint. He strangles the Indian in his own cabin, and kidnaps Sanchez's daughter Lola, knowing this will bring Sanchez back to the old ghost town. Sanchez follows them, and having killed all of the last outlaw's men, and trapped Sanchez, Jack tries to persuade Peter to rape Lola. Peter, horrified, stabs Jack, who thanks him, and shoots Sanchez. Peter and Lola flee as the saloon, and the ghost town, collapse during a fierce storm.

The film

It's hard to simply describe this bleak, dark, low-budget Spaghetti Western. Its primary location – the ghost town – resembles the set of a horror film, and the stagey collapse of the set, superimposed over a shot of Black Jack's corpse, recalls Corman's *Fall of the House of Usher* (1960). The on-screen violence is pretty intense, and Robert Woods' performance extreme: he eats up the scenery when he's tortured, but this is just a prelude to the grisly transformation he undergoes. The rape and scalping happen off screen, in the manner of *Titus Andronicus*, or a Jacobean revenge drama. And like those theatrical works, *Black Jack* has a strong moral sense.

Black Jack is no conventional, cool and distant Italian Western hero/killer. Woods – like Ben Johnson, a genuine cowboy, who grew up on a Colorado cattle ranch – plays the role entirely against type. He suggests from the very beginning that there's something wrong with Jack – a semi-hysteric, living with his sister, dressing as Ringo, or Arizona Colt. After Estelle is murdered and Jack is shot in the legs, Woods adopts Frankenstein's monster posture, and dresses as if he's been thrown down a salt mine, en route to a funeral. Like a Buñuel character, especially Archibaldo de la Cruz, Black Jack fetishises his dead sister's nightdress, which he strokes, and keeps in a drawer.

So it's a relief when he abandons his faithful, decent girlfriend – who has self-sacrificingly nursed him and Peter back to health – and heads off on his vengeance trail. There are no surprises here. Indeed, never did any revenger have an easier time. His first victim is so unpopular that Black Jack simply pays his neighbours to kill him. His second and third victims, the miners, are soon dispatched. When Jack plays cards with his fourth betrayer, Reb, he won't even show his hand: he just *says* he has four aces. He wants to provoke Reb, of course, and give him his knife back: seething, dirty and rail-thin under a big cowboy hat, Woods is pretty provoking. Indian Joe is a fine character, played

218

by Mimmo Palmera in the manner of Trintignant: entirely mute. Palmera had a good face, looked like a movie Indian, and he pulled it off. But the ease with which Jack invades his cabin, and strangles him with his own sister's scalp, suggests a certain lack of Native American frontier skills, on Joe's part.[20]

20 *It's interesting to speculate what Fistful of Dollars would be like if Leone had been able to cast his first choices. Henry Fonda would have made a fine Joe – but it's hard to imagine the stoic, impassive Mimmo Palmera replacing Gian Maria Volonte, constantly in motion, convincingly* mexicano, *with his powerful, active presence and deep, expressive eyes.*

Jack's final act of revenge is the most disgusting of all. First, he walks into Sanchez's ranch, asks to see his daughter, and kidnaps her. No one makes much of an effort to prevent this. In the ghost town, having beaten Sanchez into submission, Jack yells repeatedly at Peter to 'take her', so that their revenge will be complete. And Sanchez begs to be killed, instead, as his daughter is innocent. This is so loathsome that it confirms Black Jack's status as a fully-fledged monster. But there is more. Peter, disgusted, has a vision of his wife being threatened by Indian Joe's knife. Blinded, he lunges forward with his knife, and stabs Black Jack, who gasps, 'Thank you.'

I've seen better Italian Westerns, but no higher drama. As Jack tumbles, dying, to the floor of the saloon, a series of dissolves and superimpositions begins. We see his corpse, Peter and Lola fleeing, and the ghost town starting to collapse. We don't see much destruction, of course, because this is a very low-budget film, with a couple of hosepipes providing a very small storm. The town was a corner of the *Dinocitta* set; New Tuscos City was Elios Films.

All the exteriors were shot in Israel, via a co-production with Desert Studios in Eliat. Today such an alliance might seem strange, but the Italian producers were constantly on the lookout for co-production partners, who might bring money and some kind of state aid. Israel in the sixties was viewed as a progressive, liberal country; unlike Spain, which throughout the Spaghetti Western period was a dictatorship ruled by a fascist, Franco (strangely, this didn't deter leftist directors from shooting there[21]). Eliat certainly offers a wider choice of deserts than Tabernas. But most of

21 *Even Luis Buñuel worked in Spain during the period of the Franco dictatorship, though the film he made there (*Viridiana, 1961*) was banned by Franco's regime. The only director who refused, on principle, to shoot in fascist Spain was Henri-Georges Clouzot: he made* The Wages of Fear *in the South of France, instead.*

the time they are quite boringly filmed. These desert ride-bys tend to be accompanied by a dire 'jazz' and church organ score, composed by Lalo Gori. So they draw attention to themselves by being bad on two counts. The director, Gianfranco Baldanello, made several Westerns, including one shot in Sardinia. A couple were *Zorro* movies. As far as I know, none of them entered the strange territory of this compelling film.

An inhuman demon is an uncommon hero in any film, particularly a Western. Corbucci's dismissive reading of *The Big Silence* held that Tigrero was the hero: after all, he won. But *Black Jack* is more in the vein of *Revengers Tragedy* or *The White Devil*. Their protagonists fascinate, but they have become monsters: Black Jack, like Vindici and Lodovico, must be destroyed. Hamlet – the revenger who prevaricates – is recognisably human, and thus an appropriate hero for more mainstream films. Marlon Brando certainly had the Prince in mind when he prevaricated, on the shores of Monterrey, in *One-Eyed Jacks*. It was only a matter of time before a Spaghetti Western Hamlet rode into town.

Johnny Hamlet

aka *The Dirty Story of the West, The Wild and the Dirty, Quella sporca storia del west, Django porte sa croix*
(Italy)

Director: Enzo G Castellari **Producer:** Elio Scardamaglia, Ugo Guerra **Screenplay:** Tito Carpi, Enzo G Castellari, Francesco Scardamaglia **Story:** William Shakespeare **Director of Photography:** Angelo Filippini, Alberto Spagnoli **Art Director:** Enzo Bulgarelli **Editor:** Tatiana Casini **Music:** Francesco De Masi **Cast:** Chip Gordon aka Andrea Giordana (*Johnny Hamilton*), Gilbert Roland (*Horace*), Francoise Prevost (*Gertrude*), Gabriella Grimaldi (*Emily/Ophelia*), Horst Frank (*Uncle Claude*), Enzo Girolami (*Ross*), Pedro Sanchez (*Guild*), Manuel Sylvester Serrano (*Santana*), Stefania Careddu (*Eugenia/Laura*)

The story

Johnny Hamilton awakes on a beach where some travelling players are performing a scene from *Hamlet*. Two gunmen stalk him, but he shoots them down. Returning home from the Civil War, he passes the crucified corpse of an outlaw, and finds his father dead and buried in the Danark Cemetery. Visiting his father's grave – a cave – Johnny is threatened by two toughs, Ross and Guild, and saved by an old family friend, Horace. Horace tells Johnny his father was supposedly killed by the bandit Santana, who is also buried here. His mother, Gertrude, is now married to his Uncle Claude, who has taken over the family farm and renamed it the Rancho El Señor.

Uncle Claude and Gertrude welcome him, but Johnny is disturbed by the excessive and luxurious environment, and suspects foul play. He grills his old girlfriend, Emily, beside the family water wheel. Ross and Guild reappear; Johnny and Horace best them again. Johnny reveals his suspicions to Horace; the players arrive in town, and Johnny sleeps with one of them, Laura. He pays the gravedigger to open Santana's grave, and finds a corpse within. Uncle Claude confronts him and offers Johnny a chance to shoot him – which Johnny doesn't take.

Back at the saloon, Johnny finds Laura dead; three thugs try to kill him. Gertrude, increasingly suspicious, gives him his father's gun. Johnny discovers Santana is alive – and involved in bandit business with Uncle Claude. Claude arranges for Ross and Guild to ambush Santana and Johnny: several Mexicans are killed, but Johnny and Santana escape. Claude murders Emily, and plants evidence implicating Johnny in her shooting and drowning: her father, the crooked sheriff, catches Johnny in the graveyard, and crucifies him.

Gertrude, desperate to know the truth, holds Claude at gunpoint, only to be shot by Guild. Santana and his men attack the ranch, and Gertrude manages to ride out to where Johnny hangs crucified. She drags herself up the hill, but is blocked by the sheriff. Horace shows up, kills and crucifies the sheriff, and frees Johnny. Johnny, crippled, returns to town, where he ties his pistol to his broken hand. Thus armed, he kills Ross; Horace shoots Guild.

Claude returns to his ranch to collect a hoard of stolen gold. But the bags break – or are shot apart by Johnny – drenching Claude in gold dust, which jams his pistol, and leaves a trail for Johnny to follow. Johnny catches up with his uncle, and shoots him in the back.

Claude dies laughing. Johnny kicks the bags apart, and the wind blows the gold dust away. Horace turns up again and he and Johnny ride off, spooking a herd of cows.

The film

This wasn't the first Italian Western based on a Shakespeare play: that honour goes to *The Fury of Johnny Kidd* (*La furia de Johnny Kidd*), a Western *Romeo and Juliet* directed by Gianni Puccini in 1967. *Johnny Hamlet* was originally Corbucci's idea. His film was to star Anthony Perkins. For some reason, Corbucci lost interest, and the producers offered the project to Franco Rossetti, who had just directed *Desperado*. They wanted Hamlet to be played by Andrea Giordana, who had starred in *Desperado*; Rossetti disagreed. He'd found Giordana inexperienced around horses and guns and didn't want to make another Western with him. I don't see anything wrong with Giordana in this regard; he seems to ride and shoot just fine. But maybe many takes were needed; or perhaps Rossetti had other reasons for not wanting the actor. In any case, stars were more important than directors, or so the producers, Scardamaglia and Guerra, thought. So they moved on – to a 30-year-old director with four Westerns under his belt: Enzo G Castellari. Castellari was the perfect choice. How well made and postmodern *Johnny Hamlet* seems! Its style is exuberant, with the camera in restless motion around the protagonist. There are dream sequences, special effects, and enough crash zooms and telephoto-shots-through-things to confirm Castellari as Corbucci's heir apparent. But he was more, besides. Castellari's editing – in particular his juxtaposition of cuts with musical beats – is very precise: more so than most of his contemporaries'. His framing is bold, with the camera frequently dollying into striking close-ups, often pushing the edges of the Techniscope frame. The opening scenes, in which the hero pursues a robed figure through a cave, then wakes on a beach as a strolling player performs the 'to be or not to be' soliloquy, could be straight from Corman's LSD drama, *The Trip* (1967). There was always something acid-ish about the Spaghetti Western: those psychedelic Lardini title sequences, Giuliano Gemma's hippyish traits. In *Johnny Hamlet*, these hints, and tropes, become the visual structure of a film. To this end, Castellari is greatly supported by his art director, and costumer, Enzo Bulgarelli – who overdresses the mansion and Santana's lair, and leaves everything else lean. Lest we forget this is an Italian Western, there is some well-staged action, and a pair of crucifixions.

Johnny Hamlet is Castellari's best, most original Western. Johnny's Uncle Claude has renamed their hacienda 'El Señor' – Elsinore – and the characters ride through a landscape of rocks resembling giant mushrooms (briefly seen in *A Professional Gun*) which suggest the pervasive growth of something fungal, if not rotten, in the state. Johnny Hamilton is supposed to be a war veteran, but he looks more like a hippie student: like Hamlet, in other words (though Hamlet probably didn't wear Giordana's spray-on orange tan). His uncle, his mother, his insipid girlfriend, and the mysterious Horace/Horatio, are all drawn from the play. The adaptation stumbles by dropping the father's ghost, and introducing a subplot involving a bandit, Santana. Why did Castellari do this? If you're going to go to all the trouble of doing Hamlet out West, why ditch that outstanding opening scene? Perhaps, in 1968, it seemed too revolutionary, too strange, too surreal, to show a ghost in a Western. Things would change, within a year.

One problem which all film versions of *Hamlet* face is what to do with the soliloquies. Does the actor simply speak them, as he would on stage? Or are they heard in voiceover? Often films opt for the latter choice (*Johnny Hamlet* and Laurence Olivier's *Hamlet* both do so). I think this is a mistake. Showing an actor's blank face, while his disembodied voice plays over it, is very crude filmmaking. It rarely works, because it draws attention to itself, and the audience starts thinking how odd it is. Thus it is here: *Johnny Hamlet* is one of that handful of Spaghetti Westerns sabotaged by an unnecessary voiceover narration. A second problem has to do with language. All films borrowing from Shakespeare or the Elizabethans must decide: do they stick with the original poetry, or update it? *Johnny Hamlet* was made in Italian, but the question still applied: should the filmmakers attempt to match the original poetry, or scrap it in favour of Spaghetti cowboy talk? Castellari and his co-screenwriters went the latter route: the one taken by *Joe Macbeth*, or Don Boyd's *King Lear, My Kingdom*. This brings us to the third problem of adaptation: devoid of its original poetry, is the story still worth telling?

In general, I think not. If you're going to attempt one of these things, I believe both intellectually and in my gut that you must retain the original language, or recreate it in translation. *Hamlet*, with its strong narrative hook and its revenge motive, may be the only exception to this – certainly Castellari comes close to pulling it off. He's helped by a fine cast in most of the principal roles: Horst Frank as Claude, Françoise Prevost as Gertrude, Gilbert Roland as Horace. These are all very good actors, giving the film their best shot: the fates of Gertrude, shot yet dragging herself up a rocky slope to save her crucified son, and Claude, smothered in gold dust, laughing himself to death, are epic stuff. But the film lingers too long on Giordana, who isn't a very interesting actor. A weak Hamlet is a disaster, and for this we must blame Scardamaglia and Guerra, the producers. They had picked a great director, and a not-great lead.

And any version of *Hamlet* in which the hero lives and rides away is ultimately doomed. *Hamlet* is a tragedy, and a tragedy is a play or film in which the hero dies, after a fall from lofty heights. Castellari, an educated man, knew this! But perhaps the producers insisted. Where I would fault the director is in his excessive attention to the minor villains, Ross and Guild. Played by Ennio Girolami and Pedro Sanchez (in reality an Italian actor, Ignazio Spalla, who had changed his name so as to get work as Mexicans), they are nowhere near as funny or as interesting as the director thinks they are. Castellari failed to learn from Corbucci and Leone, who created great subsidiary bad guys, but kept them in the background. (Castellari was the son of a director, Marino Girolami. His brother, Ennio, was the actor who played Ross/Rosencrantz.)

Johnny Hamlet is also one of the first Italian Westerns to feature choreographed acrobatic stunts. The athletic Giuliano Gemma was always up for a back-flip, of course, but Castellari's were crowd-pleasing acrobatics of a more structured kind: a double leap-and-shoot by Johnny and Horace, Johnny back-flipping off his horse, Johnny jumping on a broken piece of landing, vanishing, and shooting his adversaries through the stairs. This was entertaining and original here – part of Castellari's all-stops-out approach to his material – but when other directors followed in his acrobatic footsteps, low comedy and, eventually, collapse ensued.

Johnny Hamlet's otherwise-European cast had room for one 'outsider' – Gilbert Roland, in the role of Horace/Horatio. Roland was a Mexican actor who had begun his career in silent films, and who specialised in playing educated and sophisticated Mexicans, somewhat different from the Fernando Sancho model. A Mexican playing a Mexican, at last! The same year, Roland acted in another of these pictures – a film both excellent in its own right, and fascinating as the first gay-themed Italian Western, *Every Man for Himself*.

Every Man for Himself

aka *Ognuno per se, Chacun pour soi, Sam Cooper's Gold, The Ruthless Four*
(Italy/Germany)

Director: Giorgio Capitani   **Producer:** Luciano Ercoli, Alberto Pugliese   **Screenplay:** Fernando Di Leo, Augusto Caminito   **Director of Photography:** Sergio D'offizi   **Production Designer:** Franco Bottari   **Art Director:** Nicola Tamburro   **Assistant Director:** Marcello Crescenzi   **Music:** Carlo Rustichelli   **Cast:** Van Heflin (*Sam Cooper*), Gilbert Roland (*Mason*), Klaus Kinski (*Blond*), George Hilton (*Manolo*), Sarah Ross (*Anna*), Rick Boyd, Sergio Doria (*The Brady brothers*), Ivan G Scratuglia, Giorgio Groden

The story

Sam Cooper, having killed his doublecrossing partner in their gold mine, heads for town. After a difficult desert crossing he is robbed by thieves who steal his food and horses, but ignore his bags of gold. Some of the gold dust he dumps into the river, the rest he buries. In town, Sam is recognised by an old flame, Anna; he collapses in her arms and spends the night in her room, at the saloon. Next morning, he intimates to Anna that he has finally found a fabulous goldmine; he sends a wire to his adopted son, Manolo Sanchez – with a draft for $100, so that Manolo can join him. When Manolo arrives, they get drunk and Sam insists that Manolo join him gold-mining; unlike their previous attempt, he promises this mission will succeed. Manolo, who can't get into a card game for lack of funds, agrees. But when his sinister friend appears – dressed as a priest – Manolo goes to pieces, and insists that the fake priest accompany them to the mine.

Sam is furious, and deeply suspicious. To even up the score, he makes a deal with his old enemy, Mason. Mason blames Sam – his former partner – for abandoning him to the law, and a malaria-infested jail, some years before. But he agrees to come along.

The four men leave town in a rainstorm, and trek across the desert toward the mine. At an abandoned mission, the local storekeeper has set a trap for them: but they detect the ambushers, shoot and bury them. Sam insists they bury their attackers' guns as well; the fake priest hides a pistol, for the return journey.

They reach the mine and begin extracting gold. The priest tries to kill Mason in a mine 'accident'. Manolo suggests to Sam that the priest and Mason are plotting against them. The priest tortures Manolo, and insists they must kill Mason. They catch a desert rat spying on them; discovering his sheriff's badge, the priest shoots him. Having extracted enough gold, they blow up the mine entrance, and head back across the desert.

When Manolo steals Mason's quinine, Sam pulls a shotgun and disarms his three partners. At the mission, he gives the priest a chance to steal his revolver; the priest attempts to shoot Mason. But the pistol is empty, and – despite the priest's hidden gun – Mason beats him to death. Distraught, Manolo attempts to intervene. Sam shoots him, and Manolo dies, bitterly, in Sam's arms.

Sam and Mason head for town with the mule train and the gold. But they are dogged by the Brady brothers – two hired killers whom Mason has contracted to protect him, in case Sam double-crosses him again. Scenting gold, the Bradys turn against their employer. In a final shootout, Sam is shot in the leg, the Bradys killed, and Mason mortally wounded. Dying, Mason gives Sam his share of the gold.

The film

George Hilton, who played Manolo, called *Every Man for Himself* 'good work on my part, and absolutely one of the best Westerns ever'.

Actors tend to say grandiose things, but I agree with Hilton in this case. The film is an excellent, tightly constructed thriller: a *Treasure of the Sierra Madre* in reverse, in which the hero loses everything, *except* the gold. And the plot is fuelled, it seems, by several gay love affairs. Kinski's character dominates Hilton's physically and psychologically. But Manolo's 'adopted son' role with Sam is also sexualised. When they're drunk, there is much talk of whether they will share a hotel room or not (luckily for them, no other rooms are available); when Manolo insists the priest join them, Sam beats him up in their bedroom – not with his fists, but with open-handed slaps. The scene ends with Manolo weeping into his pillow. And the scene where Sam, Manolo, Mason and the Brady brothers first meet is set in a steam-bath.

Of course, not every steam-bath is an exclusively gay hang-out. A hetrosexist might point to the steam-bath scene in *The Wild Bunch* as evidence that hyper-heteros also frequent bath houses. But there's a gay subtext to Peckinpah's film, as well, and I think the comparison proves the point. Both pictures refer constantly to *Treasure of the Sierra Madre*. The end of *The Wild Bunch*, when, dying, Pike and Dutch share a few last words, is similar to the last scene of *Every Man for Himself*, where Mason and Sam – too badly shot up to move, unable to see each other – say their goodbyes.

Marco Giusti reckons this is the best film of Giorgio Capitani, previously a director of light comedies. The script was co-written by Fernando di Leo, who intended Lucio Fulci to direct it. But the producers didn't want Fulci, and hired Capitani instead. Di Leo – a director in his own right – wasn't happy with the result. He complained that Capitani had introduced unnecessary 'psychoanalytical' elements. But these seem completely integrated into the film (original title: *Every Man for Himself – And God Against All*). It's hard to imagine how this small gem of a Western could be much improved.

When I first saw Capitani's film, I thought it 'in the American style'. This is true in that Sergio D'Offizi's photography is mainly discreet: extreme close-ups are rare, only used for real emphasis. In the shoot-outs, most of the bullets miss their targets, and a realistic amount of time is spent reloading empty guns – again, the American manner. But, today, I notice *many* Spaghetti Western flourishes. Particularly in the nameless character played by Klaus Kinski, and in the fight between Mason and the priest, with Gilbert Roland punching the lens of the camera. *Every Man for Himself* begins with a Corbucci-esque crash zoom in on the mine, and ends with an iris-in on the sunset, like a silent movie. It's a fusion film.

And how perfect that Van Heflin, co-star of *Shane*, should play Sam Cooper. Some writers have remarked that Heflin was a heavy drinker, who gave a weak performance. But his work seems fine, to me. He plays his role as tired and slow moving, but Sam Cooper is *supposed* to be an old man, clapped-out by years of prospecting, baked by the sun, untrusting, untrustworthy, half-mad. And alcoholism – while a major problem in many professions – isn't necessarily an impediment to the job of acting. I have witnessed a very skilled and gracious actor demolish a bottle of vodka in a few hours, remaining word-perfect and giving an excellent rendition of his role. Heflin was presumably in this category.

Marcello Crescenzi, the assistant director, liked him: 'I just had to make sure Van Heflin's wig was on straight, and that his bourbon glass was full, and he gave me no problems.' He recalled Gilbert Roland as *simpaticone*. Roland is fine as the malaria-ravaged, double-dealing Mason. He plays it pretty camp, and rumbas to himself while waiting for the shootout to start at the mission. According to Hilton, both Roland and Heflin had difficulties with their co-star, Kinski. As the fake priest (in the credits called Blond, but nameless in the film itself), Kinski is increasingly demonic. He plays it like a fey Tigrero, hiding a gun for future use, draping a sack over his head when he's in the mine, wrapping himself in a black burnoose – Kinski of Almería – when the characters cross the desert. No wonder he annoyed the other actors! But, given the strangeness of his character, who lacks even a name, none of this dressing up seems wrong.

George Hilton does a splendid job with the least promising of characters. Manolo is bogus, amoral and vain. Hilton shows his valiant side during the action sequences, and lets him die bitching and unredeemed. Unlike his co-stars, he got on well with Kinski, as did the assistant director, Crescenzi – who recalls only one problem: Kinski was apparently arrested, one night in Almería, standing in the middle of the main highway, holding a chandelier.

Like any gold-mining expedition, *Every Man for Himself* took its time. Interiors were shot in 1966, exteriors the following year; an Italian-German co-production, it was filmed entirely in Spain. The film was released in 1968. The censor insisted on the removal of a scene where the fake priest stabs Manolo in the hand with a cigar. Since this comes at the end of a slow zoom, the cut is as obvious as it was unnecessary. Most of the reviews were favourable – even the Vatican rating service praised Capitani's direction and the plot – but the film didn't do huge business, and has been hard to find. This is a shame because, as a thoroughly entertaining action film, with world-class leads, which anticipates (somewhat less romantically) *Brokeback Mountain*, *Every Man for Himself* is in a class of its own.

Today It's Me, Tomorrow You!

aka *Oggi a me... Domani a te!*
(Italy)

Director: Tonino Cervi   **Producer:** Franco Cucca, Tonino Cervi
Screenplay: Dario Argento, Tonino Cervi   **Director of Photography:** Sergio D'offizi   **Art Director:** Carlo Gervasi   **Costumes:** Giorgio Desideri
Editor: Sergio Montanari   **Assistant Director:** Mauro Sacripanti
Music: Angelo Francesco Lavagnino   **Cast:** Brett Halsey (*Bill Kiowa*), Bud Spencer (*O'Bannion*), William Berger (*Colt Moran*), Tatsuya Nakadai (*Elfego*), Wayde Preston (*Jeff Milton*), Stanley Gordon (*Bunny Fox*), Dana Ghia (*Mirana Kiowa*), Franco Gula (*Old man in saloon*), Jeff Cameron, Doro Corra, Vic Gazzara, Aldo Marinecci, Michele Borelli, Franco Pecchini

The story

Bill Kiowa is released after five years spent in jail for an unspecified crime. He has spent those years practising his draw and aim with a wooden gun. Two renegades trail Bill to the nearest town. He buys a revolver and guns them down. From an old man in a shack, he collects a large sum of money; he plans to raise a gang of killers and pursue an outlaw, Elfego. The burly O'Bannion eludes him in a barbershop, but he tracks him to his campfire. Bill offers O'Bannion $5,000 up front, another $5,000 when Elfego is killed.

With O'Bannion on board, Bill recruits a rifle-toting sheriff, Jeff Milton, and a young ladies' man, Bunny Fox. In Abilene, he attempts to buy the freedom of a gambler, Colt Moran, from jail – but Moran, once freed, pulls a pistol and bolts. Bill and company track Moran to a gambling house where he's fallen foul of a crooked crowd. They massacre the other gamblers, are absolved by the sheriff, and recruit Moran.

Elfego and his Commancheros attack a stagecoach guarded by US soldiers, and steal the consignment of cash. Bill and his band split up, agreeing to meet at Madigan's post. Two Commancheros spot Bill and O'Bannion en route to the trading post; Elfego orders his *segundo*, Moreno, to follow them there. At the post, O'Bannion makes short work of the aggressive Commancheros – but Elfego and the rest of the band arrive. Bill and O'Bannion are tied up and beaten by the bandits. Elfego torments Bill – in a flashback, we witness Elfego's rape and murder of Bill's Indian wife, Mirana, and Bill being framed for murder and robbery. Elfego leaves for another raid, planning to frame Bill and O'Bannion for this crime too. But in his absence Milton, Fox and Moran arrive at Madigan's post, kill the guards, and free the prisoners.

Bill leads his men into the wilderness, knowing that Elfego and the Commancheros will follow their tracks. In the forest, Bill and company split up and lay traps for the Commancheros, killing them one by one. Night falls and Elfego keeps sending his men out in small groups, in search of Bill. None of them returns. In the morning, Elfego wounds O'Bannion; the remaining Commancheros are killed; and Bill confronts Elfego in a clearing. Elfego torments Bill, claiming he has always been faster with a gun. But Bill reminds Elfego that he has been practising – if only with a wooden gun – for five years. They draw. Bill blasts two guns out of Elfego's hands and, having disarmed him, shoots him in cold blood.

Milton, Fox, Moran, and the wounded O'Bannion opt to ride south with Bill.

The film

Tonino Cervi was a producer. He gave Bernardo Bertolucci his first directing gig (*The Grim Reaper*), and made films with Rosi, Antonioni,

Pasolini and Fellini. But what he really wanted to do was to direct. *Red Desert* (1964) had won the Golden Lion at Venice, but had also gone way over budget, and ruined Cervi financially. So he decided to dedicate himself to cheaper, more popular fare: a comedy, *Excuse Me, Do You Like Sex?*, and a Spaghetti Western. Though he wasn't a professional writer, Cervi started working on the script himself – helped by a young critic, Dario Argento, who was also collaborating with Sergio Leone. Their working title was *Revenge is a Dish Best Eaten Cold*. Inevitably, someone – maybe the distributor – suggested Cervi direct it himself.

The result it a near-perfect revenge Western.

All its characters are archetypes. None of them falters. Brett Halsey (an American, obliged to become 'Montgomery Ford') is spot on as the revenger, unsmiling and obsessed. 'Bud Spencer' (an Italian, Carlo Pedersoli, whom Cervi had known in his theatre days) provides the prototype for all his performances hereafter. Wayde Preston is stoic as the mercenary sheriff, Milton. William Berger gives an ur-William Berger performance as a too-handsome gambler with shifting loyalties: the part he'd played in *Face to Face*, and would play in *Sartana*, and *Sabata*. And Tatsuya Nakadai as the villain, Elfego... this was casting of an inspired nature. Nakadai, a superb actor, who would later play King Lear in Kurosawa's *Ran*, had been the most tenacious villain in *Yojimbo*. *And* he'd had a small role in *Seven Samurai*. Bill Kiowa may be the hero, but the film is all about Elfego. Structurally, *Today it's Me, Tomorrow You* hinges around his stagecoach robbery. In the first half of the film, he's absent. Bill Kiowa gets out of jail, collects his money, and gathers a posse of killers sufficient to bring him down. Only after Bill's clan is assembled do we see Elfego: pursuing two US soldiers who have escaped the massacre, killing them – like a samurai – with a machete. Unlike Bill Kiowa, who never smiles, Elfego goes through multiple emotions in a matter of seconds. Blowing open the strong box, Elfego *smells the money*, then lets it blow out of his hands, staring, wide-eyed and questioning, at his men, as if to say, 'What is this that we so prize?' Laughing, furious, bemused, Nakadai delivers the goods in an outstanding portrayal of a genuine madman. Speaking no English or Italian, he does it in Japanese.

The final showdown between Bill and Elfego takes place in a forest glade. The two men stand facing each other. Unusually for a Spaghetti Western, the shot is held for a long time – some 20 seconds – in which the characters remain motionless, each waiting for the other to make the first move. This is a reference to the climax of Kurosawa's *Sanjuro* (1962); the final showdown in which the *yojimbo*, Sanjuro Tsubaki, faces his enemy, Hanbei Muroto. That shot, held for more than a minute, ends with both men drawing their swords, and Hanbei – pierced through the heart – dying in a welter of gushing blood. Hanbei, of course, was played by Nakadai. So there is a marvellous fusion here – both in cast and in composition – of the worlds of *chambara* and the Spaghetti West.

For his cinematographer, Cervi chose Sergio D'Offizi, who had just completed *Every Man for Himself*. They shot late in the year, and the production circumstances confuse the seasons a little: on the Elios Films set, outside Rome, it's clearly winter, with long shadows and the horses' breath visible. Bill Kiowa and O'Bannion trek across a field of snow. But earlier in the picture, and later, during the forest showdown, it's autumn – the trees golden brown. So the film was shot out of sequence, at the end of 1967, and perhaps early in 1968. Offizi's photography – still keeping the characters at a slight distance, but relying more on tracks which often follow the cast through doorways – makes the whole thing gel. And the art deptartment, run by Carlo Gervasi, is particularly hard-working. A real effort is made to fill the interiors with dressing, in the true Victorian style: drapes, painted walls, reproductions of Constable landscapes, advertisements for Beecham's Pills. Likewise the costumes are specific and elaborate. Beneath his Django cloak, Bill Kiowa wears an extremely smart grey-black jacket; Moran is a dandy who expects his fluffy Hamlet-shirts to last at least two years; Elfego and his Commanchero aide, Manolo, favour black suits and white shirts, while his gang in the flashback sport stylish silk waistcoats.

According to some sources, Dario Argento co-directed *Today it's Me, Tomorrow You*. Brett Halsey said that, no, Argento only visited the set a couple of times, as a pal of Cervi's. Either way, their script deserves considerable praise. There are multiple, classic Western situations, usually played with a twist: like the old-timer (Franco Gula) who, questioned by the sheriff, says he's glad to be alive to have witnessed such a great shootout; or the storekeeper, who – seeing Kiowa kill two outlaws with a pistol he's just bought – vows to stock more models of that gun. Spaghetti Western auteurs sometimes pretended to be founts of Western knowledge, but Argento and Cervi actually provide an interesting historical sidenote: since the Kiowa tribe is matrilineal, when Bill married Mirana, he took his wife's name.

Predictable it may be, but it's very good. As well-made, entertaining, self-aware movies which didn't insult their audience then, and don't today, *Every Man for Himself* and *Today it's Me, Tomorrow You* are exemplary. In cheap but splendid films like these, the Spaghetti Western seemed to have reached its apogee. But more, and stranger, things were about to occur – starting with Gianfranco Parolini's *Sartana*. And in the sequel-filled Spaghetti Gold Rush which followed Parolini's picture, one much-talked-about sequel strangely *didn't* go into production: *Today We Kill... Tomorrow We Die*, directed by Tonino Cervi.

Sartana

aka... *Se incontri sartana, Prega per la tua morte,*
Gunfighters Die Harder, If You Meet Sartana, Pray for Your Death
(Italy/Germany)

Director: Gianfranco Parolini **Producer:** Aldo Addobbati **Screenplay:** Renato Izzo, Gianfranco Parolini, Werner Hauff **Story:** Adolfo Cagnacci, Luigi De Santis, Fabio Piccioni **Director of Photography:** Alessandro Mancori **Art Director:** Giorgio Desideri **Editor:** Edmondo Lozzi **Music:** Piero Piccioni **Cast:** Gianni Garko (*Sartana*), Klaus Kinski (*Morgan*), William Berger (*Lasky*), Fernando Sancho (*General Tampico*), Sidney Chaplin (*Jeff Stewall*), Gianni Rizzo (*Hollman*), Andrea Scotti (*Perdido*), Carlo Tamberlani (*Pastor*), Franco Pesce (*Dusty*), Heidi Fischer (*Evelyn*), Maria Pia Conte (*Jane*), Sabine (*Saloon Girl*)

The story

A black-clad gambler, Sartana, sees an old couple and their driver shot at a distance by a well-dressed killer, Morgan. Morgan's bullet misses

Sartana, however; Sartana kills six of Morgan's accomplices and – when Morgan opens fire again – is able to dodge his bullets.

In town, two businessmen, Hollman and Stewall, and a Mexican general, Tampico, watch a large consignment of gold loaded aboard a stagecoach. Moreno, a bandit working for Tampico, attacks the stage. A young killer, Roy Hughes, murders the passengers. Lasky, a snuff-taking outlaw, appears. His men kill the Mexicans and seize the strongbox. Lasky executes Roy, his assistant in the raid.

At the scene of the robbery, Sartana pockets a musical watch belonging to Moreno. At a nearby waterhole, Lasky's men consider stealing the strongbox for themselves. They are machine-gunned by Lasky, who discovers that the box is full of rocks. Sartana steals Lasky's machinegun.

Lasky demands money from Hollman and Stewall, his partners in the robbery. In the saloon, Sartana bonds with the local undertaker, and beats Lasky at cards. He shoots three other gamblers, and follows Lasky on horseback into a quarry, where he terrifies the outlaw with the sound of Moreno's musical watch.

In a barbershop, Sartana issues an obscure challenge to Lasky and Morgan. Morgan follows Sartana into the undertaker's warehouse; a knife and gun duel ensues, among the coffins. The battle ends abruptly when Sartana knocks a row of coffins over, and Lasky is impaled on his own knife.

Lasky and a new gang pursue Sartana back to the quarry and shoot at him. He jumps to safety, and kills off Lasky's men. Again, Lasky is terrified by the musical watch, which Sartana has hidden in a skull. Sartana demands half the missing gold from Lasky; disarmed, Lasky flees. Lasky reports back to Hollman, Stewall and Hollman's wife Evelyn (who is having an affair with Stewall). The strongbox full of rocks shows up on Hollman's doorstep. Jane, the widow of the late mayor, visits Stewall. They too are having an affair. Stewall lets slip that the gold is really buried in the coffin of the mayor.

Lasky and a prostitute attempt to lay a trap for Sartana in the saloon. But Sartana outwits them, and Lasky sails out of the window, tied by a rope. At his ranch, General Tampico assumes Moreno has betrayed him, and appoints a substitute, Perdido. Outside, he finds his men unconscious, and Moreno's watch. Hollman and Stewall convince Tampico to sign a paper which they say is an insurance claim for the missing money. They finger Lasky as Moreno's killer, and tell Tampico that the gold is buried in the mayor's grave.

The Mexicans beat up Lasky, then find Moreno's corpse hanging from Tampico's front door. The General sends his men in pursuit of Sartana, but the fleeing figure on horseback is a straw dummy. Stewall romances Evelyn, but Sartana appears and demands $5,000 blackmail money. At dawn, Stewall has several black-cloaked men dig up the mayor's coffin. All are killed by the Mexicans' throwing knives. Tampico and his men carry off the coffin – observed by Lasky and Sartana who are, apparently, now partners.

Evelyn reports Stewall's death to Hollman. Hollman tells her he has killed Jane. Evelyn is affectionate and loving again. The Mexicans, opening the mayor's coffin, are massacred by Lasky, who has sneaked into their hacienda with his machinegun, unseen. Sartana appears; he and Lasky open the coffin, which contains the mayor's corpse, and more rocks. Lasky shoots Sartana in the head with his rifle, and departs. Evelyn murders her husband, Hollman, and runs to Lasky, her other lover, in her nightdress. She takes him to the undertaker's warehouse, where the gold is stored in a showpiece coffin, aboard a hearse.

Lasky stabs Evelyn, and prepares to depart with the gold. Sartana appears. He sets up an elaborate showdown. When Lasky tries to cheat, Sartana kills him. He shows the undertaker how he has used a metal plate – an old trinket of the undertaker's – in order to render his hat bulletproof. Sartana rides the hearse with its golden cargo out of town, leaving the undertaker with the bodies of Lasky and Evelyn.

The film

If *Today it's Me, Tomorrow You* was a perfect Italian Western, it was among the last of those straight-ahead films. The highly imperfect *Sartana* points the way ahead. A new hybrid emerges: born of Vincenzoni's greed-crazed contests, the muscular rituals of the gladiator movies, the high technology and ingenious pitfalls of the James Bond films, plus circuses, and gymnastic events, and children's games.

Sartana was, at first, the project of the producer, Aldo Addobbati. Addobbati wanted to make a Western with Gianni Garko. He sent Garko a couple of revenge-themed scripts, which the actor rejected, thinking the 'revenge thing' was being overused. Garko wanted to develop a new character, a gambler whose only interest was in acquiring money. He had in mind a Roman proverb, *Tra i due litiganti, il terzo gode*: when two people are fighting, the third one wins. Addobbati seemed interested, and Garko – pushing his luck – suggested two writers who were friends of his, Renato Izzo and Franco Bucceri, to write the script. When the producer agreed, a contract was signed. The only thing Addobbati insisted on was that Garko's character be called 'Sartana'. Later, the actor learned that *$1,000 on the Black* had been a big success in Germany, where it was titled *Sartana*, after his character. Addobbati had convinced his German investors that these were the further adventures of Garko's 'General Sartana'. But General Sartana was the villain of *$1,000 on the Black*, and Garko had other ideas. He wanted *this* Sartana, unlike the traditional, scurvy Spaghetti crew, to be elegant and sophisticated. Not someone who'd get beaten up, or stained with blood, not Eastwood or Brett Halsey, but a black-clad gentleman, in the Van Cleef/Colonel Mortimer mould.

Gianni Garko's preferred director was Guido Zurli, who'd just made another Western, *A Man Called Amen* (*O tutto o niente*, 1968), with Izzo and Bucceri. But Zurli was suing Addobbati over some other matter, and the producer offered the film to Gianfranco Parolini instead. Parolini had worked on a couple of Italo-German Westerns and directed one of his own, *Johnny West* (1965). He'd also directed six gladiator movies, and an acrobatic martial-arts picture, *Three Fantastic Supermen*, for Addobbati. *And* he'd directed a series of fast-moving spy films starring a character called 'Kommissar X'. Parolini went by many false names, usually 'Frank Kramer'. Neither brilliant, nor original, he was a reliable director of repetitious action scenes.

The film couldn't officially be called *Sartana* since the Germans had already used that title. So Parolini, who had a sense of humour, called the new picture *If You Meet Sartana, Pray For Your Death*. I've described the plot in detail because I want to stress *how entirely meaningless it is*. Lots of stuff happens. Event follows event. Many, many men are shot, or killed with throwing knives. I can't bring myself to write 'they ride across the desert' because there is no desert: all the exteriors take place in what looks like a quarry, dug by bulldozers on the outskirts of Rome. Part of *Django Kill* was shot in a quarry, too: but everything in that film speaks of originality, desperate ingenuity, and a low budget. *Sartana* wasn't short of money, judging by its many extras, elaborate costumes, and specially constructed sets. It looks like it was shot in a quarry for the same reason that the Elios Films set looks like a second-rate, recently painted cowboy set: *Parolini didn't care.*

Consider *Once Upon a Time in the West*, made the same year: think of the care taken by Leone and Delli Colli with the images, the efforts of Carlo Simi's team to make the sets look authentic, and inhabited. Consider the work it took to cover the Elios location with 'snow' for *The Big Silence*. By 1968, Italian Westerns had bested their American counterparts when it came to authenticity of look, or real period detail. Parolini didn't give a damn. He threw this heritage of visual beauty and innovation out of the window. He wasn't making a Western, he was making a James Bond rip-off, and that meant a change of location every five minutes, brief subplots involving sexy women, and a narrative punctuated by rapid-fire, repetitive action.

Why bother to go to Almería, or the Pyrenees, or Monument Valley, when you can shoot the action in a landfill? The sets needn't look good, or realistic: just make them *big*. *Sartana*'s sets are gigantic. Whether it's the hero's hotel room, the villain's mansion, or the General's hacienda, every interior is vast – to accommodate all that jumping and falling. Money not spent on locations or the art department could be spent on acrobats, and actors: hence the stellar line-up of Garko, Berger, Sancho and Kinski. Kinski is briefly glimpsed, but highly prominent on the poster: this would become common as producers, increasingly short on ingenuity, sought to shore up sagging narratives with briefly glimpsed guest stars.

I can think of few other Westerns in which so much effort was expended to so little apparent purpose. Why does Sartana ally himself with Lasky, rather than General Tampico, or Morgan, or one of the banker-villains? How can he jump out of the path of bullets? Why is Lasky so scared of a musical watch? What's with the medallion which

Lasky produces and keeps fingering, but which never receives a close-up or a pay-off? Why does Sartana return carrying a box of dynamite? There are no answers to these questions. Nothing in *Sartana* has any meaning. Everything happens for some instantaneous effect.

Everyone betrays everyone else. The bad guys tumble like skittles. The only survivors are Dusty, the annoying 'cute/funny' undertaker, and the ubiquitous Sartana. Sartana, dodger of bullets, appears and disappears as if by magic: he is the first authentic Spaghetti Western *superhero*. Always ironic, never outsmarted, he speaks in heavily emphasised aphorisms. His first line is, 'I am your pallbearer.' Like Django and Joe, he has an affinity for coffins. Unlike them, he shows no rudimentary traces of morality, nor mortality. He invites an attractive prostitute into his room to lay a trap for Lasky; having bested Lasky, he throws her out. Sartana has no interest in sex, no plans to buy a 'little ranch', no revenge motive. Devoid of any moral sense, yet strangely priggish (he lectures Dusty on the importance of pursuing one's dream!) Gianni Garko's gambler becomes a simple, deadly, money-accumulator.

A superhero for the Reagan/Thatcher years, Sartana was a character ahead of his time.

The film's episodic plot and specific characters were borrowed for a number of sequels, official and unofficial. Some were directed by Parolini, others by a very similar director, Giuliano Carmineo ('Anthony Ascott'). I think of these as *Circus Westerns*. *Sabata*, *My Name is Nobody*, and the egregious *Trinity* films all fall into this category, though *My Name is Nobody* is broader in its reach. Overpopulated, jammed with acrobatics and explosions, peppered with loathsome 'cute/funny' characters, these films were very similar, and very popular, for a while. The Spaghetti Western had found a formula, at last.

Another prescient film made this year was Giuseppe Colizzi's *Revenge in El Paso* (*I quattro dell'ave Maria*, aka *Ace High*). This was a variant on *The Good, the Bad and the Ugly*, with four characters instead of three.

Eli Wallach repeated his bandit role – now as a Greek – and Brock Peters played an acrobatic former slave. Carlo Pedersoli and Mario Girotti ('Bud Spencer' and 'Terence Hill') appeared, for the first time, as a team: they'd appeared separately in Colizzi's previous Western, the splendidly titled, mostly dull *God Forgives... I Don't* (*Dio perdona... Io no!*, 1967). The film did well, and the Spencer/Hill chemistry experiment was soon repeated.

Unfortunately, I haven't seen Lina Wertmuller's 1968 Spaghetti Western, *Belle Starr*, starring Elsa Martinelli and Robert Woods. I *have* seen, much to my regret, *Rainbow*, aka *Shoot Gringo Shoot* (*Spara, gringo, spara*), the only Western directed by Sergio Corbucci's brother, Bruno. Derivative and boring, it's a reminder that talent as a director is not inheritable, or a family trait. By contrast, Giuseppe Vari's *A Hole in the Head* (*Un buco in fronte*) makes several attempts to be original, with a debased, alcoholic hero, acrobatic gunfights, three-way sex between the villain and prostitutes, and bandits arm-wrestling over metal spikes. The casting is weak, but the ideas are good: particularly the early scenes in a monastery, where a monk wielding a football rattle reminds the brothers that death is close at hand (the priestly body count is the highest of any Spaghetti Western).

Giuliano Gemma, erstwhile Ringo, hadn't made a Western in more than a year. Till this year he'd seemed synonymous with the Italian Western. Now, like Eastwood, he was nowhere to be seen. His only 1968 release, *A Sky Full of Stars for a Roof* (*... E per tetto un cielo di stelle*) was shot the previous year by Giulio Petroni. Once again, Gemma plays a 'transformational' character: for the first hour of the film he carries no gun, claiming to suffer from delicate nerves. He handles the move from mawkish dolt-boy to stone-cold killer extremely well. Like the drunken hero of *A Hole in the Head*, Billy Blood, Gemma's character, Billy Boyd, plants a slug in the middle of each enemy's forehead. He has a solid, wicked adversary in Rico Boido's scarred and dandified outlaw, Roger Pratt. And the opening of the film, a stagecoach robbery in the bone-dry Tabernas desert, with cruel, pointless killings, followed by a burial, is beyond splendid.

But, after this stark and shocking opening, *A Sky Full of Stars...* descends swiftly into 'cute/funny' comedy involving Gemma and his co-star, Mario Adorf. Scene after scene of dull outwittings follow, many taking place in the circus. When Billy Boyd finally draws a gun and kills five bad guys, we are reminded what *professionals* Gemma and Petroni can be. But when Billy and Harry bitch at each other like a TV comedy couple, sharing a room with twin beds, we are in the tedious territory of the *buddy movie*. So what if Gemma and Adorf anticipated Hill and Spencer, or Butch and Sundance? Who cares?

1969

Hollywood, whose Westerns had become entirely moribund, fought back in 1969. This year saw the release of three significant American Westerns: *True Grit*, *Butch Cassidy and the Sundance Kid*, and *The Wild Bunch*. *True Grit*, like *The Searchers*, plays with the tough, wry, cantankerous cowboy character John Wayne had created: it also comments on the actor himself – on his chequered career; on what, as a reactionary public figure, he had become – even as it tells the story of a tough old lawman, hired by a young girl. For all its mainstream nature and familiar style (it was directed by a hack, Henry Hathaway), *True Grit* is a fusion picture. Its protagonist is a feisty teenager, Mattie Ross, played by Kim Darby; her sidekicks are a country-music star, Glen Campbell, and Wayne, as Rooster Cogburn. The director of *Easy Rider*, Dennis Hopper, plays an outlaw punk, who dies in Cogburn's arms.

Butch Cassidy and the Sundance Kid has dated more, but it was, in its day, a box-office sensation, reclaiming status for the American form. Today, it seems less like a Western than a de-fanged *Bonnie & Clyde*: instead of Arthur Penn's doomed lovers, George Roy Hill gives us doomed buddies.

The Wild Bunch, on the other hand, has fared brilliantly. It borrows from Huston and the Italians – and why not? Rare is the film which doesn't refer at some stage to some other picture. *The Wild Bunch*, like *True Grit*, exists in the mainstream tradition of American Westerns. It's full of American movie stars, one of whom – Ben Johnson – had played the lead in 'Pappy' Ford's *Wagonmaster*. Yet *The Wild Bunch* simultaneously exists outside that tradition. Like *¿Quien Sabe?* or *Once Upon a Time in the West*, or *The Big Silence* (or non-Westerns like *Citizen Kane*, or *2001*, or *Performance*, or *The War Game*), it is a film so good that it endures in its own right, on its own terms. Time doesn't wither films like these. Years after they were made, they remain extraordinary.

Soon the American Western would disappear – replaced by imitation Spaghetti Westerns like the one Eastwood had made with Ted Post, *Hang 'Em High*, or by Grand Guignol massacre tales which depended on the blood-spurting techniques of Peckinpah, minus his moral compass or his storytelling skill. No matter. In 1969, the Americans back-footed the Italians, with a trio of highly successful, mainstream cowboy films. On the international level, *Once Upon a Time in the West* had faltered, and *The Big Silence* remained unseen. How would the ever-innovative Italians respond?

The most noteworthy Spaghetti Western of 1969 also has the distinction of being the most *political* Western ever made. Directed by Sergio Leone's assistant, on the sets of *Once Upon a Time in the West*, and starring Giuliano Gemma, it was called *The Price of Power*.

The Price of Power

aka *Il prezzo del potere, Texas, La muerte de un presidente*
(Italy/Spain)

Director: Tonino Valerii   **Producer:** Bianco Manini   **Screenplay:** Massimo Patrizi (and Ernesto Gastaldi)   **Director of Photography:** Stelvio Massi, Ricardo Andreu   **Art Director:** Carlo Leva, Angel Arzuaga   **Costumes:** Giorgio Desideri   **Editor:** Franco Fraticelli   **Music:** Luis Enriquez Bacalov   **Cast:** Giuliano Gemma (*Bill Willer*), Van Johnson (*President Garfield*), Warren Vanders (*Arthur McDonald*), Maria Jesus Cuadra (*Lucrezia Garfield*), Ray Saunders (*Jack Donovan*), Jose Suarez (*Vice President*), Fernando Rey (*Pinkerton*), Benito Stefanelli (*Sheriff Jefferson*), Manuel Zarzo (*Nick*), Pepe Calvo (*Dr Strips*), Antonio Casas (*Pa Willer*),

Julio Pena (*Governor*), Angel Del Pozo, Franco Meroni, Paco Sanz, Luis Rico, Massimo Carocci, Maria Luisa Sala, Jose Canalejas, Francisco Brana (*Mortimer*), Lorenzo Robledo (*Brett*), Ralph Neville, Angel Alvarez, Norma Jordan, Carlos Bravo, Joaquin Parra (*Slim*), Massimo Carocci, Luis Rico Pelaez, Lisardo Iglesias, Luis Rico, Franco Meroni, Riccardo Pizzuti, Carlos Bravo, Roberto Camardiel

The story

Dallas, TX, 1880. Pa Willer goes to see Sheriff Jefferson and asks him to put his son, Bill, in jail for a few days: he fears an attempt on the life of the president, shortly to visit Dallas, will be blamed on the unpopular Bill.

In Washington, DC, an aide, McDonald, warns President Garfield and his wife, Lucrezia, of a conspiracy against him, based in Texas. His reforms have made him many enemies; nevertheless, Garfield insists he'll visit Dallas. Sheriff Jefferson escorts Pa Willer back to his ranch; but, as a member of the conspiracy, he has alerted his partner, Wallace, who murders Willer with a red-hot poker. Bill and his friend Jack Donovan discover Pa's body, and Bill vows revenge. Bill and Jack discover and foil a plot, by Jefferson's deputies, to blow up the presidential train. In a flashback, we learn that – during the Civil War – Bill, fighting for the North in a mixed-race regiment with Jack, refused to shoot his own father, a Confederate, and was jailed for four years. However, he tells the grateful president, he bears no grudge.

In Dallas, a cabal controls the vice president. Its members include a rich banker, Pinkerton; the Texas governor; Sheriff Jefferson; and Wallace. Wallace prepares another ambush for the president; Jefferson sees that Jack – an escapee from his jail – is recovering from his wounds in a room overlooking the parade route. The next day, Wallace's snipers assassinate Garfield as he rides in a carriage through town. Bill escorts the carriage to the home of Dr Strips, where the president dies. Jefferson's deputies arrest Jack for the crime.

Pinkerton insists that the VP take the oath of office immediately. Alone with McDonald, the vice president confesses that he is being blackmailed by the Texans, who want him to start another Civil War. He enlists McDonald in an effort to recover documents which incriminate him. Bill and a crippled journalist, Nick, capture one of the assassins, Slim, and torture him till he reveals Wallace's name. McDonald intervenes and

– pretending to be on the side of the southerners – returns Slim to the sheriff's office. Jefferson sends Slim to escort Jack to another jail; both are killed in another of Wallace's ambushes. Bill forces the crooked sheriff, Jefferson, to sign a confession; McDonald confiscates it.

In the saloon, Jack is tried *in absentia*. His mistress, a prostitute, condemns him as the lone assassin. But McDonald, acting for the defence, calls two doctors: Strips, who says the president was killed by a frontal shot, and the presidential surgeon, who says the shot came from the rear. On cross-examination, the surgeon reveals he hasn't really seen the corpse. McDonald demands that the case against Jack Donovan be dismissed – just as Bill arrives bearing Jack's corpse, and Jefferson escapes through the window.

Bill chases Jefferson, but is captured by Wallace. Pinkerton entertains McDonald, who asks point-blank for the documents which incriminate the VP. In return, he offers Pinkerton a *limited hang-out*: a conspiracy will be revealed, but it will involve only Jefferson and Wallace. Pinkerton declines.

In Wallace's ghost-town hideout, Bill warns Wallace and Jefferson that they are being sold out. Wallace, perturbed, rides for Dallas. Jefferson plays Russian roulette with Bill as the target, till Nick shows up with a rifle concealed in one of his crutches and dispatches the guards. Bill kills Jefferson, then, with a bullet in his leg, races for Dallas. He finds Pat, the newspaper editor, intimidated into compliance, and Dr Strips fatally shot. Strips extracts the bullet before he dies.

Wallace visits Pinkerton and demands the documents, at gunpoint. Having got them, he shoots his boss. Bill catches up with Wallace, kills him and acquires the papers. McDonald demands them; Bill refuses to give them up. But, next day, Bill meets McDonald at the station and hands them over. He remains on the platform, uncertain, as the train leaves.

The film

The Price of Power is the first filmed drama to present a critical perspective on the Kennedy assassination. It supports the dissenting viewpoint (consistently held by a majority of Americans) that President Kennedy was killed in a conspiratorial crossfire, on 22 November 1963.

Tonino Valerii sets his story in Dallas, Texas, in 1880. But the issues, and the events, are those of 1963. A liberal president, who must visit Dallas for political purposes, is murdered there. A suspect is quickly arrested, interrogated by the police, then killed in transit between jails. Government agents collect information, which disappears. Local right-wingers and journalists die in mysterious circumstances. The official verdict is that the assassin acted alone.

Bill Willer, helped by a lone honest newspaperman, sets out to break the real story: that the murdered 'patsy' was innocent; that the president was shot by multiple assassins in the pay of wealthy South-ern racists; and that the vice president is in the pocket of this cabal. A complex character, Bill – a Texan – fought for the North during the Civil War, then spent four years in a Northern jail. His goal is neither to save the new president nor preserve the Union, but to avenge his father, and his friend.

Valerii takes vivid images from Dallas, 1963, and places them in his imaginary Dallas, 1880. This city is flyposted with *Wanted for Treason* posters, bearing the president's face. On her arrival in Dallas, the first lady is given red roses instead of the yellow ones Texas visitors tradi-tionally receive. The race to the hospital is overexposed, out of focus, a visual panic. Later, stained with her murdered husband's blood, the widow declines to change her clothes. Just as Lee Harvey Oswald was convicted, after his death, by the Warren Commission, so Jack Donovan is tried *in absentia* in *The Price of Power*. The necessary assumptions of the conspiracy film (almost-universal racism, total cor-ruption of the police, double-dealing by the forces of authority) are already those of the Italian Western, so there is no conflict of interest. What is striking, in fact, is how close Valerii's version comes to our understanding of the Kennedy assassination today.

Of course, as with any controversial, influential event, there are multiple versions. Gerald Posner, Vincent Bugliosi, and other authors have parroted the Warren Commission line that the 'patsy' had no con-nections to anyone, and acted alone. Others, like Mark Lane and Sylvia Meagher, did the painful groundwork which showed the deceptions of the Warren Commission and pointed a finger at the CIA. A later generation of researchers, including John Newman and Anthony Sum-mers, located many of Oswald's secret CIA files, and uncovered his

FBI informant number. While some authors still blame the Mafia, and others an amorphous 'military-industrial complex', there is by now a substantial body of evidence that Texas oilmen with strong links to the CIA were behind the murder. Like the business group run by Pinkerton in *The Price of Power*, a Texas *oil*igarchy financed Lyndon Johnson's political career and had the goods on him. LBJ and his Texas-based associates were under investigation for corrupt practices; it was widely believed that Kennedy would drop him after winning the 1964 election. Johnson is reported to have employed a hired killer, Mac Wallace. Among Wallace's victims was one John Kinser, killed for dating LBJ's sister: convicted of first-degree murder, Wallace received a *suspended sentence* in the case. An LBJ crony, Billy Sol Estes, told a grand jury that Johnson had also ordered Wallace to murder a Department of Agriculture worker, Henry Marshall, who was investigating their mutual rackets.[22]

22 *Robin Ramsay provides a synopsis of evidence regarding LBJ and 'Mac' Wallace in his book* Who Shot JFK? *(Pocket Essentials, 2002). That LBJ was behind the Kennedy murder was the thesis of a documentary broadcast by The History Channel in the United States on 22 November 2003:* The Guilty Men. *What is most interesting about the documentary may be the response of Jack Valenti, head of the Motion Picture Assocation of America – another powerful LBJ crony – who got the film suppressed.*

In *The Price of Power*, the corrupt vice president – excellently played by Jose Suarez – explains it this way:

> As a young political candidate, I was helped by certain corrupt southerners. Now they're aiming to use their influence on me as President of the United States.

Lyndon Johnson would have put it more colourfully, but his situation was the same. The VP wins over the presidential aide, McDonald (Warren Vanders), by telling him that the Texas oligarchs want to rekindle the Civil War. He insists he will commit suicide before starting another war. McDonald, impressed, promises to help him. In 1963, Lyndon Johnson used the same threat of war to make Earl Warren chair the kangaroo court that hung Oswald, and to make Senator Richard Russell serve on it. LBJ told both Warren and Russell that he was under pressure to go to war – against Cuba, maybe even Russia – and that it was essential to establish that Oswald had acted alone. McDonald, the presidential aide, acts like J Edgar Hoover's FBI: intimidating witnesses, hoovering up all the evidence – whether of assassination or political corruption – then concealing it till he can use it for political gain.

All this is part of the rich, unfolding tapestry of JFK assassination research in the early twenty-first century. But how did Valerii and his writers, Massimo Patrizi and an uncredited Ernesto Gastaldi, come up with such a complex, yet viable, conspiracy theory in 1969? LBJ's use of a war threat to railroad the 'patsy' wasn't known until decades later. And where did the name *Wallace* come from? *George* Wallace was a famously racist southern politician, and when I first saw *The Price of Power*, I assumed this was an obvious reference to him. But George Wallace was governor of Alabama, the victim of an assassination attempt himself, who later renounced racism. *Mac* Wallace, unknown to most of us in 1969, was a low-level, racist thug and killer: just like the Wallace of the film, whom the aristocratic Pinkerton so gravely underestimates.

It would be four more years before a Hollywood movie dealt with the Kennedy assassination: *Executive Action* (1973). This is a strange, somewhat stilted film – nowhere near as well made or as exciting as *The Price of Power* – about a conspiracy between business interests and the CIA to murder the president. Robert Ryan plays the head of the corporate plotters, and Burt Lancaster the intelligence-connected organiser; neither is as good as Fernando Rey or Benito Stefanelli, who play the same roles, with considerably more gusto, in Valerii's film. *Executive Action* was directed by David Miller, best known for his fine adaptation of Ed Abbey's *The Brave Cowboy: Lonely Are the Brave* (1962).

The Price of Power is about very important things; appropriately, it gives the impression of being a 'big' picture. Only on a second viewing does one notice the absence of extras: there seem to be about 40 of them, so whenever a small crowd gathers, the streets of Dallas are deserted. Much of the budget probably went to pay Gemma and Van Johnson. What gives the film its big look is its spectacular locations: the city of Dallas, the massive Willer ranch house, and the presidential train. These are the locations of *Once Upon a Time in the West* – Carlo Simi's 'Flagstone' set, the McBain ranch, and Morton's private coach and locomotive. Tonino Valerii had been Leone's assistant on that film; Carlo Leva, the designer, had been Carlo Simi's assistant. And Leone's tough-guy regulars – Stefanelli, Jose Canalejas, Frank Braña and

Lorenzo Robledo – are prominent among the cast. Inevitably, Leone and his masterpiece cast long shadows across *The Price of Power*.

Which raises the question: whose idea was this? Corbucci wasn't interested in the JFK business at all; his sorrow was reserved for the murdered revolutionaries, Che and Malcolm. So why did Valerii, whose first solo Western, *Day of Anger*, was devoid of politics, make this intensely political film? I suspect the hand of Leone. The Master didn't direct a Western in 1969, but he was certainly in the vicinity – preparing a new film about the Mexican Revolution, for Peter Bogdanovich to direct. Bogdanovich was the director of *Targets*, another sniper-assassin thriller. And when another Leone assistant, Giancarlo Santi, directed his first Western – *The Big Duel* – he too chose assassination/conspiracy as his theme. Coincidence? Or was Leone, with his eye on the big picture, and the international dimension, pushing his collaborators somewhere he didn't dare to go?

In distribution, some of the foreign-language titles emphasised *The Price of Power*'s Kennedy connection: in France, the film was called *Texas*, with a poster featuring a sniper's-eye-view of the parade; in Spain, like William Manchester's book, it was called *La Muerte de un Presidente*.

Even today I can't watch the uncensored Zapruder film without being moved to tears by the tragedy of it, and by the outrage that such a conspiratorial murder could occur, and its perpetrators still profit from it. And I was similarly moved when I watched Valerii's parade of open coaches, in *The Price of Power*, turn into a tragic rout. The film is beautifully photographed, by Stelvio Massi, who uses split diopters in the scenes where the cabal puts pressure on the VP. These filters split the focus of the lens, so that a figure in the distance and a face in the near foreground are both sharp: Robby Muller used one in *Repo Man* and, while the actors must keep within certain boundaries or go out of focus, the effect is striking. Also of great note is Luis Enriquez Bacalov's score: an epic piece, his best since *Django*.

The Price of Power is a well-made, thought-provoking Western thriller, with very few failings. Its only annoying factors are the piousness of the president (who intones, 15 years after the Civil War, 'I wonder when we'll be able to abolish slavery... for everyone') and the constant beating up of the black character, Jack Donovan. The film ends ambiguously, with Gemma's character turning secret documents over to the government agent, played by Vanders. 'You need these more than I do,' he says. But Gemma remains on the platform as the agent's train pulls out, in a great heroic shot, and his expression says he isn't sure of this at all. And nor are we. Will McDonald prevent a war? Or will he just facilitate a sleazy cover-up, and business-as-usual?

Gemma admired the film, and was excited to work with Van Johnson, whom he considered 'one of the legends of the American cinema'. Of Ray Saunders, who played Donovan, he recalled: 'He was a very capable American, but the poor guy was mentally unstable... he easily became depressed. One time, he painted himself white.' As Gemma remembered it, Saunders commited suicide. A sad story, indeed – but not uncommon among the expatriate actors who made their careers in the Italian Westerns. Some of the foreigners working on these films were starting to feel very lonely, and isolated. Frank Wolff killed himself, as well; Al Mulock fell out of a hotel window in Guadix; the Austriaco-American, Willam Berger, was busted for drugs and sentenced to years in jail. Berger's 'replacement' was another sandy-haired, too-handsome gringo: Dean Read. Read, like Lee Harvey Oswald, had defected to Russia in the sixties. Unlike Oswald, Read had stayed, becoming a top pop star in the former Soviet Union. Inevitably, he started acting in films. Read died in mysterious circumstances, shortly before Communism did the same.

Cemetery Without Crosses

aka *Une corde, un colt, The Rope & the Colt*
(Italy/France)

Director: Robert Hossein   **Producer:** Jean-Charles Raffini, Jean-Pierre Labatut, Vincenzo Buffolo, Giulio Sparigia   **Screenplay:** Robert Hossein, Claude Desailly, Dario Argento   **Director of Photography:** Henri Persin   **Art Director:** Jean Mondaroux   **Editor:** Marie-Sophie Dubus   **Music:** Andre Hossein   **Cast:** Robert Hossein (*Manuel*), Michele Mercier (*Maria Cain*), Lee Burton (*Thomas*), Daniele Vargas (*Will Rogers*), Serge Marquand (*Larry Rogers*), Pierre Hatet, Philippe Baronet, Pierre Collet (*Sheriff*), Ivano Staccioli, Beatrice Altariba, Michel Lemoine (*Eli Cain*), Anne-Marie Balin

(*Diana Rogers*), Benito Stefanelli (*Ben Cain*), Angel Alvarez (*Barman*), Chris Huerta (*Hotel owner*), Lorenzo Robledo, Carlos Bravo, Simon Arriaga, Jose Canalejas, Alvaro De Luna

The story

A sheep farmer, Ben Cain, is lynched on the orders of Larry Rogers, a despotic cattleman. Cain's brothers share their money with his widow, Maria, after Rogers burns their ranch. She takes her share to a ghost town in the dunes, inhabited by a killer, Manuel. She asks him to take revenge, on her behalf. Manuel declines, then does so.

When vigilantes attempt to run the Rogers boys out of town, Manuel sides with the Rogers. As a result, he is arrested. They bail him out of jail, and take him to the ranch, where Larry Rogers offers him a job as foreman. Manuel accepts. He dines in silence with the Rogers and their hands; that night he opens their corral and frees the horses. When the Rogers take off after their mounts, he kidnaps Diana, Larry's daughter.

Back at the ghost town, Manuel and Maria Cain wait in the street while Ben's brothers rape Diana. Maria forces Rogers to re-bury her husband in the town cemetery. Rogers captures the Cain brothers; and in return for $2,000, one of them, Eli, promises to return Diana at the church, that night. But his attempt to surprise Manuel fails; Manuel and Maria shoot him dead. His horse returns his body to the rendezvous, and Larry orders his brother dragged to his death. While Manuel returns Diana to her ranch, the Rogers attack Maria Cain's place. Manuel goes to return her money, and finds her dying.

Back in town, Larry Rogers and his three sons are waiting. Manuel shoots them all. He is, in turn, gunned down by Diana. She rides away; he dies in the sand.

The film

This film – like *Once Upon a Time in the West*, and *One-Eyed Jacks*, and *El Topo*, and *The Last Movie* – is an Art Western. The visuals are striking, the acting good, the sets amazing. And what is really striking is the *absence of dialogue*. John Ford said a Western was good when it was 'long on action, and short on dialogue'. In reality, there is a lot of jawing in Ford's films. Hossein, on the other hand, took the Master at his word.

There is a long dinner scene, played entirely mute. The only sound is the clatter of cutlery against plates. During the course of the meal, the paid revenger, Manuel, becomes more and more uncomfortable. He realises everyone is looking at him. Do they suspect him? Nervously he fingers a· big jar of mustard – and the top flies off, letting a devilish jack-in-the-box spring forth. Both dinner tables, high and low, erupt with laughter. This is a great Spaghetti Western scene. How complicated a situation it describes! Manuel has infiltrated the Rogers clan so as to destroy them; but now he isn't just a guest – he has been teased – accepted as a friend. His situation, as proxy avenger, is now untenable. Previously the Rogers gang have been distant monsters, murderers. In close-up, they're human, fallible, frail. The episode is so strong because it's played without dialogue. Some say that Sergio Leone directed the dinner scene. He and Hossein had become friends – Hossein dedicates *Cemetery Without Crosses* to Leone – and some sources claim Leone acted in the picture. Leone was certainly in Spain, at the time, preparing *Once Upon a Time in the West*, so his participation is both possible, and unnecessary. For Hossein, in his determination to follow Ford's dictum, goes *beyond Leone*.

Leone's films all have memorably mute beginnings; usually followed by big chunks of expository dialogue. In *Cemetery Without Crosses*, many scenes are played in total silence, or with just a few words, spoken off-screen. Another outstanding sequence, where Manuel and Maria basely acquiesce to Diana's rape, is also entirely mute. Hossein had seen *The Big Silence*, perhaps. Despite the presence of Leone, his master-of-arms, Benito Stefanelli (who plays the hanged man at the beginning), and several Spanish actors, the crew and cast of *Cemetery Without Crosses* is largely French. The cinematography of Henri Persin is very good; unnecessarily, the film begins and ends in sepia tones, but it's otherwise impressively composed and lit throughout. And the design of Jean Mondaroux is quite superb. These French were nothing if not ambitious! On the Llano del Duque, in the Tabernas desert, they pulled down the old *Bounty Killer* set, and built two new ranches – a big one for the Rogers, a small one for the Cains. And on the sand dunes near the beach at Cabo de Gata, Mondaroux constructed a brand-new ghost town. This is a surreal location, wonderfully used in the film – isolated and toy-like, like the matte-painting fortress in *$1,000 on the Black*. Literally built on shifting sands, it vanished once the film was done.

As a director who must earn a living, I have a natural hostility to actors who decide that they, too, can direct. But Hossein does a dynamite job. Though subject to Costner-itis (giving himself bigger close-ups than his leading ladies), Hossein is visually inventive and unafraid to cast himself as a despicable character. Like Archibaldo de la Cruz and Black Jack, Manuel is sad and fetishistic: fantasising that his ghost-town saloon is a bustling casino; keeping his black, leather 'killing glove' in a jewel box. The storytelling is admirably simple; Diana's rape is played off-screen, on the faces of the pair who have, disgracefully, allowed it to occur. Only one thing lets the film down: the director's tendency to forget, at times, his brilliant mute aesthetic, and to allow certain characters to babble. At Ben Cain's funeral, a priest intones lengthily that 'there is a time to live and a time to die', and much more besides. We know this. And the end, otherwise most affecting, is undermined by a long 'we could have been happy together' *schpiel* from Michele Mercier, as the dying Maria. Perhaps, as first-billed actor, Mercier demanded a tedious exhange of sentimental dialogue at this point. But I doubt it. She's too good an actor elsewhere, intelligent as well as beautiful; what a great moment this might be if it, too, were played in silence.

Despite this, *Cemetery Without Crosses* is a tremendous film. No Western, other than *The Big Silence*, communicates such an authentic sense of *sadness*. Hossein's film succeeds both as Art and – even more impressively – as a simple, entertaining Spaghetti Western. It was among the last of these. The film was shot in early 1968, though not released until the following year: their work done, Benito Stefanelli and Lorenzo Robledo headed north to Guadix, to begin *Once Upon a Time in the West*.[23] Leone's model – a simple story, convoluted into something grand, and

23 *And did Leone act in it? It depends who you ask. Frayling and Leone's later biographer, Marcello Garofalo, are both convinced Leone played a hotel clerk in the film. Like Leone, the character is bearded and wears glasses, but according to the credits the actor is Chris Huerta. Marco Giusti says it's Huerta, not Leone: Leone had invited Hossein to play a role in* Once Upon a Time in the West, *and Hossein returned the invitation. But Hossein doesn't appear in Leone's film, and Giusti speculates that – if Leone did act for him – he hated his performance and persuaded the director to reshoot it with Huerta. That would explain his quote in Frayling's book, 'When I saw myself in the film, I decided I would not repeat the experience: the horses acted better than I did.' Lars Bloch acted opposite Huerta and knew Leone well: he says the clerk is definitely Huerta.*

great – was Hossein's model, too. Few other directors seemed so interested in stripping away the subplots and the baroque detail, to reach the raw kernel of the Western. Instead, Baroque Spaghetti Westerns, in the *Sartana* style, were multiplying like mushrooms; and Gothic Spaghetti Westerns, heavily influenced by Italian horror films, *in which the hero was already dead*, were about to appear.

Django the Bastard

aka *Django il bastardo, Stranger's Gundown,*
La horde des salopards, El bastardo
(Italy/Spain)

Director: Sergio Garrone   **Producer:** Pino De Martino   **Screenplay:** Sergio Garrone, Antonio De Teffe   **Director of Photography:** Gino Santini   **Art Director, Costumes:** Giulia Mafai   **Editor:** Cesare Bianchini   **Assistant Director:** Roberto Bessi   **Music:** Vasco Mancuso
  Cast: Anthony Steffen (*Django*), Lu Kamante (*Luke Murdoch*), Paulo Gozlino (*Rod Murdoch*), Rada Rassimov (*Alida Murdoch*), Furio Meniconi (*Sheriff*), Teodoro Corra (*Williams*), Jean Louis (*Howard Ross*), Riccardo Garrone, Carlo Gaddi (*Brett*), Victoriano Gazzara (*Sam Hawkins*), Tomas Rudi (*Roland*), Pietro Torrisi (*Mexican*)

The story

Django, clad in a black poncho, plants a cross in the main street of a near-deserted town. On it is the name of 'Sam Hawkins'. Hawkins and several cronies emerge from the saloon. There is a brief, sepia-tinted flashback of rifles firing. Django kills Hawkins and company.

At the Murdoch ranch, a game of dynamite throwing is in progress. Rod Murdoch, presiding, thinks he sees Django – but Django disappears. Django shows up at a carpenter's and asks for a cross with the name 'Ross Howard'. The carpenter offers to make the cross for free. That night, the wealthy Howard and his wife discuss Murdoch's claim to have seen Django. Ross sits down to work on his accounts – and Django appears in his living room. Another brief sepia flashback – then Howard follows Django outside. Django lures him to the graveyard, where Howard finds a cross with his name on it, and an open grave. He's still insisting Django is dead, when Django kills him.

Rod Murdoch sends his henchman, William, to buy the widow Ross's farm for a low price; and instructs his enforcer, Brett, to raise a large, armed gang. Ross's beautiful sister-in-law, Alida, spies on him. She demands money, reminding him that she has only married his brother, Luke, in return for a regular salary. Luke, meanwhile, spies on the two of them, popping pills.

William heads to the bordello to celebrate; Django appears and tears up Murdoch's money. When William asks who he is, Django replies, 'A devil from hell.' William and the brothel's customers attempt to confront him; Django guns them down.

Brett hires Roland's gunfighters, offering them $1,000 each. Django crucifies William on the Murdochs' fence. He finds Alida, bound and gagged. Released, she scours the bodies of Murdoch's dead henchmen for cash.

Luke Murdoch drags a man behind his gig, to teach him some respect. When the sheriff and the mayor complain, Luke guns them both down. Rod, annoyed, slaps his brother. Luke has an epileptic fit; Alida alone can calm him. On the way to town, Roland's gunmen are decimated by a dynamite bomb set by Django, who permits Roland to escape.

In town, a cross with the name 'Rod Murdoch' and the next day's date appears. Rod orders the town searched and evacuated. Django sits in the saloon, playing solitaire, while the gunmen force all the townspeople to leave. Brett offers Django a job, but he declines, preferring to finish his game of solitaire.

After three dead gunfighters ride, crucified, into town, the surviving gunmen are uneasy. Night falls and Django enters the Murdochs' town house. The sight of a bottle of whiskey induces a third sepia flashback, in which – 13 years previously – Django and a regiment of Confederate soldiers were betrayed by their officers, and massacred. The officers were Lieutenant Hawkins, Captain Ross and Major Murdoch. Alida finds Django and offers to show him where the money is stashed; he insists he isn't interested in money. Instead, 13 years late, he delivers a bottle of whiskey to Rod Murdoch, berates him, and vanishes.

During the night, Django shoots, strangles and dynamites Rod's henchmen. But the deranged Luke manages to shoot him in the arm.

Django hides out while a gun battle erupts between Murdoch's loyal henchmen, and those who want to quit. Luke catches Django a second time, in the chapel, and tries to hang him from the rafters. But Django cuts the rope and Luke falls to his death.

Dawn comes. Outside the church, another cross with Rod's name on it has appeared. Rod grieves over his dead brother, then emerges for a showdown with Django, and is killed. Alida is overjoyed to have her hands on the Murdoch fortune. She invites Django to help her spend the money, saying they'll be rich forever.

'We won't live forever,' Django replies. And he's gone.

The film

In 1969, Sergio Garrone and Antonio de Teffe ('Anthony Steffen') made two Westerns: *No Room to Die* and *Django the Bastard*. These are very different films. *No Room to Die* (*Una Lunga Fila De Croce*) starts from an unusual premise – the smuggling of cheap agricultural labour from Mexico into the United States – and turns rapidly into a routine and conventional picture. *Django the Bastard* starts with the most conventional material, then becomes something unique: the Western whose hero is a ghost.

Given its solid, uninteresting director and its routine leading man, *Django the Bastard* is a remarkable film. Stylistically it resembles a sixties horror movie. In particular, the scene where Ross Howard sits doing his accounts – his office, his flouncy tie, his quill pen, his ticking clock – recalls one of Corman's Poe films. Here Garrone uses no music and the tension is intense: later, when Howard follows Django to the graveyard, a ghostly score of the 'musical saw' variety plays – this dissipates the tension, but increases the similarity to a bad horror flick. Likewise, the scene where mad Luke has a fit – shot from above – and is calmed by his treacherous wife, might come from any horror film by Corman, or Bava, or Margheriti. In this context, the more traditional Spaghetti Western elements – the sepia flashbacks, say – don't work so well: they jar, and interrupt the tightly told horror tale.

Graveyards and crosses are part of the *Django* repertoire, of course – but the Christian symbolism is more perverted here: this Django crucifies his enemies, claims to be a devil from hell, and kills a man in church. While most of the so-called *Django* movies had nothing to do with Corbucci's original, I think this one does. It begins with a shot of water dripping into a mud puddle in a ghost town; Steffen's costume is almost identical to Nero's, minus the Union Army pants. As it progresses, it becomes an *alternative history of Django*. What if, Garrone and Steffen ask, Django had fought not for the Union, but for the South? Their answer is the same: betrayed by his own officers, he would end up a killer of wealthy, ex-Confederate aristocrats, after the war. Paolo Gozlino is cast in the Major Jackson/racist villain role of Rod Murdoch, a vicious yet proper killer who insists to Alida that, 'My brother and I come from one of the best families in the country.' Indeed. But Garrone and Steffen take things further than Corbucci did. Their Django doesn't ride a horse (the only time he's seen on horseback, it turns out to be a dummy) because he is, demonstrably, a ghost. We see him shot dead in the flashbacks. He appears in inaccessible places – Howard's study; the balcony of the Murdochs' town house; Ross's office; a saloon filled with bounty hunters, all of whom are searching for him. Steffen simply slides into frame, like Bronson in *Once Upon a Time in the West*, or is revealed in the background, as other characters clear frame. Unlike the original, this Django disdains money. If he's a devil, or a ghost, this makes sense: what is he going to do with it?

Alida, on the other hand, is a very *lively* character, and my favourite Italian Western villainess. She's played by Rada Rassimov, a good-looking, sharply featured actor who appeared briefly in *The Good, the Bad and the Ugly*. Alida is beautiful, intelligent, strong, and money-mad. Django rejects her overtures, yet nothing bad happens to her: she isn't killed or unduly humiliated, and she gets all the money. At a time of increasingly pessimistic and mysogynistic Spaghetti Westerns, this qualifies as a happy end.

The music, by 'Vasco and Mancuso' (Vasili Kojucharov and Elsio Mancuso) is passable, Gino Santini's lighting is good, though his photography sometimes parades invention to no purpose, as in the opening tracking shot, from directly overhead, of Django's hat.

There's a fine Spaghetti Western/Horror moment – when three crucified bounty hunters ride, dead, into town. This is witnessed by Rod Murdoch, the aristocrat, Luke Murdoch, a madman dressed as

Hamlet with bleached-blond hair, and Alida, clad in a ball gown. Whatever his limitations as an actor, Steffen/de Teffe certainly deserves credit as a screenwriter. Laden with symbols, his script also makes frequent references to games. Django turns down the enforcer's offer of $1,000 – to find and kill himself – in order to 'finish his game'. And, as the last night of the Murdochs descends, Luke and Alida play with a jigsaw puzzle.

> ALIDA: With a bit of patience all the pieces fall into place.
> LUKE: And that's the end of the game.

Luke resembles the blond epileptic Tomas Milian played in *Death Sentence*. It seems like weirdness for weirdness' sake, but, as a madman, he has a special place in this haunted film. Only two characters are able to track Django down: Alida, convinced that he, like she, is money-mad, and the lunatic Luke. When all the other bad guys are convinced that Django is a ghost, or a devil, Luke insists he *isn't*. Previously treated as the sick boy, Luke, slavering, now leads the group of frightened outlaws through the night – yelling, 'Look! This is his blood! *This is his blood!*'

Again, we are in horror-movie territory. The same territory which Clint Eastwood would ride into in *High Plains Drifter*. Steffen/de Teffe bore a certain resemblance to Eastwood, and made his living playing Clint-type roles. So it's a nice irony that Eastwood ended up imitating Anthony Steffen, in his own, derivative, ghost-revenger-horror-Western film. Once again, Eastwood the director was shooting blanks. As with *The Big Silence*, the Italians went there first, and did it better.

And God Said to Cain...

aka *E Dio disse a Caino...*, *Fury at Sundown, Duel in the Wind,*
Et le vent apporta la violence
(Italy)

Director: Antonio Margheriti **Producer:** Giovanni Adessi **Screenplay:** Antonio Margheriti, Giovanni Adessi **Director of Photography:** Luciano

Trasatti, Riccardo Pallottini   **Art Director, Costumes:** Mario Giorsi
Editor: Nella Nannuzzi   **Assistant Director:** Edoardo Margheriti
Music: Carlo Savina   **Cast:** Klaus Kinski (*Gary Hamilton*), Peter Carsten
(*Acombar Sr*), Marcella Michelangeli (*Maria Acombar*), Antonio Cantafora
(*Dick Acombar*), Giuliano Raffaelli (*Doctor*), Alan Collins, Lee Burton
(*Santamaria Brothers*), Lucio De Santis, Furio Meniconi (*Mike*)

The story

Gary Hamilton, breaking rocks on a desert chain gang, receives an amnesty and is abruptly freed. Outside prison, he discovers his Confederate dollars are now worthless. On the stage to town, he meets a pleasant young man, Dick Acombar. He advises Dick, 'Tell your father Gary Hamilton's in town – and I'll see him at sundown.'

The news of Gary's arrival terrifies the wealthy Acombar Sr. As a storm rises, Acombar vows that Gary will never arrive alive. But Gary avoids an ambush by the Santamaria brothers – Acombar's lieutenants – and enters town under cover of a dust storm. He's followed into a dank, dripping tunnel by Acombar's Indian henchman, whom he kills.

Intercepted in church by the priest, Gary insists that, after ten years in jail, he's earned the right to kill. One by one he murders Acombar's men, and leaves their bodies hanging in the chapel. The Acombars dine while a gun battle rages outside. But Acombar Sr goes to pieces when he discovers Gary has killed the Santamaria brothers. In a panic, he pistol-whips then murders the minister. Meanwhile, Dick confronts Gary, who tells him why he's out for revenge. Dick is angry, but sides with his dad.

Still searching for Gary, two more henchmen, Frank and the butler, Juanito, shoot each other. Acombar's wife, Mary, comes on to Gary; he slaps her for betraying him, ten years ago. Acombar Sr kills his son by accident. He blames Mary for Dick's death and shoots her. Falling, she knocks over a lamp and sets the mansion ablaze. Gary kills Acombar, and the tornado finally dies. Departing, Gary tells a townsman, 'Dig under the ruins and you'll find more than enough to rebuild your town.'

The film

Like *Django the Bastard*, this is a fusion of horror film and revenge Western. In contrast to the norms, it all takes place within 24 hours, in one location. There's no back story, no riding through landscapes, no gath-ering-of-the-gunfighters, no flashbacks. Instead, there's a near-classical unity of place and time, in this story of a single night's revenge.

Though made of flesh and blood, and fresh out of prison, Gary Ham-ilton has all the qualities of a ghost. He slides in and out of shadows, appears and vanishes mysteriously. At night, he spirits Acombar's men away, unheard, unseen. The film has a claustrophobic air with lushly decorated, overdressed interiors: the colour red predominates. There is a graveyard; catacombs; a mirror-lined, candle-lit music room; a church with a tolling bell. The photography, with constant circular track-ing shots, low angles, and zooms, reflects the 'look' of contemporary horror films. Antonio Margheriti was a versatile director who had made gladiator movies, spy films, and other Westerns – the most interesting of which, *Vengeance* (*Joko... invoca Dio... e muori*, 1968) has elements of Corman's horror movies, and of *The Trip*. He was happiest with the horror genre: *The Long Hair of Death* (*I lunghi capelli della morte*, 1964) is a tremendous film. Unlike some other directors, Margheriti appreci-ated Klaus Kinski: his *Web of the Spider* (*Nella stretta morsa del ragno*, 1972) would star Klaus Kinski as Edgar Allen Poe.

Here, Kinski's character can't really be a ghost – *and yet he acts like one*. Windows fly open and birds of prey cry out whenever his name is mentioned. One waits for the scene when he'll reveal all, and tell us who he is and what Acombar Sr did to him. The moment never comes. Whenever mention is made of Gary's motives, or of Acombar's past, the scene shifts; and when Dick finally confronts Gary and demands an explanation, Margheriti cuts to Acombar Sr, searching his hacienda for his son. The explanation, when finally offered, is cursory and incom-plete: something to do with money, and Acombar stealing Gary's girl. It just doesn't matter – it certainly can't justify this insane night of death. Yet the killing continues, and the corpses are laid out in the church.

In the absence of an explanation, the whole thing depends on Kinski, and Kinski, clad in a black cape and red shirt, is explanation enough. Whereas in *Sartana* he might be accused of 'phoning in' his cameo performance, Kinski is entirely present here. Languid, men-acing, strong, mad, Gary Hamilton is one of his best Western roles. For a revenger, Gary is unusually loquacious – insisting to the priest that he'll take revenge 'even if God chooses to punish me for it'. His allies are predictable – garrulous old man, kindly saloon girl, ageing doctor – but the villains are remarkable for their sheer lack of villainy. Given the film's classical, 24-hour structure, there isn't time to establish Acombar, or the Santamaria brothers, as paragons of evil. Instead, they come over as a pleasant bunch – like the Rogers clan in *Cemetery Without Crosses*. Acombar plays with toy soldiers, and plans a political career for Dick; Mary appears to be a glamorous, loving mother; the Santamarias are a trio of jokers who line up 'at attention' to welcome Dick home from West Point.

So why all the killing? Acombar Sr is guilty of something, and Gary Hamilton has returned in order to release the violence, the evil in these men: he achieves this in a matter of hours. When Dick learns of his father's past, he sticks by him: like any sane person, Dick cares more for the unity of the family than for some old outsider's grudge. Seeking to resolve matters by violence, he too dies. Death follows a pattern. As Gary's rampage progresses, his victims die more exotically: one Santamaria brother is hanged from a bellrope; another is crushed by the falling bell. Acombar's murder of the priest is particularly Gothic: dying, the pastor strikes the keys of his organ with bloody fingers, till Acombar shoots him again. The final showdown, between Gary and Acombar, takes place in a mirrored, burning room.

There is a remarkable symmetry between this film and *Django the Bastard*. It's the best of Margheriti's Westerns, though apparently he disliked making it, and some scenes were shot after he left the picture. For a long time I puzzled over the coincidence that two similar, Gothic-horror-Westerns should be made the same year. What zeitgeist produced *that* in 1969?

Marco Giusti's *Dizionario* explains and complicates things. Though Giovanni Adessi, the producer, and Margheriti take the sole screenwriting credits for *And God Said No to Cain*, Giusti reveals that the film is a remake of *A Stranger in Paso Bravo* (*Uno straniero a Paso Bravo*), an Italian Western made the previous year. Not only is the story very similar, but *the principal character names are identical*. So Eduardo Fajardo plays Acombar Sr, Franco de Rosa plays Acombar Jr, Jose Jaspe plays Paquito Santamaria, and *Anthony Steffen* plays Gary

Hamilton. Clearly, Steffen/de Teffe – who co-directed *A Stranger in Paso Bravo* with Salvatore Rosso – was impressed by their film and wanted to expand on its notion of an otherworldly hero. (At the start of *A Stranger in Paso Bravo*, Gary Hamilton simply walks out of an empty desert, without a horse or a gun.) When Adessi and Margheriti saw it, they felt the same: they found a great actor to play the ghost, ripped off the character names, then weakened Gary's ghostly status, by putting him on the chain gang.

Producer antics? Or Margheriti's idea? It's puzzling, and strange, and wonderful that the Spaghetti Western could expand its horizons to include a ghostly protagonist. Yet note, at the same time, how *cemented its expectations* have become. Each of these films depicts an obsessed, near-infallible revenger. The majority feature a businessman, not a bandit, as their principal bad guy. These Westerns, inventive and crazy though they may be, are all *In a Colt's Shadow*: especially the one we turn to next.

Sabata

aka *Ehi, amico... C'e sabata, hai chiuso!*
(Italy/Spain)

Director: Gianfranco Parolini   **Producer:** Alberto Grimaldi   **Screenplay:** Renato Izzo, Gianfranco Parolini   **Director of Photography:** Sandro Mancori   **Art Director, Costumes:** Carlo Simi   **Editor:** Edmondo Lozzi   **Music:** Marcello Giombini   **Cast:** Lee Van Cleef (*Sabata*), William Berger (*Banjo*), Pedro Sanchez (*Carrincha*), Franco Ressel (*Stengel*), Robert Hundar (*Oswald*), Antonio Gradoli (*Fergusson*), Linda Veras (*Jane*), Gianni Rizzo (*Judge O'hara*), Nick Jordan (*Alley Cat*), Spartaco Conversi (*Slim*), Ken Wood, Romano Puppo (*Rocky*), Marco Zuanelli (*Sharkey*), Luciano Pigosi (*False Father Brown*), Frank Marletta (*US army captain*), Rodolfo Lodi (*Father Brown*), Fortunato Arena, Angelo Susani, George Wang

The story

Black-caped Sabata arrives one windy night in Daugherty City, just as the bank is being robbed. Sabata meets a drunken Mexican, Carrincha, who claims to be a hero of the American Civil War. In the saloon, he humiliates the innkeeper, Fergusson, who has been running a crooked dice game, and sees an old, bell-wearing, hippie friend, Banjo.

A dying soldier staggers into the saloon and alerts the town. Out in the desert, Sabata intercepts the wagon carrying the stolen loot and kills all those aboard. He returns the safe and the corpses to Daugherty, and receives a reward of $5,000 from the army, whose money was in the bank. Sabata takes a room at the saloon, and reconnects with Banjo, who – like Carrincha – criticises him for not keeping the money.

At the ranch of Stengel, an aristocratic landowner, Judge O'Hara argues with his criminal partners. Stengel, Fergusson and O'Hara have set up the bank robbery, in order to fund Stengel's appetite for land and power. O'Hara is afraid that the army will investigate, and wants to leave town. But he is more afraid of Stengel – and his dart-throwing cane. Stengel tells his henchman Oswald to take care of the Virginian Brothers: acrobats who participated in the robbery. Oswald and his men kill the acrobats, but Sabata intercepts their attempt to make off with the brothers' wagon. Stengel intimidates, then murders, Oswald – the last witness to the robbery. Sabata shows up at the ranch, demanding $10,000 in exchange for the acrobats' wagon. He sends the wagon, booby-trapped with dynamite, into the ranch. When Stengel blows it up, Sabata demands $20,000.

Back in town, for $200, Banjo warns Sabata that Stengel, Fergusson and O'Hara won't pay him. Several killers, led by Stengel's man, Slim, arrive to shoot him, but, via an elaborate ruse, Sabata fools them, kills them, and tells Slim he wants an invitation to supper. A meeting with Stengel, at a long table in an ornate dining room, follows. But there is no dinner. Instead Sabata demands $30,000, and when Stengel threatens him with his dart-throwing cane, Sabata warns him that if he doesn't return to Daugherty, 'Colonel Rafferty will be informed of everything.'

In town, Stengel discusses Sabata with his co-conspirators. O'Hara fears Sabata is a government agent; Stengel thinks he's just a drifter – so it's cheaper to have him killed. Fergusson hires Sharkey, a young killer who lives with his harridan mother, to kill Sabata for $1,000. But

Sabata kills Sharkey; a pair of Earp-type brothers; and a fake priest, all hired by Fergusson. Five old enemies of Banjo's arrive, seeking a gunfight: having a rifle concealed within his instrument, Banjo kills them all. Fergusson, impressed, hires him to kill Sabata – who by now wants a $60,000 bribe – for $100,000. But Sabata out-draws Banjo, and lures Stengel's mounted horde into a dead-end canyon, whose entrance he and Carrincha dynamite. Sabata, Carrincha and Carrincha's Indian sidekick, Alley Cat, attack the ranch, with knives, guns and dynamite, and kill some 50 of Stengel's men. Stengel shoots Fergusson, and attempts to trick Sabata with the same mechanical duelling contraption which killed Oswald. But Sabata kills the grandee with his own dart-throwing cane.

Next morning, Sabata and Banjo face each other in a duel in Daugherty City. Sabata dies – but the duel has been faked between them. Sabata departs with $80,000 of O'Hara's money, leaving Carrincha, Banjo and Alley Cat to split the army reward of $5.000. Carrincha asks Sabata who he is. Sabata doesn't say.

The film

Gianfranco Parolini was scheduled to direct a sequel to *Sartana, I'm Sartana... I'll Dig Your Grave*. But he and the producer, Aldo Addobbati, fell out, and Addobbati offered the film to another director, Giuliano Carmineo, instead. So *Sartana* returns as *Sabata*. This was the first of a successful series of Spaghetti Westerns involving the black-caped gunfighter, initially portrayed by Lee Van Cleef. In it, Parolini was able to pursue the Spaghetti Western's acrobatic tendency – like a Hong Kong kung-fu auteur – blowing up countless stuntmen with dynamite, and seeding gymnastic stunts into every action scene. Even the middle-aged Sabata (most likely Van Cleef's stunt double, Romano Puppo) vaults a second-floor balcony rail and lands in the street with ease. This is a world either of supermen, or of muscle-bound gymnasts.

Gianni Garko had wanted Sartana to resemble Colonel Mortimer: now Lee Van Cleef was actually playing the part. Sabata has Mortimer's dress sense, and his high-tech, extendable repeating rifle. Like Sartana, he packs a multiple-barrelled Derringer pistol, is described as a 'pallbearer', and aspires to be a blackmailer. Ignazio Spalla ('Pedro Sanchez'), who plays Carrincha, isn't a bad actor, but he's given too much screen time and too little to do. William Berger and Gianni Rizzo repeat their *Sartana* roles. Parolini hired *Sartana*'s cameraman, and screenwriter, and editor, and used the same set, at Elios Films. So, couldn't he have brought the *original* fake Mexican, Fernando Sancho, along for the ride as well?

Maybe Sancho wasn't available: the same year he acted in an Italian biopic, *Simon Bolivar*, in Venezuela. Or perhaps Grimaldi, Parolini's new producer, cut him out: after all, his deal was with the Americans. Lee Van Cleef was a big star now, and UA were happy with him: happier than they would have been with Gianni Garko. They were also in favour of William Berger – another white guy, who, with his bells and long hair, they could imagine was a representative of 'hippie' culture: rumour had it that he'd been Keith Richards' flat-mate. Fernando Sancho was by far the better actor. But he was a big, fat, dark-skinned actor, who threw himself into the role and made no effort to charm the audience. So the Americans had no interest in him. Nor, it seems, in Klaus Kinski, who has no cameo here. Not that Kinski or Sancho were short of work: Italian popular cinema was booming, and there were plenty of roles for this iconic pair. But, as replacements, Sabata gives us the under-powered duo of Sanchez and Aldo Canti ('Nick Jordan') as an acrobatic Native American muscleman, as bland as he is mute.

Still, when Parolini made an effort he could do good things. Daugherty City – filled with signs and false fronts and new paint jobs, by Carlo Simi – is a credibly bustling place. At the Villa Mussolini, the director shows us, in one shot, both interior *and* exterior of the ornate dining room, with Stengel's men waiting in the huge courtyard, watching the windows, so that we understand the owner's wealth, and his epic vision of himself. In many of these Westerns, when Mussolini's place is used for a location, it seems out of proportion: more like a palace or an embassy than a ranch house. But now, as Stengel's residence, it makes perfect sense.

Sabata is the best of the circus Westerns, a sub-sub-genre which Parolini either invented or enthusiastically made his own. It succeeds thanks to the high skill levels of all concerned, a great art department and soundtrack, and the presence of Franco Ressel as the principal bad guy, Stengel. Ressel had played the sadistic aristo-villain of *In a Colt's Shadow*; with Stengel, he took this prototype to a higher level: to the camp, flamboyant level of Fergusson in *Requiescant*, or the criminal aesthetics of Sorro, in *Django Kill*.

Stengel is a bizarre, fantastic villain, splendidly portrayed. A self-educated Texan elitist, he reads books praising hierarchies and repeats this stuff as if it were his own. Sabata puts him in his place ('Sit down, Stengel!') but everyone else is simply terrified by him. His henchman, played by Claudio Undari, is named Oswald: shades of *The Price of Power*. This is a nice casting touch, since, as 'Robert Hundar', Undari had been the star of numerous small Westerns. All the villains follow Ressel and Hundar's lead, and take themselves very seriously: among them Spartaco Conversi, as Slim, and Marco Zuanelli (Wobbles from *Once Upon a Time in the West*) as the moronic murderer, Sharkey.

Sabata, on the other hand, is a problematic character. Not only is he a long-distance back-shooter, he's also a blackmailer/extortionist, and – worst of all – respectful of authority. Carrincha and Banjo both criticise him for not simply stealing the army's money. Sabata replies, 'It might be lousy, but it's legal.' So he works within the system! As does the villainous grandee Stengel, robbing his own bank to fund a real-estate scam. Both Stengel and Sabata are racketeers. They are also technocrats: Stengel with his mechanical duellists and dart-shooting cane; Sabata with his extendable rifle, his multi-barrelled pistol, and his phonograph-recording system. But what makes a villain fascinating makes a hero seem smug and unappealing; when Sabata warns Stengel not to harm him, or 'Colonel Rafferty will be informed', he becomes simply pathetic. Not even the wimpish heroes played by Tony Anthony or Mark Damon appealed to higher authority just to avoid a fight.

Van Cleef had a good time making the *Sabata* pictures, but had little regard for them. When, as a young pup, I interviewed him about them, he said:

> I enjoyed them, but they weren't like the Leone films. I don't think it's Parolini's fault – it's as much the fault of the script. I did as good as I could. But if things aren't in the script you can't direct them and you sure can't act them. You can try to add to it

as best you can, but if they aren't there to begin with, you got a wee bit of a problem.

Indeed, there are so many incomplete plotlines and oblique references in *Sabata* that one wonders whether scenes have been cut. There's at least one missing sequence: in which Sabata visits Stengel with sticks of dynamite woven to the inside of his cloak. This is a third instance (cut from the English-language version, it exists in the novelisation of the film!) of Spaghetti Western hero as potential suicide bomber – hard to imagine in a popular entertainment today.

Marcello Giombini's score is very good: funny, big, and lively, self-reflexive like the film itself. As the robbers loot the bank – rolling the purloined safe along a set of dolly rails! – a church organ plays. A play-er piano jangles cheerfully through a shootout, then winds down. And the orchestral whirlwind which accompanies Stengel always makes his presence big, as well as sinister. Parolini said of Giombini, '*Era un scherzoso como me.*' My Italian dictionary translates *scherzoso* as playful. And this is the problem with *Sabata*, overall. It is very well made, and a lot of money went into it – as with *Sartana* – but it is too playful by far. Van Cleef and Berger smirk, as if in on some secret joke. Stronger actors, like Sancho and Kinski, are absent. Only the villains – particularly Ressel, and Hundar – are up to true Spaghetti Western snuff. One feels that Parolini likes the film, likes his crew, likes his ac-tors, but, as with *Sartana*, doesn't really give a damn. Nor did Alberto Grimaldi, busy producing *real* movies: *Satyricon* for Fellini, and *Burn!* for Pontecorvo. It was a game called 'spend the Americans' money, and have a good time'. Whereas, with Questi, or Leone, or Corbucci – in his great films – there is no doubt that the director was *seriously invested* in his work. They weren't being *playful*. They *meant it*. And they made great films, as a result. *Sabata* isn't a great film, but it's an entertaining one. Many entertainments, along these lines, would follow.

By the time *Sabata* appeared – 1969 in Italy, 1970 in the USA – the Italian West was no longer particularly wild: crime had become the province, not of bandits, but of highly placed embezzlers such as Stengel. Franco Ressel played the first of these grandee-businessman-crooks in *In a Colt's Shadow*. In three years they had become the norm. Bankers are villains in *Death Rides a Horse*, *The Big Silence*, *Navajo Joe* and *The Price of Power*; wealthy ranchers are the bad guys in *Requiescant*, *The Hills Run Red*, *The Big Gundown*, *Texas Goodbye*, *Django Kill*, *I Want Him Dead*, *Sartana*, *No Room to Die*, *And God Said to Cain...*, *Django the Bastard* and *Cemetery Without Crosses*. And these are just a few examples.

At the end of 1969, a new Western by Corbucci appeared. In a year without a Leone film, this was, potentially, a most exciting development. An Italo-Franco-German co-production, the film was called *The Specialist*. In the past, Corbucci had demonstrated his capacity to create the sublime, and also to roll out the ridiculous. Which would this be?

The Specialist

aka *Gli specialisti, Le specialiste, Drop Them or I'll Shoot*
(Italy/France/Germany)

Director: Sergio Corbucci   **Producer:** Paolino Mercuri, Neue Emelka, Attilio Ricci   **Screenplay:** Sergio Corbucci, Sabatino Ciuffini   **Director of Photography:** Dario Di Palma   **Camera Operator:** Gilbert Dassonville   **Art Director:** Riccardo Domenici   **Costumes:** Enrico Job   **Editor:** Elsa Armanni, Enzo Alabiso   **Assistant Director:** Filiberto Fiaschi   **Music:** Angelo Francesco Lavagnino   **Cast:** Johnny Hallyday (*Hud*), Gastone Moschin (*The Sheriff*), Sylvie Fennec (*Sheba*), Mario Adorf (*El Diablo*), Francoise Fabian (*Virginia Policutt*), Gino Pernice (*Cabot*), Serge Marquand (*Boot*), Lucio Rosato (*Deputy Sheriff*), Remo De Angelis (*Romero*)

The story

Mexican bandits have held up a stagecoach among snow-capped mountains. They rob the passengers, and throw four hippies into a crater filled with mud. Hud, a gunfighter hanging out at the stagecoach

267

depot, kills all but one of the bandits. He sends the survivor fleeing back to his boss, El Diablo.

Hud is returning to Blackstone, whose citizens lynched his brother Charlie. Everyone in town is obsessed with the whereabouts of the gold Charlie allegedly stole from the city bank. The new sheriff, meanwhile, has banned firearms within the town. Hud surrenders his guns to the sheriff, but 'borrows' one back when two men try to ambush him with rifles. Hud meets a pretty girl, Sheba, who lives with her evil father, Boot; and a bad but attractive woman, Virginia, who owns the bank. Virginia is having an affair with the saloon keeper, Cabot. Her attempt to seduce the sheriff is interrupted when Hud and Boot are involved in a knife fight: in the absence of guns, Hud crushes his adversary with a cash register.

Hud visits El Diablo, who was his childhood friend. The sheriff and El Diablo engage in a head-butting match. The hippies smoke dope and menace Sheba. Hud finds the money buried in a grave; the sheriff confiscates it and returns it to Virginia. She and her lover, Cabot, murder the deputy sheriff and steal the money. Virginia guns Cabot down, as well, but is captured by El Diablo, who determines that the money is fake. He and his men drag her to town and demand the real money; the townspeople hide. El Diablo orders two of his thugs to make Virginia talk. Unarmed, the sheriff tries to intervene. El Diablo shoots him. Hud belatedly comes to her aid – but he is shot and stabbed, and Virginia, bizarrely, jumps into a horseless wagon which rolls backwards, through a barn door, into the middle of the gunfight. All Diablo's men are killed. Dying, Virginia expresses her hatred for Blackstone and its denizens, and tells Hud where the real money is.

Hud goes to Virginia's house to get the cash. Wounded, El Diablo follows him. El Diablo instructs his biographer to write the report of their gunfight truthfully; he loses. Hud takes the money out onto Virginia's balcony, and burns it. In the saloon, the women attempt to tend his wounds. But when Sheba runs to get the doctor, she is caught by the hippies, who have stolen the late sheriff's guns and forced all the townspeople to strip naked and crawl on the ground.

Donning his bullet-proof, chain-mail vest, Hud staggers into the street, carrying an empty gun. His imposing presence terrifies the hippies, who run away. Ignoring Sheba, naked save for a blanket, Hud rides into the sunset.

The film

Sergio Corbucci had told all who would listen that he was tired of Westerns, that he didn't want to make any more Westerns. So, naturally enough, after shooting *A Professional Gun* (another Western he didn't want to make), Corbucci found himself in the French Alps, and on the Elios Films backlot, filming a Western. And not just any Western: a Franco-Italian-German co-production, starring a French pop singer, Johnny Hallyday. How he must have hated it! No wonder *The Specialist* is so shaky, veering between a soap opera involving the daily life of the plodding sheriff, and a catalogue of Corbucci's four current dislikes: strong women, bankers named Policutt, grasping capitalists, and... hippies. Of these dislikes, the hostility to women is surprising, and the hatred of hippies verges on the obsessional. Corbucci gave an interview to a French magazine, in which he explained *The Specialist* as follows:

> The idea was to show that I was against the hippies. Listen, at this time the Manson business hadn't happened... But there are too many real problems in the world for me to accept the disinterested passivity of these people. Yesterday, Jimi Hendrix died shooting up, in London. I am against drugs and hippies. I wanted to denounce them in *The Specialist*... I'm really violently against their attitude, and I hate *Easy Rider*.

Does Corbucci sound like John Wayne, here? Or Ronald Reagan? Given his leftist politics, this may seem strange. But what Corbucci is doing is understandable: he is displaying the traditional, holier-than-thou, *intolerance of the left*. Corbucci was a fan of Malcolm X, of Che Guevara; he made films with simple politics, in which self-sufficient collectivists are protected, by a violent hero, from the greed of urban capitalists and exploiters. For a traditional, working-class leftist, fast approaching middle age, the hippies – with their philosophy of disengagement, drug-taking and sexual experimentation – might, indeed, seem intolerable. Consider the Zapatistas' charismatic representative, Sub-Comandante Marcos. How long did this traditional leftist get away with insulting pot-heads and anarchists, before agreeing to confront his own addictions – tobacco and Coca-Cola – and *their* political implications?

Corbucci was no anarchist. He was no more likely to love hippies than John Wayne was. Wayne hated *Easy Rider*, too. Yet his professed loathing doesn't explain all the conflicting signals in his films. Consider the costumes of Enrico Job, here, and in *The Big Silence*: they are heavily influenced by hippie fashions. Corbucci didn't object when Klaus Kinski wore a shawl under his hat, or Trintignant wrapped himself in fur and leather. He *must* have known where those costumes were coming from. And, if he didn't like hippies, why have them in his film at all? Why not just ignore them, or kill them early on, the way he used to do with priests? Instead, the hippies are a constant and annoying presence in *The Specialist*: hanging around town like stray dogs, they have as much screen time as Hud, and almost as much as the tedious sheriff, who dominates the film.

Mysterious hippie tendencies pop up throughout the film. Hud hates money; he sets the townspeople's treasure trove ablaze, and kills Boot with a cash register. The sheriff is a practising pacifist, who has banned guns, carries daisies in his rifle barrel, and confronts El Diablo unarmed. When El Diablo kills him there is a sudden fast montage of flash-cut, back-and-forth close-ups, like the transitions between scenes in *Easy Rider*. And the film is unique among Corbucci's Westerns for the amount of nudity it contains. Both Virginia and the nameless hippie girl entice men with their bodies, and when the hippies show up with guns, they force all the townspeople to get naked and crawl on their bellies. This isn't very sexy, having all the awkwardness of an amateur production of *Hair*. But, if Corbucci didn't like this stuff, why did he imitate it?

The Specialist is *The Big Silence* superlite. Instead of snow-covered mountain ranges we have wet hills in the off-season. Instead of a few scenes with Frank Wolff as a funny sheriff, we have many scenes with Gaston Moschin as a would-be-serious sheriff. The villain, once again, is a banker named Policutt. And the bad guys round up a bunch of hostages and threaten to kill them all unless the hero shows his face. But who cares? In *The Big Silence* something was actually at stake, since the hostages were genuine innocents: the townspeople in *The Specialist* are greedy, grasping jokes with bad hairpieces and false moustaches. And *The Big Silence* had a real hero and at least two truly evil villains. The audience *cared* about Jean-Louis Trintignant's fate, whereas no one in their right mind can be bothered either way about Johnny Hallyday.

Not that Hallyday is entirely bad: he's your average rock-star-actor, no better and no worse than Kris Kristofferson: facially, he somewhat resembles 'Rick Boyd' and might, like Boyd, have made a career playing minor Spaghetti Western villains, if he'd kept at it. The action sequences are few but good, particularly the fight, with knives, ice blocks, and cash register, in the saloon. And Virginia (Françoise Fabian) is a handsome and effective villain, with extraordinary grey eyes and a streak of white hair; doomed by Corbucci to an unnecessarily cruel and sexist fate. Why does her character hate the town of Blackstone so? She dies without revealing the details. Gino Pernice, so memorable in Corbucci's earlier films, is wasted here. Mario Adorf – Gemma's comic 'buddy' from *A Sky Full of Stars for a Roof* – is unconvincing as the one-armed bandit, El Diablo. And Elios Films – so well used in *The Big Silence* and *Sabata* – never looked more like a run-down old movie set.

I regret to inform the gentle reader that this film was released in England as *Drop Them! Or I'll Shoot*. In France, the film was called *Le specialiste*. In Italy, it was *Gli Specialisti: The Specialists*. Hud is called a 'specialist' by the sheriff, but he's the only one. The rest are amateurs. Was Virginia the other specialist, perhaps? Corbucci didn't seem to think so. He told *Image et Son*:

> Eroticism is already in the violence of a Western. I think it's better not to put women in these films – if *The Specialist* didn't work, it must be the woman that's to blame...

What a marvellous example of a director displaying no self-knowledge or perspective on his own work! All of Corbucci's Westerns up till now had featured strong women characters, most of whom survived and were not so basely treated. *The Specialist* doesn't work because Corbucci didn't care about it, and really didn't want to make it. Worse was to come.

1969 saw various Spaghetti Westerns of minor note, including Enzo Barboni's first film as a director, the boring *Unholy Four* (*Ciak Mull, l'uomo della vendetta*); a co-directed, MGM-funded, Tortilla-train-heist film titled *The Five Man Army* (*Un esercito di 5 uomini*); a Western shot by Italians in Brazil, *O Cangaceiro*, with Tomas Milian; another ur-*Trinity* film by Giuseppe Colizzi, *Boot Hill* (*La collina degli stivali*); another Tony Anthony/Alan Klein sequel, *Stranger in Japan* (*Lo straniero di silenzio*), shot, as the reader might guess, in samurai territory; and a well-acted, dark, gay-themed Western, *El puro* (*La taglia e tua... l'uomo l'amazzo io*), starring Robert Woods, Mark Fiorini, and Mario Brega.

The biggest-budget Western of the year was probably Duccio Tessari's new one, *Alive, or Preferably Dead*. Though made by Italians, this picture barely qualifies as a Spaghetti Western at all. Instead, it's an acrobatic, slapstick *Butch and Sundance* spoof, featuring mud-wrestling hunks in the shapes of Gemma and Nino Benvenuti. There is little death, no danger, and much cuteness. It's blameless, rootless and uninteresting. Howard Hughes reckons that by 1969 the Spaghetti Western was losing ground to horror films; he credits the form's survival to *Sabata*, with its circus atmosphere, its somersaults, its tongue-in-cheek. Thanks to Grimaldi and the American deal, the film was widely seen and – like *Sartana* – much imitated. But several forces were now in play: competition at the box office from other genres; actor and director availability; and investor confidence in these 'older' forms, as the market changed. No one watched gladiator films any more – how long before the audience tired of Westerns? As a new decade loomed, no producer or distributor wanted to be stuck with outmoded product. Would they play it safe, and stick to established formulas – even if this made the Italian Western more predictable, and less open to startling visions, or political parables?

The Seventies

'Leone's pictures are cynical, which Ford never was. There's no poetry in them. The problem is they do in a way reflect a change in American mythology: and they're rather fascist in implication.'
– **Peter Bogdanovich**

Around 1970, the Spanish government erected a gigantic antenna on the Sierra de Nijar, south of the Tabernas desert, where most of these Westerns were filmed. The hideous construction dominated the landscape, changed all the possibilities. Suddenly the 360-degree view, which Sergio Leone had praised so highly, was gone – instead a massive, red-and-white radio, TV and communications mast dictated what angles a Western could, and could not, use. Soon after, high-tension power lines ran across the Llano del Duque, killing the 360-degree panorama there, as well.

This is just happenstance, no doubt, but the new decade – and the destruction of that pristine, desert view – marks the continued growth, and swift decay, of the Spaghetti Western.

Compañeros

aka *Vamos a matar, compañeros*
(Italy/Spain/Germany)

Director: Sergio Corbucci   **Executive Producer:** Antonio Morelli
Screenplay: Dino Maiuri, Massimo De Rita, Fritz Ebert, Sergio Corbucci
Based on an idea by: Sergio Corbucci   **Director of Photography:** Alejandro Ulloa   **Art Director:** Adolfo Cofiño   **Costumes:** Jurgen

273

Henze, Giuseppe Capogrosso   **Editor:** Eugenio Alabiso   **Music:** Ennio Morricone   **Music Director:** Bruno Nicolai   **Cast:** Franco Nero (*Yolof Petersen*), Tomas Milian (*Basco*), Jack Palance (*John*), Fernando Rey (*Prof Xantos*), Iris Berben (*Lola*), Francisco Bodalo (*Gen Mongo*), Karin Schubert (*Zaira*), Edoardo Fajardo (*Colonel*), Gerardy Tichy (*Lieutenant*), Lorenzo Robledo, Jesus Fernandez, Luigi Pernice, Alvaro De Luna, Claudio Scarchilli, Giovanni Petti, Gianni Pulone, Nello Pazzafini, Victor Israel, Simon Arriaga, Rafael Albaicin, Jose Canalejas

The story

Lola and Basco – two revolutionaries – are about to get married when Basco is forced to face a Swedish arms dealer, Yolaf Petersen, over a business deal which went sour. As the two prepare to shoot it out, we flash back to Basco's political transformation: he goes from being a shoeshine boy to an army officer to a shoeshine boy for a rebel general, Mongo. Basco, deputised by Mongo, arrests the Swede and plans to kill him. But Mongo returns and begins negotiations with Petersen instead.

Petersen and Mongo plot to open a safe in Mexico: they believe a huge quantity of rebel wealth is cached within. The only person who knows the combination is a rival rebel leader, Professor Xantos, currently held prisoner in the United States. Petersen volunteers to go to the US and rescue him; Mongo sends the naive Basco to assist him. Petersen and Basco are stopped by an army patrol which has orders to take all *peones'* pictures, and issue them with ID cards. Basco kills several soldiers and escapes, followed by Petersen – who loses his passport. With the aid of a group of prostitutes led by Zaira, Petersen and Basco infiltrate the US Army prison and set it on fire, so as to liberate Xantos.

They are just in time. US interests, keen to control the outcome of the Revolution and unable to make a deal with Xantos, have hired a professional killer, John, to murder him. Dressed as monks, Petersen and Basco attempt to sneak the Professor back into Mexico in a coffin. But John intercepts them and a gun battle ensues. Peterson and Basco manage to return Xantos to the village where the safe and General Mongo are. After lecturing them all on pacifism and non-violence, Professor Xantos opens the safe to reveal only an ear of corn – symbolic of the true wealth of Mexico – within. Mongo attempts to kill him, but is shot by Xantos' followers.

The showdown between Petersen and Basco is interrupted by the arrival of John, who has a long-standing grudge against the Swede. Professor Xantos takes up a rifle and attempts to save Basco. John shoots him. Petersen sets off a time bomb aboard his armament-packed railroad car; blowing John up. Professor Xantos dies in his followers' arms, and Petersen leaves for the border. But, seeing a cavalry detachment approaching, he returns, and throws in his lot with the rebels.

The film

A remake of *A Professional Gun*, with Franco Nero and Jack Palance reprising their roles, and Tomas Milian replacing Tony Musante. What is surprising about *Compañeros* is that it's a decent film: faster, crazier, better than the one it imitates. Corbucci imports scenes from *Django* (such as the Trojan horse of prostitutes, gaining entrance to a fort), and hires actors from *Django*: Eduardo Fajardo, Gino (now 'Luigi') Pernice, and Jose Bodalo. So it seems he was having fun, at last.

The *Monthly Film Bulletin* remarked, 'Saddled with some embarrassing revolutionary sentiments by the dubbed dialogue, the student revolutionaries... are an exceptionally risible crew.' Indeed they are. The film's politics are a sort of leftist pie-fight. Corbucci clearly believes in the therapeutic application of revolutionary violence, at all costs, in all circumstances. Every situation, for him, involves irreconcilible class conflicts, to be resolved with dynamite and machineguns, at once. So he is opposed to the pious pacifist, played by Fernando Rey. Rey had the same role in *Navajo Joe*, as well: this time he changes his mind, and totes a rifle for the grand finale. What is Corbucci telling us? Xantos' attempt is useless: he is quickly shot. So why have him take up a gun at all? To make some point about the hypocrisy of non-violence? But who, in the Wild West or Revolutionary Mexico, was seriously preaching this?

Our director is on more solid ground with Palance, playing one of his crazier villains. Like the hippies in *The Specialist*, John is a pot-smoker. So we know he's dangerous, apt to giggle and get hair in his eyes. Unlike the hippies, he is a reliable bad guy. And there's a classic Corbucci back story: not too long ago, we are told, the Swede nailed John's prosthetic to a tree. John was unable to get it loose, and so his pet falcon (Mary Jane in the English version, Marcia in the Italian) had to bite his hand off. Now John has a wooden prosthetic and a grudge, and has been looking keenly for Yolaf Petersen. What a pity John's sad story doesn't receive a red-tinted flashback! But Corbucci was at least enjoying his old mutilation trip, with John's screw-on wooden hand, and his deaf Chinese henchman, tiny speaking-trumpet attached to his ear... The director's widow, Nori Corbucci, told Katsumi Ishikuma that they saw a UFO while on the set of *Compañeros*, and filmed it. So there was much to enjoy.

And Corbucci liked Tomas Milian, just as he continued to approve of Nero. Milian was still in his heroic-actor-peasant phase, so the role was perfect for him. And Nero certainly knew how to play an ironic gringo gun-runner. Milian found Nero a bit strange. 'He was very self-conscious of his looks,' he told *Westerns All'Italiana*. 'I remember Franco was going to make-up. Franco was, at the time, I think 23, 24 years old or something like that. He was in make-up three hours, and the make-up man was painting wrinkles and putting gold in his moustache and things. I said, "Franco, why do you want to look older?" He said, "You know why? Because when I am old, when I am 50, the audience will always see me in the same way. I will look like I never aged because I'm going to be an actor forever."' It *was* a strange-sounding strategy: directors never cease to marvel at the weird game-plans actors can come up with. But Nero remained an ageless leading man, so his strategy appears to have worked.

I saw *Compañeros* when it came out, and didn't like it much. It seemed a bit feeble and very simplistic, compared to *¿Quien Sabe?* or *Tepepa*. But its simplicity was the message, perhaps. Corbucci thought of himself as a political filmmaker, just as Sollima did, just as Bertolucci did. They all wanted their work to say something, to communicate ideas – leftist ideas – to the largest possible audience.

Christopher Wagstaff has pointed out, in *Popular European Cinema*, that in 1970 Bertolucci's *The Conformist* earned half a billion lire at the box office, while *Compañeros* took 1.5 billion lire. *Il Conformista* is a better film than *Compañeros* – it is one of the best films *ever!* – but which reached a wider audience? Which was seen by the working-class masses whom leftist filmmakers, presumably, desired to entertain, and influence? Which picture, ultimately, was more effective, in political terms?

1970 was an uncertain, transitional year. *The Beast* (*La belva*) was a bizarre attempt at a Western vehicle for Kinski, in which the star played a drunken and depraved rapist and murderer. If anyone could have sustained such a project, it was Klaus Kinski, but the lack of talent in every other area – script, direction, production, cast – proved fatal. Giorgio Gentili – director of *The Bang Bang Kid!* – took over an Italian-American Western filming in Spain, after Dino De Laurentiis fired his first director, Vic Morrow. The film, *A Man Called Sledge*, is a good heist-robbery-caper movie in the Spaghetti style, starring James Garner and John Marley. Rainer Werner Fassbinder shot *Whity* entirely in Almería, using the 'El Paso' set. But the film, a family story about racism and murder, isn't really a Western, nor is it one of Fassbinder's great melodramas. Gianfranco Parolini shot a *Sabata* sequel, without Lee Van Cleef: unable to agree upon a price with the obvious actor, the producers cast Yul Brynner instead. The result, *Indio Black*, was retitled *Adios Sabata* when the French insisted it be a sequel. Pop star/spy Dean Read fills in for an incarcerated William Berger. And Anthony Steffen donned a 'Hamlet' outfit for *Apocalypse Joe* (*L'uomo chiamato Apocalisse Joe*), in which he played a gunfighter/Shakespearean actor.

But I am avoiding the elephant in the room. For all the big-budget, international co-productions made this year, the one film which matters is an inexpensive, comic Italian Western starring the team Giuseppe Colizzi had created. Written and directed by *Django*'s cameraman, it was *They Call Me Trinity*.

They Call Me Trinity

aka *lo chiamavano Trinita*
(Italy)

Director: Enzo Barboni   **Producer:** Italo Zingarelli   **Screenplay:** Enzo Barboni   **Director of Photography:** Aldo Giordani   **Art Director:** Enzo Bulgarelli   **Costumes:** Luciano Sagoni   **Editor:** Antonio Siciliano, Giampiero Giunti   **Assistant Director:** Giorgio Ubaldi   **Music:** Franco Micalizzi   **Cast:** Terence Hill (*Trinity*), Bud Spencer (*Bambino*), Farley Granger (*Major Harrison/Harriman*), Steffen Zacharias (*Jonathan*), Dan Sturkie (*Tobias*), Gisela Hahn (*Sara*), Elena Pedemonte (*Judith*), Luciano Rossi (*Weasel*), Enzio Marano (*Timid*), Remo Capitani (*Mescal*), Michele Spadaro (*Peon*), Michele Cimarosa, Ugo Sasso, Riccardo Pizzuti, Gigi Bonos

The story

Trinity, a Western layabout who travels in a travois, kills two bounty hunters and delivers their wounded prisoner to his brother, Bambino, who appears to have become a sheriff. Bambino is in fact an outlaw waiting for his gang to arrive; he has shot the real sheriff and stolen his identity. Trinity and Bambino befriend a group of Mormons, who are building a settlement nearby. This brings them into conflict with Major Harrison, a cattle rancher who wants the Mormons to move on. Harrison hires killers to dispatch them, but Trinity, with his unerring aim and super-fast draw, and Bambino, who is incredibly strong, run them out of town.

Harrison teams up with Mescal, a comic Mexican outlaw, to destroy the Mormons' settlement. But Trinity has fallen for two blonde Mormon girls, Sara and Judith; he, Bambino, and Bambino's imbecilic henchmen teach the Mormons how to fist-fight, disarm the bad guys, and participate in a lengthy brawl, which the Mormons win. Bambino discovers that Trinity has given Major Harrison's herd of stallions – which he had planned to steal – to the Mormons. Defeated, Harrison heads for Nebraska. Trinity, realising a life of toil and prayer is not for him, follows Bambino and the gang west, towards California.

The film

They Call Me Trinity was originally intended as a vehicle for two other actors, Peter Martell and George Eastman ('Luigi Montefiore'). Enzo Barboni had directed one other Western, *Ciak Mool/The Unholy Four*, under the pseudonym of 'EB Clutcher'. Unlike Massimo Dallamano, as a director Barboni abandoned any attempt at visual quality. *They Call Me Trinity* is a particularly boring-looking Italian Western: mostly wide shots of uncomfortable extras and stunt men, its medium shots centrally placed, in television style. But Barboni wasn't into aesthetics here. Leave that to the Sergios. He'd been hired, by producer Italo Zingarelli, to write and direct a broad, popular 'buddy' comedy. So that was what he did. Instead of Martell and Eastman, he cast two actors who had already been paired, for comic purposes, by Giuseppe Colizzi: Terence Hill and Bud Spencer.

Frayling and Hughes observe that the Trinity/Bambino team is a variant on Laurel and Hardy in *Way Out West* (1937). Both films depend upon an ill-matched pair of partners; both begin with one of the partners being dragged through the desert on a travois, and drenched in a river crossing. The main difference is that *Way Out West* is a funny movie, with real actors and good photography. Sergio Leone said that *Trinity* killed the Spaghetti Western, by reducing it to farce. Sergio Corbucci called the film 'a moral blow to the Italian Western'. These men took their storytelling seriously – or thought they did – and both were offended by Barboni's film. Yet it enjoyed a box-office triumph: having cost 400 million lire, it earned between six and seven *billion*. Only Bertolucci's *Last Tango in Paris* did better in terms of receipts, and – as Barboni observed – ticket prices almost doubled between the releases of *Trinity* and *Last Tango*. Like Gianfranco Parolini, Enzo Barboni injected a lease of lifeblood into the Spaghetti Western: at least, into its sentimental, formulaic, farcical variant.

1971 saw another Western version of *Hamlet*, *In the Dust of the Sun*, (*Il sole nella polvere*), by a French director, Richard Balducci. And there was also a *Trinity* sequel. *Trinity is Still My Name* (*...Continuavano a chiamarlo Trinita*) followed the same menu of fast-draw displays and brawls, in a more episodic format. So mainstream had these films become (and so difficult the life of a Western movie actor) that Dobe Carey – costar of *Wagonmaster* – played a cameo role as the heroes' father. A less-official, overtly leftist sequel also appeared: Mario Camus' *Trinity Sees Red* (*La colera del vento*) is a Tortilla Western in which Trinity (Terence Hill) renounces his slothful ways and follows the Revolutionary path – just as Franco Nero's character did, in *Compañeros*. Giuliano Gemma and Michele Lupo teamed up for a forgettable 'buddy' movie in the *Trinity* manner: *Ben & Charlie* (*Amico, stammi lontano almeno un palmo*). Pasquale Squitieri directed an 'Indian-loving' Western in the style of the revisionist American picture, *Jeremiah Johnson*: it was entitled *Apache* (*La vendetta e un piato che si serve freddo*) and, in the light of the American Western fight-back, Squitieri reverted to an American *nom-de-film*, 'William Redford'. A Western with hardcore porno scenes was also shot – *The Price of Death* (*Il venditore di morte*). The sex seems to have been dropped from the finished film. And Parolini and Van Cleef revisited Elios, for *Return of Sabata*, in which Sabata is a government agent pursuing counterfeiters, and circus action predominates.

So, by 1971, The Spaghetti Western seemed doomed to expire in a cemetery of imitative sequels, parodies of parodies, signifying nothing. Two films came along to shake up this otherwise irrelevant year: one from the Master, Sergio Leone, the other from a surprising source. First, the Master.

Duck, You Sucker!

aka *Giu la testa, Il etait une fois... la revolution, A Fistful of Dynamite*
(Italy/Spain)

Director: Sergio Leone   **Producer:** Fulvio Morsella   **Screenplay:** Luciano Vincenzoni, Sergio Donati, Sergio Leone   **Story:** Sergio Leone,

Sergio Donati   **Director of Photography:** Giuseppe Ruzzolini   **Art Director:** Andrea Crisanti   **Costumes:** Franco Carretti   **Editor:** Nino Baragli   **Special Effects:** Antonio Margheriti   **2nd Unit Director:** Giancarlo Santi   **2nd Unit Photography:** Franco Delli Colli   **Music:** Ennio Morricone   **Cast:** Rod Steiger (*Juan Miranda*), James Coburn (*Sean Mallory*), Romolo Valli (*Dr Villega*), David Warbeck (*Sean's friend in flashbacks*), Maria Monti (*Woman on stagecoach*), Rik Battaglia (*Santerna*), Franco Graziosi (*Don Jaime, The Governor*), Domingo Antoine (*Col Gunther Reza/Gutierrez*), Goffredo Pistoni (*Niño*), Roy Bosier (*Landowner*), John Frederick (*American*), Antonio Casale (*Notary*), Jean Rougeul (*Priest*), Furio Meniconi (*Executed revolutionary*), Nazareno Natale, Benito Stefanelli

The story

Mexico, 1913. Juan Miranda and family rob a richly appointed stage-coach, killing the guards and driver, and stripping, raping and humiliating the passengers. Sean Mallory, a former IRA dynamiter, rides by on his motorcycle. Juan shoots a hole in his rear tyre. Sean retaliates by blowing a hole in the stagecoach roof – and Juan has a vision of Sean as the key to realising his lifelong dream: robbing the Mesa Verde bank.

Juan tries to persuade Sean to join him in this enterprise. Sean claims he has a job in a silver mine, and escapes on a passing train. Juan and his sons ride the next train to Mesa Verde. Two policemen try to arrest Juan; he is saved via the intervention of the mysterious Dr Villega. In Mesa Verde, Juan sees the bank he has always dreamed about – and runs into Sean again. Sean reveals that he and Dr Villega are revolutionaries; they want help in liberating the contents of the bank. Juan is delighted to assist.

The bank robbery takes place under cover of an insurrection. Juan breaks into the bank, losing several sons in the process, and shoots open the vaults. But the strong boxes contain not money but men. Too late, Juan realises that Sean has tricked him into freeing political prisoners. The unwilling Juan is now a hero of the Revolution.

The rebels retreat into the mountains, pursued by the Germanic General Reza in his armoured car. Sean and Juan remain behind to harrass Reza. They blow up a bridge and decimate his forces. But all the other rebels, who have retreated to a cave, are massacred – including

Juan's father and his six remaining sons. Juan is captured, and Sean sees Dr Villega, a broken man, collaborating with Reza.

In a series of flashbacks, we learn how Sean's best friend betrayed their IRA cell to the British Army, and how Sean killed him.

Sean saves Juan from the firing squad, and they board a cattle car for the United States. Also attempting to escape aboard the train is the state governor, Don Jaime. But the train is ambushed, and Juan shoots Don Jaime. Once again, he is a hero of the Revolution. Their trip to the US is postponed, a major operation against Reza planned. Sean picks Dr Villega as his partner aboard the locomotive which will ram a cargo of explosives into Reza's train. Aboard the loco, he confronts Villega about his treachery. Sean jumps clear, but Villega, stricken with guilt, remains aboard the train.

A night-time battle ensues around the wreckage of the trains. Reza shoots Sean; Juan kills him. Dying, Sean assures Juan he will be a great hero of the Revolution, and explodes.

The film

Sergio Leone did not want to direct this. He had just been offered *The Godfather*, and turned it down. Leone had his own gangster project, but, once again, was under pressure to make a Western. In 1968, he'd hired Sergio Donati to write the first draft of a Tortilla Western, provisionally entitled *Mexico*. But the two men fought over the script – Donati felt Leone wasn't really into the project – and parted company. Leone approached Eli Wallach about playing the lead: this time the 'Ugly' character would be the hero. But when United Artists became involved, a 'more famous' actor was called for. Leone un-invited Wallach (this is a very bad thing to do, though most directors have done it, on occasion). Somehow, his relationship with Vincenzoni was patched up, and Vincenzoni started working on a new draft, now called *Once Upon a Time...The Revolution*: he was pleased to be back in the territory of *A Professional Gun*, but with an even bigger budget.

Leone invited Peter Bogdanovich, 30 years old and highly regarded, to direct the picture, which Leone would produce. Bogdanovich came to Rome in October 1969, and they began a series of meetings. These went badly; directorial egos immediately clashed. Their styles clashed, too: Bogdanovich favouring a 'retro' approach of medium shots and wide masters, while Leone was famous for his filmic 'postmodernism' – fast cuts, loud music, super-tight close-ups. Bogdanovich either quit, or was fired, and in an article for *New York* magazine he wrote: 'Sergio wanted me to believe he was a great director; *he* didn't believe it, which is perhaps why it was so important that those who worked for him did.' Throughout the process of making these films, Leone seems to have veered between long periods of boundless energy and confidence, and crippling passages of insecurity: the insecurity which Clint Eastwood hadn't been slow to exploit, in the belt-and-suspenders incident.

Meanwhile, the title had changed again: to *Giù la Testa*, which means 'Keep Your Head Down' or 'Get Out of the Way'. Leone apparently believed that the English equivalent of this common Italian phrase was 'Duck, you sucker' and that this should be the English title of the film. Before he left, Bogdanovich tried to talk Leone out of it: '[Leone] insisted that "Duck, you sucker" was a common American expression. I said to him, "They don't say that *ever*, Sergio, *anywhere* in America." "No. It is a big expression in America." Eye block. He seemed to think I couldn't be a real American at all if I hadn't heard of it.' Chris Frayling, understandably, loathes the title and calls the relevant chapter in his Leone biography *Keep Your Head Down* instead.

Leone claimed later that Sam Peckinpah agreed to direct the movie, but that UA didn't want him. Vincenzoni said that Peckinpah didn't, in fact, want the job. The other producers suggested Leone's assistant director, Giancarlo Santi, and Leone agreed. Santi began directing the film, but survived only a short while. Rod Steiger and James Coburn, the two American stars, had signed on believing Leone was to be the director. They refused to allow him to replace himself with Santi, and insisted that Leone direct, or they would quit. Perhaps this was what Leone had wanted, all along: to direct the film but only by stepping in late, to save the project. That way, maybe he could escape the blame if *Duck, You Sucker!* didn't turn out to be his biggest, most expensive, most highly regarded opus yet.

Of all the Tortilla Westerns – Italian films supposedly set during the Mexican Revolution – this is the least 'Mexican'. The art department is good, and the locations, at Almería station, in Gergal, in Guadix, in Burgos, and in Ireland, are excellent. The massacre, filmed in an abandoned sugar mill, is very impressive, so massive and so cruel that it could, indeed, have occurred in Revolutionary Mexico. But the film's other incidents, and the faces of the participants, are quite un-Mexican. The actors look like Italians, in an Italian movie about partisans, fighting against the fascists, in the Second World War. Given Leone's obsession for details and bizarre fragments of authenticity, a certain wilful ignorance went into his art department's creation of a prop book titled '*The* Democracy', by Bakunin. It was the same triumph of ignorance that gave the film its title; the same determined know-nothingness which set its story in 1913, and made its co-protagonist an IRA man (as Frayling points out, the IRA was not formed until 1919). Leone himself said, in the aftermath, 'The Mexican Revolution is only a symbol.' But it had already been a symbol, and a powerful one, for Damiano Damiani, and for Giulio Petroni. Both directors used the Mexican Revolution as a means of depicting other, more modern, conflicts between high-tech armies and *guerrillas*, other interventions by the Colossus of the North.

What is the message of this film? That making a Revolution hurts? Even Corbucci's Tortilla larks told us that, and a bit more. The lengthy quote from Mao Tse Tung ('The Revolution is an act of violence,' etc) which precedes the film was unlikely to surprise audiences. The customers expected machinegun massacres, explosions, flying stunt men, and a certain cynicism about the triumph of the Revolution. These same working-class, Italian audiences might well be offended by the film's sentimental finale, in which Sean returns the crucifix which Juan, in his anger against God, has thrown away. Again, this is the kind of stuff included to please studio executives in Hollywood. The *real* Mexican Revolution was intensely, popularly anti-clerical, with priests taking up arms in open warfare against the population (just as they did during the Spanish Civil War). Christian terrorists – called *Cristeros* – fought violent rear-guard actions against successive Revolutionary governments. What a Spaghetti Western that would have made!

Instead, Leone borrows from other films: the locations of ¿Quien Sabe? and Tepepa are recycled; Sabata's dynamite-filled coat turns up, worn by James Coburn. The liveliest moments in the picture are a bank robbery (borrowed from Vincenzoni's script for For a Few Dollars More) and the blowing up of a bridge (borrowed from Vincenzoni's script for The Good, the Bad and the Ugly). A subplot, told in flashbacks, about Sean and his buddy's love for the same girl, and the friend's betrayal of their unit to the British, is in the sentimental vein of Ford's The Informer and The Quiet Man. British politicians and media people who celebrate our 'special relationship' with the US might wish to ponder Duck, You Sucker! – a film financed by a Hollywood studio, whose Irish hero (played by an American movie star) shoots dead two British soldiers, on duty in the province of Ireland.

The film has fine technical credits. It's beautifully photographed, by Pasolini's cinematographer, Giuseppe Ruzzolini. The acting is good: Steiger and Leone had certain misunderstandings on set, but he gives a decent performance, and Coburn does his usual cool, minimalist stuff. The film is very well directed. The wordless scene where Sean watches as Dr Villega betrays his former comrades is as good as anything Leone ever did. Santi – relegated to second unit – delivers some good crowd scenes. Santi's cinematographer was Franco Delli Colli, who had shot Django Kill.

But good technical credits don't stop a film being stupid, or boring, or base, and Duck, You Sucker! is all those things. Frayling writes, of the rape, 'It is a difficult scene to watch.' He is, as ever, discrete in his judgements. This scene, where Steiger's character, Juan, rapes one of his prisoners, played by Maria Monti, is horrible: annoying, self-satisfied, sexist and stupid. I've got tired of repeating the crass, mysogynistic plot-lines of some of these Spaghetti Westerns; the later Westerns of Leone and Corbucci are the most wearisome of all, in this crass regard. Other than this nameless woman, and another one in the flashbacks (who appears to symbolise the spirit of Irish Republicanism), there are no women in the film. After Once Upon a Time in the West, it was a return to the boys-only world Leone and Vincenzoni apparently preferred.

Duck, You Sucker! is the first of these films to rely extensively on post-production effects and model shots. The sign which appears over

Sean's head, making him the patron saint of bankrobbers, is the first matte in an Italian Western since *$1,000 on the Black*. There are also composites and miniatures when the train wreck occurs. The model shots look too much like model shots, which I would guess is not the filmmaker's intention; it's more obvious because some of the footage – the 'B' camera, presumably – was filmed in a 1:1.33 ratio and inserted into the otherwise anamorphic film, giving them a crudely stretched-out appearance. One doesn't normally highlight the miniatures via glaring, obvious mistakes; I wonder if Leone, who hadn't done post-production special effects since his gladiator days, just failed to pay attention to them.

The other '71 Spaghetti Western of note comes from Ferdinando Baldi, a not-very-noteworthy director, and Tony Anthony, an actor worthy of little or no note at all. Despite their plodding pedigrees, the two came up with – in the face of buddy Westerns and circus Westerns – an old-fashioned, bad-taste Spaghetti, based on a Japanese *chambara* film, heavy on traditional bloodshed and violence, but with added sexism. The model was *Zatoichi Monogatari*, Kenji Misuma's samurai film, made in 1962. The film was *Blindman*.

Blindman

aka *Il cieco, Il pistolero cieco*
(Italy/Spain)

Director: Ferdinando Baldi   **Producer:** Tony Anthony, Saul Swimmer, Roberto Infascelli   **Screenplay:** Vincenzo Cerami, Piero Anchisi, Tony Anthony   **Director of Photography:** Riccardo Pallottini   **Art Director:** Gastone Carsetti   **Costumes:** Marco Ambrosini, Silva Corso   **Editor:** Roberto Perpignani   **Music:** Stelvio Cipriani   **Cast:** Tony Anthony (*Blindman*), Ringo Starr (*Candy*), Lloyd Battista (*Domingo*), David Dreyer, Lucretia Love, Isabella Savona, Magda Konopka (*Sweet Mama*), Agneta Eckemyr (*Pilar*), Ken Wood, Raf Baldassare (*El General*)

The story

Blindman, a blind gunfighter, is trying to find 50 mail-order brides whom he is under contract to deliver to miners in Utah. His former partner, Skunk, has betrayed him: he says he has sold the women to a Mexican bandit, Domingo. Pausing only to dynamite Skunk and his colleagues, Blindman heads on his seeing-eye pony, Boss, for Mexico.

In Mexico, a naked prostitute attempts to seduce Blindman. But he just wants information as to Domingo's whereabouts. Domingo refuses to return the women to Blindman: he says he intends to sell them to the Mexican Army. Domingo's sister, Sweet Mama, runs their bandit operation out of an abandoned fort; his brother, Candy, thinks only of a blonde woman, Pilar, who keeps resisting his charms. Sweet Mama and her henchmen massacre a squadron of Mexican soldiers while Domingo kidnaps their general, to hold for ransom. Candy and co beat up and imprison Blindman.

But Blindman overpowers his jailer and escapes; with the General's and Pilar's help, he frees the 50 women, and humiliates Pilar by tying her, naked, to a post. In the desert, Domingo and his men catch up with the women, murder several, and re-imprison the rest. Blindman kills Candy, and Domingo stages an elaborate funeral for him; insisting to the priest that Pilar marry Candy's corpse. Blindman murders Sweet Mama and rescues Pilar, but the two are tracked down by Domingo and his surviving men, in a graveyard. The General intervenes; his men kill Domingo's men, and he blinds Domingo with a cigar so that a fair fight between Blindman and the bandit may follow. Blindman kills Domingo.

The General says goodbye to Blindman, and departs, taking all the surviving women with him. Blindman asks Pilar to help him locate his charges; she tells him the General has them aboard his wagons. Amazed, Blindman gallops off in pursuit.

The film

Blindman was financed by former associates of the Beatles: Allen Klein, their disastrous manager, and Saul Swimmer, co-producer of *Let it Be* and director of George Harrison's *Concert for Bangladesh* film. Second billing goes to Ringo Starr, the ex-Beatles drummer who was looking for acting roles. And two small roles – Skunk's villainous associates – are played by Klein and Beatles roadie Mal Evans. With so much peace, love and transcendental energy in their sails, it's interesting to speculate how these guys made such a cynical, sexist, and slapdash film.

Not that cynical, sexist and slapdash are deal-breakers: this is a Spaghetti Western, after all. But to pull such things off, a film has to be technically very, very good: like Hitchcock's *Psycho*, or *Rope*, or one of the better horror films of Dario Argento. This isn't. The idea of 50 women, who wear only nightdresses, kidnapped by Mexican bandits (one of whom is from Liverpool) and rescued by a blind gunfighter is, in a Spaghetti Western context, a very good one. Unfortunately, Anthony treats it as a remake of *A Stranger in Town*, with a bigger budget and better production design. All the incidents are boring and implausible, the loathing of women similar, but on a bigger scale. Scenes are recycled: again, the hero is menaced by a sadistic woman; again, he murders her. The murder is more protracted, but no more plausible here.

Of the women characters, only two – Pilar and Sweet Mama – have names. The 50 kidnappees are anonymous; all the same size and shape (tall, skinny, big-breasted), and mainly blondes. The scene where the women, in their nightdresses, attempt to escape and several are shot down or beaten to death is bad: it would be worse if it were done graphically, in the American manner of *The Hunting Party* or *Soldier Blue*. But it is still bad. The scene where the brides, all naked, are washed by gypsy harridans throwing bucketloads of water at them, is, by contrast, played in the background. Anthony and his director, Ferdinando Baldi, seem much more interested in filming women killed than washed. I wonder why, and if their audience was of the same persuasion.

Ringo Starr is not strong in the role of the bad younger brother, Candy. Gifted actors like Eli Wallach and Rod Steiger had to work hard to even attempt a Mexican accent. Ringo couldn't pull it off. By contrast, he showed talent as a film composer: he appears to have written a score for *Blindman*, only to have it rejected by the producers. All that remains is the 'B' side of his single *Back Off Boogaloo: Blindman*, a dirge-like theme song which actually works well, in the context of the film. Instead, Anthony and co went with a lazy score by Stelvio Cipriani.

The art department, headed by Gastone Carsetti, is unusually fine. None of his previous work, on Westerns like *Get a Coffin Ready* (1968) and *Boot Hill* (1969) was anything like this. Carsetti uses some of the newer locations – in particular a fort built by the Americans for their Lee Van Cleef–Jim Brown Western *El Condor*, and a *cortijo* which Leone had found near Guadix, and used at the start of *Duck, You Sucker!* But his triumphs are a ghost ranch, surrounded by a mesa-sized cemetery, and Domingo's town – which, after the death of Candy, he insists on painting black, anticipating *High Plains Drifter*'s city-painting schemes by several years. The images of a jet-black settlement with a white-walled church, surrounded by the Tabernas desert, are sensational. These, and the lines of *penitentes*, clad either in white brides' dresses or black *Semana Santa* hoods, make Candy's funeral the high point of the film.

Lloyd Battista, Raf Baldassare, and Magda Konopka give solid, uninspired performances. The hippies who play their henchmen are mostly ridiculous. For once, despite his vanity and ill-advised multi-tasking, Tony Anthony does a decent acting job. He plays his strange, blind, sexless hero with an uncharacteristic degree of sympathy and range. Blindman is less a gunfighter than a desperate, money-hungry bumbler. Most of the jokes are at his expense: breaking mirrors, falling off his horse, dropping his hat or gun and having to go back for them. He milks goats, shares watermelons with his horse, and kills his enemies largely by luck, emptying his guns in their direction. And he remains a naive and trusting character: marching like Requiescant into lions' dens, and remarking to Pilar what a nice man the General is, just after the latter has kidnapped his mail-order brides. This is the only time I've seen Anthony give a performance of any substance, or play a likeable personage. Indeed, second only to the horse, Boss, Blindman is the most appealing character in the film.

Anthony, and Klein, and Baldi would make other films together, but this was the high point of their collaboration. Now they were on a downward learning curve, with genre-busting Westerns, 3-D Westerns... Well, never mind. *Blindman* is far from a great film, but it has sadistic style and imaginative elements which recall the golden years of 1966–68. It could have been worse, and for that reason alone – as the form stumbled and began to lose its way – enthusiasts still recall it fondly.

1971 also saw the release of a new *Sartana* sequel – *A Cloud of Dust, A Cry in the Night... Sartana's Here* (*Una novola di polvere, un grido di morte... arriva Sartana*) – directed by Giuliano Carmineo, whose style and aspirations were very similar to Gianfranco Parolini's. The film is memorable for two reasons – the murder, at last, of one of those 'cute/funny' characters (in this case the old coffin-maker) – and because of its structure, with copious flashbacks, as a murder mystery. Admittedly, it's a boring mystery, resolved with the aid of robots and a pipe-organ machine-gun. But the notion of Western-as-Whodunit took root, and, the following year, Sergio Leone oversaw one of his own: *The Big Showdown*.

The Big Showdown

aka *Il grande duello, The Grand Duel, Storm Rider, Hell's Fighters*
(Italy/France/Germany)

Director: Giancarlo Santi **Producer:** Pietro Innocenzi, Ettore Rosboch, Enrico Chroscicki **Screenplay:** Ernesto Gastaldi **Director of Photography:** Mario Vulpiani **Art Director:** Franco D'andria **Editor:** Roberto Perpignani **Assistant Director:** Fabio Garriba, Claude Othnin-Girard **Music:** Luis Enriquez Bacalov **Cast:** Lee Van Cleef (*Clayton*), Peter O'Brien (*Philip Vermeer aka The Jesse Kid aka Newland*), Horst Frank (*David Saxon*), Marc Mazza (*Eli Saxon*), Klaus Grumberg (*Adam Saxon*), Jess Hahn (*Peacock*), Dominique Darel (*Elisabeth*), Anthony Vernon (*Hole*), Sandra Cardini (*Anita*), Remo Capitani, Furio Meniconi, Romano Puppo

The story

Clayton, a sheriff, is riding on a stagecoach. Its progress is halted by a roadblock: the stage station up ahead is occupied by Philip Vermeer, an accused murderer. Surrounding the post is a host of vigilantes and bounty hunters. Clayton intervenes and promises to protect Vermeer; the outlaw surrenders; the bounty hunters kill off their allies so as to concentrate the reward money; but, true to his word, Clayton escorts Vermeer to Saxon City, where he is alleged to have killed the town's founder.

Here, the youngest Saxon boy, Adam, clad all in white, provokes an old man into a gunfight. He kills the oldster; the townspeople, also clad in white, take off their shoes and beat them together, as a symbol of disapproval. Clayton realises that Vermeer isn't safe with the town marshall, Eli Saxon, and lets him escape. Overcome with emotion, Eli recalls – in the first of numerous flashbacks – how their father was shot dead at the railroad station in nearby Jefferson. Vermeer was present at the time, and Eli and Adam blame him for the crime. Vermeer, meanwhile, blames them for his own father's murder.

David, the oldest Saxon brother, introduces himself to Clayon in his saloon. Unlike his siblings, he doesn't believe the patriarch's murder will ever be solved. As he attempts to win Clayton over to their side, a wagon train attempts to leave Saxon City, in search of a better life. Adam and his henchmen bomb and machinegun all aboard to death in a ravine. Killing his last henchman, Adam departs. Vermeer discovers the massacre and brings a wagonload of bodies – men, women and children – back to town.

Captured by Marshall Saxon, Vermeer is marched to the gallows to be hung. But Clayton intervenes again, insisting he killed Saxon Sr, and challenging the sons to a duel. The showdown occurs in the corrals outside town. No one will draw first, till Vermeer shoots Clayton's hat off – then guns flash, and Clayton kills David, Eli and Adam. He rides off, leaving Vermeer in the arms of Elisabeth, Adam's mail-order bride.

The film

Giancarlo Santi, the reader may recall, was Sergio Leone's assistant director. Placed in an invidious position on *Duck, You Sucker!* he was fired by the actors, who wanted Leone to direct them instead. Santi was given his chance to direct a Western the following year. Leone doesn't receive a producer credit, but – given his relationship with Santi, and the film's similarity to *The Price of Power*, I perceive his influence.

The Big Showdown has a similar plot, and title, to *The Big Gundown*. Again, Van Cleef plays a redoubtable lawman, who comes to believe the killer he's hunting is innocent. It is also a whodunit. In this case, the audience is asked to guess who killed the patriarch of the Saxon clan, and why they did it. There is a problem here. Murder mysteries, in my experience, tend to offer a potential array of suspects, any one of whom may have done the deed. *The Big Showdown*, on the other hand, doesn't offer many suspects. Vermeer is accused, so he can hardly be the guilty party. The only established characters not present at the railroad station shooting are Sheriff Clayton and David Saxon. As the flashbacks progress, each adding more visual information, we learn that both Clayton and David *were* present, and fired pistols that night. So David may be his father's killer; or it may be the mysterious man in black at the end of the platform (who is obviously Van Cleef, or his double, Romano Puppo!).

Thrilling, no? Either one or the other of two thinly sketched characters may, for his own reasons, have shot the patriarch: an unpleasant-looking old man in a top hat, whose assassination is his only appearance in the film. The problem is, of course, who cares? What does it matter who shot the old capitalist? We know nothing about him, other than that he fathered a nest of rich, viperish sons. Two of the three sons are pretty interesting. The middle son, Eli, is permanently angry, permanently bald, and saddled with a dull brown suit. David and Adam dress all in white. David is like an ambitious Kennedy, or Rockefeller, aspiring to great things, simultaneously hushing other things up:

> DAVID: Undisputed masters of the whole state! And one day there will be Saxons in Washington – and even in the White House!
>
> ELI: You know who killed our father, don't you?
>
> DAVID: Never ask me that question again.

David keeps repeating this, insisting to his brothers, and to Clayton, 'Half the state had reasons to kill the patriarch. We will never know the truth,' and 'The case of the patriarch's death is closed.' So he is deeply suspect. And the conspiracy angle is also pushed by Clayton, who starts discussing bullet trajectories, like a Dealey Plaza analyst: 'The bullet that went through the patriarch's head came from in front of him. And Philip was behind him. So it couldn't have been Philip.'

Adam Saxon doesn't concern himself with fine points like who killed his dad, or why. As played by Klaus Grunberg, he is a fine Spaghetti Western psycho, white gloved, white hatted, distinctly Bowie-esque, his face covered either with cigarette burns or pox. His introduction is tremendous: through sheer evil energy, and strength of will – and an intense, trilling Bacalov score – Adam forces an old man to draw his gun, so that the Thin White Duke can have the pleasure of shooting him, with his silver pistol. If only there were more of this intense, insane stuff. But the bulk of the picture is pretty routine. There are Hong Kong-style acrobatics, and pole-vaulting, by Alberto Dentice ('Peter O'Brien'), who plays Vermeer. And, as was increasingly common, there are many hippies in extra roles. Indeed, only the Saxon brothers seem able to afford haircuts. Van Cleef has let his hair grow; ragged ringlets around the collar of this middle-aged man do not suit him. The decline of the Spaghetti Western can be seen, here and in *Blindman*, in these henchmen who follow the principal villains around. In the glory days of the sixties, such roles were filled by tough-looking *men* like Kinski, Sambrell, Stefanelli and Brega. By the early seventies, these *actors* had been largely replaced by fat-faced, stoned-looking hippie *extras*, all sporting long, freshly washed hair.

A certain infantile seediness pervades *The Big Showdown*: as in the bizarre 'joke' where Vermeer's horse is shot – the stunt looks very dangerous – and the camera zooms in on its asshole. The bad guys apparently think Vermeer is hiding in a hole: 'This is the only hole I see around here, boys,' says one. This is so pathetic that one again suspects the presence of Leone, and the bathroom humour he had come to favour, in *Duck, You Sucker!* and *My Name is Nobody*.

Ernesto Gastaldi was a good screenwriter – he'd written *Arizona Colt* and *$1,000 on the Black* – whose heroes are strangely blank, self-regarding characters. Vermeer and Clayton certainly fit that bill. Whereas Gastaldi's villains were baroque and splendid. Here the Saxon brothers, having imprisoned the hapless Elisabeth in her room, plan their political futures (she is a senator's daughter) and drink a toast, to 'Peace, law, and order'.

The big showdown of the title takes place in a series of corrals. This involves a lot of opening of big gates, and some exaggerated, but effective, choreography.

As a filmmaker, you enjoy it because you know there's a crew member hiding out of shot, who grabs the gate and stops it flying back and hitting Lee Van Cleef. But why does David Saxon (played by the redoubtable Horst Frank), having thrown open his gate, walk backwards, in unison with brother Eli (Mark Mazza)? It looks good, and it's done in time to the music. But doesn't walking backwards while maintaining eye contact with Lee Van Cleef put you at a disadvantage? All is sacrificed for the conceit of the shot, and to the Spaghetti Western convention that villains, about to be shot, will stand in a straight line.

DAVID: Don't jump the gun, Eli. Wait. In a minute.

ADAM: We must draw soon. We mustn't let Clayton start this. He's faster than we are.

Vermeer, who also knows this, shoots Clayton's hat off – provoking Clayton to draw, and shoot 'em all. While the big showdown isn't nearly as prolonged as Leone's had become, it's very distinctive. Santi was clearly a good student of showdowns. But he didn't persist with them: this was his only Western.

Some credits list four editors on *The Big Showdown*; Roberto Perpignini, the first credited, says the other three did not exist. Perhaps they were invented for co-production reasons. This might also explain the odd musical credit: supposedly the composer was one Sergio Bardotti, and the musical director 'Luis Enrique'. According to Marco Giusti, Bardotti had nothing to do with the project; all the music was composed by Bacalov. Certainly the recycled chunks of score from *Django* (also reused in *¿Quien Sabe?*) suggest the score is his.

1972 saw two new Corbucci Westerns, *What Am I doing in the Revolution?* (*Che c'entriamo noi con la rivoluzione?*) and *Sonny & Jed* (*La banda J&S – cronaca criminale del far West*). I haven't seen the first of these, apparently a Tortilla Western starring Vittorio Gassman and Eduardo Fajardo. I *have* seen the second, a mean-spirited 'comedy' Western in which Tomas Milian mistreats Susan George for 98 minutes. About this film, the less said the better. It serves to illustrate only how Corbucci had by this stage given up everything that had once been important to him: original action scenes; perverse, anti-clerical violence; and strong women characters. He would direct one last Western, the following year.

The same year, the acrobatic Hong Kong influence was at last incorporated as a plot element, along with a Chinese hero: *To Kill or Die*, aka *The Fighting Fists of Shanghai Joe*.

To Kill or Die

aka *Il mio nome e Shanghai Joe, The Fighting Fists of Shanghai Joe, The Dragon Strikes Back*
(Italy)

Director: Mario Caiano   **Producer:** Renato Angiolini, Roberto Bessi, Carlo Alberto Alfieri   **Screenplay:** Mario Caiano, Carlo Alberto Alfieri, Fabrizio Trifone Trecca   **Director of Photography:** Guglielmo Mancori   **Art Director:** Riccardo Domenici   **Costumes:** Orietta Nasalli-Rocca   **Editor:** Amedeo Giomini   **Assistant Director:** Cesare Nola   **Music:** Bruno Nicolai   **Cast:** Chen Lee (*Shanghai Joe*), Klaus Kinski (*Scalper Jack*), Katsutoshi Mikuriya (*Samurai*), Carla Romanelli (*Christina*), Gordon Mitchell (*Sam Il Becchino*), Robert Hundar (*Pedro Il Cannibale*), Carla Mancini (*Conchita*), Giacomo Rossi Stuart (*Tricky*), George Wang (*Master Yang*), Rick Boyd (*Slim*), Francisco Sanz (*Jesus*), Piero Lulli (*Spencer*)

The story

1882. Joe, a recent immigrant from China, arrives in San Francisco. He turns down offers of laundry and dish-washing work, and buys a ticket on the stage to Texas – where he learns that Chinese, blacks, and Indians, must ride outside.

Abandoned by the stagecoach driver at an isolated outpost, Joe is pestered by three local racists. He reveals himself a master of the martial arts, demolishes them, and heads for a local ranch, to find work as a cowboy. The racist foreman insults and whips him, so Joe gives the guy a pasting, and helps himself to a horse. At another ranch, five racist cowpokes lose all their money to him at poker. When they attempt to beat him up, Joe renders them all senseless. Next day, he's invited to come and work for Stanley Spencer, a big rancher whose herd is supposedly being rustled.

Instead, it turns out he's been hired to guard a group of Mexican slave labourers, imported by a Southern plantation. When the Mexican Army is reported to be nearby, the cowboys massacre the guest workers. Joe helps one of the wounded Mexicans to escape. Spencer himself catches up with Joe and has him beaten. Joe watches as Mexicans are forced to stand on barrels, hung, and then shot by Spencer and his family and friends. Then he is forced into an arena, with his hands tied, to confront Spencer's fiercest bull. But Joe escapes, kidnaps Spencer and takes him out to the desert, where he lectures him on what being a true American is, and departs.

Joe denounces Spencer to the sheriff, but the sheriff is in Spencer's pay. Spencer's cohorts suggest he hire a quartet of killers to get rid of Joe: Pedro the Cannibal, Valiant Sam, Tricky the Gambler, and Scalper Jack. Joe kills Pedro easily. Sam kidnaps Christina, daughter of the Mexican Joe helped; he is impaled in his own spike-filled pit-trap. Christina develops a raging fever, and Joe rides for Linkville, where he is told there is a doctor. There, he is lured to the saloon, by Slim, henchman of Tricky. But Joe switches clothes with Slim, who is promptly gunned down by Tricky's men. In a foot-and-hand battle against Tricky's men, Joe triumphs. Tricky tries to make a deal with him, but, when he reaches for his concealed gun, Joe blinds him.

Christina recovers thanks to the doctor and Joe's ministrations. But the doctor is waylaid, and scalped, by Scalper Jack. Jack shoots Joe in both legs, and ties him and Christina up. After playing with his doll, he proposes to scalp them. But Joe breaks loose, kills him, and sends Jack's scalp back to his employers. Spencer wants to execute a *peon* a day, on the grounds that this will make the Mexicans turn Joe over;

but his partners insist that another martial-arts specialist will do the job more reliably.

Joe recovers in a cave, with Christina. In a flashback he describes his arduous study, under his martial-arts tutor, the venerable Yang. Then he returns to town to face his former fellow-student, the Samurai. After a bout of kung fu and swordsmanship, Joe defeats the Samurai, and tears out his heart. Bidding goodbye to Christina, he departs, vowing to do further good on behalf of Asians and Latinos.

The film

What sounds like the most awful, throwaway cross-genre picture – the first kung-fu Western! – turns out to be both a decent film and a latter-day surrealist Spaghetti Western. Joe is a particularly naive immigrant, who finds himself working for the worst oppressors imaginable:

JOE: I thought slavery was illegal here.

COWBOY: What do you mean, slavery? Why, those greasers are tickled pink to find work here, instead of stayin' at home, starving to death. The boss pays a fair price to the recruiter in Mexico, then sells the lease to a Southern plantation owner. Nothin' illegal about it.

Moments later the Mexican Army is reported to be approaching, and the gringos open fire on their guest workers: a Spaghetti Western shooting spree in the *Django* style, enhanced by Peckinpah-esque exploding blood capsules. While modern in its violence, *Shanghai Joe* is refreshingly old-fashioned in other ways – like Cipriani's fine Western, *Every Man for Himself*. Social issues – like racism and the exploitation of different races for the benefit of rich capitalists – are the substance of the film. In this way it is unlike the *Sartana* school of Circus Westerns, where nothing matters. Yet it manages to avoid the sugary rectitude of the *Trinity* films. 'Go home and tell them that slavery is worse than hunger,' Joe advises the Mexican he has saved.

Chen Lee is a very appealing actor, who does all as he should. The principal bad guy, played by Piero Lulli (the gangster, Oaks, from *Django Kill*), is excellent: in the English-language version he was dubbed either by Jack Palance, or someone capable of a first-rate Palance imi- tation! Lulli is a lively actor and it's a pleasure to see him, six years later, shift from the hoodlum to the grandee role. All the bad guys are good, as they appear and are summarily killed. The horrible fate of Tricky (Giacomo Rossi Stuart), whose eyes are torn out by our likeable hero – *in close-up* – is far worse; this one moment catapults *Shanghai Joe* into another world – the hell-world of *Django Kill.* And so, the casting of *Django Kill*'s actors, Lulli and Paco Sanz as the old Mexican, begins to make sense. *Shanghai Joe* no longer a comic knock-off with a Chinese star: it's a surrealist horror-Western, in the Questi and Cor- bucci tradition.

Totally in keeping with this, after the mass killing in the saloon, Joe brings a doctor to see Christina. She is concerned:

CHRISTINA: You were gone a long time.

JOE: Some friends in the saloon...

They kiss. The director, Mario Caiano, was the same 'Mike Perkins' who, almost a decade previously, had directed *Bullets Don't Argue* back-to-back with *Fistful of Dollars.* This was quite a different film, and, in an interview with Ishikuma, Caiano recalled, regretfully, how they had removed the tearing out of the samurai villain's heart.

1973 saw another kung-fu Western, *Blood Money,* starring Lo Leih and Lee Van Cleef; and *Those Dirty Dogs!* (*Campa carogna... la ta- glia cresce*), a *Sartana* derivative in which Gianni Garko played a hard- drinking, Koran-reading, Muslim gunfighter. Interviewed years later, Garko could remember nothing about this film. He is a wise man. *Cut- Throats Nine* (*Condenados a vivir*) was a Grand Guignol chain-gang horror Western, tightly directed by Joaquin Romero Marchent, an old Spanish practitioner: if your taste veers towards Gordon Herschell Lewis and spilled entrails, this is the film for you. Somehow, March- ent's offering was eclipsed by the new, big-budget production from

Sergio Leone: allegedly directed by Tonino Valerii, and starring Terence Hill and Henry Fonda, it was sold as Leone's take on the phenomenally successful *Trinity* films. The reality was more complex.

My Name is Nobody

aka *Il mio nome e nessuno*
(Italy/France/Germany)

Director: Tonino Valerii   **Producer:** Claudio Mancini   **Screenplay:** Ernesto Gastaldi   **Story:** Fulvio Morsella, Ernesto Gastaldi, Sergio Leone   **Director of Photography:** Giuseppe Ruzzolini, Armando Nannuzzi   **Art Director:** Gianni Polidori   **Costumes:** Vera Marzot   **Editor:** Nino Baragli   **2nd Unit Director:** Sergio Leone   **Music:** Ennio Morricone   **Cast:** Henry Fonda (*Jack Beauregard*), Terence Hill (*Nobody*), Jean Martin (*Sullivan*), Piero Lulli (*Sheriff*), Leo Gordon (*Red*), RG Armstrong (*Honest John*), Remus Peets (*Big Gun*), Mario Brega (*Pedro*), Antoine Saint Jean (*Scape*), Benito Stefanelli (*Porteley*), Mark Mazza (*Don John*), Franco Angrisano (*Engine driver*), Alexander Allerson (*Rex*), Angelo Novi (*Barman*), Tommy Pulgar (*Juan*), Carla Mancini (*Mother*), Antonio Luigi Guerra, Emile Feist, Geoffrey Lewis, Antonio Palombi, Neil Summers (*Squirrel*), Steve Kanaly, Humbert Mittendorf, Ulrich Muller, Claus Schmidt

The story

Jack Beauregard, a famous gunfighter, is trying to locate his brother, the Nevada Kid, and sail to Europe. But he is constantly dogged by killers. In a frontier barbershop, three assassins attempt to ambush him; he shoots them and moves on. His brother's associate, Red, dies in his arms – shot by bandits. Sullivan, a mine owner, is hassled by the leader of the Wild Bunch: his attempts to kill Jack Beauregard are drawing attention to their primary scam – via which stolen gold is converted into 'new' gold from Sullivan's played-out mine.

In another small town, three more men try to kill Beauregard with a bomb; they are thwarted by Nobody, a younger gunfighter who repeats the names of Jack's victims, and the dates they were killed. Nobody wants to see his hero, Jack, confront the Wild Bunch: a gang of 150. Jack declines. He runs into Nobody again at Acoma Pueblo, and finds his brother buried there. Jack challenges Nobody to a gunfight, shooting his hat off. Nobody declines to fight.

Nobody shows up in Cheyenne City; the circus is in town, and he gets involved in various comic fights. Sullivan hires him to kill Jack; but Nobody instead helps thwart Sullivan's ambush. The Wild Bunch arrive and extract their tithe from the town. Jack and Nobody kill several secondary enemies; then Jack goes to the mine and extracts money from Sullivan: $500 for passage to Europe, and two bags of gold. Outside, Nobody is disappointed that Jack hasn't killed Sullivan. Jack says money is more important than revenge. Sullivan's recycled gold is loaded aboard a train, which Nobody steals. Out on the prairie he stops the train to watch Jack confront the Wild Bunch beside the tracks. Nobody reminds Jack of the dynamite sticks in the Bunch's saddlebags. Jack's bullets detonate the dynamite, killing most of the Bunch, as Jack's exploit enters history.

In New Orleans, Nobody challenges Jack to a duel. A crowd gathers to watch; a photographer takes a picture; Jack is apparently killed. But, in fact, he and Nobody have faked his death, so that he can retire to Europe. From aboard his ship, Jack writes Nobody a letter, passing on the gunfighter's mantle.

The film

Although Tonino Valerii is credited as the director, its *auteur* is the omnipresent Sergio Leone. Leone was the (uncredited) producer, who, with his brother-in-law, hired Ernesto Gastaldi to write the screenplay, based on an idea of Leone's. According to Gastaldi, it was the first time he saw a film made *exactly* as he'd written it, in the script. The first director to be considered was Giuliano Carmineo; Michele Lupo was also on the cards. But one of Leone's old assistants, Valerii or Santi, was bound to get the job – since what Sergio really wanted to do was direct.

According to Giusti, Leone directed 'second unit' for Valerii: no small assignment, since it included all the American shooting – the first 40 minutes of the film, plus the gunfight in New Orleans, and the epilogue – *and* the scenes with the Wild Bunch. This is all the action in the film. The opening scenes, shot in Cabezon and Mogollon, New Mexico, are very boring; but the scene between Henry Fonda and Terence Hill in Acoma is excellent. Leone and Valerii have been attempting a synthesis of various Western forms up until this point: particularly the *Trinity* phenomenon, here present in Hill and in the 'cute' burping, farting, Morricone riff which follows Nobody around. At the start, the locations are dull, the jokes are flat, the film looks headed for the dumpster, and then comes the Acoma Pueblo scene. There is some real acting, some emotion on Fonda's part, and the film is swept up by one of Morricone's best showdown scores: ticking clock, guitar and trumpets. Acoma and the surrounding mesas help enormously: the American location no longer seems like a grandiose backdrop – the way it was in *Once Upon a Time in the West*. Instead, the action of the actors seems a part of the natural setting: as it is at the end of the film, in the French Quarter of New Orleans.

If Leone shot these scenes, all that remained for Valerii to shoot were the dreadful 'hall of mirrors' and circus freak scenes featuring Hill, Mazza and Stefanelli; the long, boring scene involving Fonda, Hill and a 'cute/funny' old man; and a 'funny' drinking and shooting scene in a bar, also involving Hill, Stefanelli and Mazza. These are the worst scenes in the film, but, according to some sources, Leone directed them, too. On the other hand, Valerii insisted to Frayling that *he* directed the gunfights and the showdowns. Certainly Leone seemed to be setting Valerii up to fail: Valerii had difficulties with his cinematographer, Armando Nannuzzi, whom Leone had advised to 'help' Valerii with the direction. And when he arrived in Spain, he found Leone had replaced Nannuzzi with another cameraman, Giuseppe Ruzzolini. Poor Valerii! Such disrespect, and yet Valerii didn't quit. I wonder if he related to Leone as Nobody does towards Jack Beauregard: impossibly in awe of the Master, eternally grateful, yet desperate for him to retire and move elsewhere?

My Name is Nobody is as imperfect as it's remarkable: one film attempting to reconcile at least *four* different types of Western – the classic American, personified by Fonda; the modern, revisionist American, in the many references to Sam Peckinpah and the Wild Bunch; the Spaghetti *alla* Leone, with its soaring Morricone scores and classic showdowns; and the Spaghetti *alla* Barboni, with Hill and baked beans and 'cute/funny' jokes. Barboni apparently admired the photography, but not the film. Among all *Nobody*'s cinematic quotes, Gastaldi even managed to reference one of his own scripts: the bandit horde exacting tribute from the townspeople, as in *$1,000 on the Black*. At times, *My Name is Nobody* plods, struggles for significance, bumps into great issues like the Death of the West, stumbles away. And then it suddenly gets its act together, with individual scenes as good as anything in *For a Few Dollars More*, or *Once Upon a Time in the West*. We might think of it as Leone's epitaph to the Italian Western, disguised as an elegy to the West itself, if he had stopped here. But he didn't. Leone's last Western was, sadly, still to be made.

My Name is Nobody is a half-great Spaghetti Western. Opening at Christmas 1973, it made more money than the original *Trinity* movie (though less than the *Trinity* sequel). Naturally, there was immediate interest in a sequel to this film, too. Leone must have thought he'd got away with it: masterminding and co-directing a film without being held responsible for the finished version. It's a strange desire, not to be accountable for your own work. But directors are strange animals, and Leone was concentrating on his gangster movie, now: his riposte to *The Godfather*. Maybe *Nobody* would become a franchise, like the *Dollars* films. He hadn't been blamed for *Nobody*; he could risk another one. Leone had just seen, and been impressed by, Bertrand Blier's *Les valseuses* (1973): an unerotic, three-way love story about French petty crooks. He thought, for some reason, it would make a good Terence Hill vehicle.

A Genius, Two Partners, & a Dupe

aka *Un genio, due compari, un pollo, Nobody is the Greatest*
(France/Germany/Italy)

Director: Damiano Damiani **Producer:** Fulvio Morsella, Claudio Mancini, Horst Wendlant **Screenplay:** Ernesto Gastaldi, Damiano Damiani, Fulvio Morsella **Director of Photography:** Giuseppe Ruzzolini **Art Director:** Carlo Simi (in the US & Spain), Francesco Bronzi (in Italy)

Costumes: Franco Carretti **Editor:** Nino Baragli **Assistant Director:** Stefano Rolla **Music:** Ennio Morricone **Cast:** Terence Hill (*Joe*), Miou Miou (*Lucy*), Robert Charlebois (*Steam Train*), Patrick MacGoohan (*Major Cabot*), Klaus Kinski (*Doc Foster*), Raimund Harmstorf (*Sergeant Milton*), Jean Martin (*Colonel Pembroke*), Rik Battaglia (*Captain*), Piero Vida (*Jelly Roll*), Mario Brega (*Stagecoach driver*), Benito Stefanelli (*Mortimer*), Furio Meniconi, Karl Brown (*Gambler*)

The story

The racist owner of a trading post, vouchsafing that he and his neighbours should disguise themselves as Indians, kill some worthless whites, and provoke an Indian war, is killed by phony Indians. A sleepy drifter, Joe Thanks, arrives in town, is hassled by the local hippies, and provokes a gambler, Doc Foster, into a gunfight. Super-fast on the draw, Joe utterly intimidates Foster, who leaves town in a rush. Joe's confederates, Lucy and Steam Train, pass Foster's hat around.

Joe, Lucy and Steam Train ride west on a railroad car fitted with a sail. They jump clear just before the end of the line. At the railhead, the employees are quitting: they haven't been paid in weeks, and there's a mountain in between them and the Pacific. The Navajo, needless to say, oppose the dynamiting of this holy place.

Joe and his partners develop a plan to steal $300,000 – belonging to the Indians – which is in the hands of the US Army. Colonel Pembroke, sent by Washington to investigate the case, is killed. Joe persuades Steam Train to impersonate Pembroke, and Lucy to pretend to be his daughter. Major Cabot, who has been attempting to drive the Navajo off their land by staging the fake Indian attacks, welcomes the 'Colonel' and his 'daughter' to Fort Christabel. But Cabot quickly sees through the disguises and imprisons them. Joe, posing as an ecologist concerned for the buzzards, visits Cabot and leaves behind him a patina of gold dust. Cabot is thus tricked into believing there is gold in an old mine, freeing his prisoners, giving the $300,000 to the Navajo in return for mining rights, and returning all lands stolen by the federal government.

After a lengthy stagecoach chase, in which Joe himself is tricked and receives a duplicate suitcase full of fake money, the Navajo chief reveals to Cabot that the ore in the mine is fool's gold. Lucy and Steam Train head west together, in her words, 'to go and screw America'.

The film

If evidence that sequels are a bad idea is ever needed, this is it. The only vestige which remains of *Les Valseuses* is Miou-Miou, who plays one of the trio of 'cute/funny' protagonists. She is by far the least objectionable. Hill is his usual cute, blank, nobody-self. And the curly-haired Robert Charlebois – playing a character supposedly in crisis because of his Native American blood – is just awful. My guess is that Girotti, the actor who played the face (but not the voice) of Hill, objected to the sexual slant of Blier's film: in any case, Leone announced that they were now making his version of *The Sting*.

Leone picked Damiano Damiani as his fall guy. It was an odd choice. Damiani was primarily a director of political films like *Confessions of a Police Captain* (*Confessione di un comisario de polizia al procuratore della republica*). His only Western was the equally political *¿Quien Sabe?* But he was viewed as a bankable, reliable director, and Leone wanted to get started as soon as possible. A script was quickly written, by Gastaldi, with input from the 'patsy', and the brother-in-law: the whites-killed-by-fake-Indians set-up was borrowed from Squitieri's *Apache*. Production, naturally, would be in Monument Valley and at the 'Flagstone' location in Spain. Leone loaded the picture with 'his' people: the excellent Carlo Simi, Nino Baragli as editor, Ruzzolini as cameraman, plus pals like Rik Battaglia, Benito Stefanelli, Mario Brega and Karl Braun – a big, tough ski instructor whom Leone had brought from Switzerland to Almería to replace the hippies who were infiltrating the edges of his films. Damiani retaliated by casting Klaus Kinski and Patrick McGoohan: famously difficult, but hugely talented actors – the exact opposites of Leone's easy-going, deferential stock company.

As Leone told it, on set in Monument Valley he realised his mistake. 'I had committed an enormous error. Damiani excels at drama, but he's not a humorist. He has no sense of farce, nor irony.' This meant, of course, that Sergio must take a hand in directing. All those involved agree that Leone shot the opening scene, a parody of *Once Upon a Time in the West*. According to some sources he directed other scenes; meanwhile, Leone's friend, Giuliano Montaldo, began shooting a second unit. Damiani, who already knew how to direct, must have been furious. Especially since he *did* have a sense of humour. Steam Train stares out at a completely barren desert and remarks, in wonderment, 'There used to be *nothing* here.' When Joe tries to tell one of his 'cute/funny' stories (like his long, boring tale of a bird 'saved' from cowshit by a coyote, in *My Name is Nobody*), Major Cabot cuts him off with a brisk, 'Young man, the desert sun sometimes affects the brain.' And consider this exchange:

JOE: You've been in the army.

STEAM TRAIN: That's right – like all white men.

JOE: What rank?

STEAM TRAIN: Deserter.

Note also the last words of Colonel Pembroke, who dies wanting to know why people keep pulling on his beard. The dialogue is funny and it gets crisper when Patrick McGoohan appears. So there is no problem with Damiani's *wit*. What upset Leone was that Damiani didn't do slapstick, or flatulence – the staples of *My Name is Nobody* and the *Trinity* films. There's one speeded-up, fast-draw gag – Joe is so fast, supposedly, that his gun leaves his holster and returns on its own – but it's more puzzling than amusing, and Damiani drops it thereafter. There are no jokes about piss, no stories about shit, no shots of horses' assholes. No wonder Leone was anxious. He, as a director and a man, was anti-intellectual, cowardly, ambitious, grandiose. He knew what the public wanted (or thought he did!). Damiani was highly intellectual, cynical, specific, and knew what *he* wanted. On set, there was tension between Damiani and the 'friends' Leone had brought on board. The only thing the two directors had in common was their distaste for the military: as a result, this is the most anti-cavalry picture since Sam Fuller's *Run of the Arrow*.

But *A Genius...* is no *Run of the Arrow*. Its energy is dissipated, slopping about in every direction, just like its title. Three mediocre heroes are no replacement for one strong one. Either Jean Martin (who plays the doomed Colonel Pembroke) or McGoohan (as the Machiavellian

Major Cabot) would be an excellent antagonist; but neither gets sufficient screentime. McGoohan appears too late to do much more than act
mean, and be kidnapped. *A Genius...* isn't entirely terrible; indeed, I like
parts of it. But it falls to pieces way before the end, and peters out into
nothingness. This may be due to a curious development which occurred
during post-production.

Apparently, the cut negative of *A Genius...* was stolen by crimi-
nals who intended to hold it to ransom. According to Giusti, the nega-
tives of Pasolini's *Salò* and Fellini's *Casanova* were stolen in the same
heist. I don't know how the producers of *Salò* and *Casanova* responded, but Fulvio Morsella, Leone's producer and brother-in-law, refused
to pay to regain the film. The original negative was not returned, and
Nino Baragli was forced to reconstruct *A Genius...* from outtakes. The
result of using only the second-best takes is entirely predictable: a
film which always seems not-quite-right, and second-best. The film's
virtues are McGoohan, its wonderful locations, and a Kubrickian Morricone score which borrows 'Für Elise' and the overture from *William
Tell*. Its vices are its weak characters and how little is at stake (of
course, the fates of the Navajo and their holy mountain *supposedly*
hang in the balance. But we don't experience this. There's only one
Navajo character. Like Cabot's alleged racism, this is an undeveloped
subplot, a bit of 'back story').

Predictably, *A Genius...* tanked, and Damiani took the fall. I sympathise with him. It wasn't his fault that Leone hired him. It certainly
wasn't his fault the negative was stolen, and the producer wouldn't buy
it back. He'd got good performances out of two
highly strung, thoroughbred actors, and done his
best with the rest. Over the years, Leone tried to
minimise his involvement in *A Genius...* In some
interviews, he claimed he'd never visited the set.

But this was not so. The location photographer
snapped evidence of Sergio Leone, Damiano Damiani and Giuliano
Montaldo together, working in happy unison towards a common goal,
on location in Monument Valley.[24]

(It's unclear who the genius of the title is, or why the film is called
this. All three protagonists are said to be a genius at one point, as is
Major Cabot. But, so what? It's risky to use a word like 'genius' in a

24 *This picture can be seen on pp 6–7
of Gilles Lambert's book* Les
Bons, les sales, les mechants
et les propres de Sergio Leone
(Solar, France, 1976).

film title. Having directed a picture called *The Winner*, I've seen, first-hand, the fate of grandiosely titled, half-good films.)

The same year, 1974, Sergio Corbucci directed his last Western, *The White, the Yellow and the Black*. There was no shortage of money here. It has a big cast, with Eli Wallach as a sheriff, Tomas Milian as a Japanese would-be samurai, and Giuliano Gemma as his usual enigmatic, never-ageing self. I wish I could say more, but it's a useless, worthless film, structurally reminiscent of *The Good, the Bad and the Ugly*. Ishikuma-san defends the film on the basis of its script, which – in the original Italian – refers to numerous Spaghetti Western titles and is thus less dull than the English version. Either way, as these films so often are, it's utterly racist, while pretending to condemn racism.

Corbucci's exhaustion was evident. His Buñuelian muse had slipped away, like tears in rain. But another Italian director stepped forth the same year with a Western so genuinely Surrealist, and politically radical, that Don Luis might actually have approved of it (if he watched Westerns, which I don't think he did). *Don't Touch the White Woman!* (*Non toccare la donna bianca*) is Marco Ferreri's only Western. A Franco-Italian co-production, it isn't a true Spaghetti Western, being more in the John Ford, cavalry mode. But it's an excellent film, suggesting – like *Cemetery Without Crosses* – that French cinema was capable of substantial, intelligent achievements *dans le Far-West*.

Don't Touch the White Woman

aka *Non toccare la donna bianca, Ne touche pas la femme blanche*
(Italy/France)

Director: Marco Ferreri   **Producer:** Jean Yanne, Jean-Pierre Rassam, Alain Sarde, Alberto Grimaldi   **Screenplay:** Marco Ferreri, Rafael Azcona   **Director of Photography:** Etienne Becker   **Costumes:** Lina Nerli Taviani   **Editor:** Ruggero Mastroianni   **Music:** Philippe Sarde

Cast: Marcello Mastroianni (*General George Armstrong Custer*), Catherine Deneuve (*Marie Helene*), Ugo Tognazzi (*Mitch*), Michel Piccoli (*Buffalo Bill*), Philippe Noiret (*General Terry*), Alain Cuny (*Sitting Bull*), Paolo Villaggio (*CIA Man*)

The story

Capitalists in evening dress sit in a domed building in Paris, agreeing that the enemy classes must be destroyed. They go to see General Terry and his daughter; he agrees to run their class-cleansing operation – even though they want the more popular General Custer to do the killing.

Custer's train has arrived in Paris, but he refuses to leave it. The General is freaking out because he's lost his comb. After a CIA 'anthropologist' helps him find it, Custer rides through the streets of Paris, abuses his troops – forcing one to eat dogshit – and is introduced to his employers, a polite society of capitalists including the lovely Marie-Helene de Boismonfray.

Custer's troops round up Indian women and children and march them into the foundations of an old chimney in Les Halles; they set it on fire and it collapses, killing all within. An Indian retaliates, shooting a cavalryman off his horse. Custer has four Indians lynched in a pedestrian walkway.

The tribes gather in a 'canyon' created by the mechanical diggers. A 'madman' proposes concerted action against the whites, as opposed to fruitless, individual acts of bravery. Sitting Bull agrees.

The soldiers try to provoke a war by cutting off an Indian's head and throwing it at the passing band. Custer abuses the Indian women, who work in a sweatshop beneath a portrait of Nixon. The anthropologist, now with a University of Denver sweatshirt, shows Custer pictures of the dead Che in Bolivia, Patrice Lumumba in Africa. Deneuve volunteers to assist the US Army surgeon, who is gutting indians and stuffing them with newspapers for a public display. Custer complains to Terry about the presence of another brash showman, Buffalo Bill, in their ranks. But the General, who has acquired a machinegun, insists that Bill is essential for public relations purposes.

A parley occurs. General Terry orders Sitting Bull and his tribe back to the reservation. Buffalo Bill and his girlfriend, Calamity Jane, harrass

Custer; Bill sticks a custard pie in the face of one of the capitalists. Followed by a singer and banjo band, Custer romances Marie-Helene. He confesses to her that influential people want him to run for president.

Next day, the army's cannon destroy the old market of Les Halles. At a war- planning session, the General orders Custer to participate in a pincer movement against the Indians: there are to be no survivors. The Indians go to a sporting-goods shop to buy rifles; they're shadowed by Custer's Indian corporal, Mitch – who tells the madman of Custer's plans. He says he will dress Custer in a beige outfit for the battle, to make him easier to kill. He confesses he hates Custer 'because he treats me like an Indian'. Meanwhile, Custer's hairdresser warns him that his hair is falling out; reluctantly, he agrees to have it cut.

At dinner, Terry dines on lobster while his men eat beans. Custer, though married, reveals his love for Marie-Helene. She panics and insists on returning to her hotel. But that night, while Custer is writing a letter to his wife, Marie-Helene, clad only in a negligee, brings him a club sandwich. They cannot resist temptation.

Next day, the General reviews his troops. Buffalo Bill arrives with a truck carrying a stuffed buffalo and two large-breasted chicks. Custer and his Seventh Cavalry set off to engage the Indians – warned by the General not to attack alone. Buffalo is unable to join the battle due to a crippling attack of indigestion. Marie-Helene follows Custer to the front, where she is the first victim of the Indians' counterattack.

The film

Ferreri and Rafael Azcona, his writing partner, clearly weren't interested in Spaghetti Westerns as such. There is little revenge here, and the heroes, white and Indian alike, are anything but taciturn. Their model is clearly *Fort Apache*, the Ford film in which a vainglorious officer played by Henry Fonda (with a daughter, played by Shirley Temple, in tow) leads his regiment to complete destruction. But the cavalry story itself is but an excuse, a template, for a radical political comedy, about American genocide against native peoples, and about the Parisian elite's attempt – via 'regeneration' – to destroy vibrant, working-class neighbourhoods.

The 'Indians' are working-class Parisians. As a conceit this works very well, though it also provides an opportunity for some broad, 'comic' acting and slapstick food-eating: things Ferreri enjoyed, perhaps more than his audience. The dialogue, on the other hand, is often spectacularly funny: it helps that this Franco-American alliance of city planners and extermination specialists is played by some of the best actors in Europe: Marcello Mastroianni as Custer, Catherine Deneuve as Marie-Helene, Ugo Tognazzi as the traitorous Mitch, Philippe Noiret as Terry, and a particularly memorable Michel Piccoli as the constantly grandstanding Buffalo Bill.

Piccoli and Deneuve were two of the most prominent actors of Buñuel's later period, of course. Buñuel didn't particularly enjoy Deneuve's acting: he only found her interesting, he said, when her characters were crippled in some way. How Don Luis might have enjoyed, then, the scene where – in the midst of simpering love talk with Custer – Marie-Helene is felled by an arrow through the throat!

Ferreri and Azcona present us with a small group of greedy, violent, wealthy monsters at war with the rest of the world. They have almost everything; the rest of us have almost nothing; they are prepared to kill us so that things stay that way. The same story plays out on the Great Plains, in Vietnam, and in Les Halles: the rich, and technologically adept, drive out the poor. So it's entirely appropriate that the photograph of President Nixon dominates many scenes; that Custer compares the Indians to the French 'Algerian problem', and that Custer's wife turns out to be the girl stamped on the base of an old-fashioned Coca-Cola tray.

No film has ever used anachronisms to better effect. Custer and Terry watch the crane and ball destroying a working-class residential district as if it were the US Cavalry sweeping through an Indian camp. And the film's 'landscapes' – wide shots of a Gothic church, the half-destroyed market, the huge 'canyon' dug out of the devastated area – really do begin to resemble the great buttes and wastelands of the desert. Etienne Becker's photography is at its finest in these great landscape shots: always the test of a good Western. And the crew and cast clearly had amazing access to the real 'action' – the destruction, by wrecking ball, bulldozer and dynamite, of Les Halles.

Don't Touch the White Woman is a funny, provocative film which has been inexplicably ignored over the years. It seems to have had a decent budget, with a fine cast, and many extras, horses, guns and uniforms. Oddly missing is the last shot which the film leads up to and requires: in which thousands of working-class Parisians, dressed as Indians, pour out of the 'canyon' and into the streets. Ferreri clearly had enough extras, and got the footage he wanted elsewhere.

So did the production suddenly run out of time and money? Or did the City of Paris – so seemingly helpful in all other ways – refuse to allow the staging of the Insurrection, outside the safe confines of Ferreri's 'canyon'?

Four Gunmen of the Apocalypse (*I quattro dell'apocalisse*), made the following year by Lucio Fulci, looks and sounds like a late-sixties TV commercial: backlit, with a soundtrack of pop songs. Fulci, director of the excellent *Massacre Time*, tried to honour traditional Spaghetti Western brutality with a vigilante 'clean up of bad elements', whose corpses are left lying or hanging in the streets; and a massacre of Christians. The latter takes place (unfortunately off-screen) at the behest of a Charles Manson-style hippie psycho, played by Tomas Milian. This was Milian's last Western role. Having perfected his peasant revolutionary and twice portrayed 'Provvidenza' – a gunfighter dressed as Charlie Chaplin's Little Tramp – Milian was done with cowboy films.

The Hostage (*L'ostaggio*), also made in 1975, was a Western featuring children in grown-up roles; a magnificent idea which surely inspired Sir Alan Parker in the creation of his directorial *magnum opus*, *Bugsy Malone* (1976). And the regrettably unstoppable team of Anthony and Baldi added a third sequel to the *Stranger* franchise, with *Get Mean!*, a genre-buster in which Anthony's Western gunfighter takes on Mediaeval Spain. 1976 saw *Keoma*, a big, old-fashioned action Spaghetti Western, starring Franco Nero, in the Castellari style. While the *Trinity* franchise seemed to have played itself out, the last burst of genre-busting continued. In 1977 a truly eccentric Western-horror-*policier* appeared: *Closed Circuit*.

Closed Circuit

aka *Circuito chiuso*
(Italy)

Director: Giuliano Montaldo   **Producer:** Mario Gallo, Enzo Giulioli
Story: Mario Gallo, Giuliano Montaldo   **Screenplay:** Nicola Badalucco, Mario Gallo   **Director of Photography:** Giuseppe Pinori   **Music:** Egisto Macchi   **Cast:** Giuliano Gemma (*Gunfighter*), Ettore Manni, Aurore Clement, Flavio Bucci, Alfredo Pea, Franco Balducci, William Berger, Tony Kendall, Brizio Montinaro, Mattia Sbragia, Marzio C Honorato, Irene Bignardi, Luciano Catenacci

The story

Rome, the sixties. Cinema patrons buy tickets to see a Giuliano Gemma Western, *Day of Anger*. In the cinema, various liaisons take place or are anticipated. Near the end of the movie, a member of the audience is shot dead.

The police are called and won't let anyone leave. They interview the patrons and staff, but learn nothing. In an attempt to gather evidence, they re-run the film and make everyone sit in their original seats. An usher volunteers to fill in for the murdered man. During the showdown scene, he too is shot and killed.

The audience panics; the police are confounded. More senior police officers arrive. The first victim's apartment is searchered; the police learn nothing. Two patrons who try to break out of the cinema are arrested. Forensics report that the bullets are .45 calibre, manufactured in the United States in the previous century. Furious, the senior police inspector orders the crime re-staged again. This time, he will play the victim. In the final showdown, the movie gunfighter, played by Gemma, shoots the inspector dead. All the witnesses flee.

Afterwards, in the darkened cinema, the police commissioner and a sociologist discuss the possibility of a 'fantastic' explanation for the murders. They find a cheroot, still smoking, at the foot of the movie screen.

The film

Closed Circuit was an experimental film project of RAI, the Italian national network. The director, Montaldo, was the friend of Leone's who had trodden on Damiano Damiani's toes during the shooting of *A Genius...* But he was also a director in his own right, having made *Sacco & Vanzetti* (1972), and *Giordano Bruno* (1973).

Closed Circuit begins like a documentary, or a docu-drama. People buy tickets for a movie, sit down to watch it, look around for other forms of action. The cinema employees do their jobs, and observe the patrons. Then, after the first murder, the police arrive, and we are in Buñuel territory. As in *The Exterminating Angel* – or an Agatha Christie thriller – the cops refuse to let anyone leave. Instead, individuals are interviewed, and when this fails to produce any clues, all present are told to sit where they were originally, and to watch the film again. As in Buñuel's film, re-creating the previous situation produces a closed-circuit kind of magic: in this case, a second murder.

None of the characters have names: there's a projectionist, a police commissioner, a sociologist, and so forth. It's one of those 'investigation films' like *Investigation of a Citizen Above Suspicion* or Damiani's *Police Captain*; but the investigation reveals nothing, goes nowhere. After his superior has been killed *by the film* – stalked by Gemma's pistol, as he moves around the cinema, trying to avoid the nineteenth-century bullet that's about to come flying through the screen – the detective in charge remains in the dark, empty cinema. The sociologist – who goes to the cinema because it's a good place to study people – proposes a 'science-fictional' explanation, something to do with a Ray Bradbury short story... But there is no explanation. Is it this mysterious Western – from what we see of it, an amalgam of Valerii's *Day of Anger* and Petroni's *A Sky Full of Stars for a Roof* – which kills people? Do all the prints of the film do this? Or is this insane, yet replicable, incident confined to this one cinema, this one day? The characters hope so, just as Don Edmundo Nobile and his guests hope they've put the horror of incarceration behind them, as they attend a liberation service, at the end of *The Exterminating Angel*. The cheroot, burning on the cinema carpet, suggests that – as for Nobile and party – the horror is uncontrollable, about to begin again.

Closed Circuit won a prize at the Berlin Film Festival, but didn't receive a theatrical distribution in Italy. It remains a fascinating, thought-provoking artefact, and a splendid re-use of the talents of Giuliano Gemma.[25] Quite an appropriate film with which to conclude this chapter, were there not another Gemma vehicle, also made in 1977, to consider. *California*, directed by Michele Lupo, produced by Manolo Bolognini, shall have the last word.

25 Closed Circuit *is also an illustration of the 'RW Culture' which Lawrence Lessig writes about in* Remix: Making Art & Commerce Thrive in the Hybrid Economy *(Penguin Press, NY, 2008): an open, creative culture where all filmmakers – not just studios – can recycle and re-use old cultural products to create new works.*

California

(Italy/Spain)

Director: Michele Lupo **Producer:** Manolo Bolognini **Screenplay:** Mino Roli, Nico Ducci, Franco Bucceri, Roberto Leoni **Story:** Franco Bucceri, Roberto Leoni **Director of Photography:** Alejandro Ulloa **Art Director, Costumes:** Carlo Simi **Editor:** Antonietta Zita **Assistant Director:** Mauro Sacripanti, Ricardo Huertas **Music:** Gianni Ferrio **Cast:** Giuliano Gemma (*California, aka Michael Random*), Miguel Bose (*Willy Preston*), Raimund Harmstorf (*Rope Whittaker*), Chris Avram (*Nelson*), Paola Bose (*Helen Preston*), Robert Hundar (*Eric Plummer*), William Berger (*Mr Preston*), Dana Ghia (*Mrs Preston*), Romano Puppo (*Gary Luke*), Malisa Longo (*Jasmine*), Franco Ressel (*Full*)

The story

The end of the Civil War. The Union Army wants to empty a prison camp so as to accommodate a new influx of prisoners. So the inmates are given a week to leave, find work or leave the state. By coincidence, work is available – for 50 cents a week. Willy Preston, a young Confederate lieutenant, resolves to walk home to Georgia. On the road, he falls in with a terse veteran who says his name is Michael

Random. They watch as a bounty hunter, Rope Whittaker, traps Confederate renegades and kills them. There is a bounty for Southerners accused of every type of crime; Rope shares an office with the Union Army staff who run the prison, and print the wanted posters.

Hassled and beaten by vengeful Northerners, Random and Willy steal a horse and escape. They hide out in a ghost town, drinking and playing cards in the ruins. But when they attempt to leave, they're bushwhacked by the Northerners, who've tracked them here. Random is dragged by his horse; Willy is shot in the back, and lynched.

Random heads for Georgia to report Willy's death to his family. He falls in love with Willy's sister, Helen, and starts working on the farm. One day he and Helen give a ride to three ex-Confederates, on their way home. But in town the men are massacred by bounty hunters, and Helen is taken hostage by the killers. Random sets out to find her. He learns she is being held at Rope Whittaker's secret hideout. In order to reach Helen, Random teams up with Rope in a bank robbery, and pretends to become his friend. He helps Rope escape the Union troops, who have new orders to stop his activities. Finally discovering the hideout, where Helen has been forced into prostitution, Random kills Rope and rescues Helen. 'Nelson', a fake reporter who is actually an army spy, and who has orchestrated much of this sordid affair, lets Random and Helen go.

The film

This, I think, is the best acting Giuliano Gemma did, in an Italian Western. He and Michele Lupo were old hands; with producer Manolo Bolognini, who brought Carlo Simi on board to design the sets and costumes, they were a 'dream team' which, for once, produced a great work. *California* is a Spaghetti Western version of *The Searchers*, and a meditation on the wreck the 'new' form had become.

None of the film takes place in California. Instead, 'California' is Gemma's character's old nickname – according to Franco Ressel, who appears as an old gambler in one scene. This doesn't matter. For most of the picture, he calls himself 'Michael Random' – a name he's picked, off the back of a tobacco box, just as 'Arizona Colt' invented his own name, out of thin air. Names don't matter here (any more than they do in *Closed Circuit*). What counts, in the aftermath of the disastrous Civil War, is how much money you have, and what colour overcoat you wear. In *California*, the Spaghetti Western's understanding of American history has matured, acquired nuances. Gemma, like John Wayne in *The Searchers*, plays a Confederate who hates the Union, because the Union hates him. Leone's and Corbucci's films touch on the *economic* aspects of war: profiteers lurk on the margins, shouting encouragement to the troops. But *California* devotes whole sequences to this economic angle: in a highly political scene, two wealthy magnates offer work to hungry Confederate prisoners. The pay is room, board, and 50 cents a week. A Johnny Reb remarks, to one of the magnates' black footmen, 'That's less than the pocket money I used to give my slaves.' But if they don't take the job, they risk a 'Wanted' poster, and being shot by Rope.

The film begins from the point of view of a young, idealistic, naive second lieutenant, Willy Preston. Then Gemma appears, and we are set up for two narrative surprises. First, the audience assumes (or, I assumed) that this will be a 'buddy' picture, in which a crusty veteran, played by Gemma, is teamed with a sprightlier, sexier, younger man (Miguel Bose). And so the film plays, right up to the moment where – in Peckinpah-esque slow motion – young Willy is shot in the back, and thrown from his horse. Random/California is dragged some distance, and returns – we expect – to save the injured Willy. Not a bit of it. In his absence, the dying Willy has been lynched by the Northerners. Close-up of the useless medal, which the lad had so prized, clutched in his hand.

At this point, the audience breathes a sigh of relief (well, I do). This isn't a 'buddy' movie after all! The younger leading man has just been slaughtered in an outrageous, *unexpected* Spaghetti Western turn! And the thing with the medal... So sick, so cynical. Now, *California* will become a story of revenge, as California/Random hunts down the Yankee murderers of his friend, and dispatches them bloodily.

Wrong, again. Lupo and his four screenwriters surprise us a second time. Gemma's character eschews the vengeance trail. Instead he heads for the kid's farm in Georgia, and reports his death to the family. Willy's father is played by William Berger, but still there is no gathering-of-the-vengeance-clan. Mr Preston disdains his son's medal ('We already got a load of metal rusting in the barnyard'), but thanks Random/California. This is the stuff of the traditional American Western, very well done. And what follows, in which Random and Willy's sister, Helen, fall in love as they restore the farm's irrigation sluice gates, is a properly sublimated Western romance, in the style of *Shane*.

But trouble is never distant in a good Western, and the bad guys in this one are particularly vile: it's hard to say whether the bounty killer, Rope, or the government spy who funds the killings, Nelson, is more despicable. As in *The Searchers*, the heroine is simply absent from the film during her captivity; like Ethan Edwards, California returns her to her family after a long and difficult pursuit. In his case, the hardest part is actually convincing Rope he is his friend; the murderer softens, ceases to be a monster, must – yet cannot – be destroyed.

Like a Peckinpah Western, this one is permeated with the notion of things being finished. The War ends, but Willy's life ends, too, and, without Willy, the farm falls apart. The English gambler, played by Ressel, says he heard California fought in the War. 'Yes,' California replies, 'and I was killed.' The first 'town' we see is a prison camp – emptying out its old inmates, to accommodate new ones: another *closed circuit*. Then, the story shifts to *ghost towns*. The first is the Elios Films set, wrecked, with the main street full of trash. Gemma and Bose ride into the saloon. They clip-clop alongside the bar – the long bar from those crowded, smoky scenes in *Django*, filled with music, violence, laughing Mexicans – and joke about how the old place must have been.

The second ghost town is the El Paso set, in Almería. In 1977 a great storm swept through Southern Spain and tore the movie sets – and much else – apart. Carlo Simi's bank survived, but the facades were torn off a whole street of buildings, including the hotel where, once, Clint Eastwood's bounty killer stayed. As at Elios, Simi filled the street with additional wreckage, extra trash. So Giuliano Gemma rides, literally, through the ruins of the West. Given that the mountains and the sand dunes remained unchanged after the storm, we might even call them the ruins of Western civilisation, Western society. Certainly Lupo and his collaborators were making a point when they had their hero enter such broken-down, gutted settlements. The ruined, empty

bars; the fallen, false-fronted buildings; the young, doomed hero mar-
velling, 'Must have been a nice place!'

California was shot by another old pro, Alejandro Ulloa. He used
muted colours – browns and dark reds – which complement the
season and the theme. And that was it. A fine, latter-day Spaghetti
Western, neither inanely funny nor bizarrely violent, great looking, well
acted, well directed, had come and gone. It made good money: more
than a billion *lire* at the box office. Gemma, Lupo, Simi, Bolognini, Ulloa, all went on to other things.

There would be many more films, but not many more Westerns.

How much further could this old mule trot? Some distance yet. In
1979, Monte Hellman directed a Western starring an Italian, Fabio
Testi, in Spain: *China 9, Liberty 37.* Co-starring Warren Oates and Sam
Peckinpah, this feels more like an American Western, like *100 Rifles* or
Doc; as such it belongs in a study of revisionist American Westerns, or
of Hellman's work. And the same year saw a Spaghetti Western version of Hammett's *Red Harvest*, *La Notte Rosa Del Falco*, starring Gianni Garko and Roberto Camardiel. About a year later, Alberto Grimaldi
told me he still owned the rights to the novel, and was planning to
make a film of *Red Harvest* with Bertolucci. So I would guess this is
an 'unauthorised' adaptation; and would love to see it! The 1980s saw
Lupo and Spencer make a comic Western, *Buddy Goes West* (*Occhio
alla penna*); Franco Nero attempt an 'official' sequel, *Return of Django*,
sans Corbucci; and new blither from Anthony and Baldi, in the form of
the only 3-D Spaghetti Western, *Comin' at Ya!* Nothing if not consistent, this too featured 50 women in nightdresses, running through the
dunes. The 1990s saw a new Spaghetti Western by Enzo G Castellari:
Jonathan of the Bears (*Jonathan degli orsi*). Also starring Franco Nero,
it was oddly old-fashioned: like Stanley Kubrick, Castellari saw no need
to change his style, as the years passed. His film has the distinction
of being the first Western made in Russia, where bears are popular
animals, and the film's title was *Dzonatan – Drug Medvedej*.

The twenty-first century has been quiet in this regard. Only the French have kept the form afloat, shooting big-budget Western TV series at Estudios Decorados and in the Tabernas desert; while *Blueberry* (2004) picked up – budget and locationwise – where Leone left off.

What more to say about these films? I have said enough. Let them speak for themselves. Sergio Leone made one other feature, and – as he wished – it was his biggest, most expensive, most critically regarded: his gangster epic, *Once Upon a Time in America*. He died, worn out by overeating, overpartying, overworrying, and overreaching, at the age of 60. Corbucci passed away a few days before his 63rd birthday, a year later.[26]

What to think about Corbucci? He directed many films, action films, period film, police films, comedies; plus 13 Westerns. His first, *Red Pastures*, was terrible; his last was worse. But in his late-30s – during the golden years – he made one Spaghetti Western which was brilliant and vastly influential, *Django*, and another, *The Big Silence*, to which that word, 'genius', can be applied.

26 *When I heard that Sergio Leone had died, I called my friend Lee Katz at the Completion Bond Company, who were bonding Leone's next picture, The Siege of Leningrad. I offered my services as a replacement director. Lee told me that the budget was $100,000,000, and that only $50,000,000 had been secured, in goods and services, from the Russians. Lee told me that if I could find the other fifty million dollars, I was welcome to replace Leone.*

Let us remember Corbucci for these great films, and hope that, as celluloid turns to vinegar, and video standards change, his masterpieces will long be preserved. And the same toast to the other Sergio! And to Questi, and to Damiani, and to Petroni, and to Lizzani, and to Castellari, and to their colleagues!

To the Spaghetti Western masters: the good and the bad; the ugly and the pretty; the live and the dead!

1608

'Between 1586 and 1631 there were at least 40 food riots, and two attempted insurrections... In 1596, Bartholomew Stere, a carpenter, and Richard Bradshawe, a miller, recruited followers from around Hampton Gay, to rise up and march on London, where they thought the apprentices would join them. After that, "yt was but a monthes worke to overrune the realm".

The date for the insurrection was set as 22 November 1596. But the night before, instead of 300, only ten rebels showed up. They went home.

Five "principal offenders" were arrested, taken to London, tortured, and returned for trial. At least two were hung, drawn, and quartered.' – **Buchanan Sharp**, *In Contempt of All Authority* (UC, 1980)

The biggest problem I faced, in trying to raise money for a feature film based on *The Revengers Tragedy*, was the language. The second-biggest problem was the characters themselves. Vindici, a fanatical murderer, Graziana, his money-hungry mother, and Hippolito, his good-for-nothing, go-along, killer brother, are what, in the trade, are called 'unsympathetic' characters. What this really means is that the gatekeepers of media production don't like certain characterisations, or certain situations (for how can character, in a film or play, or in real life, be divorced from its circumstances?), and will prevent them from being seen.

The need for 'sympathetic' characters, often expressed quite wistfully by soulless, chromium-plated financiers, as if this were a basic tenet of storytelling, literature, or art, is a modern form of censorship: a twenty-first century Hays Code. Finance can get away with this because film money – and the cash for TV drama – is highly concentrated over just a few sources: so political or moral censorship, in the guise of protecting a large investment, by choosing 'name' actors, 'safe' storylines and 'sympathetic' characters, is easy to maintain.

It was not ever thus. In the 1960s, Italian producers faced an increasing demand for genre movies: action films, horror films, sex films, gladiator films, Westerns. Tastes changed – the gladiator market collapsed, and for ten years making a Western almost guaranteed a financial return. This was partially because they were popular, and so the actual ticket revenue from the box office, recycled via the producer, paid for the next film. But there were also state subsidies to be had; banks which would lend money; and additional cash and resources, if you could structure your project as a European 'co-production'. The big demand for films, and the wide variety of funding sources, guaranteed the producers, and the directors they hired, a lot of autonomy.

Because his money came from Italian producers and a European co-production deal, Sergio Leone didn't need to pay attention to the Hays Code. Because there were no gatekeepers, transgressive films like *Django*, and *Django Kill*, and *The Big Silence* could be made. Because there were no 'co-branding' deals to be done with the Pentagon, all of these films shared a hostile attitude to the military, and a horrified focus on the detritus of war. These are, for the most part, anti-capitalist, anti-interventionist, radical films, which – in the guise of cowboy movies – severely critique the foreign and domestic policies of a superpower, the United States. Even Leone, as he developed an eye for the American market, continued to insist that businessmen and their money were the root of all evil. Damiani, Petroni, Corbucci, Questi and others went much further, exploring the darkest possibilities of the Western form.

So this was a lucky time for filmmakers – a time when, like Giulio Questi, you might receive a phone call from a producer friend: 'I need to shoot five Westerns quickly – have you any ideas?' It seems to me, if this isn't too strange to contemplate, that the circumstances of the original play, *The Revengers Tragedy*, were pretty similar.

In both cases, the Spaghetti Western and the Jacobean revenge tragedy, we're talking about a radically new form, derived from another style of drama, itself not very old. Westerns are as old as the cinema, and when the Spaghetti Westerns appeared, the cinema was reckoned to be 65–70 years old. The English revenge drama begins around 1589 with Thomas Kyd's *Spanish Tragedy*, which established both a genre, and a dramatic style which would be used in many other types of plays. Like the Spaghetti Western, Kyd's work – which involved the placement of a gallows on stage, to compete directly with another popular entertainment, hangings – was frowned on by the politer powers-that-be. The Lord Chamberlain waged a constant battle against playwrights and actors – financially beneficial to him, since he received a fee for permitting plays to be performed; sometimes very costly to the artists. Kyd's friend, Christopher Marlowe, was a particular problem for the authorities, both secular and religious. Marlowe was rumoured to be an atheist, and also a spy, and was violently killed in mysterious circumstances: after his death, his plays were re-written, to make them conform more to current precepts, and Kyd was tortured by the state.

So there were dangers associated with being a playwright in Elizabethan England, just as there was risk involved in going to the theatre itself. Audience members were killed, on occasion, when special effects went wrong. But this didn't seem to stem their enthusiasm for scenes of killing and fighting, enhanced with entrails and bladders filled with blood. To be followed (as in a John Ford film!) by dancing, because no good play concluded without a jig.

As with films, these early plays were a tremendously popular art form. And people enjoyed revenge stories, even while the supposed message of the story was that people should never take revenge. Plays were expected to have a moral purpose – that was how they got their licences – so it was necessary to see a bad man punished, a feckless rich person fall from high estate, an atheist killed with an axe. But there was another moral and political aspect to the plays as well: in addition to the enjoyment of the crimes – the killing and the revenge – the audience could take pleasure in the secret knowledge that these events, supposedly set in Italy, *happened in England, too*. This was the *double entendre* of the Elizabethan theatre, the bargain between artists and state: playwrights could make political statements, show bad nobles and poisoning priests, as long as these events occurred in another country. Italy had the popular reputation as the 'apothecary shop of man-slaughter' so it was always favourite – but Denmark and France would do, too. Yet nobody in that audience doubted that something was rotten in their own state; they knew the names of famously corrupt nobles, which priests had fathered whose children. In the same way, only a *very* uninvolved person, watching *¿Quien Sabe?*, could fail to draw a parallel with American intervention in the third world, *now, today.*

These trade-offs produced great art: culminating, around 1600, in that revenge classic, *Hamlet.* Inevitably, the free-for-all of the English theatre produced rip-offs, and parodies of the rip-offs. *The Revengers Tragedy*, first performed in 1608, was one of these. The Elizabethan and Jacobean audiences were tough. They felt no need for 'sympathetic' characters – only for interesting ones. Hamlet, a mad Catholic prince, pointed towards hell by his demon dad, yet dragging his feet, was certainly interesting. So was Vindici – constructed by Thomas Middleton as the *anti-Hamlet*, Vindici jumps into action every time Hamlet delays, only to be thwarted, or presented with a new enemy. In the same way, in the 1960s, Joe and Django stepped into a narrowly defined, heroic universe, shot all those present, and changed the rules.

What fun for the audience! What puzzlement for the authorities, if they were paying attention. But as long as the fiction was maintained: that these events were fictions, and that they happened exclusively in far-off countries, in long-ago times, the game went on. Italian producers and directors created scathing critiques of contemporary injustices... disguised as cowboy films. These films were sometimes postponed, or banned, or re-edited, allegedly on account of violence. But there was something inherently subversive about a Spaghetti Western – popular entertainment with a loud soundtrack and a radical political analysis – which the authorities could neither understand, nor suppress. So individual films, like *Django* and *The Big Silence* suffered, at the behest of a censor, or a studio exec.

Late in the cycle of Jacobean revenge tragedies, a young writer called John Webster wrote a couple of plays, *The White Devil* and *The Duchess of Malfi*, which broke even the theatre's own, mad rules. Without labouring this, I want to suggest that Webster created a Good,

323

Bad and Ugly set-up in his scenarios, for the same reason as the Italian Western did: to incorporate, as a heroic character, someone of 'lower' birth. In *The White Devil* (1612), there are no 'good' characters. The most attractive of them, Vittoria Corombona, is a murderess; she is pitted against a duo of aristocratic gangsters, a Duke and a Cardinal; in between them is a lower-born, mercenary character, Count Lodovico, who begins and ends the play. In *Malfi* (1613), the Duchess is definitely 'Good', her brothers Ferdinand and the Cardinal entirely 'Bad', and lowly hit-man, Bosola, resembles Leone's or Lupo's 'Ugly' character: far from good, caught up in the swirl of events, recognisably human – a character with whom the audience will identify.

Not a sympathetic character, note. Tuco's crimes are read aloud before each of his hangings in *The Good, the Bad and the Ugly*. He is a vicious killer, and worse: like Lodovico, and Bosola, and all the gangsters in *Women Beware Women*, trying to behave like high society, falling out, and killing each other off.

Webster's plays deal with women treated as chattels by men; a theme which Middleton addressed in his comedies and tragedies – especially *Revengers* and *Women Beware Women* (1623). And this, of course, is a constant – the worst constant – of Spaghetti Westerns, where women usually appear 1) as a wife or mother, raped and killed and provide a revenge motive, or 2) as a prostitute, probably to be killed at some point. It may be said that this is how the West was; that the Spaghetti Western shows these things in order to condemn them. But I don't really buy that. Both the Jacobean theatre and the Italian Western, for all their rebelliousness, take too much pleasure in two dark, reactionary myths: the myth of racial superiority, and the myth of the inferiority of women. These, of course, are the dark, reactionary myths which sustain Western 'civilisation' as well. It would be surprising if workers in the Elizabethan theatre or on the Elios Films set delved deeply, on a daily basis, into the meanings of the work they did. It was enough that there *was* work, and that it was fun, at times, as well.

And the very amount of work that was done – *hundreds* of English plays; *thousands* of Italian, popular films – enabled some extraordinary artists to flourish, for a while. Even late in the day, when all seemed to have degenerated into a meaningless mish-mash of parodies, strong voices were still heard: John Ford with *'Tis Pity She's a Whore* (1628), Gemma, Lupo and company with *California.*

The Jacobean revenge play and the Italian Western appeared in times of ferment. There was simultaneous social mobility and repression. Wars and insurrections had radicalised people. The threat of violence was never absent. Huge social change – a revolution – seemed to be at hand. 'Popular' art, if it's any good, reflects what goes on around it. For all their flaws, and their hypocrisy, I think the revenge drama and the Spaghetti Western were progressive in this way: they presented images of radical social upheaval, of the overthrow of corrupt systems, and of the triumph – in some shape or form, however messy – of justice.

VINDICI: Great men were gods, if beggars couldn't kill 'em.

Index

INDEX

INDEX

INDEX